The Time of Our Lives

CONTEMPORARY APPROACHES TO FILM AND MEDIA SERIES

A complete listing of the books in this series can be found online at wsupress.wayne.edu

General Editor
Barry Keith Grant
Brock University

Advisory Editors
Robert J. Burgoyne
University of St. Andrews

Caren J. Deming
University of Arizona

Patricia B. Erens
School of the Art Institute of Chicago

Peter X. Feng
University of Delaware

Lucy Fischer
University of Pittsburgh

Frances Gateward
California State University, Northridge

Tom Gunning
University of Chicago

Thomas Leitch
University of Delaware

Walter Metz
Southern Illinois University

The Time of Our Lives

DIRTY DANCING AND POPULAR CULTURE

Edited by

*Yannis Tzioumakis
and Siân Lincoln*

WAYNE STATE UNIVERSITY PRESS   DETROIT

© 2013 by Wayne State University Press, Detroit, Michigan 48201. All rights reserved. No part of this book may be reproduced without formal permission. Manufactured in the United States of America.

17 16 15 14 13   5 4 3 2 1

Library of Congress Cataloging-in-Publication Data

The time of our lives : Dirty dancing and popular culture / edited by Yannis Tzioumakis and Siân Lincoln.
    pages cm. — (Contemporary approaches to film and media series)
    Includes bibliographical references and index.
    ISBN 978-0-8143-3624-3 (pbk. : alk. paper) —
ISBN 978-0-8143-3625-0 (e-book) (print)
    1. Dirty dancing (Motion picture)   I. Tzioumakis, Yannis, editor of compilation.   II. Lincoln, Siân, 1974- editor of compilation.
    PN1997.D4965T56 2013
    791.43′72—dc23

                                                                    2012040549

∞

Designed and typeset by Newgen North America
Composed in Feijoa Medium and Whitney

For Roman

CONTENTS

Acknowledgments   xi

    Introduction   1
    YANNIS TZIOUMAKIS

I   *DIRTY DANCING* IN CONTEXT

    Introduction   21
    YANNIS TZIOUMAKIS

  1. Vestron Video and *Dirty Dancing*   25
    FREDERICK WASSER

  2. Bringing Up Baby: Generic Hybridity in *Dirty Dancing*   43
    TAMAR JEFFERS MCDONALD

  3. Is *Dirty Dancing* a Musical, and Why Should It Matter?   59
    JANE FEUER

  4. White Enough   73
    RICHARD DYER

  5. *Dirty Dancing* as Reagan-era Cinema and "Reaganite Entertainment"   87
    CYNTHIA BARON AND MARK BERNARD

  6. Dressing and Undressing in *Dirty Dancing*: Consumption, Gender, and Visual Culture in the 1980s   105
    PAMELA CHURCH GIBSON

II. QUESTIONS OF RECEPTION

    Introduction   127
    SIÂN LINCOLN

7. *Dirty Dancing*: Feminism, Postfeminism, and Neo-feminism   131
   HILARY RADNER

8. "There Are a Lot of Things About Me That Aren't What You Thought": The Politics of *Dirty Dancing*   151
   OLIVER GRUNER

9. "You Don't Own Me!": *Dirty Dancing* as Teenage Rite-of-Passage Film   167
   SIÂN LINCOLN

10. Heteros and Hustlers: Straightness and Dirtiness in *Dirty Dancing*   183
    GARY NEEDHAM

III. THE PRODUCTION OF NOSTALGIA

Introduction   203
SIÂN LINCOLN

11. "(I've Had) The Time of My Life": Romantic Nostalgia and the Early 1960s   207
    BILL OSGERBY

12. "It's a Feeling; a Heartbeat": Nostalgia, Music, and Affect in *Dirty Dancing*   223
    CLAIRE MOLLOY

13. Dancing in the Nostalgia Factory: Anachronistic Music in *Dirty Dancing*   239
    TIM MCNELIS

IV. BEYOND THE FILM

Introduction   259
YANNIS TZIOUMAKIS

14. A Dance Film with Legs: The *Dirty Dancing* Franchise   263
    AMANDA HOWELL

15. From Screen to Stage: *Dirty Dancing* Live   281
    MILLIE TAYLOR

16. *Dirty Dancing* and Its Stage Jukebox Dansical Adaptation:
    The Dancing Male in a Teenage Female Fantasy of Desire
    and Sensuality   297
    GEORGE RODOSTHENOUS

Contributors   315

Index   321

ACKNOWLEDGMENTS

There are a number of people who made this collection possible and whom we would like to thank.

First and foremost, we would like to thank our contributors. They all responded with an overwhelming enthusiasm to our invitation for this volume and were extremely supportive during the editing stage. It was a real pleasure and honor to work with you all.

Some of these contributors tested ideas for their chapters as part of the "Declarations of Independence: (Re)discovering *Dirty Dancing*" panel at the 2011 SCMS Annual Conference in New Orleans. The panel included contributions from Frederick Wasser, Tamar Jeffers McDonald, Pamela Church Gibson, and Yannis Tzioumakis, and we had many opportunities to discuss the film and the reasons why it has remained so popular twenty-five years after its release.

Then we would like to thank Wayne State University Press for commissioning the volume. More specifically, we would like to thank Annie Martin, who steered this project from the very beginning and who was a pleasure to work with, and Barry Keith Grant, who agreed to have this volume as part of the Contemporary Approaches to Film and Media Series, of which he is the general editor. We would also like to thank our copyeditor, Dawn McIlvain Stahl, for her painstaking work, which certainly improved the manuscript, and the rest of the team at Wayne State University Press who ensured the smooth production of the volume: Carrie Downes Teefey, Maya Whelan, Emily Nowak, and Kristina Elizabeth Stonehill. A big thank you also must go to Lisa Grazley and Alyssa Mervyn at Lionsgate for arranging permission to use the image from the film that decorates the front cover of the book. We really appreciate all your help.

We would also like to thank a number of colleagues, friends and family who supported us throughout this project. A big thank you must go to Julia Hallam, who arranged a semester long research leave for Yannis, during which he did a lot of the work on this book. Also great many thanks to Karen Ross, Lydia Papadimitriou, and James and Jo Frieze for their support and encouragement from the very beginning. A special thank you must go to Colin Fallows, whose friendship and generosity in the past few years have been invaluable, as has been his advice to "open up" the volume and reach out outside the fields of film and cultural studies. He will be happy to see that we took his advice and that it made for a better, more complete collection. The three of us have spent many an hour talking about art and culture and having luncheon in old pubs in the suburbs of Liverpool, and it was always a great pleasure.

Finally, we would also like to thank Panayiotis and Christina Tzioumakis, Leonidas Tzioumakis, Patroula Vrantza, Eleftheria Thanouli, Warren Buckland, Peter Krämer, Chris Holmlund, Panayiotis Koutakis, Dimitra Kavatha, Harris Tlas, Rigas Goulimaris, Roger and Maggie Lincoln, Carys and Alex Damon, Fiona and Richard O'Mahony, Paula Noble, Nathan Casson, Becky Finnigan, Vicki Maguire, Melanie Green, Sarah Wharton, Hayley Trowbridge, and Louise Wilks. Louise also assisted with the production of the index and, as always, did a stellar job.

This book is dedicated to our son, Roman, who was born during this project.

INTRODUCTION

YANNIS TZIOUMAKIS

dirty gardening. dirty hiking. dirty scrubbing. (missed it at the movies? you must get it on DVD. it's the love story of a young cleaner at an upscale holiday retreat in 1960s America who teaches the teenage son of a middle class couple to become a whizz with a mop and bucket). and, OK, dirty dancing, especially the foxtrot in a muddy field. all of these, as well as sweaty jogging, warrant a shower with this gel from anatomicals, the world's most crazy (or should that be Swayze?) bath and body company. we only want you for your body.

An Increasingly Strong Presence: *Dirty Dancing* at Twenty-Five

This unusually long marketing message can be found printed on one of the four sides of Anatomicals' Cypress and Thyme Body Cleanser container that is readily available in department stores and from online retailers. On another side of the same container there is a small drawing of the "likeness" of Patrick Swayze and Jennifer Grey taking a shower together. Swayze is standing behind Grey and is ready to brush body cleanser down her arm, which she has extended to embrace him. They both seem to be losing themselves in the moment, their faces almost touching each other, their lips ready to meet. On the front of the container, the product's name, "'I've Had the Thyme of My Life'

Cypress and Thyme Body Cleanser," appears in striking white and black lettering against a strong green background, promising an unparalleled cleansing experience that will make one's body feel the way it has never felt before.

For anyone who has seen the film *Dirty Dancing* (Emile Ardolino, 1987), the name of the product, the drawing of the shower scene, and the fictitious film about the young cleaner teaching a middle-class teenager how to mop are all unmistakeably signifiers of the film. Indeed, all three references are variations of the film's plot (replace "cleaner," "son," and "a whiz with a mop and a bucket" with "dancer," "daughter," and "a whiz on the dance floor"), of one of the film's most iconic scenes (remove the shower and the body cleanser and imagine that the characters are rehearsing a dance number), and of the trademark song of the film (replace "thyme" with "time"). Even without the presence of such tells as mentioning the act of "dirty dancing" and "[Patrick] Swayze," the film's male lead, these three playful references invoke *Dirty Dancing* in an effort to relate pleasures associated with audiences' experiences of the film to the product.

The tie-in of a beauty and body product to an American film is certainly not new or unusual.[1] However, the tie-in of "'I've Had the Thyme of My Life' Cypress and Thyme Body Cleanser" to *Dirty Dancing* highlights a number of remarkable qualities that characterize this particular film, especially in the context of today's franchise-driven, media-saturated environment. First, it represents licensing from a film that is a quarter of a century old. Despite the recent global success of its stage adaptation, *Dirty Dancing: The Classic Story on Stage*, for the majority of the twenty-five years since the film's release in 1987 *Dirty Dancing* has not been subject to any major or coherent franchising plans beyond the first couple of years following its surprisingly successful theatrical release. These plans included a concert tour featuring some of the artists whose songs were heard in the film and in the two soundtrack albums that accompanied its release, and, far less successfully, a spin-off television show with the same title that lasted only a few episodes.[2] Even its once eagerly awaited sequel/remake, *Dirty Dancing: Havana Nights* (Guy Ferland) came out as recently as 2004 (coinciding with the opening of the stage show in Australia) and had little impact, box office or otherwise, compared to its predecessor.[3]

Dirty Dancing failed to establish a significant commercial afterlife partly because the rights to the property changed hands several times since its theatrical release, the company that produced and distributed the film having gone out of business in 1990. In this respect, potential plans to further exploit *Dirty Dancing* in the market had to be abandoned and later redesigned by a parade of successive copyright-holding companies (LIVE, Artisan, and Lionsgate). Each of these companies occupied a different position in the marketplace and had questionable abilities to franchise a property in the manner of a major Hollywood studio.

Arguably more important, however, the failure to franchise *Dirty Dancing* for most of its history had to do more with the fact that the film had few points of contact with the *franchisable* blockbusters of the last twenty-five years, which targeted primarily young male audiences. As a period piece that was based on an original screenplay by novelist and screenwriter Eleanor Bergstein and geared primarily toward young female audiences, *Dirty Dancing* had little in common with the expensive, effects-driven action spectacles that were based on pre-existing properties and generated merchandising that would support a significant film afterlife. *Dirty Dancing* also seemed to share few characteristics with the small number of Hollywood films that targeted women and succeeded in becoming franchises or "event films" in the 2000s, such as *Legally Blonde* (Robert Luketic, 2001) and *Sex and the City: The Movie* (Michael Patrick King, 2008).[4] Despite the fact that *Dirty Dancing* did share an emphasis on romance, escape, and, arguably, validation with the above films, it was not interested in questions of consumerism and beauty, which, according to Ashley Elaine York, represent qualities that also characterize the more recent event films targeting women.[5] Furthermore, it was certainly not marketed with an emphasis on "spectacle aesthetics and a focus on ancillary marketing and foreign box office," elements that, for York, are foundational in the marketing strategies of all blockbuster films, irrespective of whether they target primarily male or female audiences.[6] Although *Dirty Dancing* was admittedly very successful in the two ancillary markets of home video and the movie soundtrack, its success in the latter market was arguably a happy accident that took even those responsible for it by surprise rather than a product of meticulous franchise design. This could also be said to be the case for the film's unexpectedly lucrative box office outside the US given the importance non-US markets place on the presence of established stars and other marketable elements, neither of which characterized *Dirty Dancing*.

On the other hand, despite the film's failure to become a franchise in the 1990s and early 2000s, *Dirty Dancing* never quite disappeared from popular culture. Its celebrated soundtrack sold more than 42 million copies by 2006, and certain sources have referred to it as the sixth biggest selling record of all time.[7] The film also generated *More Dirty Dancing*, an album that contained the songs from the film that did not make it onto the original soundtrack, and *Dirty Dancing: Live!*, a collection of live versions of many of the songs. All three albums have been widely available since their release. Furthermore, *Dirty Dancing* was re-released in theaters both in 1997 and 2007 to mark its 10th and 20th year anniversaries. The film has always been readily available in every new home entertainment format, from VHS to LaserDisc to DVD and Blu-ray, including several special and anniversary editions; this suggests the continuing existence of an audience in the years following its success in theaters. The franchising efforts that took place from the mid-2000s onwards, when the film's rights were bought by successful mini-major Lions Gate (later Lionsgate), were built on solid foundations. These efforts included, among others, the release of *Dirty Dancing: Havana Nights* by Lionsgate, the extremely successful launch of *Dirty Dancing: The Classic Story on Stage* (2005–present) first in Australia and later in the UK, and the reality television dance competition show *Dirty Dancing: The Time of Your Life* (Living TV, 2007–2009), and proved that the film did have the potential for the kind of commercial exploitation that is associated with blockbuster films despite not sharing most of their constituting elements. This makes *Dirty Dancing* a very rare phenomenon in the American film industry, and of course justifies the decision by a modern body products company like Anatomicals to strike a licensing deal for a twenty-five-year-old film.

Between Hollywood and Independent Cinema

Second, the strong presence of *Dirty Dancing* in contemporary popular and consumer culture is even more impressive if one considers that it is not a Hollywood film, but a film the origins of which are located in the so-called "independent sector" of American cinema, a sector that was enjoying a small boom in the 1980s before companies like Miramax and film showcases like the Sundance Film Festival helped transform it into a hugely commercial and popular market from the 1990s onwards. In an authoritatively constructed appendix of American independent theatrical releases between 1984 and 1994,[8] *Dirty Dancing* was listed among such 1987 independent films of distinction as *The Hollywood Shuffle* (Robert Townsend) and *Matewan* (John Sayles).[9] This is because *Dirty Dancing* was one of the first films from Vestron Pictures, a theatrical production and distribution organization that branched out from the home video market in the mid-1980s. At a time when VHS penetration in the US market was still increasing by 40% annually (1986–87),[10] Vestron decided to create a production and distribution facility that would make relatively low budget films that, after a brief theatrical release, would be exploited further by its core business, the home video division.

The film's independent credentials might come as a surprise both to the many fans of the film who are not aware of its production history and to lovers of American independent cinema who might fail to detect in the film any characteristics of independent film production in the 1980s. These typically included stylistic and narrative departures from pillars of Hollywood studio filmmaking such as continuity editing and cause-effect narrative logic, a slower narrative pace, and an emphasis on subjects and issues deemed non-commercial by Hollywood standards (for instance, unionization or the experiences of ethnic minorities, among others).[11] And yet on a closer look *Dirty Dancing* does contain a surprising number of such characteristics, including its focus on a young woman's journey from adolescence to adulthood, the presence of a secondary plot revolving around the non-commercial subject of abortion and its mature, matter-of-fact handling by the narrative, the extremely prominent role of class politics in a film that is supposed to be about a summer romance, the strong presence of ethnic minorities (especially Jewish but also African American and Latino/a), and a relatively ambiguous ending that does not entirely support the lasting formation of the heterosexual couple. In this respect, it is neither surprising nor coincidental that the *New York Times* review of the film compared it to *Baby, It's You* (John

Sayles, 1983), another 1960s-based film about a young couple's problematic relationship that featured a strong focus on class politics.[12]

On the other hand, despite these characteristics, the film had a number of points of contact with Hollywood studio productions. Indeed, while it was financed, produced and distributed away from the major studios of the time, *Dirty Dancing* also seemed to model itself on studio filmmaking. For instance, it carried the substantial budget of $6 million at a time when the budgets of key independent films tended to be below or near the $1 million mark;[13] it featured actors with some marquee value—if not full-fledged star status—like Patrick Swayze; it was distributed in almost a thousand theaters in the US (which was comparable to the release of many studio films); and, as part of its marketing formula, its distributor also released an original soundtrack that included a mix of period songs and songs commissioned specifically for the film (which, as noted earlier, became one of the best-selling records of all time). Furthermore, *Dirty Dancing* was characterized by such Hollywood studio film elements as a straightforward, cause-effect driven narrative structure, a functional and fairly conservative visual style, participation in a number of clear and well-established film genres, and even the use of certain stylistic elements associated with the high-concept films that were the epitome of Hollywood cinema in the late 1980s. According to Stephen Prince, *Dirty Dancing* was a high-concept film characterized by "a catchy narrative premise," which he summarizes in 15 words as "spoiled girl vacationing in the Catskills, learns about life from a sensual working-class performer."[14] In this respect, and despite citing comparisons with *Baby, It's You*, the same *New York Times* review also compared *Dirty Dancing* to Adrian Lyne's *Flashdance* (1983),[15] a film widely considered a paradigmatic Hollywood high-concept film.[16]

This peculiar combination of independent and mainstream filmmaking choices has been responsible for the creation of a hybrid film and example of proto-Indiewood cinema, a predecessor of that category of filmmaking in which "Hollywood and the independent sector merge or overlap"[17] that was not popularized until at least a decade after the release of *Dirty Dancing*. The unusual mixing of production, narrative, stylistic, and political elements from these two different modes of filmmaking might go some way to explain why the film has managed to maintain a strong presence in popular memory

Introduction 7

following the end of its lucrative theatrical run. Resembling a Hollywood production enough to be distributed as a major motion picture and attract a mass audience but also utilizing enough characteristics associated with the quality independent film sector to make it stand out from the crowd, *Dirty Dancing* managed to achieve a rare feat in American cinema: to tell an extremely conventional story in a way that circumvented many of the clichés and pitfalls of commercial Hollywood studio filmmaking. However, rather than avoiding clichés through the use of irony, alienation techniques, or other more pronounced aesthetic and political choices, *Dirty Dancing*'s weapons of choice were often subtlety, understatement, and even a refusal to fully embrace hallmarks of the lovers-from-different-backgrounds story. These strategies helped undermine many of the conventional and formulaic aspects of its narrative and allowed the film to speak to the audience in a way that comparable Hollywood films (*The Karate Kid* [John Avildsen, 1984], *Pretty in Pink* [Howard Deutch, 1986], and *Cocktail* [Roger Donaldson, 1988]) rarely could while also reaching a mass audience.

More specifically, the narrative of *Dirty Dancing* presents a number of elements that deviate from or complicate the *Romeo and Juliet* narrative formula on which it heavily draws. First, the spectator's guide to the narrative is a young girl (Baby) rather than the young male character (Johnny), to the extent that the audience never gets to experience Johnny's perspective in the narrative world except when he is in the presence of Baby.

Second, and contrary to Prince's view that *Dirty Dancing* is a film about Baby learning "about life from a sensual working-class performer," the film actually ends with a public admission by Johnny that he has learned about life from Baby and her actions in the narrative. Such a male character transformation into an "ideal" posed by a woman is, according to Kristin Thompson, "certainly an unusual [feature] of a Hollywood film,"¹⁸ as it breaks from the patriarchal viewpoint that structures Hollywood cinema and suggests that *Dirty Dancing* is an atypical American film that firmly stands its ground when it comes to privileging a female perspective.

Third, for a film that deals with rites of passage, summer romance, and a love story involving a couple that tries hard to go past seemingly insurmountable obstacles, the fact that neither of the two leads ever say "I love you" to each other is another element that differentiates the film from similar ones. Even in their goodbye scene, after Johnny has been fired and is ready to leave Kellerman's (seemingly) forever, the two protagonists embrace in an awkward fashion, with Johnny uttering "I'll never be sorry" and Baby responding "Neither will I." No emotional outbursts, no indictment of the restrictive environment that crushed the romance, no long speeches, no "I love you." Compare this to the equivalent scene from *Dirty Dancing*'s contemporary, *Pretty in Pink*, in which the working-class heroine, in an outburst of emotion, pressures her rich boyfriend into admitting that he is splitting up with her because of her class background, causing him to cry in the process. Through such narrative choices, *Dirty Dancing* subtly avoids a major Hollywood cliché, while arguably making the point through the non-diegetic rendition of the song "She's Like the Wind" sung by Patrick Swayze.

Fourth, the film also avoids a number of climactic sequences that are normally expected when the narrative finally deals with the fate of the couple's antagonists (in this case, Robbie the waiter, Vivian Pressman, Max and Neil Kellerman, and Jake and Lisa Houseman). Despite ample opportunity for dramatic showdowns with the numerous obstacles to the realization of the couple, the narrative once again opts for understatement, which, on the one hand, makes for a more realistic outcome to the story, while, on the other, does not detract from the fantasy of the climactic dance sequence at the end of the film. With the exception of Robbie and Vivian, whose punishments are still light and rather symbolic (the former loses his tip from Dr. Houseman and the possibility to develop a serious relationship with the cold-hearted Lisa, while the latter is punished by not being able to get Johnny), the other antagonists are last seen "dirty dancing" alongside the main couple in the final sequence. Again, the comparisons with films like *Cocktail* and *The Karate Kid*, in which the working-class male character punishes his antagonists through the use of violence, or with *Pretty in Pink*, in which the upper-middle-class Steff (played by James Spader) is confronted and exposed as a sad failure who could not buy the female protagonist with his money, are interesting.

Last and most importantly, the film supports the formation of the couple only partially. Despite the undisputed triumph of Baby and Johnny at the end of the film, which comes with the approval of the whole community (barring Vivian) at Kellerman's, it is questionable whether couplehood is in this case a long-term prospect or a very short-term arrangement. On the one hand, there is an indirect (and subtle) acceptance by Dr. Houseman of Johnny and of Baby's maturity. The film ends with the couple dancing the night away, celebrating their victory and their integration to society. On the other hand, this narrative closure, strong as it is, does not carry with it the expectation that "they lived happily ever after." The couple's abstinence from the discourse of love, Baby's willingness to accept her fate (and a place in a corner) as soon as Johnny leaves and not to actively fight to reverse things, the narrative's refusal to open up any possibilities for a long-term future for the couple until perhaps the very last moments, and the extremely strong emphasis from both characters on standing up for people and for one's principles (which also provides the context for their own relationship) all point toward the conclusion that the formation of the couple in the film is a short-term arrangement—the culmination of a summer romance before everyone goes back to their normal lives once vacation is over. Both Johnny and Baby (who by the end of the film is called by her real name, Frances) are transformed characters at that point, ready to grapple with the challenges of a middle-class adult life (for Frances) and the injustices of a tough class system (for Johnny). However, the extent to which they can face these challenges together is certainly debatable, which marks the final dance as both their beginning and end as a formal couple.

These little deviations, based on subtlety and understatement, have helped the film both stand out from a large crowd of similarly themed films and, perhaps, achieve the longevity it has. Specifically, the film's reluctance to succumb fully to a number of formulaic elements readily embraced by other films, in tandem with the privileging of a female perspective in the narrative, creates a very particular effect whereby the narrative structure of *Dirty Dancing* comes across as *originary*, as a point of departure for the formula, before its conventions were further developed and refined by other similarly themed films such as *Cocktail, Never Been Kissed* (Raja Gossnell, 1999), *She's All That* (Robert Iscove, 1999), and many others. This is undoubtedly helped by the fact that this 1987 film is set in the early 1960s, while the narratives of comparable films from the 1980s are set in contemporary times (with the exception of *Baby, It's You*). The narrative of

Dirty Dancing then is set in the more "innocent" times of the 1960s (as compared to the 1980s from when the protagonist remembers her youth in the voiceover at the beginning of the film) and constructed as a more innocent story that is not spoiled by the usual clichés and conventions that characterize similar 1980s (and later) films. In this respect, the absence of "I love you," the light punishment of the antagonists, the debatable state of the couple at the end, and so on, help construct an otherwise typical love story of two young people from different backgrounds as "original," and therefore utterly enjoyable. Indeed, many fans treat the film as a "guilty pleasure," as something that, recognizing its formulaic character, they should not have liked or been taken in by, but which they could not resist.[19]

Approaching *Dirty Dancing*

Since the success of *Dirty Dancing: The Classic Story on Stage* and Lionsgate's more concerted efforts toward franchising the property, the original film has enjoyed a remarkable revival in popular culture. According to Lionsgate executives, the film's DVD has consistently sold a million copies a year,[20] while a vast range of merchandising associated with the film or licensed to use its title or logo (including the Anatomicals body cleanser) has saturated the market. Contemporary films such as *L'arnacoeur* [*The Heartbreaker*] (Pascal Chaumeil, 2010) and Warner Bros.' *Crazy, Stupid Love* (Glenn Ficarra and John Requa, 2011) have reproduced whole sequences from *Dirty Dancing*, while a Season 2 episode of the successful television show *Glee* (Fox Television, 2009–present) features a performance of "(I've Had) The Time of My Life." The *Dirty Dancing* "Connections" page on the Internet Movie Database lists over 100 films and television programs that make direct references to the film, including spoofs, re-enactments of iconic scenes, and quotations.[21]

However, the two most important elements in bringing the film into greater prominence in recent times were Patrick Swayze's death in 2009 and Jennifer Grey's comeback following her victory in the US reality television show *Dancing with the Stars* in 2010. Both events created a media frenzy that involved a relentless circulation of images, clips, and interviews associated with the film on a global scale, demonstrating clearly the special place that *Dirty Dancing* occupies in

Introduction

popular culture. If in doubt, one can check the film's Facebook page, which as of July 22, 2012 boasted 14,239,116 "likes" (compare this with 8,367,519 "likes" for the *Star Wars* page and 9,747,196 "likes" for *The Lord of the Rings* trilogy page, both billion-dollar franchises).[22] The logical extension of this *Dirty Dancing* fever took place on August 9, 2011, when it was announced that Lionsgate had given the green light for a remake of the film with Kenny Ortega, the choreographer of *Dirty Dancing*, as director.[23] The decision prompted extreme reactions from the film's fans, including a few Facebook "boycott the remake" groups (though membership is relatively low, with just a couple of thousand people having signed up).[24] The new film is scheduled for release in 2014.

In many respects, the genesis of this volume took place at the time when *Dirty Dancing* was enjoying this undeniable revival, even though both my co-editor and I had noticed for some time that, despite the film's availability and its great popularity across generations, there was very little scholarly work dedicated to the film.[25] This volume offers the first in-depth examination of *Dirty Dancing* from a number of perspectives, with an intention to discuss the film and the phenomenon at a time when its stamp on popular culture can no longer be ignored. Bringing together work from scholars from the areas of film studies, cultural studies, popular music studies, media sociology, popular theater studies, dance studies, and media industry studies, the volume aims to provide a diverse range of answers to the question of why *Dirty Dancing* has become such an important aspect of popular culture in the past twenty-five years.

As the essays that appear under each of the four sections that structure this volume ("*Dirty Dancing* in Context," "Questions of Reception," "The Production of Nostalgia," and "Beyond the Film") will be briefly presented in the respective introductory passages that precede each section, this general introductory chapter will finish with a few remarks on the scope of the collection, the rationale behind its structure, and the challenges we faced as editors in our effort to examine the film from a variety of disciplinary backgrounds. Given that the number of scholarly collections dedicated to the study of individual films is still relatively small—especially compared to the number of (short) monographs that several publishers commission, primarily as part of book series[26]—I hope that the brief discussion below will inspire colleagues to undertake similar studies and thereby open up further avenues for bringing film studies closer to other disciplines, with a view toward promoting novel approaches to the study of popular film.

Given that the main question that has been driving this study was to locate the reasons for the film's unusually strong hold on popular culture, we envisaged a collection that would focus on more than *Dirty Dancing* as a film text. Although textual analysis is still at the core of the volume's overall approach, with particular emphasis on questions of genre, race, class, gender politics, and the production of nostalgia, we also wanted to conceptualize the film in other ways. One of these ways involved examining the film's industrial location and was based on two different conceptualizations of the film: *Dirty Dancing* as a product of the American film industry at a very specific, historical juncture and as a *franchisable* property with a long (if uneven) history in a variety of media outlets. In this respect, we solicited essays from film scholars whose work is often located outside traditional, text-based film studies. This work is influenced by industrial film history and by the recent surge of "media industry studies," a body of methodological, historical, and theoretical work that often brings together formerly disparate approaches to the study of media (and film).[27] Besides adding new and interesting dimensions in the examination of the film, these industry-based studies have demonstrated the extent to which the film's box office success and much-celebrated afterlife are often intricately linked to the host of companies that have exploited it commercially and their place in the global entertainment industry.

Alongside the collection's focus on the film as text and industrial product, the reader can find an equal level of emphasis on questions of the film's reception. Taking as a starting point Janet Staiger's often-quoted foundational principle that reception studies researches "the history of the interactions between real readers and texts, actual spectators and films,"[28] the collection brings together film scholars, cultural studies scholars, and media sociologists in hopes of understanding the "*Dirty Dancing* phenomenon" as it has manifested itself in the (often extreme) ways in which people have engaged with the film. Given the film's undisputed cult status and its popularity around the world, examining its reception in detail could have generated many

Introduction

more book-length volumes of work; perhaps this is an area of research that future studies might wish to develop further.

Within this collection, we decided to focus on three areas surrounding the film's reception, two rather obvious and one much less prominent. The first of these areas revolved around the extent to which viewers of *Dirty Dancing* and the critical apparatus debated its feminist credentials, focusing on the ways the film might empower women and politicize the female experience. The second dealt with the ways in which the film has taught young girls how to navigate the tricky transitional years from adolescence to adulthood. Perhaps less expectedly, we've also included a chapter about the (latent) pleasures the film might offer gay audiences, especially given its strong focus on the production of heteronormativity and traditional couplehood, primarily exemplified by the dancing (heterosexual) couples. Together, these chapters highlight some of the diverse ways in which viewers have interacted with the film, although, as mentioned earlier, there is scope for many more studies that could perhaps look at the reception of the film in different geographical and cultural contexts.

The question of nostalgia could not have been excluded from the collection, and indeed this was one of the first subjects on which we solicited contributions. This explains why it stands as an individual section under the title "The Production of Nostalgia." Due to the multifaceted nature of the concept, we approached scholars from three different disciplines: youth culture studies, film studies, and popular music studies. Within the context of cultural studies, the emphasis is placed on questions of representation and the ways in which nostalgia in this film does not gloss over problems and conflicts (as is often expected). The film studies perspective tackles questions of affect and the complex ways in which nostalgia is constructed, especially for contemporary audiences who are more likely to connect with the time of the film's release in the 1980s than its setting in the 1960s. Finally, the popular music studies perspective focuses on the prominent use of anachronistic songs and the ways in which they manage not to disrupt the nostalgia for the 1960s. The role of music is explored in-depth in all three essays, but each emphasizes different aspects, highlighting the complexities of the topic and justifying the inclusion of essays from different disciplinary backgrounds.

Although there were numerous other areas relating to the film that we also considered (e.g., *Dirty Dancing* as a teen film, Patrick Swayze and stardom), given our emphasis on the film *and* the phenomenon we also decided to include work that dealt with other manifestations of *Dirty Dancing*. Two of the chapters we have included focus on the stage adaptation of the film and were written by theater and performance studies scholars. Despite the affinities between theater and film, there have been few opportunities for representatives of the two disciplines to coexist within the same project,[29] and we believe that the inclusion of these chapters represents a great opportunity for a renewed dialogue between the two disciplines. This is especially illustrated in these two chapters discussing the concepts of "memory" and "fantasy," concepts that have had a long-established history of research in the field of film studies. We would have liked to include chapters on the 2004 sequel/remake, *Dirty Dancing: Havana Nights*, or the reality television show *Dirty Dancing: The Time of Your Life*, especially in terms of the ways they engage with the original film; given the fact that the stage show had a much greater impact on popular culture than the sequel or television derivatives, however, we decided to focus on that.

All this work goes some way toward examining *Dirty Dancing* in an effort to understand the reasons behind its success and continuing popularity. Some of these reasons, however, are intricately linked to the manner in which the film represents identity politics and privileges particular representations over others. This necessarily means that the film takes positions on matters of gender, class, race, and sexual politics, many of which are problematic for particular social groups with a history of marginalization and exclusion. Indeed, despite its huge global fan base, the film has also attracted a number of negative responses from critics and the public,[30] while for many *Dirty Dancing* remains a politically suspect and ideologically manipulative Hollywood product. As the first scholarly publication on the film, *The Time of Our Lives* had to accommodate discussions of *Dirty Dancing* that represent these viewpoints, emphasising specifically the ways in which the pleasures the film offers are not necessarily for everyone (see in particular chapters 5 and 10).

Whether negative, positive, or neutral in tone, whether written by scholars who are fans of the film or who do not like it, and whether arguing for or against the pleasures it offers, the sixteen essays in this volume take *Dirty Dancing* seriously. The film has been an increasingly significant part of global popular culture, especially since the 2000s, but academia has steered clear of bestowing on it the attention it deserves—until now. Besides throwing ample light on the film and its impact, the editors of this collection hope that the included essays will prompt more work on the subject and, more broadly, on the junctures between film studies and a number of other cognate disciplines.

Notes

1. Even as far back as the 1930s, LUX soap and Max Factor cosmetics were habitually attached to films, such as MGM's *Dinner at Eight* (George Cukor, 1933). See Charles Eckert, "The Carole Lombard in Macy's Window" in *Movies and Mass Culture*, ed. John Belton (Brunswick, NJ: Rutgers University Press, 1996), 113.
2. For more details, see Amanda Howell's essay in this volume.
3. *Havana Nights* recorded a US theatrical box office gross of just over $14 million, compared to the $63 million that *Dirty Dancing* had recorded fourteen years earlier. The figures were taken from The Internet Movie Database, http://www.imdb.com/title/tt0338096/ and http://www.imdb.com/title/tt0092890/business, respectively. Accessed on October 1, 2011.
4. Hilary Radner, "*Sex and the City: The Movie* (2008): The Female Event Film" in *Neo-Feminist Cinema: Girly Films, Chick Flicks and Consumer Culture* (London: Routledge, 2010), 153–70.
5. Ashley Elaine York, "From Chick Flicks to Millennial Blockbusters: Spinning Female-Driven Narratives into Franchises," *Journal of Popular Culture* 43.1 (2010): 4.
6. Ibid.
7. Veronica Lee, "There's a Secret Dancer Inside Us All," *The Telegraph*, September 23, 2006, http://www.telegraph.co.uk/culture/theatre/3655489/Theres-a-secret-dancer-inside-us-all.html. Accessed on October 14, 2011.
8. John Pierson, *Spike, Mike, Slackers & Dykes: A Guided Tour across a Decade of American Independent Cinema* (New York: Hyperion Books, 1995).
9. Ibid., 341–42.
10. "The 1980s: A Reference Guide to Motion Pictures, Television, VCR, and Cable," *Velvet Light Trap* 27 (1991, Spring): 86.
11. Annette Insdorf, "Ordinary People, European Style: How to Spot an Independent Feature," *American Film* 6.10 (September, 1981): 58.
12. John Sayles, the director of *Baby, It's You*, was one of the most prominent independent filmmakers of the 1980s. Samuel G. Freedman, "'Dirty Dancing' Rocks to an Innocent Beat," *New York Times*, August 16, 1987, 19.
13. For instance, fellow 1987 independent production, *Hollywood Shuffle*, was made for $100,000, while *Stand and Deliver* (Ramon Menendez), one of the most successful independent films of 1988, cost $1.37 million to produce.

David Rosen with Peter Hamilton, *Off-Hollywood: The Making and Marketing of Independent Films* (New York: Grove Weidenfeld, 1990), 130, 202.
14 Stephen Prince, *A New Pot of Gold: Hollywood Under the Electronic Rainbow, 1980–1989* (Berkeley: University of California Press, 2002), 309.
15 Freedman, "'Dirty Dancing,'" 19.
16 The poster for *Flashdance* decorates the cover of the main study on high-concept filmmaking. See Justin Wyatt, *High Concept: Movies and Marketing in Hollywood* (Austin: University of Texas Press, 1994).
17 Geoff King, *Indiewood USA: Where Hollywood Meets Independent Cinema* (London: I.B. Tauris, 2009), 1.
18 Kristin Thompson, *Storytelling in the New Hollywood: Understanding Classical Narrative Technique* (Cambridge, MA: Harvard University Press, 1999), 147.
19 Some of these comments about *Dirty Dancing* as a "guilty pleasure" can be found in the reviews section of the film's page on IMDb. See, for instance, Thesar-2, "Each Dance is The Time of My Life," the Internet Movie Database (February 6, 2011), http://www.imdb.com/title/tt0092890/reviews?start=40; and Jackal_17, "Girl Goes to Camp, Girl Meets Boy, Girl Learns to Dance, Complications Ensue," the Internet Movie Database (January 17, 2006), http://www.imdb.com/title/tt0092890/reviews?start=20. Accessed on November 1, 2011.
20 Sandy Brown, "Lions Gate Grabs Swayze Rights," *The Street* (July 14, 2005), http://www.thestreet.com/stocks/sandybrown/10232495.html. Accessed on November 1, 2011.
21 "Movie Connections for *Dirty Dancing*," the Internet Movie Database, http://www.imdb.com/title/tt0092890/movieconnections. Accessed on November 10, 2011.
22 See http://www.facebook.com/OfficialDirtyDancing; http://www.facebook.com/StarWars; http://www.facebook.com/lordoftheringstrilogy Accessed on July 22, 2012.
23 Ben Child, "Kenny Ortega Set to Direct *Dirty Dancing* Remake," *The Guardian*, August 9, 2011, http://www.guardian.co.uk/film/2011/aug/09/kenny-ortega-dirty-dancing-remake. Accessed on November 1, 2011.
24 See for instance the *Boycott Dirty Dancing* Remake page, which as of July 22, 2012 had just over 2000 "likes." http://www.facebook.com/BoycottDirtyDancingRemake. Accessed on July 22, 2012.
25 Indeed, for such as a successful and influential film, we found only a handful of scholarly essays discussing it. See, for instance, Lesley Vize, "Music and Body in Dance Films" in *Popular Music and Film*, ed. Ian Inglis (London: Wallflower Press, 2003), 22–38; and David R. Shamway, "Rock 'n' Roll Soundtrack and the Production of Nostalgia," *Cinema Journal* 38.2 (Winter 1999): 36–51. See also Markus Rheindorf, "The Multiple Modes of *Dirty Dancing*: A Cultural Studies Approach to Multimodal Discourse Analysis" in *Perspectives on Multimodality*, eds. Eija Ventola, Cassily Charles, Martin Kaltenbacher (Amsterdam: John Benjamins Publishers, 2004), 137–52.
26 See, for instance, the BFI Modern Classics series and Edinburgh University Press's American Indies series.

27 Douglas Kellner, "Media Industries, Political Economy and Media/Cultural Studies: An Articulation" in *Media Industries: History, Theory, and Method*, eds. Jennifer Holt and Alisa Perren (Chichester: Wiley-Blackwell, 2009), 102.
28 Janet Staiger, *Interpreting Films: Studies in the Historical Reception of American Cinema* (Princeton: Princeton University Press, 1992), 8.
29 One such exception is research on playwright-turned-filmmaker David Mamet, whose work has attracted the interest of both theater and film scholars in a number of collections featuring work by scholars from both disciplines. See, for instance, Christopher C. Hudgins and Leslie Kane, eds., *Gender and Genre: Essays on David Mamet* (Basingstoke: Palgrave, 2001).
30 For instance, there is also an "I Hate *Dirty Dancing*" Facebook page, though it has had only slightly over 100 "likes" at the time of writing. See http://www.facebook.com/pages/I-hate-Dirty-Dancing/183432081669612. Accessed on May 25, 2012.

1 *DIRTY DANCING* IN CONTEXT

Introduction

YANNIS TZIOUMAKIS

"Dirty Dancing in Context," the first of the four sections in this volume, places the film within a number of important critical frameworks, starting with its production location. Frederick Wasser's in-depth examination of Vestron Pictures, the company that produced and distributed the film, demonstrates the unusual circumstances that gave birth to Dirty Dancing. As one of the first productions of a new company that branched out from the home video market and tried to carve a niche between the Hollywood majors and the low-budget independents, Dirty Dancing was made at a time when the American film industry was changing in fundamental ways due to the great success of home video technology and the increasing significance of ancillary markets. Dirty Dancing was the ideal property for Vestron, Wasser argues, whose unique circumstances as a start-up company gave the film its distinctive shape.

Chapter 2 examines the generic status of Dirty Dancing, and Tamar Jeffers McDonald argues that its success owes a lot to its remarkable ability to co-opt elements from an unusually large number of film genres. However, it is the family melodrama and the romantic comedy "wrong partner" subplot, Jeffers McDonald argues, that dominate the film's generic mix. This is because the film's main dramatic nexus is located in the relationship between Dr. Houseman, Johnny, and Baby, and the fact that Baby needs to swap the "wrong partner" with whom she has been paired at the beginning of the film—her father—for the right one, Johnny.

Chapters 3 and 4 continue the examination of the film's generic qualities but focus primarily on its status as a musical and the ways it negotiates racial identities. In chapter 3, Jane Feuer categorizes the film as a "Jewish folk musical" that also manages to pass itself as a non-ethnic film, especially for audiences with no knowledge of the Jewish culture of the 1950s. Feuer re-conceptualizes the film's emphasis on class politics as intricately linked to the politics of race, revealing the structural complexity of the film, and concludes with a discussion of both the film's links to classical examples of the genre and its undeniable influence on more recent musicals. In chapter 4, Richard Dyer focuses primarily on questions of race within this musical film, and especially on the place of African Americans, who register an unlikely presence in a Jewish resort in early 1960s America. This presence, however, is gradually eliminated, with the film increasingly celebrating whiteness, especially in its final sequence. For Dyer, this elimination takes with it the strong historical relationship between black and Jewish music, while Jewishness itself, despite its strong presence in the film, "all but disappears in the light of whiteness," the default identity for Americans within the context of the film.

The final two chapters in this section place *Dirty Dancing* within the political and cultural milieu of the 1980s, the decade in which the film was produced, and which has emerged as an historical period with its own political and cultural specificity. In chapter 5, Cynthia Baron and Mark Bernard discuss the film as a representation of Reagan's America and as an example of Reaganite entertainment. In terms of the former, the authors argue, *Dirty Dancing* presents a particularly pessimistic view of working-class people like Johnny, who is characterized by "feelings of guilt at not having made it." As an example of Reaganite entertainment, however, the film offers reassurance and satisfaction. "Disturbances and problems," Baron and Bernard suggest, "are magically resolved before they spoil the fun," so long as they stay in the distant past of 1963 and the self-contained world of Kellerman's that bears no resemblance to the outside (1980s) world. The film's ability to entertain is also examined by Pamela Church Gibson in chapter 6. She places her emphasis on the film's relationship to the changing landscape of 1980s visual culture, which saw radical shifts around both gender roles and consumer habits. Takings its cue from the images of the "New Man" in advertising and from the nostalgic look associated with Fifties retro, *Dirty Dancing* cultivated an extremely attractive image of masculinity. This particular image, however, Church Gibson argues, was able to coexist with the idea of a strong female agency that was also emerging in 1980s America. These two trends find a material embodiment in the film's costumes, which enable the two main characters to register the changes in identity politics during the decade.

The above critical frameworks (chapters 2-6) allow for a comprehensive examination of the film's race, class, and gender politics, which are characterized by an interesting mix of politically progressive elements, especially in terms of gender, together with more problematic representations, primarily in terms of race and class politics. Irrespective of the nature of the representations, what is abundantly clear in all these discussions is that the film is not just escapist entertainment for young audiences. It engages with serious political issues, often head on, which is another reason why it stands out among other youth films of the time. Equally, its production history (chapter 1) demonstrates the possibilities for filmmakers away from the Hollywood center, if not for the companies that operated in its shadow. The film's central themes of transition and change are very much metaphors for American cinema in the late 1980s, which was entering irrevocably into a new era of conglomeration. "*Dirty Dancing* in Context," then, explores from a number of perspectives the reasons behind both the film's production and its complex textual politics.

1 VESTRON VIDEO AND *DIRTY DANCING*

FREDERICK WASSER

Introduction

The success of *Dirty Dancing* (Emile Ardolino, 1987) was a surprise twenty-five years ago. The fact that it is well-remembered to this day is a bigger surprise. But just as big a surprise is the name of the studio that made it. That is because few remember Vestron Pictures, and the company itself has been out of business for more than twenty years. It was the short-lived production division of Vestron Video, itself a once remarkably successful company that would not survive the 1980s and whose rise and fall tells us much about the revolutionary circumstances in that decade in the history of the American film industry. Vestron's history may even reveal something about the unique magic of *Dirty Dancing* itself.

Vestron Video is now as remote from us as the floppy disk, while the movie lives on forever. Why worry about Vestron when it is easy enough to imagine that some other studio made *Dirty Dancing*? Is the company that made the film important to understanding the film? Would the audience notice the difference? To answer no to these questions would be to deny the film its historical status. It was a story that could only be expressed when the creators found a studio willing and able to produce it. It was a unique road and it made for a unique film that only Vestron managed to make, one time. And then not even Vestron could duplicate it.

Dirty Dancing is set in a resort hotel in the midst of the leisure revolution of the 1960s. Toward the end of the movie the owner complains that resorts in the Catskills were coming to an end since affluence meant that summer frolickers and tourists had so many other choices. He might as well have been talking of the circumstances of Vestron in the 1980s. Vestron had helped usher in its own leisure revolution, which was the rise of home video rental, and now was falling victim to its own success. Home video was initially marketed as an extension of the television set. The movie studios were relatively agnostic about its introduction, but within a few years the use of home video was being used all over the world for movie-watching, and Hollywood had to take notice. Vestron Video was foremost among the pioneering companies driving this change in home video usage. Producing *Dirty Dancing* became a "do or die" moment in video's reformation of the American film industry. Was *Dirty Dancing* going to propel a video company into the heart of Hollywood, or would it go the way of the late, great resorts of the Catskills?

MGM was once first among the great movie companies of the studio era. But its decline was rapid in the 1960s, and by 1985 it could rarely mount a high-risk production. The executives had read a script of *Dirty Dancing* and were interested in producing it, but they finally felt they had to pass.[1] The writer, Eleanor Bergstein, shopped it to other studios with similar frustrations when she was directed to Vestron. Perhaps she had never heard of Vestron Video before, since few writers would have bothered about a company whose only business was distributing videotapes. Nevertheless, Vestron had now decided to make a film, and its CEO, Austin Furst, liked Bergstein's script. Another executive, Mitchell Cannold, was even more enthusiastic; finally, Ruth Vitale, the head of the newly formed production division Vestron Pictures, gave it the green light.

This is only the tip of the story. Investigating the circumstances surrounding how Vestron Video made this film leads to a deeper story about the changes that were culminating in the American filmed entertainment industry in 1987. (Notice how I use the expression "filmed entertainment." It was being used more and more in the business reports of the time precisely because the nature of film and movies was changing so much that no one wanted to use the older, simpler terms.) From an economic perspective, we may say that the commodity nature of film was changing; how and where people would watch movies was changing, and there were questions surrounding whether the recently emerged video market would develop new cultural expressions and/or change Hollywood itself.

Blockbusters and the Video Revolution

The analysis begins with the changing status of film as a commodity since the end of classical Hollywood in the 1940s, when approximately half a dozen integrated studios ("the majors") dominated the production, distribution, and exhibition of films. At that time, changes in American lifestyles and the introduction of television had shifted movie-going habits. The majors responded to the loss of their theatrical audience and the corresponding rise in risk by off-loading production. They encouraged independent producers to make movies with their own money and then bought the rights to distribute these movies to theaters. This kind of deal was known as a "negative pickup." This allowed the studios to produce relatively few films with their own money while maintaining a full distribution schedule. The overall result was that there were fewer major films in the market.

Meanwhile, theaters still needed new movies. Several producers and other entrepreneurs were inspired by this product drought to bypass the majors and distribute movies directly to theaters. But independent distribution was still a daunting endeavor, since the most efficient distribution systems were national, and therefore the overhead for such systems was prohibitively high for companies with less than a dozen films per year.[2] Many smaller companies specialized in certain kinds of film in order to facilitate relationships with theaters. These specializations included European art films, exploitation titles (particularly for teens), and horror movies. This did not lead to increased financial stability for major studios, and the enduring volatility of the situation changed the content and style of American filmmaking. More audiences were being addressed in new and different ways by the films of the 1960s than before, and the causal correlation between the diversity of films and the growth of independent producers and distributors was self-evident. The mix of majors, independents, in-house productions, and negative pickups continued into the next decades. But then the relative power of the majors increased and the diversity of audiences and content subsided. This was due to the relatively stable formula that the success of the mid-1970s blockbusters provided the major studios with. Films such as *The Godfather* (Francis Ford Coppola, 1972), *The Exorcist* (William Friedkin, 1973), *Jaws* (Steven Spielberg, 1975), and *Star Wars* (George Lucas, 1977) showed that single films could attract huge audiences, and Hollywood majors started to redesign their business models around making these blockbusters.

The majors self-produced the blockbusters and used them as the tentpoles of their schedules. This gave them added power in dealing with theaters, since the theaters were quite anxious to book these blockbusters and would arrange for favorable showtimes and subsequent bookings of other offerings by the majors in order to get the blockbusters. Sometimes these practices would circumvent laws against "block bookings," but there was little that anyone could do about such deals. Similarly, the majors made sure to control all aspects of selling the blockbusters to ancillary markets. "Ancillary" was defined as anything except North American theatrical markets, and ranged from foreign theater, video, and television to US TV and video to music and merchandising. The blockbusters represented huge investments, however, and the majors could only afford to make a handful per year while continuing to rely on negative pickups to fill out the rest of their schedules. This ensured enough products in the pipeline to maintain efficiency of distribution. However, the majors continued to allow independent producers to retain the ancillary rights to their movies.

In the 1970s, independent distributors survived by continuing to service the various niche audiences while exploring new technologies of distribution. Cable was beginning to purchase original films. Consumer-oriented video began when the Sony Corporation introduced the U-matic three-quarter-inch videocassette in 1969. It was designed for the educational market, and Time-Life was among several independent film companies to use it as a secondary market for a series of educational and theatrical films. Other users of the U-matic were distributors of adult films, and they would also figure into the story of film's changing status. The real changes in the status of film came after Sony's Betamax half-inch videocassette recorder (VCR) was introduced in 1975. This quickly overtook the U-matic and other video and laser playback machines on the market to become an international success in the consumer market. The reason for its immediate success was Sony's decision to market it as a machine that could time-shift television viewing. Therefore, many of the Hollywood majors tried as much as possible to ignore the introduction of the VCR; however, two of them, Universal and Disney, went even further and instituted a lawsuit against the new technology, charging Sony with contributing to copyright infringement. The lawsuit was finally decided in favor of Sony in 1984, but its pursuit created a hostile atmosphere ranging from passive wariness to aggressive hostility between the Hollywood majors and the new technology.

Therefore, the majors were reluctant to sell their films on videocassette. Twentieth Century Fox hesitated for two years before allowing Andre Blay to transfer films that were four years old or older to tape for sale in 1977. His company, Magnetic Video, assumed all the risk, so he decided to price the tapes high at more than $50.[3] Nonetheless, the offering was a success, and within a year Twentieth Century Fox bought Magnetic Video and placed Blay as the executive in charge of video sales within the film company. Within the next three years other Hollywood majors followed suit by either forming a video distribution division or operating one in partnership with a non-Hollywood company (e.g., CBS/Fox and RCA/Columbia). We must remember that the only video releases the majors had were the films for which they had retained the ancillary rights. Many new video companies were able to snatch up the rights to other high-profile films that the majors had not secured.

Vestron Begins

Meanwhile, Time-Life had decided to rationalize its filmed entertainment divisions. Its Home Box Office (HBO) had become very successful since Time had placed Gerald Levin in charge in 1973. His fellow executive at HBO, Austin Furst, was given the assignment of selling off other assets so that the company could focus on its cable operation. He sold both the Time-Life film production and theatrical distribution divisions to Twentieth Century Fox and the television division to Columbia Pictures in 1981. But no one would buy the home video division. Furst came up with the idea to buy the home video rights himself and form his own company. He could see enterprising outsiders such as Andre Blay and Noel Bloom (creator of Family Home Entertainment) starting to exploit the void that the majors had created by not snapping up and distributing all the films with outstanding video rights. Home video distribution was a rare opportunity that could reward individual risk-taking.

In 1981, Furst persuaded the other Time-Life executives to sell him the home video rights to the Time-Life films. He resigned from HBO to go into business for himself at age 38. His daughter suggested the Vestron name after the Roman goddess of the hearth, Vesta, and the Greek word for instrument, Tron. Furst recruited another Time-Life executive, Jon Peisinger, a former record company executive, to preside over the new company in the summer of 1981. Vestron Video began operations in February 1982, offering titles such as the Time-Life production *Fort Apache, The Bronx* (Daniel Petrie, 1981), starring Paul Newman, that Twentieth Century Fox had distributed to the theaters. Another Vestron Video release that had an interesting pedigree was the Burt Reynolds hit *The Cannonball Run* (Hal Needham, 1981). This was produced by the famous Hong Kong studio Golden Harvest. Once again, its American distributor, Twentieth Century Fox, had not bought the video rights by the time Furst made his offer.

Video rental was becoming important. Northern Europe led the way with stores opening up to rent both the VCR machine and the videotape. It was thought that Americans did not care to rent, but US tape rental (without the machine) did become popular using an infrastructure pioneered by adult film clubs. Club members had been exchanging tapes using credit cards as security. It was rather easy to proceed from these exchanges to in-store rentals. The majors were aghast that their films could be rented without their consent. They tried to stop these practices through contracts stipulating that tapes could not be rented, through offers to rental stores to lease the tapes, and through legislation. None of these strategies had any effect except to alienate video rental store owners from the majors. Into this new void, Vestron again moved boldly, promising the store owners its complete cooperation and to help them with their promotions of various rental tapes.

Furst and Peisinger were not looking back as they rolled over the money they got from selling tapes into acquiring more titles for distribution. Contemporaries remember how Vestron sales personnel would swarm over film festivals and small markets, placing bids on video rights with every producer they could find.[4] Furst announced that their business model was derived from the publishing industry (in contrast to the theatrical distribution models within which the majors were working). There was less emphasis on marketing individual tapes and more on offering many different types of tapes. Fictional films were just part of the mix. Vestron was willing to put out travel tapes, educational tapes, and even tapes on current events such as papal visits. Vestron became part of a groundbreaking collaboration with cable when it partnered with Showtime and MTV to produce and sell *The Making of Michael Jackson's Thriller* (Jerry Kramer) in 1983. This was an hour-long documentary that was shot about the production of the fourteen-minute music video. It was designed to fill out the video in order to promote sales of a full-length tape, and it worked. Vestron marketed the tape at the relatively low price of $30. It sold 900,000 units.[5]

Furst commanded respect as the foremost distributor and spokesperson for the emerging video market. Despite this success at co-production, Furst was not moving toward actual film production at this time. He avoided production centers such as Los Angeles and New York City by locating the company in Stamford, Connecticut, a location more typical of a publisher than of a media mogul (and, incidentally, closer to his home). His immediate competitors were fast establishing links with film production divisions. They were other specialty video distributors such as Media Home Entertainment, IVE (Noel Bloom's expansion of Family Home Entertainment), and Embassy. Media Home Entertainment had distributed John Carpenter's *Halloween* (1978) and continued to be associated with low-budget horror films. Bloom's IVE had a children's entertainment division but was now moving into horror, and Embassy also increasingly worked in the horror genre. But the publishing strategy of Vestron was clearly distinct, and the company had a completely diversified library of titles. In 1982, they scored a coup by contracting to do the video distributing for Orion Pictures, a mini-major created by former United Artists executives in 1978. For the next few years Orion's library was a major revenue source for Vestron Video. The library had titles in many different genres dating back to the 1960s.

By 1986, the home video market was returning as much money to the film producers as the theatrical market.[6] This was a new world. Not even the profound changes introduced by television in the 1950s changed the business model for theatrical filmmakers as much as the expanding flow of video money. Film companies' revenue streams attracted attention from other media corporations. In 1985, major cable pioneer Ted Turner acquired MGM for a brief period of time. Within a few months a more permanent conglomeration was in place when News Corporation bought Twentieth Century Fox, while by the end of the decade both Columbia Pictures and Warner found themselves parts of entertainment conglomerates; after a seven-year period under the corporate umbrella of the Coca-Cola Company, Columbia was bought by Japanese electronics manufacturing giant Sony, while Warner went on a merger spree that culminated in 1989 when Time-Life bought Warner to form the largest media conglomerate in the world, Time Warner. The point is that video and cable inspired the merger of major film studios with media conglomerates. The conglomerates wanted the production and distribution arms of the studios, and the studios wanted the deep pockets of the conglomerates. Costs were increasing precisely because film was now being sold to theaters, cable, and video.

In particular, costs went up when producers, who felt they were being shortchanged on video, increased their asking price for the rights. If in 1983 Vestron could buy video rights for a couple of hundred thousand dollars, now it had to negotiate for a couple of million. This forced even relatively small distributors into the uncomfortable position of picking winners and losers, since only a few movies would justify such expensive video rights. In addition, this became a picked-over market, since the majors were locking down all the sure winners. Because of this new competiveness, Vestron felt compelled to acquire *Prizzi's Honor* (John Huston, 1985), a movie with two major stars, for $4.5 million. It made a profit by selling 150, 000 units, but profit margins were slim and Vestron was becoming nervous.[7]

In 1985, Furst was eager to take the company public to make some personal money and to get better access to capital and credit. But there was pressure to change Vestron's way of doing business in order to have a successful stock sale. One Wall Street analyst stated that Furst's price was too high since Vestron was "only one of the top five [video distribution] companies that d[id] not own its own film production operation, so it [had to] compete in an increasingly difficult market."[8] It did not take much diligence to discover that Orion would soon start to self-distribute its videotapes and therefore not renew its contract with Vestron. This represented the loss of a major asset. Wall Street investors wanted to know what would be the future inventory for Vestron Video. The successful sale of stock came at the end of the year when Furst lowered the price of the initial public offering and made some assurances to direct Vestron to start making its own programming.

Production Strategies and *Dirty Dancing*

By January 1986, Jon Peisinger announced that Vestron Pictures was being created as an in-house feature film division. It was the first film production division developed by a videocassette distributor and was the only major attempt to do so in the history of the video era. Peisinger promised to put out a full slate of pictures, up to twelve a year.[9] They hired William J. Quigley away from the Walter Reade Organization to be the senior vice president with responsibilities for the distribution and marketing of films. (Quigley was the third generation of a prominent film industry family.) Mitchell Cannold was also hired to be the vice president of production. He had gone the independent route to produce *Go Tell the Spartans* (Ted Post, 1978) and executive produce *Hit and Run* (Charles Braverman, 1983). Ruth Vitale had worked her way up through Vestron to be selected as the vice president of feature film production. This became the team that guided *Dirty Dancing* through the corporate level.

Vestron had several executives who had worked in the music industry. There was no conscious decision to pursue musical productions, but when the *Dirty Dancing* script arrived it quickly found favor with readers who sympathized with the heavy use of pre-British invasion rock 'n' roll in the storyline. There was a string of profitable dance and music films that began with *Saturday Night Fever* (John Badham, 1977) and *Grease* (Randall Kleiser, 1978) and accelerated several years later with *Flashdance* (Adrian Lyne, 1983), *Footloose* (Herbert Ross, 1984),

Purple Rain (Albert Magnoli, 1984), *Breakin'* (Joel Silberg, 1984), and *Breakin' 2: Electric Boogaloo* (Sam Firstenberg, 1984). Vestron had made money with Michael Jackson, and even the first film that Vestron used as a trial run for theatrical distribution was a romantic musical from Australia entitled *Rebel* (Michael Jenkins, 1985).

The tricky question was how to budget *Dirty Dancing*. The average budget for a major studio film was inching up to $20 million (MPAA).[10] The majors had been using the new revenues from video to increase both the production and the marketing budgets of their movies rather than increasing the number of movies being made. Some independent producers, notably the legendary Italian producer Dino DeLaurentiis and his imitators Andrew Vajna and Mario Kassar, were also increasing their budgets to match the majors. Other independents were lowering their budgets in order to increase the number of movies that they could make and release to video. Many low-budget producers tended to follow genre formulas such as horror, fantasy, and thrillers. However, one low-budget production company, Cannon, was rather eclectic in its genre range. It made romances, music/dance, action, and even art films. Menachem Golan and Yoram Globus, the two Israeli cousins who ran the American company, were promiscuous in their choice of genre ever since they decided that the video market would support expanded production in all areas. Their formula was to make as many movies as possible. Their theory was that ancillary markets such as video would limit losses and that the more titles they had in distribution, the more likely it was that one would be a breakout hit. Unfortunately for Cannon, the breakout hit never really materialized, although several films did well.

The high-end contrast was the strategy pursued by DeLaurentiis. He was an independent working in the United States since the 1970s who made one or two big budget movies a year. By the mid-1980s, two other non-Americans, Vajna and Kassar, would also use the DeLaurentiis formula of self-financing a few big-budget (above the MPAA average) movies and controlling the global distribution. Based on the runaway success of *First Blood* (Ted Kotcheff, 1982), which was budgeted at $14 million, they put together $44 million in order to produce the sequel: *Rambo: First Blood Part Two* (George P. Cosmatos, 1985). This movie went on to sell movie tickets worth over $300 million all over the world.[11] Vajna and Kassar named their studio

Carolco, and produced other big-budget films such as *Terminator 2* (James Cameron, 1991). Both DeLaurentiis and Carolco would sell off their movies as negative pickups to a big Hollywood distributor (Paramount and Tri-Star, respectively) while taking control of distributing the movie to the rest of the world. These producers had access to international credit lines and the connections to set up deals with foreign distributors even before the film was made (a practice that was known as pre-selling). Cannon also relied heavily on international pre-sales. Carolco used its foreign credit to refinance IVE (at which point it was renamed LIVE) in order to handle video distribution of its big productions.

Vestron had had video successes in the international market but did not follow either the Cannon or Carolco formulas, and was more inclined to follow the model of Orion, Hemdale, and some other mini-majors. These companies were less oriented to the international market and therefore less interested in action films than Cannon, Carolco, and DeLaurentiis. Their films had younger Hollywood actors who might make an impression on American audiences, not the older international stars that DeLaurentiis favored. Hemdale budgets ran well below the MPAA average and hovered in the $6 million range. Orion was more flexible, with both $4 million and $13 million films in production at this time.[12] But they avoided action precisely to keep down the budgets and because they were targeting English-speaking audiences interested in romance and other dialogue-centric genres.

Vestron Pictures contemplated these lessons from the non-major production companies that were comparable in status and financial resources to itself. They decided not to compete with Hollywood in making blockbusters and initially had an instinct against low-budget exploitation films and high-budget action films. When *Dirty Dancing* was given the go-ahead, the producers hired actors familiar to the American scene who would not charge very high sums (notably Jerry Orbach) to bring the budget down to $6 million. The director was a semi-neophyte Emile Ardolino, who had not yet done a major feature film. Jennifer Grey was the lead, and she had yet to prove that she could support a major film; perhaps the studio trusted that she was strong enough to do so because of her pedigree as the daughter of veteran Broadway actor Joel Grey. Her co-lead, Patrick Swayze, had had strong roles in *The Outsiders* (Francis Ford Coppola, 1983) and *Red*

Dawn (John Milius, 1984) but had yet to obtain star status. He contracted for a fee of $200,000.[13] The use of such young yet-to-be stars and relatively modestly priced veterans (including Jack Weston) was in keeping with the middle path formula.

Theatrical releasing has always been a hard task and a major barrier against new film distributors. Vestron reports that it did not have major problems when the time came to release the film on the third weekend in August 1987. They had allowed a generous post-production period of ten months after the end of principal photography. The distribution team was waiting to get the theaters they wanted and managed to book almost a thousand theaters (a standard wide release) in the relatively uncompetitive part of the summer season. Orion's *No Way Out* (Roger Donaldson) and Buena Vista's *Can't Buy Me Love* (Steve Rash) had opened a week earlier. *Dirty Dancing* did not immediately surpass these films and got only mixed reviews, but word of mouth gave it "legs."[14] It sold a respectable $3.9 million in its opening weekend, topped out at $4.9 million two weeks later, and accumulated $58 million in the first twenty weeks of release. Overall, domestic ticket sales were in excess of $63 million. *Dirty Dancing* was the biggest independent, and overall was the eleventh biggest grosser, of 1987.[15] The top ten films were all from major studios.

A bigger pleasant surprise was its foreign box office grosses, which *Boxofficemojo* estimates at $150 million.[16] Grosses represent ticket sales that the distributor splits with the theaters after expenses. There are various formulas to determine how much of the ticket revenue is returned to the distributor, and one can imagine that Vestron got back $25 million from the domestic release. The foreign return is more difficult to estimate, but might be higher than $60 million. Of course, Vestron had more clout and experience in the video release of the movie. It sold 300,750 units by February 1, 1988.[17]

Failure in Spite of Success

Yet despite the hit and despite the earnings, Vestron had reached its limit and was now in an irreversible downward spiral. The problem was that no film company had survived with only one hit since before the days of D.W. Griffith. The tide was turning even faster against small, one-hit operations in the mid-1980s, because the major movie companies had upped the ante and were increasingly financed by bigger media conglomerates. It was ironic that increases in marketing budgets for films (averages were now $6.9 million, which was higher than the production cost of Dirty Dancing[18]) came about because of the very success that Vestron and others had had in creating the video market. The immediate problem for Vestron was to find more successes, and here is where it became obvious that Dirty Dancing had not broken down barriers. The movie did not lead to a franchise, and no one at Vestron could figure out how to reassemble the audience that came together for this film.

The company's main step toward exploiting Dirty Dancing was a spin-off television show under the same title. Produced by Vestron Television, a Vestron division that had not been particularly active, and aired on the CBS network, the series failed to match the success of the film and proved short-lived. Despite sharing with the film a number of common elements, including Johnny and Baby (the latter now the daughter of Kellerman's resort owner), the same setting, and the use of songs associated with the film, with the exception of Kenny Ortega, who choreographed the dance sequences and directed a few episodes, none of the original above-the-line talent was involved with the TV show. Premiering in late October 1988, the show was canceled ten episodes later in January 1989.

The failure of the show put a stop to discussions about a sequel to the film that perhaps would have stood a better chance of success, especially if Swayze and Grey had agreed to reprise their roles (which had gone to Patrick Cassidy and Melora Hardin in the TV series). But if the movie could not be cloned, perhaps Patrick Swayze might become his own franchise. He had demonstrated the strength and charisma of a genuine movie star. Vestron had already cast him as the lead in Steel Dawn (Lance Hool, 1988), a low-budget apocalypse film that did very little at the box office. Swayze went looking for a bigger outfit that could do bigger films and found one when he starred in Road House (Rowdy Herrington; Silver Pictures and United Artists) in 1989. Ruth Vitale also left to pursue independent productions with a major studio. Jon Peisinger had managed to open Dirty Dancing wide and to give it an adequate advertising budget (although its success was, arguably, due more to word of mouth than to the marketing campaign), but Vestron was not prepared to back its other films to anywhere near the same degree. For example, *Steel Dawn* had a much smaller release and advertising budget.[19] Over the next two years, Peisinger had only two more opportunities to give a movie the same marketing launch as *Dirty Dancing: Earth Girls Are Easy* (Julien Temple) and *Dream a Little Dream* (Mark Rocco). Both fizzled in 1989.[20]

Vestron Video lost money in 1987, its first year of losses. In 1988, on the strength of *Dirty Dancing*, it returned to profits, and Austin Furst capitalized on this to negotiate a $100 million line of credit with Security Pacific.[21] Nonetheless, time was running out. It was not just the cost of producing seven or eight movies per year (below their stated target but still a hefty number) but also the higher and higher cost of doing business in the video market. The executives decided that there was a limit to the publishing model and that the market was turning against obscure films that had not had the exposure of a theatrical run. Therefore they continued to seek out films that might receive some critical notice, such as John Huston's last picture, *The Dead* (1987), and to pay top dollar for Hollywood ensemble films such as *Young Guns* (Christopher Cain, 1988).

Vestron's return to profits was short-lived, and Security Pacific got cold feet (not just with Vestron but also with other mini-majors). The bank refused to honor its commitment to give the credit line, and Furst shut down production and declared bankruptcy. There was no re-organization. Most executives jumped ship, and Vestron went out of business in 1990. Furst pursued a lawsuit against Security Pacific (which was soon bought and bought again). By the time Furst won his lawsuit, it was against Bank of America, and he personally gained as much from the lawsuit as from his half a dozen years of building Vestron.

Vestron became the poster boy for all the mini-majors and independent distributors that were going out of business. DeLaurentiis, Cannon, Carolco, the Samuel Goldwyn Company, Hemdale, and even Orion were all fading out or going bankrupt by 1992. Miramax was the only rising independent in the early 1990s, and a large part of its success was that it could buy films from the bankrupting companies. Even Miramax was a cautionary story; only three years after Furst started selling off Vestron, Miramax allowed itself to be purchased by the very major Walt Disney Company. Another surviving independent, New Line, also sought refuge within the corporate giant Time Warner.

One way of looking at the demise of Vestron treats *Dirty Dancing* as an irrelevant fluke. Vestron had taken advantage of a small window of opportunity. It snapped up available rights and built the video market. When the market hit a critical mass, video rights reverted to those studios that had the power to make films and market them—the major studios. Vestron could then only find less desirable rights and products and would either fade away or go out of business. Business analysts dubbed this "the Vestron Law," and even now it receives attention on the Internet. Joseph Esposito explains that when "publishers or content producers in non-print media license rights to third parties, over time the pressure builds to revert those rights."[22] What happened to Vestron actually resembled what happened in the early days of television, when secondary movie producers made money in the 1950s syndicating their movies to television stations until the networks and the major studios finally agreed on a price for mainstream movies in the 1960s. Years later, Furst observed that video behaved just like the early days of television, and stated that because of that "home video came right back to the [film] industry."[23] This suggests that at some point he realized that the publishing model had been victimized by the "Vestron Law." The Vestron Law is currently observed operating in various platforms such as YouTube and Facebook.

But industry observers still have a romantic regard for Vestron because the company beat the odds with *Dirty Dancing*, its first movie. If *Dirty Dancing*'s millions could not make a new studio competitive, what could? The very fact that *Dirty Dancing* did not lead to success for the company points to the new status of movies at that time. Either they had to be a franchise or at least of a type or genre to which the same large audiences would return in various media and in various iterations of different movies.

What type was *Dirty Dancing*? It was a romance, a dance film, a music film, and a period piece. None of these categories represented a viable production strategy. Vestron was not in a position to really capitalize with other recognizable "chick" flicks. Such films, if well-written, are snapped up in development by the major studios. Vestron managed to get an offbeat one, *Earth Girls Are Easy*, starring Geena Davis and Jeff Goldblum. This had been developed originally by Warner Bros. and it went into production with DeLaurentiis. By the time Vestron got it, the production budget had gone to $10 million, and Vestron had to clear several legal hurdles before they could present it to an audience.[24] It did not reach profits. Mitchell Cannold had developed some other hard-to-categorize movies such as *Parents* (Bob Balaban, 1989) in-house at Vestron, but they were not romances and did not get enough critical attention to find another audience grouping to reach profits.

Instead, Vestron Pictures pursued various genre productions from horror to oddball. Industry critic Anne Thompson cited film executive Sam Kitt's charge that Vestron was too eclectic to get marketing momentum.[25] Vestron might have followed the strategy that Goldcrest Films had stumbled upon earlier after the success of *Chariots of Fire* (Hugh Hudson, 1981). That company felt it had identified an educated middle-aged audience who were not attracted to the youth-oriented fare of the period. Goldcrest pursued this audience by producing and marketing small-budget films. Inevitably, the strategy failed, as success led to irresistible pressure to increase the budgets, and other film companies started to compete for the same upscale audiences. After several expensive flops, Goldcrest became dormant by the late 1980s.

Independents have briefly emerged since the demise of Vestron. Miramax certainly benefited from the wholesale bankruptcies of the 1980s and then cleverly sought shelter in the deep pockets of the Walt Disney Company. New Line did the same with Time Warner. LIVE inherited many of Vestron's assets before being taken over and renamed Artisan Entertainment, which briefly gained attention with the cult hit *The Blair Witch Project* (Eduardo Sánchez and Daniel Myrick, 1999). But small companies such as Artisan and Trimark that were the last vestiges of the independent video distributors have more recently been folded into Lionsgate, the successful Canadian film studio. Vestron executives have spread throughout the entertainment industry into music and video games and independent film productions, and many of their individual efforts have shown the legacy of being at a company that pioneered the video market. The cinematic charms of *Dirty Dancing* will be explored in other chapters; the industry lessons that Vestron learned from making the movie were rather rougher. The film was made in improvised circumstances, as are many films. Other producers could have made it, but it was the unique circumstances of Vestron that shaped this unique film.

Notes

1. Michael Wiese, *Film & Video Marketing* (Los Angeles and Stoneham, MA: Michael Wiese Productions and Focal Press, 1989), 122.
2. Suzanne Mary Donahue, *American Film Distribution: The Changing Marketplace* (Ann Arbor: UMI Research Press, 1987).
3. Anon., "Conversation with Andre Blay," *Videography* (June, 1979): 53.
4. James Bryan, independent filmmaker, interview with the author (April 4, 1990).
5. Foreign sales were more important than domestic, and the foreign market was particularly open to music titles. See Geraldine Fabrikant, "As Video Soars, Vestron Slips," *New York Times,* May 23, 1987, Section D, 34.
6. Goldman Sachs, "Movie Industry Update," *Investment Research Report* (1991).
7. Frederick Wasser, *Veni, Vidi, Video: The Hollywood Empire and the VCR* (Austin: University of Texas Press, 2001), 172.
8. Geraldine Fabrikant, "Wall Street Awaits Video Wunderkind," *New York Times,* September 19, 1985, Section D, 1.
9. Geoff Mayfield and Tony Seidman, "Vestron Video Forms 'Modes' Film Division," *Billboard* (January 18, 1986): 1 and 62.
10. MPAA, *U.S. Economic Review* (Encino, CA: Motion Picture Association of America, 1990).
11. The Internet Movie Database (IMDb), http://www.imdb.com/title/tt0089880/business. Accessed on June 1, 2011.
12. IMDb, http://www.imdb.com/company/co0001995/. Accessed on March 12, 2011.
13. Ben Child, "Kenny Ortega Set to Direct Dirty Dancing Remake," *The Guardian,* August 9, 2011, http://www.guardian.co.uk/film/2011/aug/09/kenny-ortega-dirty-dancing-remake. Accessed on October 26, 2011.
14. "Legs" is a showbiz term indicating that a show or a movie continues to attract a strong audience even after the opening days of its debut or release.
15. All figures for *Dirty Dancing* were taken from *Boxofficemojo,* http://boxofficemojo.com/movies/?id=dirtydancing.htm. Accessed on June 1, 2011.
16. Ibid.
17. *Vestron Annual Report* (1987).
18. MPAA (1990).
19. IMDb, http://www.imdb.com/title/tt0094033/. Accessed on March 12, 2011.
20. Wasser, *Veni,* 175.
21. Austin Furst, Vestron's Chief Executive Officer, interview with the author (November 2, 1995).
22. Joseph Esposito, "Vestron's Law: The Propensity for Rights to Revert to the Original Publisher," http://scholarlykitchen.sspnet.org/2011/01/24/vestrons-law-the-propensity-for-rights-to-revert-to-the-original-publisher/. Accessed on June 1, 2011.
23. Furst, interview.
24. Bryan, interview.
25. Anne Thompson, "Another Indy Bites the Dust," *Los Angeles Weekly,* August 4, 1989.

2 BRINGING UP BABY: GENERIC HYBRIDITY IN *DIRTY DANCING*

TAMAR JEFFERS MCDONALD

Introduction

Consider the following iconic film moment: We are backstage, amid the hubbub of a company getting ready for the big show. Stagehands mosey around; the pianist resolutely thumps out the tune while the star rehearses in the foreground. But in the background, riveting the camera's, and thus the viewer's, gaze, is our heroine, painting scenery. Come opening night, we know the established star will be eclipsed as this heroine, the newcomer, takes center stage and commands the spotlight.

There is something undeniably pleasurable in this upsetting of the balance of power, regardless of whether this familiar moment comes from *42nd Street* (Lloyd Bacon, 1933), *My Dream Is Yours* (Michael Curtiz, 1949), or *The Boyfriend* (Ken Russell, 1971). In this instance, however, the pleasure derived from this revolution is enhanced by the fact that the overlooked one, the "newcomer," is more talented than the current singing "star," who has the voice and dancing skills of a crow. The Cinderella moment, when it comes, is heightened still further: The two rivals are sisters. But this is not a backstage musical. This is *Dirty Dancing*.

While *Dirty Dancing* may seem on the surface a simple love story, further attention shows that it also possesses attributes of a dance picture, even a musical, despite the fact that the performers do not sing. When *closely* examined, the film can actually be seen to draw on conventions, tropes, and iconography from a remarkably large number of other genres. In this chapter, I will examine how and why the film was constructed to absorb aspects from so many different genres of film. While approaching the topic from different points of view, film theorists such as Steve Neale[1], Janet Staiger[2], and Rick Altman[3] have documented this filmic tendency toward the incorporation of tropes from a proliferation of genres, with the former two speaking of film's "generic hybridity" and Altman using "fluidity" and "poaching" as his terms. I will first explore the notion of generic hybridity in *Dirty Dancing* and then continue by examining in particular how the film employs certain tropes and conventions borrowed from the romantic comedy genre, reworking them to serve its own specific narrative aims.

In exploring the film's use of these conventions, and the manner in which it co-opts and sometimes subverts them, I want to ask: What does the film gain by its promiscuous generic borrowings?

Genres

The opening of *Dirty Dancing* seems to establish the film's generic allegiance in an immediate and straightforward way. With apparent transparency, it sets the film firmly within the bounds of the nostalgia film, which presents a fond look back at bygone, personal events. The voiceover, the retro car, music, and fashions, the traditional familial relationships, and the golden-lit cinematography, all assert that this will be a dip back into the heroine's past.

David Shumway distinguishes the film from others in this genre such as *American Graffiti* (George Lucas, 1973) or *The Big Chill* (Lawrence Kasdan, 1983), but although *Dirty Dancing* does not merely gesture toward, but actually *supports*, a liberal and libertarian agenda, the film still maintains the fetishization of objects from the past common to its peers. What Shumway calls "commodified nostalgia"—"the revival by the culture industry of certain fashions and styles of a particular past era"—is very apparent in these opening shots.[4] While, as we will consider later, the objects and outfits surrounding the characters of "Baby" Houseman and her family do serve to pinpoint specific character traits for each of them, these same objects and outfits also clearly highlight the *pastness* of the setting. Similarly, both the music heard over the credits and the script's cultural references serve to highlight the retro feeling of the opening. Script and music, however, go beyond mere pastness, counteracting the vagueness of the specific time being evoked by the scene's other elements, to provide a more concretely locatable *periodization*. While the costumes and car could be pointing us to any time in the late 1950s or early 1960s, the music and references to President Kennedy and the Beatles affirm that this is 1963. The film is, significantly, set at a time not only when the country still preserved its confidence and innocence (before Kennedy's assassination), but also, as the summer of 1963 setting indicates, *just before* the wide availability of female birth control and *just after* the publication in February of that year of *The Feminine Mystique* by Betty Friedan, events that helped kickstart the second wave of the Feminist Movement.[5] The narrative thus sets this story of *personal* change at a time of imminent *historical* change, pinpointing us in time so that we, with hindsight, can appreciate the short period this golden moment has left to run.

However, the film does not simply commit itself to playing out within the nostalgia or historical genre conjured up by this beginning. Although the narrative devotes itself to unfolding the story of its female hero's maturation, granting Baby both desire and agency as she attempts to negotiate the twin etiquettes of dance and romance in the summer of 1963, the film soon moves beyond its interest in mere nostalgic remembrance of the heroine's rites of passage to proliferate not only the inspirations but also the images, elements, conventions, and tropes it draws on from a variety of sources, skillfully co-opting material from other genres. For example, *Dirty Dancing* becomes a musical in those scenes where it presents various dance sequences, showing the ensemble or couple exhibiting their skill, grace, and *joie de vivre*. It turns itself into a romantic drama when it displays moments of intense romantic passion, telling the story of a love affair threatened because its protagonists come from "different sides of the tracks." But this protean film also utilizes familiar elements from still further categories of films.

Baby's initial clumsiness and lack of skill at dancing make for much humor, and the film presents enjoyable forays into comedy. *Dirty Dancing* trivia holds that when Johnny performs the dance move caressing Baby's side, the film shows us not just Baby's but *Jennifer Grey's* spontaneous reaction to being tickled in this way.[6] Thus, a potential outtake was left in the movie by the director, who was charmed by the performer's evident enjoyment of the moment. Other comic interludes that are more overtly constructed by the film abound as well, however; one such comedic highlight is the sequence that plays as a female-inflected version of a training montage like the one in *Rocky* (John Avildsen, 1976). Here, Baby is shown repeatedly traversing the outdoor steps to the staff quarters while practicing her dance steps. As we watch her rehearse, attempting to internalise the rhythm and master the maneuvers, we not only see Baby go—comically—from clumsily inept (via furious and grimacing) to being finally confident, but also witness a change in her costumes: Her outfits evolve from tomboyish clamdiggers worn with blouses to overtly provocative short shorts and skimpy tops more in keeping with both the sultry summer weather and the sexualised moves of the Latin (read: passionate) dance.

In other momentary plundering, this protean film makes allusions to the genres of teen pic and juvenile delinquent movie. When Johnny's crew are seen together enjoying their dirty dancing, or worrying as a group about what will happen to Penny after her backstreet abortion, the teen pic is evoked; when working-class Johnny squares

A female Rocky: Baby's solo training

up to privileged, Yale-bound Robbie, the camp Lothario, for an insult to Baby, the brief fight scene between young men recalls other movie "rumbles." Indeed, the fighting outside the staff cabins that breaks the tension brewing between waiters and entertainers throughout the film hints for a moment that matters could get out of hand in an interesting, summer camp twist on *West Side Story* (Robert Wise and Jerome Robbins, 1961). But at times the film seems more concerned with accruing references to genres than sustaining these references, and so the moment passes, as the film moves on to hoover up another generic quotation. Even the swashbuckler genre is given a nod when Johnny and Baby are training outdoors and Johnny shows off his excellent balance on a tree branch that has fallen across a river.

Why does the film allude to and borrow from so many different genres? Let's look more closely at that brief evocation of the swashbuckler for clues. When Johnny balances on the branch before coaxing Baby out to join him in another dance sequence, he poses for an instant as if holding a sword or fencing foil. The gesture made by his wrist as he extends his arm indicates that this posing is not accidental but meant to evoke the flourish of a swordsman offering a challenge or preparing for a bout. The iconographic quotation adds momentarily to the good-humored feeling of the scene; instead of being his usual stern taskmaster self, here, out-of-doors, Johnny is more relaxed, fun to be with, and intent on entertaining Baby. The visually rich scene, with its lush green foliage and lively flowing water, contrasts with those of the indoor rehearsals, which are set in the hot, claustrophobic studio.

But the use of the swashbuckler motif also makes a further character point beyond showing that Johnny can be fun at times and is only so serious about dancing because it is his job. It also evokes Robin Hood, the heroic, handsome, altruistic class warrior who, though born into nobility, sided with the common people, "robbing the rich to give to the poor." Johnny, who feels the inequities of being lower-class in a supposedly classless society, is ennobled through his comparison to Robin Hood, as it makes his anger at being judged lowly less personal and more an affront to all his working-class peers. There is also the hint in this fleeting moment that previous sparring between Johnny and Baby—as with that between Little John and Robin on their first meeting in the famous log-bridge battle—is just a hiccup on the way to their becoming inseparable. So, although this shot lasts only a few seconds, and *can* be read as being motivated by its illustration of Johnny/Swayze's poise and grace, it *also* has a frisson generated by this quoting.

What conclusions can we draw at this point about the film's catholic mix of sources and inspirations? *Dirty Dancing* seems to be proliferating its visual and thematic touchstones primarily in order to keep audiences entertained; the different conventions employed, always skillfully integrated into the dominant narrative and timeframe, provide something for everyone, so that if the romance gets to be too much for some viewers the comedy or the brief eruption of violence in the fight scene can offer compensations. However, in drawing specifically on *filmic* conventions—Johnny is not just like Robin Hood, he is like *Errol Flynn* as Robin Hood—*Dirty Dancing* seems to go beyond this pragmatism to become a more self-aware text. Roger Ebert's damning review on the film's release suggests that *Dirty Dancing*'s creators cynically milked the old formula of "love between kids of different backgrounds," and that the only new thing added to the mix is the provocative title.[7] My feeling, in countering this, is that the film is fully aware of the filmic and generic quotations and evokes them not in an exploitative but in a knowing way. If we next turn to the film's co-opting of elements from two final genres, it might help to cast some light on its achievements.

"The Wrong Partner"

We've seen how the film borrows from many other genres, whether for a fleeting moment or a more sustained co-option. In plundering aspects from the romantic comedy genre, however, *Dirty Dancing* makes very particular use of a specific trope, intriguingly ensuring that the evocation of the light-hearted rom-com genre turns darker by coupling it with another kind of film. Furthermore, what *Dirty Dancing* takes from romantic comedy fascinatingly does not involve the central romantic couple, Baby and Johnny, despite the ease with which rom-com elements could have been subsumed by the narrative.

For example, the film could easily have made more out of the character oppositions of the leads. The common trope of "hate at first sight," that instant spark of animosity between female and male protagonists, could have been incorporated into the movie's trajectory. Friction between Baby and Johnny does occur while he is trying to train her to dance, but while each seems at times irritated by the other, this never develops into active dislike. Similarly, the standard "meet cute" is avoided. Both of these traditional rom-com elements are ignored chiefly because the film is told from Baby's point of view. Baby first sees Johnny when she herself is hidden from view and has time to appraise his looks and behavior, so that when she sees him again she is already interested and keen to make him like her. Privileging Baby's viewpoint and emotions, the film avoids the parity rom-coms engender when they bring together mutual strangers in an awkward or comic way to initiate a shared antagonism or an immediate reciprocal attraction. Similarly, *Dirty Dancing* does not go down the route of arranging the pair's class differences along screwball lines, with physical Johnny helping book-learned but sensuously clueless Baby to feel instead of think. Although the film clearly shows the importance of comic moments, of play and fun, to their burgeoning relationship, it does not shape them into recognized romantic comedy ingredients like those listed here. Instead, it utilizes a component that is generally kept to less dominant characters. Significantly, it also uses this component, perhaps uniquely, to bind the film into participation in yet another genre, the family melodrama.

The film's principle co-option from romantic comedy is the employment of an archetypal character Steve Neale calls "the wrong partner."[8] Neale defines the wrong partner as someone whom the central character must outgrow and forego, and who is usually in place at the start of the narrative. In *Bringing Up Baby* (Howard Hawks, 1938), for example, the wrong partner for hero David Huxley is his fiancée, Miss Alice Swallow. Alice is overdetermined, through the weight of narrative and her costume and performance, as the unattractive option which David must decline in choosing the right one, Susan Vance.

Neale goes further, however, to suggest that the wrong partner is not merely wrong emotionally but also represents some quality or ambition in the central character that needs eradication.[9] Both Miss Swallow and the characteristics of David that made him choose her—his dull *sexlessness* and arid dedication to work at the expense of pleasure—must be excised from his life. Whereas Alice is determined to work through her honeymoon, Susan is happy to have all the fun of the honeymoon *before* a wedding, if David will only let her. The film supports this as the most healthy attitude, and by choosing Susan over Alice at the film's end David indicates that he has not only elected the more wholesome alternative but also given up the dreary aspects of himself that were tempted otherwise. Besides Susan's tame leopard, David is seen to be the "Baby" of the film's title, and to need weaning away from both Miss Swallow and those characteristics within himself that have made them a couple.

Because of its subject matter as conveyed in its title, *Dirty Dancing* inherently suggests that the central character will find a partner. Beyond this, the film's poster and tagline ("First dance. First love. The time of your life") both suggest the formation, during the narrative, of a heterosexual couple. The narrative itself begins with the voice of the radio disc jockey announcing "Our summer romances are in full bloom and everybody, but *everybody's* in love!" which similarly coaxes audiences to expect that there will be a romance in the story line. Having then set up these initial resonances, the film is quick to present us with a potential partner for Baby in Billy, the cute bellhop who notices Baby when she helpfully takes the baggage out of the car with him and to whom she seems initially attracted. The Houseman family is soon also introduced to Neil Kellerman, the hotel owner's grandson; although he seems to think he is perfect for Baby, he appears so comically arrogant and self-satisfied that we know fairly quickly that he is not right for her. It might be a straight fight between wealthy but insensitive Neil and poor but sympathetic Billy, but then into the film walks Johnny. As noted, not only does the film privilege Baby's subjectivity by showing us her first encounter with Johnny when he is not aware of her presence, enabling both character and audience to study him, but we are also in a position to register the effect that Johnny's appearance has on Baby: She straightens as if suddenly alert, physically aroused at the sight of the man. From this point in the narrative onwards, there is no doubt about who the *right* partner will turn out to be, but there is an unusual profusion of wrong ones. The film lines up potential rivals to Johnny for Baby's affections in Neil and Billy, but then boldly exposes Dr. Jake Houseman, Baby's father, as the real threat.

Bringing family dynamics into its generic mix in this way, *Dirty Dancing* makes overt in its narrative that a girl has to stop viewing her father as the greatest man in the universe in order to achieve an appropriately mature sexual identity. The tensions shown within the family unit brought about by Baby's journey to maturity firmly underline the film's participation in the melodrama. Baby's actions, and her father's *reactions*, shown in scenes of tense family meals, of confession and confrontation, show how the film directly inhabits similar territory with films such as *Rebel Without a Cause* (Nicholas Ray, 1955) or *Imitation of Life* (Douglas Sirk, 1959), which both involve as part of their plots the emotional journeys their young protagonists must take in order to work out what kind of man or woman to become. Although very different central emphasis is given in these films to the struggles of Jim Stark (James Dean) and Susie Meredith (Sandra Dee), the teenagers must both learn to separate themselves from their parental role models—Jim to become a stronger man than his father and Susie a softer, less selfish woman than her mother. *Dirty Dancing* shows that another separation is necessary for teenagers, too, from the parent of opposite gender. Baby must move through the film from her position of idolizing her father to finding another man— Johnny—to be her right partner.

From the start of the film, Baby is shown to be partnered with her father, as *Dirty Dancing* charts the evolution of her emotional separation from him. The following four scenes in which their relationship is either displayed or discussed show how the film attempts to "bring up Baby."

As noted earlier, the mise-en-scéne of the film's opening serves not only to conjure up a sense of its historical period but also to suggest initial characterisations. In the car on the way to Kellerman's, we first meet Baby reading a book, before the camera pans left to show us her sister, Lisa, flirting with herself in a hand mirror. Furthering this obvious cerebral/corporeal opposition, the former wears a white shirt and blue denim shorts while the latter is dressed in more feminine garb, a pale lavender blouse and pale blue skirt. Baby is presented as the brainy tomboy who has serious matters of world import on her mind rather than anxiety about bringing insufficient pairs of shoes to the summer camp, the topic exercising Lisa's imagination by the time they arrive.

The camera pulls forward from the primping Lisa to the elder Houseman couple. Apart from their clothing, which again provides confirmation of the early-1960s setting of the film, there appears to be nothing overtly significant about the couple. There certainly seem to be no character clues via objects guiding our initial viewpoints on the parents as there were with their daughters. However, their positions in the car do perhaps serve to do this: Mrs. Houseman sits in the passenger seat while her husband drives. This reinforcement of then-traditional family power structures, with passive mom and in-charge, active dad, are shown to play out across the rest of the narrative. Almost at once Dr. Houseman is shown to have more importance in the nexus of relationships than the others in the car. As we see Baby lean forward and put her arms around him, her opening voiceover mentions her father: "That was the summer of 1963—when everybody called me Baby, and it didn't occur to me to mind. That was before President Kennedy was shot, before the Beatles came, when I couldn't wait to join the Peace Corps, and I thought I'd never find a guy as great as my dad. That was the summer we went to Kellerman's." The stage is obviously set for Baby to change her mind about her dad's greatness, and the last line of this opening narration indicates the setting for this change, the holiday hotel. Characters and actions at this locale will act from the very first to separate the film's initial couple and show Baby that Daddy is the wrong partner she must leave behind.

The Housemans' first organized holiday activity is to take some dance lessons, led by former Rockette Penny. We meet her teaching the assembled guests the dance moves, but she, like the radio DJ before her, seems to have been recruited also to advertise the importance of summer romance and thus set the scene for the unfolding narrative. As she instructs the men to dance behind her in one circle and the ladies to form an inner one, she informs the latter group, "Now, ladies, when the music stops, you're going to find the man of your dreams."

When she yells stop, Baby and her father can clearly be seen making toward each other instinctively. Baby and her Daddy are thus almost partnered together in the first dance of their holiday; given Baby's musings earlier, we can understand she believes her own father is, in Penny's words, the man of her dreams. However, just as they are about to join hands and dance together, Penny suddenly comes between them and dances with him, forcing him backward and away from his daughter, who ends up partnered with a little old lady. Baby's wistful glance sideways at the couple as they dance together registers

Bringing Up Baby: Generic Hybridity in Dirty Dancing

Penny stops Baby from finding the man of her dreams during the merengue.

her disappointment in being blocked from being partnered with her father. On a symbolic level, Penny will come between Baby and her father within the narrative as well as here in the dance; since Baby cares for Johnny and Johnny for Penny, Baby is driven to help the woman by providing the money for her abortion, by replacing her in the dance exhibition, and by fetching her father when the termination goes wrong. Both Penny and Johnny have roles to play in Baby's maturation process, Johnny by being the right partner she must learn to dance with, and Penny by effectively blocking Dr. Houseman from being with his daughter.

Another key sequence that furthers our understanding of Baby being with the wrong partner—her dad—comes in the scene where Baby advises sister Lisa not to sleep with Robbie because "the first time should be with… someone you sort of love." Lisa responds by denying that Baby proffers this advice because she cares about her sister's sexual and romantic well-being; instead, she insists, "What you care about is that you're not Daddy's girl anymore." Lisa thus ignores Baby's tacit declaration of having lost her virginity, responding instead with a seeming non sequitur: she asserts that Baby resents sacrificing her longstanding familial status as Daddy's favorite. Lisa's apparently random line actually exposes the film's alignment of Baby's rebellion against fatherly authority with the sexual act, since she sleeps with Johnny immediately after her father tells her she is never to see "any of those people" ever again. In seeking Johnny out not only to carry on being his friend but to initiate a sexual relationship with him, Baby shows that she is moving on from the wrong partner toward the right one. As part of its project of bringing up Baby, the film encourages her to pursue secret and illicit physical activities with Johnny—both dancing and romancing—rather than the paternally sanctioned serious book study with which she has been associated up to that point. This shift from thinking to doing, reading to acting, corresponds with the shift in male objects of identification and desire. As with *Bringing Up Baby*, the central character must forsake the internal qualities that attracted the wrong partner, and, as in the earlier film, too, it is passive book-learning that must be foregone in order to experience the more physical thrills occasioned by the right partner.

Finally, while the new, right couple is constituted through energetic action (both vertical and horizontal), only the original coupling between Baby and her wrong partner is permitted to have its relationship defined by the familiar romantic confession, when she has her big dramatic scene with her father. After she has provided Johnny with an alibi for the theft of which he is wrongly accused and thus outed herself as his lover to Max Kellerman and her whole family, the next scene shows Baby going to find her father. Leaves are falling and the mise-en-scéne underlines the content of the scene: summer is nearly over, and both the season and Baby are changing. Although Jake Houseman does not say anything throughout the sequence in response to Baby's impassioned remarks, this is the big declaration scene in the film. Baby says, "I'm part of this family and you can't go on giving me the silent treatment. There are a lot of things about me that weren't what you thought but if you love me you have to love all the things about me, and I love you, and I'm sorry I let you down, but you let me down too."

What I particularly want to draw attention to here is that Baby says "I love you." These words are never spoken between her and Johnny. Baby's emotionally overwrought scene here with her father, with her declaration of love and the tears from both of them, is a much more typically romantic scene than that in which the actual lovers say goodbye to each other. *They* have a much more restrained, slightly awkward leave-taking, which contains a remarkable comment for a love story:

JOHNNY: I'll never be sorry.
BABY: Neither will I.

This is *not* a romantic exchange! It takes in the entire story of their relationship, the idea that they will never be sorry they met, had sex, and danced together, that she stood up for him, that he got fired anyway and had to leave his job and friends and go off on his own. The potential (if minute) bit of romance in this exchange is thus toned down even further by its real-world, contingent feeling. They never declare their love for each other; Baby delivers this traditional romantic line only to her father. This highlights the intensity of the father-daughter relationship at the heart of the film; while Johnny is constructed by the narrative as being definitively the right partner for Baby's physical and emotional progress toward maturity, the pair's love story is denied the use of customary romantic phrasing. Although repudiating her father's overly possessive style of love for Johnny's more liberal affection, Baby solemnizes *only* her relationship with Dr. Houseman with the traditional three little words.

Furthermore, the scene between Jake and his daughter also links, via its emphasis on tears and crying, with the consummation scene. The question "Don't you feel like cryin'?" is asked repeatedly in the song "Cry to Me" that marks Baby and Johnny's transition from close friends to active lovers. The recording, by Solomon Burke, was released in 1962, and as such contributes to the soundtrack of carefully selected contemporaneous hits (combined with original songs written especially for the film). Its lyrics insist that, in the face of loneliness, frustrated desire, and abandonment, the natural reaction is to weep.

Moreover, the song and its lyrics have a special resonance given the narrative's intent to trace the progress of Baby's sexual maturation and the key role this plays in her transfer of affections from Dr. Houseman to Johnny. It might profitably be asked: To whom is the song addressed? It begins with the line, "When your baby leaves you all alone," but if we capitalize "Baby," the line seems to be asking Dr. Houseman what he will do now that his daughter's love and hero-worship are being re-routed. This bears out the emotional intensity of Baby's relationship with her father; Baby is not shown weeping when Johnny has to leave her, but only cries in the scene where she declares both her love for and separation from her father. Dr. Houseman too is shown wiping his eyes after she has delivered her speech and walked away, showing how moved he is by Baby's accurate diagnosis of his snobbery, as well as her declaration of separation.

What, then, does Baby have to outgrow in Daddy, in recognising that he is the wrong partner and represents a part of her that, along with him, must be rejected? It is that sense of entitlement and class prejudice which she finally condemns in their big scene together. Her dad has never said so but obviously tacitly agrees with Robbie's Ayn Rand formulation: "Some people count, and some people don't."[10] Daddy is a middle-class snob—his dislike of Johnny is based not merely on the erroneous belief that he is the "one who got Penny in trouble," but also on the threat he poses to middle-class family stability with his lower-class, rough masculinity. Baby matures past this snobbish view through her relationship with the right partner. Johnny, as the film takes pains to show, is remarkably like Dr. Houseman: kind, nurturing, talented, and clever. Importantly, the two differ not because of Johnny's youth and sexual attractiveness, or even his lower-class status, but because of his lack of snobbery. Johnny is prepared to befriend anyone who has likable qualities; Jake prefers his protégées, like Robbie, to come with Ivy League credentials. This is a point that Baby openly challenges in the part of her speech to her father that precedes her declaration of love: "I'm sorry I lied to you, but you lie too. You told me everyone was alike and deserved a fair break, but you meant anyone who was like you." Baby's big scene with her father is thus both a renunciation and a reaffirmation: She rejects his snobbery, as she has been shown by Johnny that people's true value lies in who they are, not to what class they belong. But she also remakes her covenant to her father, assuring him of her continuing love, even as she subtly shifts the emphasis of this love away from their past special relationship as partners to her more appropriate place as "a member of this family."

Conclusion

To return to my initial question, then: What *does Dirty Dancing* gain by its promiscuous borrowings? Perhaps *Dirty Dancing* is successful because it has something for everyone. Audiences can be fairly well-assured that somewhere amongst all its generic plunder there will be something in the film to please most viewers, whether it is the dancing, the romance, the comedy, the nostalgia, or any one of the other elements co-opted and skillfully integrated into the narrative mix. In offering something for everyone, the film backs up the theory advanced by genre theorists, including Altman and Neale, that a text that proliferates genres also proliferates audiences. It should be recognized, however, that, despite the potentially excessive nature of this magpie borrowing, each purloined generic element is tightly linked to the overall narrative, carefully, painstakingly plaited in with all the other strands to serve the dominant trajectory. We have already looked at the tiny moment where Johnny is presented as Robin Hood in a gesture that not only celebrates his/Swayze's graceful poise but also evokes a heroic figure of myth who, like Johnny, stands up for the downtrodden lower classes. One more instance can serve to confirm the film's care to bind its generic allusions to its main trope. The sequence where Baby is seen practicing the tricky dance steps on her own has already been mentioned as one which brings comedy into the film, largely through the character's fury at her initial inability to master the maneuvers. Baby grows up before our eyes in this scene, too. Increased confidence in her control over her body is shown in her humorous, overdramatic dance poses, but beyond the clowning lies the revelation that she is becoming a fitting partner for Johnny, both on and off the dance floor. The metonymy of using dancing as a symbol for sex is not a new one, but its subtle figuring here in a solo comic rehearsal scene indicates how *Dirty Dancing* makes all its generic borrowings work together to serve its overarching theme. The trope that ties all the disparate generic elements together is Baby's maturation, the development of her adult sexuality, and what she needs to do in order to fulfill its potential.

The employment of the wrong partner trope from romantic comedy seems to be the film's most audacious steal, however. By setting up

Baby's *father* as this archetypal character, a person who, in the heterosexual romance storyline, is generally seen as wrong but not *taboo*, the film comments on what it really meant to be a daddy's girl in early-1960s America and how hard Baby has to struggle to achieve sexual maturity during this era. The film realigns Baby's desires so that she may become *socially* transgressive by choosing her own, lower-class lover, because in so doing she abandons her more sexually taboo position as Daddy's wrong partner. *Dirty Dancing* thus uses this rom-com convention to underline the dangerously intense feelings that could be generated by the traditional American family nexus. In a similar way, all its generic borrowings serve to highlight this point, even if at times they seem to camouflage the boldness of the storyline.

Notes

1. Steve Neale, "Questions of Genre," *Screen* 31.1 (1990): 57.
2. Janet Staiger, "Hybrid or Inbred: The Purity Hypothesis and Hollywood Genre History," *Film Criticism* 22.1 (1997): 5-16.
3. Rick Altman, "Reusable Packaging: Generic Products and the Recycling Process," *Refiguring American Film Genres: History and Theory*, ed. Nick Browne (Berkeley: University of California Press, 1998), 1-41.
4. David R. Shumway, "Rock 'n' Roll Sound Tracks and the Production of Nostalgia," *Cinema Journal* 38.2 (1999): 30.
5. Betty Friedan, *The Feminine Mystique* (New York: W.W. Norton and Co., 1963).
6. The Internet Movie Database, http://www.imdb.com/title/tt0092890/trivia. Accessed on July 1, 2011.
7. Roger Ebert, "Dirty Dancing," *The Chicago Sun Times*, August 21, 1987, http://rogerebert.suntimes.com/apps/pbcs.dll/article?AID=/19870821/REVIEWS/708210301/1023. Accessed on July 1, 2011.
8. Steve Neale, "The Big Romance or Something Wild?: Romantic Comedy Today," *Screen* 33.3 (1992): 284-99.
9. Ibid., 289.
10. This quotation is from Ayn Rand's *Fountainhead*, a book that Robbie carries with him and cites as a major influence in his life.

3 IS *DIRTY DANCING* A MUSICAL, AND WHY SHOULD IT MATTER?

JANE FEUER

The Vicissitudes of Diegetic Singing

A commonsense definition of a musical film would be that it is a film that has a lot of music in it. It is not a question that your average person would consider worthy of asking. For better or for worse, the scholarly study of musicals has evolved a bit further than this. And yet, we still disagree as to just how much music a film must contain to be called a musical, how that music must relate to the diegesis (the narrative world of the film), and what proportions of singing and dancing there must be. A very basic issue involves the diegetic nature of the music: Almost all films contain large amounts of non-diegetic music on the soundtrack, music that is not heard within the narrative world of the film. And many films feature singing and dancing in realistic performance settings; in fact, Rick Altman identifies an entire subgenre of "show" musicals.[1] In this way, a film can have wall-to-wall music and yet not be considered a musical (e.g., *American Graffiti* [George Lucas, 1973], or a concert film). Intuitively, we call a film a musical when it contains diegetic singing: songs or numbers that contribute to the telling of the film's narrative. Interestingly, we are not so concerned about diegetic dancing. If we were, the numerous "silent" films that used dancing as part of the narrative with an off-screen piano or orchestral accompaniment would register as musicals. Yet there seems to be a consensus that the musical film genre emerges with the coming of recorded sound to Hollywood films.

I would like to speculate a bit about diegetic singing and why it seems so crucial to defining a film as a musical. This will provide a way in to examining *Dirty Dancing* as a film with almost no diegetic singing and yet one which some people would classify as a musical.

Live singing is the very soul of stage musicals.[2] Ironically, no film musical contains live singing, although many contain diegetic singing. But the diegetic singing in musicals, even when it reproduces the singer's own voice, is always recorded or, more often, pre-recorded. To be annoyingly accurate, we should not say, "Judy Garland was a great singer" but rather, "Judy Garland was a great lip-syncher." Being a great lip-syncher is no small achievement, because it creates the illusion that we are hearing live singing when we view Judy Garland's films, and this expresses a very powerful illusion indeed. It was not just the quality of her voice that made Judy great; it was also her ability to render the illusion of actually singing on film.

The question of diegetic singing is a tough one for music videos as well. Because of their miniaturization and fragmentation, most videos do not achieve the same effect from diegetic singing as classic musicals do. Although there may be a narrating voice, such a voice is more likely to be addressed to the camera and to be constantly interrupted by other images. Although such films as *Flashdance* (Adrian Lyne, 1983), *Dirty Dancing*, and *Strictly Ballroom* (Baz Luhrmann, 1992) may be said to have an "MTV aesthetic," because of their overall narrative arc, the numbers seem more diegetic than do music videos, even when, ironically no diegetic singing emerges from the characters. *Dirty Dancing* thus manages to use "numbers" such as we used to find in classic musicals without necessarily using diegetic singing at all. The film represents a break from classic musicals, but it also represents a break from the extreme fragmentation and direct address of music videos. For example, preceding the "number" "Hey Baby," Baby and Johnny are caught in a downpour, and he breaks the car window and they drive to the creek. Non-diegetic 1980s music (Zappacosta's "Overload") plays on the soundtrack until they are on the log and talking without background music, just the sound of the waterfall. The semi-diegetic music to the number commences just before they begin to dance on the log as he beckons her to try it. I call it "semi" because, although it is narrative in function, it does not involve diegetic singing, just diegetic dancing. The steps on the log are amateur dance steps to the rhythm of the song. The dance on the log does not have the fast cutting associated with music videos. "Hey! Baby" continues to play over a cut to the couple practicing the lift in a meadow, at which point the dialogue emerges over the music. As Johnny says, "You know the best place to practice lifts? In the water," there is a jump cut to them doing just that. The non-diegetic music of "Hey! Baby" continues over the cut and then dies out as he lifts her in the water. Although there are jump cuts from scene to scene, there is no *fast* cutting; rather, a series of long-take, long shots allows room for overlapping music and dialogue. In fact, dialogue regularly occurs while a song is being played on the soundtrack. As the couple continues the lift in the water, there is no MTV-like song; rather, the leitmotif "(I've Had) The Time of My Life" plays on the soundtrack in the manner of older Hollywood movies and musicals. Likewise, when Baby comes to Johnny's room and they dance/make love, the diegetic record player miraculously changes track as they begin to move. The number is shot in long takes for the same reason as the Fred Astaire and Ginger Rogers films of the 1930s: to show us the dance and to show us that the dancing is real.

For those who prefer stage musicals over film musicals, the experience of live theatrical singing is ontological. As Walter Benjamin and others have observed, the "aura" of live performance, the spatial co-presence of the singer and the audience, is a unique experience that cannot be reproduced on film.[3] But does the experience of live *dancing* operate in the same manner? We know that dancing can be "dubbed" through a practice known as "dance doubling," usually with less believable results than with singing. Yet the experience of theatrical dance is no more "live" than the experience of unamplified singing. Gene Kelly and Vincente Minnelli each talked about how difficult it is to transfer dancing to film. As Kelly said, "It is so remote from the empathy of live theatre."[4] Yet *Dirty Dancing* gives us the impression that the dancing is diegetic, but the music is not. I said that *Dirty Dancing* has "almost" no diegetic singing because the diegetic singing it does have is of a limited nature, typically comical or ironic. Lisa's singing with hilarious gestures at the amateur talent show is a prime example. One could also cite the lip-synching the couple does in the "Love is Strange" number, where Baby mocks Johnny by reversing roles and teaching him to dance. Notably, their lip-synching is not performative, because they are clearly singing to the diegetic music on the record player. The number is thus naturalistic, as is the diegetic singing of the Kellerman's "anthem" at the end of the summer amateur show. This kind of amateur singing with untrained voices is typical of the folk musical, a subgenre of the classic musical that, as we shall see, has much in common with *Dirty Dancing*. By classifying *Dirty Dancing* as a "Jewish folk musical," I hope to be able to explain the contradictory sources of the music at the end of the film.

The song "(I've Had) The Time of My Life" has its diegetic components. It starts out emitting from a record player, but as it continues, the sound is clearly studio-recorded—and not in 1963. The male and female voices of the song stand in for Baby and Johnny; the lyrics narrate their experience, yet the voices are clearly not their own voices. This becomes obvious when Johnny briefly lip-synchs to Baby as they dance, a miming that is not meant to be actual diegetic singing. As the community dancing evolves, the music seems to be taken up by a diegetic orchestra whose instrumentation and scoring would have been realistic for the Catskills in 1963. So although the soundtrack is prerecorded in a studio, the many amateur touches in the scene give it a "folk" quality. The finale does not quite capture the feeling at the end of a show musical, when professional entertainers achieve success in front of a paying audience. It is more like the putting on of a show in a barn or like the finale of *Summer Stock* (Charles Walters, 1950), in which a group of professional entertainers put on a show with the participation of farmers in the farmers' barn. Baby never quite becomes a professional dancer, and Johnny's future remains open at the end of the film.

Dirty Dancing as a Jewish Folk Musical

Rick Altman's division of the musical into three subgenres puts *Dirty Dancing* in the center of the genre, especially since all three of Altman's subgenres are present in a pastiche.[5] The syntax of *Dirty Dancing* follows the model of Altman's "show" musical. As the film unfolds, we see a series of rehearsals moving toward the performance of a final show. As Altman describes it, the success of the show depends upon the central couple falling in love, but the love relationship depends on the success of the show.[6] In *Dirty Dancing*, the show is the final evening of the summer at Kellerman's resort. Baby and Johnny cannot succeed as a couple unless they dance together, using his steps, in the final show. And the couple cannot come together until, in traditional "New Comedy" fashion,[7] Johnny tells the father that nobody puts Baby in a corner. Also typical of New Comedies since Ancient Greece and Shakespeare, when the couple dances together on stage, the community is renewed. This rebirth of the community is celebrated in a community dance that brings the film to a close, although not precisely to closure. How will this communal dancing reconcile the tremendous class differences that separate the couple? If the film is successful, the audience will forget to ask this question, just as it has for decades at the finales of countless other musicals.

Yet *Dirty Dancing* cannot be classified entirely as a "show" musical. It also borrows semantic and syntactic elements from the fairy-tale musical, which, according to Altman, takes place in a fairy-tale kingdom or hotel, features ballroom dancing, and ends with the return to order of the hotel or kingdom after the couple's class differences have sent it into chaos.[8] Kellerman's resort becomes the defining fairy-tale element for the film, and the fact that the fate of the resort is tied to the success of the couple locates *Dirty Dancing* firmly within the fairy-tale tradition of such films as *Top Hat* (Mark Sandrich, 1935). On the other hand, the fact that Kellerman's is so precisely historically and ethnically located separates the film from the mock-serious tone of the 1930s. In *Dirty Dancing*, the fate of Kellerman's is taken very seriously because it represents an authentic historical and ethnic community whose way of life is threatened by the cultural changes emerging in 1963. I would therefore argue that for those who need to place the film in a subgenre, the best choice would be to label *Dirty Dancing* a "folk" musical.

Unlike many post-classic "musicals" with an MTV aesthetic (e.g., *Flashdance*, *Footloose* [Herbert Ross, 1984], and *Strictly Ballroom*), *Dirty Dancing* is a very Jewish film. Not only is the writer/creator Jewish, but the setting is profoundly linked to Jewish-American entertainment traditions and thus to the history of the Broadway musical, also a Jewish-American entertainment form.[9] As Eleanor Bergstein has explained, *Dirty Dancing* is based on her memories of the Jewish resorts in the Catskill Mountains that thrived in the decades just before the early 1960s when the film takes place.[10] As Jeffrey Rubin-Dorsky has written, "the extent to which Jews have preserved 'Jewishness' in the succeeding years is debatable, but the first generations of twentieth-century American Jews created in the Catskills a collective enterprise that, above all, through its humor and entertainment, kept *Yiddishkeit*—the culture, traditions, and customs of the Eastern European Jews that would soon vanish—alive."[11]

Dirty Dancing was supposed to be filmed in the Catskills but had to be moved to North Carolina for production logistics. The film displays an insider sensibility toward the assimilated Jewish culture that created the Broadway musical and that faded with the ascendency of precisely the kind of music to which youths could "dirty dance." In fact, Bergstein borrowed the term "dirty dancing" from her own youth in this transitional period in American popular music. Of course, "dirty" or highly sexualized dancing had always been associated with African-American culture, and certainly it existed before rock and roll. But the assimilation of such highly sexualized dancing into mainstream white and/or Jewish-American culture is associated with the emergence of rock and roll music circa 1955. Moreover, what scholars now identify as "Jewish" music—the sounds of Tin Pan Alley and Broadway—had been a musical tradition heavily reliant upon (one could even say stolen from) the African-American tradition of jazz and other syncopated, non-European sounds.

Thus, *Dirty Dancing* has its roots in cultures—Jewish and Black—that are not represented as central in the mainstream Hollywood musical, which (although created at least in part by Jews and paying lip service to Blacks), always liked to "whitewash" its references to American folk culture by setting folk musicals in American small towns or farms.[12] Except for eight all-black musicals, all but one of which Arthur Knight labels "folk" musicals,[13] *Dirty Dancing* is one of the most "ethnic" musicals ever made (with the additional exception of explicitly Jewish films such as *Funny Girl* [William Wyler, 1968], *Yentl* [Barbra Streisand, 1983], and *Fiddler on the Roof* [Norman Jewison, 1971]). *Dirty Dancing* acknowledges its debt to Catskills culture, yet it does so without ever explicitly identifying its setting or characters as Jewish. The film occasionally slips into Yiddishkeit and even into Yiddish, as in the scene where Kellerman and his African-American music director, played by Honi Coles, discuss the decline of the Catskills just before the final performance begins, using the Yiddish words "landsman" and "zayde" to date them just as much as when Kellerman asks if they can get the "sheet music" for Johnny's final dance.[14] The film gets to have it both ways—to an audience even somewhat familiar with Catskills culture, it is full of "insider" references, yet to a mass audience, it merely represents class barriers between Baby's family and Johnny. For example, the Internet Movie Database (IMDb) describes the film as follows: "Spending the summer in a holiday camp with her family, Frances ("Baby") falls in love with the camp's dancing teacher." This description illustrates how both class and ethnicity can be drained from the film's body, leaving only a generic story about American "folk" culture.

Not only does *Dirty Dancing* represent a denuded but legible Jewish film, it also uses that specificity to deal directly with class differences, also left unacknowledged by the IMDb description. *Dirty Dancing* participates in a long tradition of film musicals that set up binary oppositions along the lines of social class differences. Rick Altman labeled a subgenre of Hollywood musicals the "fairy tale" musical, according to this reliance on class difference between the male and female leads. However, he based this binary opposition on very early musicals with roots in European operettas. Thus, the class differences had little to do with ethnicity and more to do with older, European differences between the aristocracy and commoners.[15] *Dirty Dancing*, filmed in 1987, could take the class issues much further, all the way to setting up an opposition between upper-middle-class, professional, college-educated Jews and the "goyim" that taught them how to dance at Catskills resorts. Here again we are dealing with an explicit, real, American situation, although in encoded form. *Dirty Dancing* reveals its structural complexity in the way it sets up class "warfare": It identifies dancing with the lower-class, "white trash" and professional respectability with the sexually repressed, Jewish upper-middle class. Thus, the dancer gets to have an abortion while the doctor/father gets to fix the consequences. A world of binary differences is associated with the Baby/Johnny pairing, but they are centered on the Jewish/white trash opposition. Typically for musicals, this opposition generates an entire chain of binaries:

TABLE 3.1 Binary Oppositions in Dirty Dancing

Jewish	White trash
Baby	Johnny
Doctor's family	Community of dancers
Upper-middle-class	Lower-middle-class
Amateur entertainers	Professional entertainers
Socially aware	Self-absorbed
Sexually repressed	Sexually expressive
Innocent	Experienced
Law-abiding	Potentially criminal
Nuclear family	On their own
Ethnic appearance	Mainstream Hollywood looks

These deeply cultural binaries have always provided a backbone for the structure of a musical. The oppositions may seem to be on the surface of the film, from Patrick Swayze's muscular body to Jennifer Grey's Semitic nose, but they also provide a more or less concealed, deep structure that enables other films to transform them. This is why *Dirty Dancing* has been able to generate so many other films that do not replicate the cultural surface of the original, for example, *Strictly Ballroom* and *Dirty Dancing: Havana Nights*.

The Influence of *Dirty Dancing*

Strictly Ballroom, with its wacky Australian setting, would seem to be far removed from a Jewish folk musical. And yet its structure is not unlike that of *Dirty Dancing*. The class and ethnic differences between Baby and Johnny are transformed into the national and ethnic opposition between a "native" white Australian and an immigrant Spanish one. As is typical for the show musical, he teaches her to dance, and the majority of the numbers in the film are "rehearsal" numbers for her debut as a semi-professional dancer. Although *Strictly Ballroom* takes place within the world of "amateur" ballroom dancing, it is obviously a profession for Scott Hastings and his family, and obviously not a profession for Fran. And yet she is the only one who has faith in his ability to "dance his own steps," again a reference to a dance style "dirtier" than the Federation Ballroom steps. In dancing his steps,

Fran discovers her sexuality. In breaking the rules of their isolated world, both find themselves in a last dance that energizes the community around them. Once again, the sealing-over of the binaries is inconclusive because, even though their world is inspired to dance, they could not possibly win the Grand Prix. Nor could Johnny and Baby ever reconcile their worlds away from the fairy-tale atmosphere of Kellerman's. Not only do the binaries coincide, but the use of non-diegetic music with dancing is quite similar. Already existing songs are made to narrate the film, as when Scott and Fran dance under the Coca-Cola sign ("Time after Time") while Mr. Hastings dances below. Diegetic singing has no place in the world of amateur ballroom dancing, and yet diegetic dancing permeates it.

A film obviously even more directly influenced by *Dirty Dancing* was *Dirty Dancing: Havana Nights* (Guy Ferland, 2004). This "remake," which its co-producer and choreographer JoAnn Jansen describes as a "revisioning," best illustrates the flexibility of what director Guy Ferland calls the "*Dirty Dancing* formula."[16] The way in which Ferland thinks about this formula very much resembles the way Rick Altman theorizes the structure of the American film musical. Ferland says: "We always had a basic structure in mind based on the first film and what I call the *Dirty Dancing* formula: the simple love story between two people who are basically polar opposites. It's dance that brings them together, and they find common ground first through dance and then an emotional common ground."

This formula, however, could describe many classic dance musicals as well, not to mention many of Shakespeare's plays and numerous New Comedy plots that have appealed to audiences for many centuries. According to Rick Altman, there is nothing new or original about the formula of the American film musical; in fact, it is entirely conventional and belongs to an ancient pattern of dual-focus narratives at least as old as the "Song of Roland."[17] In some ways, the aesthetic quality of musicals has to be judged on the basis of how a particular film "tweaks" the formula, and in studying musicals (and making new ones) we are faced with the acknowledgment of very small differences indeed. In some ways, every new musical is like Gus Van Sant's (1998) exact remake of Alfred Hitchcock's *Psycho* (1960). The title of an article about this remake, "101 Ways to Tell Hitchcock's *Psycho* from Gus van Sant's," could serve as an analytic frame for just about any new musical.[18] The question "How close is too close?" always emerges, and the problem of "too close" is the reason why fans of the earlier film are usually opposed to remakes. Indeed, there is already organized fan opposition to the proposed remake of *Dirty Dancing*. On the Facebook page "Boycott *Dirty Dancing* Remake," fans have organized against the current production, which they describe as "the desecration of a classic" and "an insult to Patrick and Jennifer" even though it hasn't been filmed yet.[19] So the perception of "too close" a remake is constantly negotiated within a genre, but for the genre critic, the issue of originality is recast within the framework of "close enough." That is why we tend to value a brilliant "revisioning" of a formula over clumsier films with more innovative content that nevertheless do not seem to understand the history of the genre. That is also why, for me, *Dirty Dancing* is the ultimate Jewish folk musical and *Yentl* is not.

This is also the reason why I have always admired *Havana Nights*—because I find it to be just close enough. Based on statements made by the director, producers, and writer, the motivation for this remake was quite similar to that behind the original *Dirty Dancing*. The film is based on the real-life story of co-producer and choreographer JoAnn Jansen, who at the age of 15 moved with her family to Cuba in 1958 on the eve of the revolution. Thus, she claims, the events of the film (including falling in love with a Latin boy) have a basis in her memory, just as Eleanor Bergstein remembered family vacations at the Catskills circa 1963. Both Grossinger's Hotel in the Catskills and pre-Castro Cuba were real sites of revolutionary historical change, albeit on a different scale. Both films use location settings, in the Carolinas and in Puerto Rico, to re-create the feel of the nostalgic sites as filtered through the memory of the producers. And both use the metaphor of the coming-of-age love story to contrast historically revolutionary moments with personal ones. Perhaps the triviality of the love story cheapens the momentous nature of the Castro revolution, but not in terms of the musical genre. Increasingly, "folk" musicals have come to rely on memories of the past that have an historical rather than mythological basis. In this subgenre at least, it seems as if audiences have come to expect a more reality-based, if not necessarily more "realistic," memory narrative. Both films are narrated from some present-day moment by the girls whose story the narrative tells, and both films begin by looking back at 1958 or 1963 from a personal perspective. In each film, the girl's exposure to a form of dirty dancing sets off her sexual awakening. Both girls travel to a foreign land, in one case literally to Havana, in the other to the underground world of Kellerman's staff, accompanied by their bourgeois parents and a sister. In each, the girl is offered "mambo lessons" at an elite country club.

Havana Nights also borrows from *Strictly Ballroom*, as when the family watches old black and white home movies of the parents when they were competitive ballroom dancers. This illustrates how the formula transforms from film to film. Ballroom dancing as a signifier shifts from representing both a leisure activity of the professional class and an underground expression of socially unsanctioned sexuality for the working class. In *Strictly Ballroom*, ballroom dancing becomes a world in itself, divided between the strictly regulated rules of the Federation and the sexually free and unregulated Spanish rhythms of the steps to which Scott wants to dance. *Havana Nights* follows *Strictly Ballroom* in allowing for competitive ballroom dancing as a suitable activity for the upper-middle classes, while at the same time identifying an earthier, Latin style of ballroom that nice girls are not supposed to dance. We even see Katey ballroom dancing with her father, though in a stately, asexual style. In each case, a bourgeois form of ballroom dancing is opposed to a lower-class, sexualized "dirty dancing." The sexualized dancing triumphs in the end only by accommodating the desire of the upper-middle classes to incorporate more sexuality into their lifestyle. This manner of setting up binaries between different kinds of dancing, one aesthetic and rule-bound, the other sexualized, permeates dance films of the last twenty years and lends itself to a great variety of settings and secondary oppositions.[20] That is why the dancing in dance films is never just ornamental; it is always ideological and discursive. For example, *Take the Lead* (Liz Friedlander, 2006) opposes ballroom to hip-hop as a way of refining the unregulated sexuality of lower-class teenagers from the ghetto. The film ends with the union of ballroom with hip-hop, but, as in *Strictly Ballroom*, we never learn if this merger is enough to overturn the rules and win the competition. Racist and other forms of ideology are exposed but never fully mediated, as has always been the case in musicals. A genre of films that appears to have total closure actually plays ideological tricks on us.

Conclusion

I will now return to the original question: Is *Dirty Dancing* a musical, and what difference does that make? Certainly *Dirty Dancing* is a dance film, but the post-1987 dance film cycle can be viewed as a transformation of the traditional Hollywood musical if one wishes to stress continuity over difference. I think it is important to at least acknowledge the continuity because I am dubious as to the notion that these films are more closely related to music videos than they are to the dual-focus narratives of Hollywood musicals. While it can be said that these newer dance films combine the narrative arc of the classic musical with numbers based on music videos, this is not the whole story. Even though music videos were made from *Dirty Dancing* footage and even though they were popular, I do not view the enduring popularity of the film being due to its MTV-derived aesthetic. *Dirty Dancing* has too much narrative continuity, too much uninterrupted dancing, too many debts to the folk musical and the other subgenres, and too little fragmentation to bear a close relationship to music videos. The film's debt to the music video is primarily in its recasting of the function of diegetic singing, taking the diegetic number of the classic musical and rendering it non-diegetic. And yet many numbers in *Dirty Dancing* are diegetically motivated. How can one not read the voices of "(I Had) the Time of My Life" as belonging to the souls—if not the vocal cords—of Baby and Johnny? Moreover, so many of the numbers in the film qualify as having diegetic source music, sources that add to the nostalgia of the folk musical: old record players, hotel orchestras, lip-synching.

So what difference does it make to say that *Dirty Dancing* is a reconstructive, but nevertheless authentic, musical? For me, it has to do with trying to establish a chain of continuity within the film musical genre so that, although one can register shifts in emphasis from diegetic to non-, from discrete subgenres to pastiched ones, from diegetic singing to diegetic dancing, from deconstructive to reconstructive, one can also see what, for the want of a better term, I would call a very long and continuous tradition in American musical entertainment. If operetta films of the early 1930s had a lot of non-pop singing and very little dancing, and if dance films post-1990 did the opposite, that does not mean that we can't view them as transformations in a film genre that is perhaps the longest and most enduring one of all.

Notes

1. Rick Altman, *The American Film Musical* (Bloomington: Indiana University Press, 1989), 126.
2. When *Dirty Dancing* was produced on the London Stage, most of the music remained non-diegetic, and one critic commented that "When somebody does break into song, it often looks like a mistake." And yet the audience for the stage show was noted to sing along with recorded music. See Lyn Gardner, "*Dirty Dancing,*" *The Guardian,* October 25, 2006, http://www.guardian.co.uk/stage/2006/oct/25/theatre. Accessed on September 10, 2011.
3. Water Benjamin, "The Work of Art in the Age of Mechanical Reproduction," *Illuminations* (New York: Schocken, 1969).
4. Gene Kelly, quoted in Donald Knox, *The Magic Factory* (New York: Praeger, 1973), 47.
5. For more on the three categories of musical, see Altman, *The American Film Musical*, 126-27.
6. Ibid., 200.
7. "New Comedy," from Ancient Greece to Shakespeare to Hollywood movies, has always involved a young couple who leaves society against her father's wishes but eventually returns to form a new society.
8. Altman, *The American Film Musical*, 139.
9. Andrea Most, *Making Americans: Jews and the Broadway Musical* (Cambridge, MA: Harvard University Press, 2004). Editors' note: see also Dyer's chapter in this volume.
10. Bergstein was interviewed for *The E! True Hollywood Story: Dirty Dancing,* September 3, 2000.
11. Jeffrey Rubin-Dorsky, "The Catskills Reinvented (and Redeemed): Woody Allen's *Broadway Danny Rose,*" *The Kenyon Review* Special Issue: Culture & Place 25.3/4 (Summer/Fall 2003): 266.
12. Thus Rick Altman writes that the African-American musicals of 1929 did not mark the inception of the "folk" musical. Altman, *The American Film Musical*, 291. See also Arthur Knight, *Disintegrating the Musical: Black Performance and American Musical Film* (Durham and London: Duke University Press, 2002).
13. Knight, *Disintegrating*, 126-27.
14. In Yiddish, "landsman" means "countryman" or "fellow Jew" and "zayde" means "grandfather."
15. Altman, *The American Film Musical*, 154.
16. All quotations from the production team of *Dirty Dancing: Havana Nights* are taken from the DVD special feature, "Inside *Dirty Dancing: Havana Nights,*" Lions Gate Films (2004), NTSC.
17. Altman, *The American Film Musical*, 330-31.
18. T. M. Leitch, "101 Ways to Tell Hitchcock's *Psycho* from Gus Van Sant's," *Literature/Film Quarterly* 28 (2000-2001): 269-73.
19. The Facebook page and the comments cited here are available at http://www.facebook.com/BoycottDirtyDancingRemake. Accessed on September 18, 2011.

20 Dance films featuring ballroom dancing include: *Dance With Me* (Randa Haines, 1998), Latin club/street versus competition; *Shall We Dance* (Masayuki Suo, 1996 and Peter Chelsom, 2004), Western ballroom/classical Hollywood musical versus youth in general—in the American version, Richard Gere goes to a hip-hop club briefly; *Love & Dance* (Eitan Anner, 2006), youth versus adult; *Marilyn Hotchkiss' Ballroom Dancing & Charm School* (Randall Miller, 2006); *Love N' Dancing* (Robert Iscove, 2009), uses dancing as reform for insensitivity, also places competition versus romance; and *Mad Hot Ballroom* (Marilyn Agrelo, 2005), the documentary that provides the basis for *Take the Lead* (Liz Friedlander, 2006).

4   WHITE ENOUGH

RICHARD DYER

The dirtiness of the dancing in *Dirty Dancing* is most obviously sexual, and fairly obviously class-based;[1] rather more equivocally, it is also racial. As Anahid Kassabian notes, the dirty dancing is "not-quite-white"[2]; I want to argue that, all the same, it is white enough.[3]

Dance and Sex

Nearly all the dancing in *Dirty Dancing* is sexual, although only some of it is explicitly so. In the well-lit arena of the public dance floor (at Kellerman's and the Sheldrake), dance has an ostensible role in sexual, and here clearly also racial, reproduction. The dancers are married couples or, more importantly, those who are encouraged to be: the boys who are set up as partners for the Houseman girls are both nice Jewish boys following the paths expected of them, Robbie at Yale and Neil at Cornell, paths that mean they are just the kind of boys Lisa and Baby, respectively, should have sex (that is, dance and have babies) with.

As the dancing is shown, it certainly lacks any sense of overt sexual drive. The occasional shots of couples dancing in the Kellerman ballroom and pavilion make it look sedate and dull, and Neil and Baby's first foray onto the floor is contrasted with a pair of children who, in adopting tango movements, at least go through the motions of erotic abandonment. Later, Billy, one of the staff and Johnny's cousin, remarks to Baby of the first time she has seen the dirty dancing, "Can you imagine dancing like this on the main floor beside the family fox-trot?"

This clean dancing, despite and because of its respectability and worthy function vis-à-vis reproduction, is certainly not endorsed by the film. Not only is it dull, but it is dishonest and often risible. Robbie turns out to be the least desirable catch in the film, abandoning Penny when she becomes pregnant by him, leading Lisa on, amused when the latter, having decided she's going to sleep with him, finds him in bed with Vivian. The latter is someone Johnny has danced with and also almost certainly slept with: the dancing is part of his job and it is, according to Max Kellerman, supposed to end there ("Teach 'em mambo, cha-cha, anything they pay for, and that's all—keep your hands off"), but it is also clear that such coupling (especially of the female clients with the male staff) goes on. Max has a disparaging term for the women involved—"bungalow bunnies"—and when Vivian's husband gives Johnny some money to give her "extra dance lessons" it is pretty likely he knows what he is paying for (Johnny refuses the money, a sign of his moral growth under Baby's influence; sex for pleasure is one thing, for pay, quite another). Neil, the nice Jewish boy proposed for Baby, is viewed critically and mockingly by the film. Once having established that Robbie is at Yale Medical School (high prestige as well as high earning prospects), Max tells the Housemans that his grandson Neil is attending the Cornell School of Hotel Management, and the timing of the line suggests that we are meant to find it amusing. Medical school at Yale trumps Hotel Management, even at Cornell. Later though, the less than prepossessing Neil (another way in which he appears less of a catch than cute Robbie) reminds Baby of what he's got that Johnny doesn't and that all the girls adore: two hotels. This vulgar materialism only serves to lessen him in the film's (and Baby's) eyes.

It is not only that dancing as a conduit to sexual reproduction is discredited by the portrayal of the nice Jewish boys Robbie and Neil but also the way in which sex-for-pleasure is shown to be present in the respectable dancing. On the one hand, this is scorned in the idea of the bungalow bunnies and Johnny's redemption from prostitution (all the more impressive in the context of his telling Baby earlier in the film that he is too poor not to prostitute himself). On the other hand, most attempts at sexiness on the public dance floor are made fun of. A merengue dance class, led by the incandescently sexy Penny (Cynthia Rhodes) to vivid dance music, is introduced by a tracking shot along the dancers' feet that shows they are clad in uncool sandals and socks; Baby steps on the feet of the man beside her and can't keep time; Penny shakes her torso and encourages the other women to do so, to a lot less sexy effect; and when she announces "When I say stop you're gonna find the man of your dreams," it is evidently untrue, and in fact Baby pairs with an old woman. In short, sex is very much on the agenda in the merengue class and mocked in the clients' attempts at engaging in it. Later, for the resort's final show, Lisa does a Hawaiian dance stiffly and awkwardly, ironing out any sense of sway and undulation and singing off-key to boot.

All this contrasts with the dancing in the staff quarters, which is at the other end of the spectrum from that on the main floor: groin to groin, and done unequivocally solely for the pleasure of doing it. Its explicit sexual dimension, already evident in the dancing itself from the first time we see it, is spelled out later when Baby and Johnny dancing in his room to "Cry to Me" leads to actual sex, and then again later when they start to dance in a sexually intimate way to "Love Is Strange" (though they are interrupted by Neil). Even when not leading to intercourse, its meaning is usually in-your-face sexual: Johnny and Penny are not lovers, but their dancing, both in the staff quarters and in their display routines, signifies sex, notably in Johnny's (Swayze's) pelvic-centered movements, and such movements from Penny as throwing one ankle up on Johnny's shoulder so that her crotch hovers above his.

There are perhaps two exceptions to the sense of dance as sexual, whether overtly or covertly. One is the delicate, easy dancing of Honi Coles, who plays the bandleader, something I shall return to. The other involves the display dances of Johnny and Baby (or, as she becomes through these, Frances). The first, for the Sheldrake show, signifies sexuality in its moves, not least because it is supposed to substitute for Johnny's dance with Penny, although in the performance what is emphasised is the tension around Baby/Frances getting it right. This process, especially the rehearsal sequences,[4] is part of the process leading to their falling in love. Their dance at the end of the film also contains sexual moves, something underlined by the audience whoops and applause, first when he brings his face close up to hers, second (and louder) when he shakes his groin at her. However, there are two other elements here. The biggest audience response comes at the moment that she leaps into the air and he catches her, holding her up on his outstretched arms, and much of the development of the number is the incorporation of everyone, first the staff, then the clients, in a routine closer in spirit to communal celebration than to the spontaneous dance formation achieved in classic musicals or, closer to *Dirty Dancing, Saturday Night Fever* (John Badham, 1977). Both the lift and the routine involve sexuality, the former perhaps suggesting the transcendence of orgasm, the latter allowing the audience to let their hair down in the key of sexuality set by Johnny and the staff. And yet, in both cases, sexuality is not what's at stake. But race is.

Not-Quite-White

Kassabian glosses her observation of the "not-quite-white" character of the dirty dancing as "Irish? Italian? Latina/o?"[5] This is the most explicit, albeit unspoken, racial/ethnic component of the dancing. Johnny was originally conceptualised as Italian-American but with the casting of Patrick Swayze became Irish-American.[6] Latin-American dance features importantly: Penny teaches the merengue and she (and later Baby) dances the mambo with Johnny (at the Sheldrake, their turn is described as "Mambo Magic"; Neil says to Johnny, "You always do the mambo"). Even among the clients there is Latin-American dance (albeit awkward, mocked, and nearly safely contained): they learn the merengue and they cha-cha in the pavilion. Neil proposes introducing the Pechanga; also, Lisa dances a Hawaiian dance, yet another non-white form. The dancers in the staff quarters, the real dirty dancers, are very mixed racially, and many might be perceived (probably correctly) as Latina/o. In all these ways, a great deal of the dancing, whether sexually awkward or abandoned, is coded as not-quite-white.

The first time Baby sees the dirty dancing, she asks Billy, "Where'd they learn to do that?" He shrugs his shoulders: "I don't know—the kids do it in the basement back home." "Home" as in where he himself comes from? "Basement" as in somewhere low and dark, where such dancing can incubate naturally? The question goes no further, for historically where the dance comes from—albeit mixed with other sources, albeit filtered and exaggerated by white perceptions—is African-American musical culture. This, though, would be "definitely-not-white."

Dirty Dancing plays fast and loose with the black component of dirty dancing. It seems simultaneously to acknowledge it and erase it. African Americans are among the dirty dancers, not only in the sequences when Baby visits the staff quarters but also in the black-and-white, slow-motion footage behind the first half of the opening and closing credits and in the final communal dance (but blink and you'll miss them). They are in some shots, not in others, with clear errors of continuity, as if the black performers were only present at some of the shoots. Even when they are present, they are mostly on the edges or in the background. They seem even less present, only glimpsed a couple of times, in the final number, itself a celebration of inclusion which seems nonetheless to have its utopian limits. However, a black couple are in the center of the final shot of the film (just behind Johnny and Frances, who are, literally, highlighted), as if at the last moment the film wants to register the source of the film's central pleasure, dirty dancing, only for the film to take this back in the last image of the closing credits (before the fade to black for the remaining credits), a close two-shot on Johnny and Frances—absent from the opening credits, the centrality of not-quite-white-but-white-enough re-affirmed.

The film comes close to acknowledging the connection of Johnny's dancing to black dance. Toward the end, he tells Neil that he wants to develop an idea he has for the final show combining a Cuban dance with "this soul dance." "Soul" has ineluctable African-American connotations, and even Cuba, as a Caribbean culture, may be thought to be blacker than continental South America. If this is what we are supposed to think he and Frances do at the final show (and the fact that they have not rehearsed would not preclude this possibility in the utopian drive of the last part of the film), it is not evident in dance terms and not at all musically (a point to which I shall return). Earlier in the film, Johnny and Baby are dancing in his studio; he's more interested in making love and starts to mime the words of the record they're dancing to, "Love Is Strange," sung by the black duo Mickey and Sylvia; Baby joins in. Whites ventriloquising blacks is the story in little of popular music in the USA. There is more of Johnny miming in the final number, "(I've Had) The Time of My Life," but this is distinctly white pop; if Johnny's dance and musical roots were showing earlier in the film, they are not by the end.

Acknowledgement and erasure also hold in relation to the blackest elements of the film: the casting of Honi Coles as the resort's bandleader and the musical soundtrack. Coles was a doyen of classic vaudeville and Broadway tap dance, historically a major form of black dance.[7] To have him there at all is to register the great tradition of African-American dance; the film may well reckon on a majority of the target audience not knowing who he is, but the way he is introduced, from a long shot of the dull dancing to a mid-shot of him turning round and being revealed to be the bandleader, shows some awareness of just who the film has on board. We only see him dancing twice. There is a brief sequence of his delicate style on his first appearance, followed by a brief duet with Max in front of the band; and, at the end, he sways joyously with the music, encouraging Max to let go and join in like everyone else. His dancing suggests a physical ease and enjoyment that might include sexuality (especially in the context of the final number) but is by no means primarily defined by it. The connection with Max is curious. Jack Weston, who plays Max, is evidently a competent dancer, but in his duet with Coles he hangs his wrist limply, is fussier in his steps than Coles, and has a supercilious grin on his face, as if he can't emulate and must thus slyly mock the subtlety and elegance of Coles' dancing, perhaps because non-blacks can't (or won't). (I guess there may be a very slight anxiety around gender and queerness with the limp wrist and dancing with a man [albeit not touching], but that doesn't seem to me to be at the forefront of this short moment.) Later, it is Coles, the only black man remotely foregrounded in the film, who persuades Max to go with the flow of the dirty—or, now, only dirty*ish*—dancing. The film cannot, however, let go even of this casting decision. Coles' character is called Tito Suarez, an unmistakably Latino name, and there is a very curious shot of him at the end of the first sequence in which he appears: a mid-close-up with a halo of blue suffusing his hair. His name and the lighting seem at least to modify the registering of Coles' ethnic belonging and the reminder it constitutes of the roots of dirty dancing.

The music in the opening sequence encapsulates the musical trajectory of the film as a whole. It opens over the black-and-white footage of dancing mentioned above, with "Be My Baby," sung by the black girl group the Ronettes; when the credits cut to the Houseman car on its way to Kellerman's, the music changes to Italian-American Frankie Valli and the Four Seasons' "Big Girls Don't Cry." The choices are resonant in narrative terms: the main character is called Baby and she is initially being sung to or for by a female group; the lesson that she must grow up (become a big girl that doesn't cry) comes at her from a male source. But the shift is also aurally one from black to not-quite-white. The film as a whole takes this shift one stage further.

The soundtrack uses songs of the period, with a high proportion of black artists: the Ronettes, the Contours ("Do You Love Me?"), Otis Redding ("Love Man," "These Arms of Mine"), Maurice Williams and the Zodiacs ("Stay"), the Drifters ("Some Kind of Wonderful"), Solomon Burke ("Cry to Me"), the Shirelles ("Will You Love Me Tomorrow?"), Mickey and Sylvia ("Love Is Strange"), Merry Clayton ("Yes"),[8] and the Five Satins ("In the Still of the Night"). This is eleven black tracks contrasted against another six white ones: Frankie Valli and the Four Seasons, Tom Johnston ("Where Are You Tonight?"), Eric Carmen ("Hungry Eyes"), Zappacosta ("Overload"), Bruce Channel ("Hey! Baby"), and the Blow Monkeys ("You Don't Own Me"). Frankie Valli and Zappacosta are Italian-American, and there is also the Hispanic group Melon providing "De Todo un Poco" for Johnny and Baby's Sheldrake number, beefing up the not-quite-white quotient.

The black tracks are especially significant in terms of sexuality. The first dirty dancing Baby sees is done to the Contours, which not only suggests dance as a progression to love ("Do you love me now that I can dance?") but also links this in the lyrics to specific black, and probably dirty, dances: the Mashed Potato and the Twist (both emphasising the groin area). Baby's first dance with Johnny, which creates a certain sexual frisson (already set up by her interested looks at him), is to Redding's "Love Man." Their first love-making is to Solomon Burke's "Cry to Me"; a later post-coital sequence has the Shirelles' "Will You Love Me Tomorrow?" playing in the background, and another sexually charged sequence involves, as noted above, Mickey and Sylvia's "Love Is Strange." The white artists' tracks have little weight in the sexual narrative, the most important being Eric Carmen and Bruce

Channel accompanying Baby learning Penny's part for the Sheldrake show. When sex seems to be rearing its head (Johnny standing behind Baby and making a caressing movement down her arm), she keeps breaking into giggles and he becomes increasingly frustrated; when we may sense that something more than professional is developing between them, when they are practicing lifts in a lake, "(I've Had) The Time of My Life" seeps in unsung on the soundtrack. The latter, along with Swayze's "She's Like the Wind," are the culmination of the sexual/romantic narrative: "She's Like the Wind" is first heard when Johnny and Baby say goodbye, and "(I've Had) The Time of My Life" is the music for their, and eventually everyone's, dance at the final show. "(I've Had) The Time of My Life" is sung by the it-doesn't-get-whiter-than-this duo Bill Medley and Jennifer Warnes. It's a number written for the film and, stylistically, clearly from the period in which the film was made rather than when it was set; it is also perhaps as far from black influence as it is possible for pop music to get (which is to say, of course, not utterly untouched by it).

It might be that the marginality of blacks in the film has something to do with realism. Perhaps few African Americans were employed by upmarket resorts in the early 1960s, or if they were perhaps there was a hierarchy even within the help, so that blacks did not even fraternise with everyone else when off-duty. *Dirty Dancing* has a liberal impulse. Characters register the particular salience of blacks in American politics in the period: when Lisa worries that she hasn't brought enough shoes with her, her father points out that this is hardly a tragedy beside "a police dog used in Birmingham," indubitably a reference to Southern black resistance; a little later, Neil seeks to impress Baby (who is set to join the Peace Corps) by telling her that he is going to go to Mississippi later in the summer on the Freedom Ride (connected with black voter registration). In gender and class terms, the film clearly promotes an ideal of complementary equality within heterosexuality and registers a sharp awareness of class inequality (notably in the intersection of class and gender in Penny's narrative, which also highlights a kind of Ivy League *droit du seigneur* as well as the potential consequences of illegal and thus unregulated abortion). It may be this liberal impulse that accounts for there being any blacks in the film at all, for the surprising casting of Honi Coles and the dominance of black music tracks, while realism prevents the film from getting very far with this for fear of falling into improbability.

This argument may account for much of what I have been discussing, and *Dirty Dancing* is in some ways quite surprisingly realist in its delineation of the class and gender politics of its period. But it is also a musical, and one that draws more and more on the genre's utopian impulses as it goes along. The story of the girl plucked from obscurity (whether in the chorus or not) to become a star is a perennial theme of dance-based films: Ruby Keeler in *42nd Street* (Lloyd Bacon, 1933), Maureen O'Hara in *Dance, Girl, Dance* (Dorothy Arzner, 1940), Judy Garland in *Summer Stock* (Charles Walters, 1950), Natalie Portman in *Black Swan* (Darren Aronofsky, 2010). All but Garland share with Jennifer Grey an evidently inferior dancing skill (evident in contrast to others in the films as well as in the eyes of dance snobs) that makes the acclaim their characters achieve all the more magical (at once unbelievable and delightful). Folding everyone into community is also a trope of the musical. The passing along of "Isn't it Romantic?" at the start of *Love Me Tonight* (Rouben Mamoulian, 1932), the work, family, and religious singing and dancing in *Hallelujah!* (King Vidor, 1929), the Busby Berkeley onstage numbers that show cross-sections of people all engaged in the same, usually amorous, pursuits, the arrival at the station "On the Atchison, Topeka, and the Santa Fe" in *The Harvey Girls* (George Sidney, 1946), Tony Manero and friends in *Saturday Night Fever*: all impossible, all intoxicating. Both of these tropes, as they are used in *Dirty Dancing*, have little to do with realism. Moreover, as they involve a musical move toward the 1980s of the film's making ("She's Like the Wind" and "[I've Had] The Time of My Life"), it might have been possible to let go of plausibility vis-à-vis the racial divisions of the early 1960s.

White Enough

In fact, what happens is that there is a whitening of the film, both visually and musically. The choreographic climax of Johnny and Frances' final number occurs when she leaps up and is caught and held aloft by him, which represents her achieving what she has hitherto (notably at the Sheldrake) failed to achieve and is also the moment of maximum whooping and clapping from the diegetic audience.

Choreography, narrative significance, and applause all suggest this as the climax of the film as a whole. In gender terms, it signifies a shift common in heterosexual couple dances in films[9] from a choreography emphasizing similarity or complementarity between the partners to one emphasising thrilling her-on-him dependency. In racial terms, Frances, spread out above Johnny, dominating the frame, is bathed in a dazzling white light that makes her look blonder, the apotheosis of the traditional affinity between light and white female glamour.[10] The transformation of their number into the final community/production number is initiated and led by Johnny in a move more common in action movies over the past twenty years, where women and non-whites are gathered in but always under the leadership of a white man (Conan, Steven Seagal, Bruce Willis, *The Matrix*, Harry Potter)—in other words, post-1960s utopian inclusion as long as the old hierarchies are still in place and blacks remain secondary.

This movement toward the white is salient in the context of the film's Jewish setting. It would be possible to see *Dirty Dancing* and not register the fact that it has a Jewish setting. You have to know that Catskills resorts and names like Kellerman, Houseman, Gould (Robbie's name), and Schumacher (the name of the elderly kleptomaniac couple) were usually Jewish, and that the screenplay was based on the personal experience of Jewish Eleanor Bergstein, in order to hear a (rare) Jewish cadence in lines like Jake Houseman's response to Lisa's concern that she has not brought enough shoes, "This is not a tragedy . . . a tragedy is a police dog used in Birmingham," and to countenance thinking that many of the characters/actors look Jewish, notably Baby/Jennifer Grey (her frizzy hair is reminiscent of Barbra Streisand, the most high-profile and insistently Jewish star of her generation, in a certain period of her career), Jake/Jerry Orbach (though Orbach's mother was not Jewish), and Neil/Lonny Price. Picking up on all this might allow one at once to see the film as "a sort of Yiddish-inflected Camelot."[11]

The Jewish setting gives particular resonances to the present-absent African-American elements in at least a couple of ways. One relates to the long history of Jews and black music in the USA, discussed by Jeffrey Melnick in his *A Right to Sing the Blues* (1999).[12] Many works that defined African-American musical identity for a wider audience were produced by Jews, notably "Alexander's Ragtime Band" (Irving Berlin,

1911), "Swanee" (George Gershwin and Irving Caesar, 1919), *Rhapsody in Blue* (George Gershwin, 1924), "Old Man River" from *Show Boat* (Jerome Kern and Oscar Hammerstein II, 1927, based on the novel by Edna Ferber), and "Stormy Weather" (Harold Arlen and Ted Koehler, 1932, featured in the eponymous 1943 film celebration of "the magnificent contribution of the colored race to the entertainment of the world during the past twenty-five years"). The strong association of Jews with jazz was also present in the figures of Sophie Tucker, billed as "the Mary Garden of Ragtime"[13] and "the Queen of Jazz," and Benny Goodman, known as "the King of Swing" from the mid-1930s on, and one of whose greatest hits was the Jewish-composed "Body and Soul" (Johnny Green, 1930). By the time of *Dirty Dancing* this may have been a forgotten history, and it may have been assumed (and perhaps still largely is) that the association of Jews with black music was never really known to a wider public. However, perhaps the most successful up-front, crossover Jewish entertainment of the last century was *The Jazz Singer*, first a hugely successful play by Samson Raphaelson starring George Jessel on Broadway, then the Warner Bros. film in 1927 with Al Jolson,[14] which led to three remakes: with Danny Thomas (Michael Curtiz, 1952), Jerry Lewis (TV) (Ralph Nelson, 1959), and Neil Diamond (Richard Fleischer, 1980).[15] The facts of choosing this property for the risky, but in the event lucrative and transformative, decision to make the first sound feature film, and of believing in it enough to remake it thrice (providing occasions in the process for leading stars Lewis and Diamond to in some measure come out as Jewish), suggest a knowledge of this story in American culture—and it is all about the relationship between Jewish and black music. In the most famous version (Jolson's), intercutting suggests an equivalence between Rabbi Rabinowitz's singing in the Synagogue and his son, Jack Robin's, in vaudeville: both have what we might now call "soul." Moreover, Jack sings mostly in blackface, milking a long, non-white but also specifically Jewish tradition of black impersonation—hugely ambivalent, often racist stereotyping, but also at times an assumption of affinity.[16] In other words, this very high profile property (above all by virtue of the status of the first film version as a decisive turning point in cinema history) insists, however hedged by qualification and appropriation, on the connection between Jews and blacks. By the time of *Dirty Dancing*, such awareness is erased, undoubtedly reflecting the shift in the perception of Jews in America away from the ghetto and the oppression-sharing status of racial inferiority. The distance between the 1920s *Jazz Singer* and *Dirty Dancing* is that between segregation and a model of assimilation, in which Jewishness all but disappears in the light of whiteness.

This move is also enacted in the narrative. By dancing, sleeping, and siding with Johnny, Frances is making a bid to marry out, having at the start been paired by her parents and the resort with a nice Jewish boy with good prospects. We do not of course know if Johnny and Frances will marry (and we could have a cynical take on the words of the final song to suggest they won't, or at least not happily: "I've *had* the time of my life"), but the conventions of romance suggest this is the logical development. Strictly speaking, Frances marrying a Gentile (and, if there is anything to Johnny's Irishness, a Catholic to boot) does not preclude the reproduction of Jewishness, but it certainly muddies the waters, and all the more so when, visually and musically, this means the eradication of the last vestiges of association with racial otherness and elevation to the blonde glow of whiteness.

Since *Dirty Dancing* was made, non-whites (notably Asians and Hispanics) have steadily increased as a percentage of the population of the USA, and a mixed-race President has been elected. The notion of whiteness as a default identity for Americans is being undermined—it is to be hoped irrecoverably. Perhaps the persistence of *Dirty Dancing*'s nostalgia for a time of optimism, liberalism, and emerging sexual freedom is also nostalgia for a time when all of that could still take place under the sign of whiteness.

Notes

1 For an account of the class dynamics of the film, see David Shumway, "Rock 'n' Roll Sound Tracks and the Production of Nostalgia," *Cinema Journal* 38.2 (Winter 1999): 45-48.
2 Anahid Kassabian, *Hearing Film: Tracking Identifications in Contemporary Hollywood Film Music* (New York: Routledge, 2001), 18.
3 I presented an earlier version of this paper in November 2008 at the Leo Baeck Institute in London. I should like to thank Daniel Wildman for inviting me and the audience, especially Michele Aaron, for their comments. I apologise for the several references to my own work in the bibliography.
4 Discussed in detail in Lesley Vize, "Music and the Body in Dance Film" in *Popular Music and Film*, ed. Ian Inglis (London: Wallflower, 2003), 27-32.

5 Kassabian, *Hearing*, 18.
6 I've not found any explicit reference to this in the film, but it is a common perception, and Swayze was of part-Irish descent.
7 Marshall and Jean Stearns, *Jazz Dance: The Story of American Vernacular Dance* (New York: Macmillan, 1968).
8 In fact, written specifically for the film.
9 Richard Dyer, "'I Seem to Find the Happiness I Seek': Heterosexuality and Dance in the Musical," *In the Space of a Song* (London: Routledge, 2011), 89-100. (First published in *Dance, Gender and Society*, ed. Helen Thomas [London: Macmillan, 1993], 49-65.)
10 Richard Dyer, *White* (London: Routledge, 1997), 122-40.
11 *The New York Times*, August, 16, 1987, quoted in http://en.wikipedia.org/wiki/Dirty_Dancing. Accessed on November 20, 2008. "Camelot" evokes both the optimistic notion of the Kennedy era and the eponymous musical play and film. Editors' note: see also Feuer's chapter in this volume.
12 Jeffrey Melnick, *A Right to Sing the Blues: African Americans, Jews and American Popular Song* (Cambridge, MA: Harvard University Press, 1999). See also Michael Rogin, *Blackface, White Noise: Jewish Immigrants in the Hollywood Melting Pot* (Berkeley/Los Angeles: University of California Press, 1996) and Richard Dyer, *Pastiche* (London: Routledge, 2007), 147-50.
13 Mary Garden was a leading opera singer of the day.
14 J. Hoberman, "On *The Jazz Singer*" and "*The Jazz Singer*: A Chronology" in *Entertaining America: Jews, Movies and Broadcasting*, eds. J. Hoberman and Jeremy Shandler (New York: The Jewish Museum/Princeton: Princeton University Press, 2003), 77-92.
15 For further discussion of *The Jazz Singer* in a Jewish context, see Hoberman, "On *The Jazz Singer*," and Vincent Brook, "The Four Jazz Singers: Mapping the Jewish Assimilation Narrative," *Journal of Modern Jewish Studies* 10:3 (2011), 401-20, the latter a detailed account of all four film versions. See also Corin Willis, "Meaning and Value in *The Jazz Singer* (Alan Crosland, 1927)," *Style and Meaning: Studies in the Detailed Analysis of Film*, ed. John Gibbs and Douglas Pye (Manchester: Manchester University Press, 2005), 127-140, for a discussion of the first version's relation to black culture.
16 On the dynamics of blackface in a Jewish context, see Rogin, *Blackface*; Melnick, *A Right*, 37-42; and Mark Slobin, "Putting Blackface in Its Place," in *Entertaining America*, 93-99. Brook notes the greater, but complex, acknowledgement of black music in the later versions of *The Jazz Singer* (Brook, "The Four Jazz Singers," 2011).

5 *DIRTY DANCING* AS REAGAN-ERA CINEMA AND "REAGANITE ENTERTAINMENT"

CYNTHIA BARON AND MARK BERNARD

Dirty Dancing ends, of course, with a scene that signifies perfect bliss: Cordoned off from the problems of daily life and surrounded by people of all ages dancing together, the young couple at the center of the dance floor celebrates. Their relationship has been blessed by the girl's morally perfect, all-knowing father. As the film tells us, nothing could be better; in fact, it *insists* that nothing could be better. Chillingly, it plays on our recognition that this movie moment offers the kind of comfort and satisfaction that is missing from ordinary life. Trained into patterns of viewing shaped by Hollywood convention, we bliss out at the sight of the happy couple. We also ignore a host of lingering problems, among them the persistent asymmetry in the couple's relationship. When Johnny (Patrick Swayze) lifts Baby (Jennifer Grey) into the air and brings her down in a close embrace, we read the gesture as a sign of adoration, not subservience. We see her coy smiles and his lip-synching to the anachronistic song "(I've Had) The Time of My Life" as a display of courtship rituals, not as a sign of his continued deference to her superior class status.

Taken on its own, *Dirty Dancing* keeps our attention focused on the pleasures promised by fictional worlds. However, when one considers it in relation to other 1970s and 1980s films that explore working-class characters' desire for class mobility, *Dirty Dancing* illuminates aspects of Reagan-era cinema and "Reaganite Entertainment" that warrant additional discussion.[1] The film reflects the dominant values of its production context *and* more broad-based developments in what Andrew Britton saw as "Reaganite entertainment."[2] This chapter discusses *Dirty Dancing* as a product of the Reagan era and as a film that illustrates how Reaganite entertainment uses threadbare formulas to satiate audiences whose interpretations emerge from their familiarity with Hollywood conventions. Many of these narrative patterns were developed in accordance with Hollywood's "industry policy." Conceived by Will Hays and Joseph Breen, "industry policy" blocks depictions that criticize the free market system, show collective action in a positive light, or treat racism, poverty, or unemployment in realistic ways. Like other examples of Reaganite entertainment, *Dirty Dancing* reveals the degree to which Hollywood's industry policy has shaped American cinema and its audiences.

Looking at the Narrative through the Lens of the Working-Class Character

With Frances "Baby" Houseman serving as what Gérard Genette would call the "voice" of the film—the central character who takes us through the story and conveys its point of view—*Dirty Dancing* is akin to films like *Moonstruck* (Norman Jewison, 1987) and *Working Girl* (Mike Nichols, 1988). At the same time, if we turn our attention to Johnny Castle, the young entertainment staff employee hired to give "dance lessons" to wealthy matrons at Kellerman's resort, it is possible to get a glimpse into what Genette would term the film's underlying "mood." As such, Johnny embodies the contradictions one finds in Hollywood narratives about working-class characters invested in class mobility.[3] Johnny's intense desire to win the approval of Baby's father and be "the kind of person" Baby is places *Dirty Dancing* on common ground with dance musicals like *Flashdance* (Adrian Lyne, 1983) and *Staying Alive* (Sylvester Stallone, 1983) and youth working-class films of the Eighties like *The Breakfast Club* (John Hughes, 1985) and *Pretty in Pink* (Howard Deutch, 1986).[4]

Of course, the film's parallels are not limited to other 1980s films. *Dirty Dancing* draws on classical Hollywood conventions. As main characters in a dance musical, Baby and Johnny are expected to be figures in a narrative that "conflates the formation of the couple with their transcendence of their class and gender differences."[5] Similarly, because the film is produced by an industrial system that codified its promotion of consumer culture in the 1920s, Hollywood's audiences know that style and fashion will be the vehicles for the working-class character's efforts to transcend his social position.

There are, however, key aspects of *Dirty Dancing* that make it a distinctly Reagan-era product. Class differences are not the only source of problems in the relationship between Baby and Johnny; the film repeatedly presents us with scenes that highlight Johnny's extreme self-loathing for being someone who comes "from the streets" and whose only chance for full-time employment is to use his uncle's connection to get into the "House Painters and Plasters Union, Local 179." Those anti-union and anti-working-class sentiments are integral features of the Reagan era. Reagan's presidency represented "the first time since the 1920s [that] direct attacks on labor emanated from the White House" and a period when unions "were deliberately made the scapegoat of an economy that increasingly seemed unable to perform acceptably at home or abroad."[6]

Thus, the Reagan era led not only to a film like *Top Gun* (Tony Scott, 1986) that glamorized militarism; it also led to a film like *Dirty Dancing* that used the conventions of the musical to envelop young, downwardly mobile (male) audiences in the fantasy of class transcendence through style and leisure activities, including ballroom dancing. That fantasy would have been especially attractive, of course, during Reagan's administration, which was an era of high unemployment, inflation, and escalating "middle-class" poverty. Manufacturing jobs were being replaced with service positions, and wealth was becoming "increasingly divided up amongst a smaller and smaller group of white professionals."[7] *Top Gun* might have hailed Reagan-era audiences as supporters of "aggressive military interventions" and as "highly competitive young people [able] to spur the economy to new entrepreneurial heights."[8] However, *Dirty Dancing* served as a strong reminder to middle- and working-class audiences that, in Reagan's America, people in the upper-class were to be seen as "higher beings who deserve more."[9] Thus, a working-class person could, as Johnny understood, "never do anything" as valuable as a man like Dr. Houseman (Jerry Orbach).

Dirty Dancing as Reagan-era Cinema

In another time, Johnny Castle and his dance partner Penny Johnson (Cynthia Rhodes) might have been presented as heirs to the legendary dance couple Vernon and Irene Castle. The Castles were international stars of the 1910s whose routines legitimized close dancing and popularized African-American jazz and ragtime music. Vernon and Irene Castle, during the brief time before Vernon was killed in a military plane crash in 1918, were known not only as performers, but also as dance instructors for the wealthy. Yet in this 1980s film, Johnny Castle is merely an object of fantasy for the young princess and a service provider for bungalow bunnies like Vivian Pressman (Miranda Garrison). In Reagan-era cinema, if you are not top gun, you are nothing.

Early on, we learn that the waiters at Kellerman's resort, who are on hiatus from classes at Ivy League schools, are encouraged to show the young guests a good time. By comparison, the entertainment staff "kids" exist in a separate caste. Like "Kellerman's own" Tito Suarez (portrayed by revered tap-dancing star Charles Honi Coles) and the African-American band members, they will be fired if they cross the color/class line by becoming intimate with any young guests. Moreover, in all the scenes set in Johnny's room, where the conventional focus of interest is the romantic coupling, it becomes clear that Johnny has thoroughly internalized the Reagan era's division between upper and lower castes. For instance, when Johnny contrasts himself with Dr. Houseman, who has saved the lives of Penny and, earlier, Max Kellerman (Jack Weston), he tells Baby: "the reason people treat me like I'm nothin' is because I'm nothin'."

Like the central working-class characters in *Rocky* (John Avildsen, 1976) and *Saturday Night Fever* (John Badham, 1977), Johnny's sense of worthlessness causes him to expend intense physical labor. While dance is a way for him to break out of the "cultural circle of class oppression," it is important to note that dance is itself a form of manual labor; moreover, the discipline required to succeed as a dancer and dance instructor "is also an internalization of guilt" over his working-class status.[10] Capturing the sentiment behind the extreme effort and self-discipline exhibited by the era's working-class athletes and dancers, Michael Ryan and Douglas Kellner explain that this is "a way of telling oneself it is one's own fault and that one should work hard to overcome one's own failure and succeed." "Class guilt," they continue, "is thus individualized, and [so] the effort to overcome structural inequality is conceived in individual rather than collective terms."[11]

Guilt for being working class makes little sense as a distinguishing trait for a young male character in a story set in 1963 when the economic futures of ordinary Americans looked bright. However, it is decidedly appropriate for a character in a Reagan-era film, considering the downturn in jobs and the changing attitudes toward labor taking place at the time. While "the proportion of net new employment that paid middle-level earning to male workers [was] 78 percent between 1963 and 1973," by 1986, the proportion of new, decently paying positions for (young) men had fallen to 26 percent.[12] Additionally, "beginning in 1978, and increasingly after the election of Ronald Reagan ... Washington began to adopt policies that effectively forced workers to accept wage concessions, discredited the trade-union movement, and reduced the cost to business of complying with government regulations."[13] Thus, while the upper-class characters in *Dirty Dancing* might be suited to the 1963 setting as they touch on America's looming cultural competition (near the end of the film, Max Kellerman expands on Baby's opening reference to 1963 as a time "before the Beatles came" by lamenting young Americans' growing interest in traveling to Europe), Johnny's anxiety and humiliation over being in the precarious situation of being a working-class youth reflects the film's Reagan-era production context.

Johnny's view that he was "balancing on shit" is indicative of American workers' sense of helplessness during the Reagan years. While one needs to avoid "a creeping industrial nostalgia" and recognize that manufacturing jobs in the postwar years represented "tough work that people did because it paid well and it was located in their communities," changes in the workplace meant that by 1982 "more than one out of ten Americans [were] unemployed."[14] Given the "across-the-board U-turn in managerial, economic, and social policy" that began in the 1970s and was motivated by companies' interest in expanding their profits, a seasonal employee like a dance instructor would be especially insecure financially (and psychologically). In Reagan's America, 80 percent of part-time workers earned less than the salary established as the "low-wage cut-off" for full-time workers.[15]

Economists have determined that the US could have met the challenges of international competition through innovation "in products and processes," but instead companies focused on reducing the cost of labor and thus caused "heightened competition at home" among workers.[16] With the government and management focused on cutting the cost of labor, individuals were consistently blamed for the country's economic problems. Cited as key factors in the downturn were "the decline in the work ethic in the United States, the erosion of public morality, or the collective failure to save and invest."[17] President Reagan identified workers as the cause of unemployment and told the country that "there were jobs for those who wanted them."[18] As Johnny exemplifies, American workers "internalized views" that served business interests; they accepted "a perception of themselves ... detrimental to their own interest."[19] Having been fired for crossing the class boundary and with no prospect of work in his future, Johnny will still "never be sorry." By being Baby's dance instructor, he has gotten a glimpse of what it would be like to be something other than working-class. If *Dirty Dancing* had followed the logic implicit

The final image of *Dirty Dancing*—if it were not a product of Reaganite entertainment.

in its imagery, it would have opened with Baby in the backseat of her father's 1963 Oldsmobile sedan and ended with Johnny driving away in his 1957 Chevrolet Bel Air coupe. But it does not end there. As an example of Reaganite entertainment, the film must return us to the safe confines of the ballroom.

Britton's Vision of "Reaganite Entertainment"

Dirty Dancing belongs to the Reagan era because it depicts and never questions the working-class character's "feelings of guilt at not having made it, of having failed as an individual."[20] Yet the film's thematic concerns, narrative design, and audience address also make it emblematic of "Reaganite entertainment," a term Andrew Britton coined in his polemical 1986 essay "Blissing Out: The Politics of Reaganite Entertainment." *Dirty Dancing* explicitly exemplifies the phenomenon's key components. In some cases, it does so indirectly. For instance, Britton identifies nuclear anxiety as the source of Reaganite entertainment's central motif of helplessness. In *Dirty Dancing*, the characters' feelings of helplessness arise from anxiety about job insecurity and the barriers to American working-class success.

For Britton, 1980s films' "highly ritualized and formulaic character" is "the most striking feature" of Reaganite entertainment.[21] According to Britton, studio-era audiences went to the movies to see how films might deviate from a particular set of conventions. Thus, the greatest successes of classical Hollywood cinema were the productions that presented "significant variation, inflection, and development."[22] By comparison, Reaganite entertainment features repetition and sameness. Its films are successful insofar as they replicate what has come before and meet, not challenge, audiences' expectations.

As Britton explains, the "ritualized repetitiveness of Reaganite entertainment" not only gives audiences what they want (over and over again) but also carves out a privileged, discursive space for "entertainment," which is praised for "its delirious, self-celebrating . . . interminable solipsism."[23] These movies tell "us that we are being entertained . . . that we are 'off duty' and that nothing is required of us but to sit back, relax, and enjoy."[24] The demarcation between the world of the movie (entertainment) and the realm of work outside the movie (reality) is important. Reaganite entertainment "defines itself in opposition to labor" and hails audiences as "off-duty" in several senses of the word.[25] Viewers are encouraged to "not work" in that they are told not to analyze the film's content too closely; after all, it is "just entertainment." At the same time, Reaganite entertainment presents the outside world as "profoundly unsatisfying"; entertainment is the only source of pleasure available to people who are assured that their pleasure will continue as long as they remain "off-duty" and uncritical of the ecstasies offered by the films.[26]

The distance between "entertainment" and "reality" that Reaganite entertainment creates discourages audiences from attempting to change the world or find pleasure outside the movies. It is fine for audiences to seek pleasure at the movies, but that pleasure-seeking must be delimited to the world of entertainment and sought nowhere else. In this sense, Reaganite entertainment offers what Britton calls a "negative utopia"—with "utopian" and "idealistic" categorized as "unrealistic" and "impracticable."[27] The premise is that real change in the real world is impossible, so there is no point in attempting to pursue satisfaction outside the realm of Hollywood movies. Reaganite entertainment makes the pursuit of pleasure in the real world seem illogical: Why would a person try to find satisfaction out there when it is so readily at hand in the movies? The more audiences enjoy the pleasures of Reaganite entertainment, the less they search for satisfaction in the outside world; it thus effectively discourages people from interrogating dominant ideology and structures of power.

Reaganite entertainment films promise unlimited pleasure, bliss, and euphoria. Yet they acknowledge that it is impossible to find lasting satisfaction in the real world. This creates a built-in displeasure that leads into the films' reliance on repetition. As Britton explains, because the films "continually reproduce the terms of 'the world as it is' while also a yearning for something different," audiences are compelled to "go back to them again and again."[28] Repetition is thus a key aspect of the films, which satisfy audiences by repeating what has been seen in other movies and by featuring "feel-good" stories that audiences want to watch over and over (not surprisingly, Reaganite entertainment is the ideal product for the VHS, DVD, and streaming video eras).

To ensure that audiences will come back to these movies again and again, Reaganite entertainment aims to maximize pleasure, and so the stories are structured to ensure a distinct lack of conflict. There is a modicum of dramatic conflict, but only on the most superficial level. Exploring this lack of dialectic in Reaganite entertainment, Britton contrasts the films to earlier utopian works of literature in which "contraries are not willed away, for the concrete nature of the authentic utopia ... depends on its including and accounting for its contradiction."[29] Britton attacks Reaganite entertainment's lack of serious dramatic conflict by citing William Blake's oft-quoted maxim that "without contraries is no progression."[30] In other words, a narrative presents a utopian vision, one that involves a positive re-making of the real world, only when "the imagery of the world transformed [is] dramatized in relation to the forces that act against [it]."[31] When weight is not given to opposing forces, a narrative offers escape rather than an idealized vision of the future.

This lack of contraries in Reaganite entertainment sets it apart from classical Hollywood films wherein the "ironic happy ending [makes] visible the ideological obligations that constrain the text by creating a felt contradiction between the dynamic of an actual narrative and the inertness of its resolution."[32] Conversely, in Reaganite entertainment, contraries are willed away, the thesis has no antithesis, and there is no synthesis. The films do not risk creating the dissonance of "ironic happy endings"; it is much safer to erase conflicts and maximize "pure entertainment" free from the drudgery of immutable and overwhelming real life.

Like Britton, Robin Wood highlights the fact that Reaganite entertainment addresses its audience as children (who are, typically, off-duty). As Wood writes: "The success of [Reaganite] films is only comprehensible when one assumes a widespread *desire* for regression to infantilism, a populace who wants to be constructed as mock children."[33] Accordingly, Reaganite entertainment seeks to set the minds of these audiences at ease in the face of the turmoil that the patriarchal family had, as Wood emphasizes, suffered at the hands of the radical movements of the 1960s and 1970s. Wood and Britton point out that Reaganite entertainment consistently works to reinstate the power of the father because this symbolic figure had been so often challenged by the counterculture. That effort also reflects the decline in high-paying manufacturing jobs and the films' reliance on repetition and predictability.

Summarizing his arguments, Britton proposes that patriarchy is "what gets reaffirmed in Reaganite entertainment: With unremitting insistence and stridency, it is the status and function of the father and [his] inheritance by the son that are at stake."[34] The films take great pains to reestablish the father as head of both the family and society. Even if, as Britton explains, the father seems at first "exploitative and reactionary," the audience learns—usually via a "melodramatic 'change of heart'"—that the father is "lovable and admirable after all."[35] Thus, the restoration of the father is a cornerstone of Reaganite entertainment and a key component of its ultimate mission to convince its infantilized audience to, as Wood puts it, "trust Father."[36]

Dirty Dancing as Reaganite Entertainment

Dirty Dancing opens with Baby telling us that she never thought she would find a guy as great as her dad. Dr. Houseman is implicitly identified as "the man of your dreams" when Penny selects him as her partner in the first dance class (and Baby gets paired with old Mrs. Schumacher). Dr. Houseman also has the last line of dialog in the film—"you looked wonderful out there [on the dance floor]"—and, except for the scene of couples on the dance floor, he is the character who holds Baby in his arms at the end of the movie. *Dirty Dancing* thus establishes Dr. Houseman as the film's father figure and model character. He provides the seal of approval not only for Johnny becoming Baby's "dance partner" but also for the film's overarching theme that "entertainment offers satisfaction that life does not."[37] The film can end once Dr. Houseman blesses Baby's desire to find meaning not from work in the Peace Corps, but instead from following her partner's lead on the dance floor, something she can do over and over again. Emblematic of Reaganite entertainment, Dr. Houseman is so powerful that he magically saves Penny's life after a botched abortion (we never see him labor as a doctor). When Johnny dreams about the woman he loves, the approval of her father is the salient piece. As he tells Baby, "[in the dream] we were walking along and we met your father and he said come on and he put his arm around me, just like he did with Robbie [an upper-class kid at the camp]." For the children, Baby and Johnny, getting the father's approval is both necessary and sufficient.

With the world of *Dirty Dancing* confined to the idyllic resort, the film can, as Robin Wood might observe, "paper the cracks" created by its demeaning representation of the working-class member of the couple. With our view limited to the lush green world of Kellerman's Mountain House (except for the brief appearance of Baby and Johnny on a dance floor outside the resort), the film muffles Johnny's plaintive cry that "people treat me like nothin' because I'm nothin'" with his final announcement to the audience in the ballroom, "I always do the last dance of the season." As in a film like *Saturday Night Fever* and its emblematic Bee Gees song "Stayin' Alive," the passing nod to working-class pain as US business and government cut labor costs ("I've been kicked around since I was born") is negated by being followed with the "permission to forget" ("And now it's all right. It's OK. And you may look the other way").[38]

In *Dirty Dancing*, characters' pain and conflict are muted in part by the pastoral setting. The film is marked by its absence of a dialectic, a journey, or any progression, for it begins and ends in paradise. While *Saturday Night Fever* "is unusually rich in a sense of ethnographic detail" and establishes "a set of oppositions between the fallen world [Brooklyn] and the redeemed world [Manhattan]," *Dirty Dancing* exemplifies Reaganite entertainment because it shows us a summer resort, a "hermetic, autonomous world which has no bearing" to an outside world.[39] Despite this contrast, both films find ways to reinforce the "ideal or figurative meaning" of their central metaphors; in *Saturday Night Fever*, the literal meaning of "the bridge as a means of conducting working people to the drudgery of another day on the job" is papered over by the idealized vision of it as representing "the transcendence of working-class life" and the possibility of "upward mobility."[40]

The dance floor in *Dirty Dancing* is a place of servitude for a character like Johnny; he spends his "free time" inventing dance moves that will keep the guests happy and makes big money only when he gives private "dance lessons." However, this concept of the dance floor is papered over by the vision of the abstract, autonomous dance floor as a fantasy space that allows people to transcend the "bewilderingly problematic" adult world.[41] It also allows them to set aside concerns about the challenges of upward mobility (for Johnny) and downward slide (for Baby). With both Baby and Johnny finding "surrogate professional and personal gratification through dance," Dr. Houseman's final blessing of the children's dance-floor coupling likely has little to do with supporting Johnny's desire to transcend his working-class status.[42] It is more concerned with condoning the business and government policies that would make it impossible for Baby to have a lifestyle comparable to his. Most importantly, Dr. Houseman's blessing confirms the dance floor's figurative meaning as a space where anyone can transcend the dissatisfaction of everyday life.

The film's obvious resolution is indicative of Reaganite entertainment. Its predictability, which serves as a "main source of pleasure," makes *Dirty Dancing* comparable to the films in the *Star Wars* (1977-1983) and *Rocky* (1976-1990) franchises that are, for Britton, examples of Reaganite entertainment because they are so clearly marked by predictability and because of their "ritualized and formulaic character."[43] Having been trained to understand the conventions of Hollywood movies, and musicals in particular, audiences know that Johnny will return, that the lovers will be united, and that the film will end with a dance. Like other examples of Reaganite entertainment, the predictability of *Dirty Dancing* satisfies audiences' desire both "to be constructed as children" and addressed as "sophisticated and 'modern.'"[44] It uses "window dressing to conceal—but not entirely—the extreme familiarity of the plot, characterization, situation, and character relations."[45]

Dirty Dancing's "active presentation of its conventions" not only invites viewers to become aware of them, it also celebrates "the spectator as the consumer of the spectacle."[46] Its "banal repetitiveness of entertainment formulae [produces] a certain kind of complicity with the spectator, a knowing sense of familiarity with the terms of the discourse."[47] Moreover, the film's reliance on various types of repetition gives the narrative a predictability and coherence that flatters and thus pleases its audiences. The film begins and ends with scenes of "dirty dancing"; after Baby's dance lessons, we often watch her repeat basic dance steps again and again; lines of dialog ("this is my dance space, this is your dance space") from an early rehearsal scene are repeated in a later one; and the dance moves of the entertainment staff "kids" feature a limited number of recognizable variations. Even the scenes of Baby and Johnny dancing tend to involve repeated performances of the same dance routine, one that had been part of Johnny's and Penny's standard repertoire. At Kellerman's resort, the guests get regular announcements for upcoming activities, and when Baby and Johnny are in his room, the stack of 45 rpm records keeps music playing regularly in the background. Like the predictability of the larger narrative, these smaller pieces of *Dirty Dancing*'s visual and aural repetition confirm that we are in the presence of entertainment "that tells us to forget our troubles and to get happy."[48]

Reaganite Entertainment as an Effect of Hollywood's "Industry Policy"

As monstrous and insidious as the rise of Reaganite entertainment might have seemed to observers like Britton, this particular strain of cinema was not without precedent. Reaganite entertainment productions like *E.T.: The Extra-Terrestrial* (Steven Spielberg, 1982) might have differed significantly from films such as *The Texas Chain Saw Massacre* (Tobe Hooper, 1974), *Taxi Driver* (Martin Scorsese, 1976), *Looking for Mr. Goodbar* (Richard Brooks, 1977), *Cruising* (William Friedkin, 1980), and *Day of the Dead* (George Romero, 1985). Britton and Wood see these films as revealing the larger ideological crisis taking place in the United States caused by the Civil Rights movement, feminism, gay liberation, and other socio-economic challenges to white, capitalist patriarchy. Yet it is crucial to remember that the films celebrated by Wood and Britton, which also include *Reds* (Warren Beatty, 1981) and *Blade Runner* (Ridley Scott, 1982), were the exception, not the rule. Reaganite entertainment may very well have been a formal and thematic admixture that the Hollywood film industry had been working toward since 1908, when public debates about film content led to New York's movie theaters being shut down on Christmas Eve.[49] In terms of film narratives about the working class, Reaganite entertainment seems to be the trajectory toward which Hollywood cinema has been aiming since labor conflict developed in Hollywood in the 1910s. As Steven J. Ross illustrates, by the 1920s the "highly polemic[al] films that explored conflict between the classes [shifted] to far more conservative films that explored fantasies of love and harmony among the classes."[50]

Britton himself, at the outset of his argument, explains that Reaganite entertainment should not be seen as directly tied to the policies and person of Ronald Reagan, if only because films like *Rocky* and *Star Wars* began appearing before Reagan's inauguration in 1981. It could be argued that an embryonic version of Reaganite entertainment had taken shape even before 1934, when Joseph I. Breen took charge of Hollywood's Production Code Administration (PCA). From the beginning of his tenure, Breen, whose devout Catholicism (and rabid anti-Semitism) has been well documented, had a clear vision for removing sex and violence from Hollywood cinema. However, one aspect of the job that Breen did not immediately understand—and that Will Hays was quick to teach him—was the enforcement of what they called "industry policy." This was the deliberately vague name given to "dealing with those films that, while technically within the moral confines of the code...were adjudged 'dangerous' to the well-being of the industry ...because they dealt with politically sensitive topics."[51] Under industry policy, tantalizing stories with a modicum of sex and violence were fine for the Hollywood screen as long as they did not criticize capitalism and the free market, depict poverty or class inequality, or point to any systemic problems within "the American way of life." For instance, a film like Warner Bros.' *Black Fury* (Michael Curtiz, 1935) may use labor unrest in the Pennsylvania coalmines as the backdrop for a hero's individual actions and specific struggles. However, the film's narrative must make no allusion to unionizing, and if it must, the unionizing must be presented as corrupt and/or unsuccessful.

It is little wonder, then, that the Hollywood film industry, under Breen's watchful eye, became the dreaded culture industry those in the Frankfurt School, like Theodor Adorno and Max Horkheimer, famously decried.[52] Industry policy and the allegiance to capitalism it demanded ensured that no serious problems with labor or free markets would ever be made visible, much less addressed, in Hollywood films. As Adorno and Horkheimer would point out, Hollywood's audiences could come to believe that social and economic problems did not actually exist, as their vision of reality evolved to become "indistinguishable from [that of] the movies."[53] If one takes *Dirty Dancing* as a touchstone, it is possible to see that Hollywood cinema's disavowal of social problems and its effacement of labor and class concerns reach full expression in Reaganite entertainment. Thus, rather than seeing it as emerging directly from the cultural zeitgeist of the late 1970s, Reaganite entertainment is perhaps better understood as the culmination of years of material circumstances wrought by policy decisions made in Hollywood's executive offices.

That is not to say that Reaganite entertainment in the 1980s was no different from what came before. As suggested by the allusion to Adorno and Horkheimer, the film's vision of the contrast between cinema and reality is crucial. Earlier products of the culture industry might aim to erase the difference between the wonderful world depicted in the movies and the drudgery outside the movie theater. However, the crisis brought on by the cultural events in the 1960s and early 1970s and material developments of the late 1970s and 1980s disallowed any filmic gesture that suggested the world outside was anything like the movies. Working from this cynicism, Reaganite entertainment self-consciously acknowledges that the world outside is unsatisfying. It positions entertainment as the only source from which to draw pleasure and insists on the futility of seeking pleasure or attempting to change things in the real world.

Some Conclusions

Dirty Dancing is emblematic of Reaganite entertainment for many reasons. Released in August 1987, in the wake of the Tax Reform Act passed in October 1986 (which again reduced the taxes for top incomes and raised the rate on the lowest incomes), the Iran-Contra scandal that became visible in November 1986, the savings and loans bailouts that began in 1986, and just a few months before the stock market crash in October 1987, the film blithely tells the viewer to not worry about these troublesome events and instead escape into a Neverland structured by ritual and repetition. *Dirty Dancing*'s insistence that we ignore problems in the outside world makes it the offspring of Will Hays and Joe Breen's industry policy. While the film ostensibly explores the social and economic differences that threaten the union of the couple, there is no class conflict because Johnny's beliefs and behaviors are in sync with Baby's and Dr. Houseman's from the beginning. In *Dirty Dancing*, disturbances and problems are magically resolved before they can ruin the fun. It is thus an apparatus that promises pleasure—if we all stay in the ballroom.

Reflecting its production context, *Dirty Dancing* places Johnny, the working-class dance instructor, in a hopeless and helpless situation.

While he might aspire to become Baby's "dance partner," his fixed, lower status makes him ill-suited to inherit Dr. Houseman's august place in the fairy-tale world. Revealing itself to be a distinctly Reagan-era film, *Dirty Dancing* shows that America's mutable class barriers had, in the 1980s, transformed into a caste system where dominant factions reasserted their position that a person's subservient (class and/or racial) identity could and should be determined by birth. Taking an analytic stance that both narrows and expands that focus, one can also see that *Dirty Dancing*'s use of Hollywood formulas places it squarely among the collection of films Andrew Britton saw as examples of Reaganite entertainment. *Dirty Dancing*'s narrative resolution is not ironic, like some films in classical Hollywood cinema, but instead insular and sugar-coated. Its entertainment and distraction value is so ephemeral that audiences find themselves returning again and again to this and/or other Reaganite entertainment films.

Dirty Dancing is thus not an anomaly, but one of many Hollywood media products that, increasingly, have prompted us to find our pleasure and satisfaction in the movies. Taking that idea one step further, the film and Reaganite entertainment as a whole need not be seen as aberrations, but are perhaps best understood as the result of the Hollywood industry's century-long position that references to "problems" in the outside world are not good for business. As such, *Dirty Dancing* is not simply a reflection of the Reagan era. Moreover, even Reaganite entertainment is not just a reflection of 1980s cultural and economic realities. Instead, *Dirty Dancing* and the many iterations of Reaganite entertainment exemplify the kind of motion picture product that eventually results from industrial practices designed to create wide markets for nondurable goods and thus ensure maximum profit for the private sector. *Dirty Dancing*'s incredible commercial success and its status as a platform for commercial remakes is a testament to Hollywood's unfailing ability to make its products desirable commodities.

Notes

1 For example, William Palmer's *The Films of the Eighties: A Social History* (Carbondale: Southern Illinois University Press, 1993), which covers Vietnam and nuclear war films, narratives about the Cold War, yuppie films, and the

oxymoronic category of "neo-conservative feminist texts," does not mention *Dirty Dancing*. Doug Kellner's discussion of *Top Gun* as a "Reaganite wet dream" in *Media Culture: Cultural Studies, Identity and Politics between the Modern and the Postmodern* (New York: Routledge, 1995) also characterizes Reagan-era cinema as distinguished by its invocation of "traditional values" and responses to the Cold War, and so does not discuss patterns in the films from the 1970s and 1980s that touch, in some way, on the lives of the millions of Americans who lost economic and social ground in the Reagan era.

2   Andrew Britton, "Blissing Out: The Politics of Reaganite Entertainment," in *Britton on Film: The Complete Criticism of Andrew Britton*, ed. Barry Keith Grant (Detroit: Wayne State University Press, 2009), 97-154.
3   Gérard Genette, *Narrative Discourse: An Essay in Method* (New York: Cornell University Press, 1980), 161-262.
4   Michael Ryan and Douglas Kellner, *Camera Politica: The Politics and Ideology of Contemporary Hollywood Cinema* (Bloomington: Indiana University Press, 1988), 120.
5   Chris Jordan, *Movies and the Reagan Presidency: Success and Ethics* (Westport, CT and London: Praeger, 2003), 106.
6   Bennett Harrison and Barry Bluestone, *The Great U-Turn: Corporate Restructuring and the Polarizing of America* (New York: Basic Books, 1988), 15.
7   Ryan and Kellner, *Camera Politica*, 301.
8   Kellner, *Media Culture*, 75, 82
9   Ryan and Kellner, *Camera Politica*, 116.
10 Ibid., 112.
11 Ibid., 112.
12 Harrison and Bluestone, *The Great U-Turn*, 126.
13 Ibid., 14.
14 Jefferson Cowie and Joseph Heathcott, "Introduction: The Meanings of Deindustrialization," in *Beyond the Ruins: The Meanings of Deindustrialization*, eds. Jefferson Cowie and Joseph Heathcott (Ithaca: Cornell University Press, 2003), 14, 15; Harrison and Bluestone, *The Great U-Turn*, 14.
15 Harrison and Bluestone, *The Great U-Turn*, 7, 128.
16 Ibid., 24, 175. See also Robert B. Reich, *The Next Frontier* (New York: Times Books, 1983), 174; Ira C. Magaziner and Robert B. Reich, *Minding America's Business: The Decline and Rise of the American Economy* (New York: Harcourt Brace Jovanovich, 1982), 4-5; Fredrick R. Strobel, *Upward Dreams, Downward Mobility: The Economic Decline of the American Middle Class* (Lanham: Rowman & Littlefield, 1993), xiii; Barry Bluestone, "Foreword," in *Beyond the Ruins*, xi.
17 Magaziner and Reich, *Minding America's Business*, 25.
18 Kenneth Root, "Job Loss: Whose Fault, What Remedies?" in *Research in Politics and Society: Deindustrialization and the Restructuring of American Industry, Volume 3*, eds. Michael Wallace and Joyce Rothchild (Greenwich, CT: JAI Press, 1988), 74.
19 Ibid., 76; See also Cowie and Heathcott, "Introduction," 1.
20 Ryan and Kellner, *Camera Politica*, 119.
21 Britton, "Blissing Out," 99.

22　Ibid., 99.
23　Ibid., 99.
24　Ibid., 100-101.
25　Ibid., 101.
26　Ibid., 101.
27　Ibid., 107.
28　Ibid., 110.
29　Ibid., 108.
30　Quoted in Ibid., 108
31　Ibid., 108.
32　Ibid., 105.
33　Robin Wood, *Hollywood from Vietnam to Reagan ... And Beyond* (New York: Columbia University Press, 2003), 147. Britton did graduate work under Wood at Warwick University, and the pair became close colleagues. Wood would later call Britton "the major influence on all [his] subsequent work" in the preface to *Hitchcock's Films Revisited*, revised edition (New York: Columbia University Press, 2002), xxiii.
34　Britton, "Blissing Out," 129.
35　Ibid., 130.
36　Wood, *Hollywood from Vietnam to Reagan*, 155.
37　Britton, "Blissing Out," 101.
38　Jefferson Cowie, *Stayin' Alive: The 1970s and the Last Days of the Working Class* (New York: The New Press, 2009), 317.
39　Ryan and Kellner, *Camera Politica*, 113, 114; Britton, "Blissing Out," 102.
40　Ryan and Kellner, *Camera Politica*, 116.
41　Wood, *Hollywood from Vietnam to Reagan*, 156.
42　Ryan and Kellner, *Camera Politica*, 113.
43　Britton, "Blissing Out," 98, 99.
44　Wood, *Hollywood from Vietnam to Reagan*, 148.
45　Ibid., 148.
46　Britton, "Blissing Out," 102, 106.
47　Ibid., 102.
48　Ibid., 101.
49　See Gregory D. Black, *Hollywood Censored: Morality Codes, Catholics, and the Movies* (New York: Cambridge University Press, 1994), 12-13.
50　Steven J. Ross, *Working-Class Hollywood: Silent Film and the Shaping of Class in America* (Princeton, NJ: Princeton University Press, 1998), xiii.
51　Black, *Hollywood Censored*, 245.
52　Theodor Adorno and Max Horkheimer, "The Culture Industry: Enlightenment as Mass Deception," in *The Cultural Studies Reader* 2nd edition, ed. Simon During (New York: Routledge, 1999), 31-41.
53　Ibid., 35.

6 DRESSING AND UNDRESSING IN *DIRTY DANCING:* CONSUMPTION, GENDER, AND VISUAL CULTURE IN THE 1980S

PAMELA CHURCH GIBSON

Baby, the heroine of *Dirty Dancing*, introduces the film in a voiceover that provides a clever and careful evocation of the particular period that we are about to see recreated on screen. It is designed to suggest a time both lost and somehow more innocent; as she says, the summer of 1963 was "before President Kennedy was shot, before the Beatles came, when I couldn't wait to join the Peace Corps and I thought I'd never find a guy as great as my Dad. That was the summer we went to Kellerman's." At the end of the film, we are reminded of this sense of imminent change when camp owner Max Kellerman confides in his bandleader, Tito Suarez, that "it all seems to be ending ... it's all slipping away."

We might adopt her technique as we ourselves look back on 1987, the not-so-innocent summer of the film's release. This might help us to understand its unexpectedly rapturous reception. We could recreate the cultural climate, at first using her approach, and then move on, in more depth and detail, to analyze the complexities of the late 1980s. It was, of course, the moment when "pastiche" itself was invading most forms of artistic practice and applied design; it became popular with architects, designers, advertising directors, filmmakers, and photographers. And if we start with the socioeconomic and political climate of 1987, we can perhaps show, with hindsight, the different elements that contributed to the film's initial, unexpected success. So, adopting Baby's style, we might say:

> It was 1987, before the destruction of the Berlin Wall, before consumer capitalism reached out to dominate every corner of the globe, when we were still trapped in the era of Reaganite economics. Yet in 1987, even if some really did believe that greed was good, there were significant political and social changes taking place. In that summer when we first watched *Dirty Dancing*, the AIDS quilt was unfurled along the length of Memorial Avenue in Washington; sex was suddenly no longer safe, and an unwanted pregnancy was not the only danger for women. And there were new gender politics at work, too.

Here we should note the behind-the-scenes changes within the feminism of that decade, now seen by many as leading into the "Third Wave" of the 1990s.[1] Women were making significant gains in the workplace, but also finding themselves trapped below what became known as "the glass ceiling." Nevertheless, there was a perception of their changing status and its apparent manifestation in the "power dressing" of the time; both were parodied in *Working Girl* (Mike Nichols, 1988).

But in the mid-1980s, most notable to many were the new centrality and the changed configurations of masculinity within visual culture. Pictures of semi-naked men were everywhere. Their giant torsos were emblazoned across billboards, and their perfectly formed faces looked out from the covers of the new glossy magazines, swiftly created to tempt customers in this new climate of consumption. Men were now buying not only clothes, cosmetics, "fragrances," and designer underwear, but their own idealized images. If the girl featured on a magazine cover is asking us to pick her up and take her home, then what of these men? Cultural critics were to begin a long and anguished debate over what these newly perfect men might be saying, and to whom.[2] They would turn to literary theory and the writings of Eve Kosofsky Sedgwick to find an answer; her concept of "homosociality" suggested that there might, therefore, be a "homosocial" gaze.[3]

We need to contextualize the film within this changing climate, with its altered marketplace and shifting gender politics, where men were newly visible, women were actively seeking power, and a new liberalism was emerging to counter the excesses of this "designer decade." All of these factors are reflected and, as I shall argue here, are carefully yoked within the diegesis of *Dirty Dancing*. The film's appeal and longevity may be attributed to its combination of four particular elements within a single text: the visual codes around the "new masculinity," a proactive heroine, impeccably liberal politics—even nerdy Neil is off to help in the Civil Rights Movement—and deployment of retro costuming, styling, and music.

Perhaps the most obvious 1980s factor reflected within this filmic text is the centrality and presentation of a very particular kind of hero. As Johnny, Patrick Swayze provides the particular combination of enhanced muscularity, emotional sensitivity, and genuine kindness that is, of course, attributed to the quasi-mythical "New Men" of the mid 1980s; all this is epitomized in the best-selling Athena poster of the time of a naked, well-built man carefully cradling a baby. This one image seemed to symbolize the decade, just as another popular Athena poster had summed up certain aspects of the 1970s (the image seen on so many bedroom walls during that decade was a rearview shot of a blonde tennis player standing on a sunlit court and pulling up her short white dress to scratch her totally naked buttocks, which seemed to reflect both the notion of new sexual freedom and the delightful frisson of what was still, forty years ago, mildly transgressive behavior).

However, what is equally important for our purposes is the way in which Johnny as New Man is styled and costumed; he is initially presented to us in the then very potent fashions of a mythical, and hybridized, American past.[4] And as a retro-styled, 1980s male pin-up, Johnny dances, throughout, in and under the gaze of Baby, the most active of cinematic heroines, an idealistic, independent, and resourceful girl. Her self-presentation, too, will form part of our way into a fuller understanding of the film's initial appeal and subsequent popularity. We need to locate this duo within the overall landscape of 1980s visual culture. But first, we might ask why cinema itself wanted to look *back*.

Jameson's Nostalgia Film: A Blinkered Look Back?

Three years before the film's release, in the essay that would form the basis for *Postmodernism, or the Cultural Logic of Late Capitalism*,[5] Fredric

Jameson had identified and defined "contemporary nostalgia culture," seeing it as a collective "desire for a past we cannot retrieve."[6] *Dirty Dancing* cleverly tapped into that very desire and so—perhaps unwittingly—ensured its long life and complex legacy. Even at the time, some might have seen how neatly it fit into a pattern that began with *American Graffiti* (George Lucas) in 1973—a film Jameson discusses, but one long since confined to history or to the occasional academic rediscovery—and that continued with *Grease* (Randal Kleiser) in 1978—a film that Jameson ignores but which also had an extraordinarily active shelf life. In 1985, two years before *Dirty Dancing*, some of the most successful commercials ever, designed to rebrand Levi's in Europe, achieved their aim precisely through their own skillful use of retro styling, and above all their deployment of 1960s soul music, something that has also helped to ensure the longevity of this film. Interestingly, these commercials, like the film, have had a long, successful, and thoroughly international afterlife. Well into the 1990s, the same advertising agency continued to make advertisements for the company with a precise blend of Fifties iconography and popular songs from the past that were always deliberately ahistorical. These commercials moved from the small screen into the multiplexes and now have a fan base on YouTube. They also gave Brad Pitt his first starring role in the cinema; he is the hero of the 1991 commercial, "Prison."

In 1985, when the first of these, "Launderette," was released, the shop American Retro opened on Berwick Street in Soho and has remained there ever since, selling this particular style—though its position in the center of London's "pink triangle" tells us about the presumed demographic of the clientele.[7] American Fifties style was suddenly cool again; as John Hegarty, the creative director of the Levi's campaign, argues, at the start of the 1980s, in the post-punk era, many had come to associate America with "Ronald Reagan, Mickey Mouse, oversized people and oversized cars."[8] The success of the film has much to do with this hybrid 1950s/1980s look. But retro styling alone is not enough, as we can see through looking at *Grease*, a film that remains popular with young people but which operates on a completely different emotional level. Although young girls may watch it and know the words to all the songs, they don't want to emulate Sandy or to end up with Danny—at least, not according to the focus group interviews on favorite films I conducted as part of the research for this essay.[9] The "retro-fantasy" here operates in a lighthearted way—and it has its own original score. But it is the clever, calculated use of recorded music from the past in both the Levi's commercials and *Dirty Dancing* that provides their potency.

Grease has a postmodern, "knowing" quality in the pastiching of and parallels between its "Thunder Road" sequence and the "chicken run" in *Rebel Without a Cause* (Nicholas Ray, 1955); sidekick Kenickie wields his comb constantly to remind us of Buzz in that earlier film. But *Grease* does not even gesture toward family melodrama and so lacks the psychic power of both the Ray film and—arguably—*Dirty Dancing*. The film and the song lyrics throughout reflect this knowing play with the 1950s, as when Rizzo sings in her cruel parody of Sandy:

> Look at me, I'm Sandra Dee
> Lousy with virginity....

But when Sandy throws aside her Peter Pan collar, saddle shoes, and full skirts to show off in skin-tight Lycra, there is again a kind of play—but with a fancy-dress 1950s style. The bad-boy image of Travolta and his friends in *Grease* had already been resurrected by the character of "the Fonz" in the television series *Happy Days* (ABC, 1974-1984), which took all the sting out of the gang from *Rebel Without a Cause* and made them seem loveable rather than threatening. Neither that series nor *Grease* showed us the generational conflict of Ray's film. *Dirty Dancing* is perhaps closer in spirit, since it moved beyond the mere adoption of dress codes and the showcasing of Chevrolet's 1950s bodywork to show family conflict and notions of betrayal. It went further, as befitted the context of the 1980s, to show us not only class conflict, but the existence of ethnic boundaries that might prove insurmountable, even for the most liberal. I will return to this and to the "otherness" within *Dirty Dancing* at the close of this essay.

Before we look at the use of Fifties retro (now combined with a soul soundtrack), first in the world of advertising and then in *Dirty Dancing*, we should first look at the "New Men" who were everywhere in the 1980s but whose "newness" was so often clad in the clothes of an imagined past.

Looking Sideways: From Men in Focus to Female Agency

The first Calvin Klein underwear campaign was shot by Bruce Weber in Santorini in 1982. Interestingly, that same year also saw the publication of Richard Dyer's seminal essay "Don't Look Now: The Instabilities of the Male Pin-up," where he argued that naked men were invariably seen in movement or in poses indicative of action; even if they were not photographed in action, "the male image still promises activity by the way the body is posed."[10] But as the muscled, semi-naked, totally relaxed and happily supine men created in the Klein campaigns moved from billboards onto the pages of mainstream magazines and the screens of the multiplex, Dyer's thesis was arguably challenged. The former need for naked men to be shown in motion, or at least *ready* for action, was confronted by the radical changes in the presentation of the male body that these notorious Klein campaigns—and the endless imitations they spawned—created. The model put forward in his essay of the traditional pattern of "looking" in the heterosexual love story was itself challenged in the same decade, as we will see, by the operation of the gaze and the patterning of the narrative in *Dirty Dancing*.[11]

Semi-naked, well-muscled men were of course familiar within cinema. The 1950s was dubbed "the Age of the Chest" in a 1958 *Playboy* article, describing Marlon Brando's grubby sleeveless undershirts and torn T-shirts as dominating the screen in *A Streetcar Named Desire* (Elia Kazan, 1951).[12] Steven Cohan used this particular phrase as a chapter title in his overview of the cinematic masculinity of that decade.[13] But these new advertisements of the 1980s were qualitatively different. They did not show us glimpses of chest; instead, the torso itself was central to and dominant within the frame, and was now totally bared, often oiled. We were invited to stare at a man who was virtually naked and sometimes reclining, seemingly with the sole intention of soliciting our gaze. When the first images were unveiled on the billboards of America and in the glossy magazines of Europe, they were nothing short of sensational. Klein's campaigns were widely imitated, and Weber's penchant for depicting taut male musculature rather than the traditional advertising images of languid women was mirrored and matched in the work of the other leading photographer of the decade, Herb Ritts.

Dressing and Undressing in Dirty Dancing

The very first Klein advertisement showed us the Brazilian pole-vaulter and Olympic champion Tom Hintnaus. Incontrovertibly a man of action given his impeccable sporting pedigree, he was photographed by Weber lying back against a gleaming white plinth that formed an undeniably phallic curve behind him in a skimpy, highly revealing pair of white underpants. The success of this campaign meant that Weber continued to work with Klein; he swiftly eschewed his color images for the moody, retro black-and-white photographs taken by his influential contemporary Herb Ritts. Interestingly, Ritts' own career had begun not with a fashion shoot but with a radical publicity picture that he created in 1978 for his friend, the aspiring film actor Richard Gere; that image, transformative as it was for contemporary photography, showed Gere wearing a white sleeveless undershirt and jeans, slicking back his hair and flexing his muscles in a San Bernardino gas station and posing in front of a 1950s convertible with exaggerated tailfins. His use of monochrome—and of men—was emulated by most photographers during the next few years. Male models, with their Greco-Roman profiles and classically proportioned, often semi-naked bodies were now firmly at the center of fashion shoots, hitherto an all-female preserve.

Weber and Ritts also worked on campaigns for the new male "fragrances" that were now jostling within the marketplace. The high streets of Europe and main streets across the United States reflected the changes in gendered behavior as the fashion industry responded in kind; men were now active consumers, demanding new shops, new styles, and new "grooming products." Many designers turned for the first time to this now-lucrative field of menswear. New magazines were launched: *Arena* in 1986, with male movie stars and rock singers on its cover, followed by the revamping of *Gentleman's Quarterly* as *GQ*. Others followed in their wake across the next two decades.

It is within this climate that we must situate Swayze-as-Johnny's beautifully proportioned torso, and the way in which both Baby and the camera gaze at it so reverentially. Yvonne Tasker sees Swayze's very stardom as predicated upon his body: "His physical grace as a dancer, as well as his physical strength as a fighter, is emphasised in his action movies. Swayze's body, his physicality, is equally central to romantic roles, as in *Dirty Dancing* and the hugely successful *Ghost* of 1991."[14]

But she does not discuss either film; her concern is with action movies. She does, however, note that a feature writer had seen these two fictional portrayals as representative of a "polarised persona"; she then reminds us of her earlier distinction between "New Man" and "Action Man," types that "cannot be understood within a simple gendered binary that opposes female/feminine to male/masculine."[15] Here, as elsewhere in the academy, *Dirty Dancing* is thus mentioned only in passing. But I would suggest that the construct "Johnny" is also given significant, recognizable *social* roles that take him beyond the New Man/Action Man dichotomy; he is not only Baby's teacher and chosen initiator, he is also that very familiar boy from the wrong side of the tracks, the putative delinquent, here all ready for redemption through the agency of our resourceful heroine. Young girls and older women can all rely on Johnny; he is both teacher and protector. As he tells the terrified Penny, "It's all right, Johnny's here. I'm never going to let anything happen to you."

But the female viewer is not only under his protection, she is also, paradoxically, in control—through her proxy, Baby. The new visual currency of the decade provides men who are there to be looked at; young women might now feel that they could exercise their seeming new power and perhaps move from looking, gazing, and longing to action. At a historical moment when it was still assumed that "woman is depicted to create appetite, not to have any of her own,"[16] Baby's "appetite" actually creates the narrative. She is swift to act on Johnny's sarcastic suggestion that she might act as a stand-in for Penny at the Sheldrake Hotel, and this, of course, means that he must immediately provide her with an intensive program of dancing lessons. Later on, she goes to his room, uninvited, where she herself initiates the sexual activity that follows. *Dirty Dancing* shows that a heroine need not be conventionally pretty, just intelligent and resourceful. Thus equipped, she can engineer her first sexual encounter and arrange for it to be both unusually pleasurable and have an inbuilt, clean-cut end. This heroine is also brave enough to stand up in public for her beliefs; she fetches a shaman when real pain and sickness threaten. When Johnny, New Man, working-class hero, and much more besides, carefully carries the distressed, pregnant Penny to safety, it is in fact Baby who has actually found her crying in the dark hotel kitchen.

Dressing and Undressing in Dirty Dancing

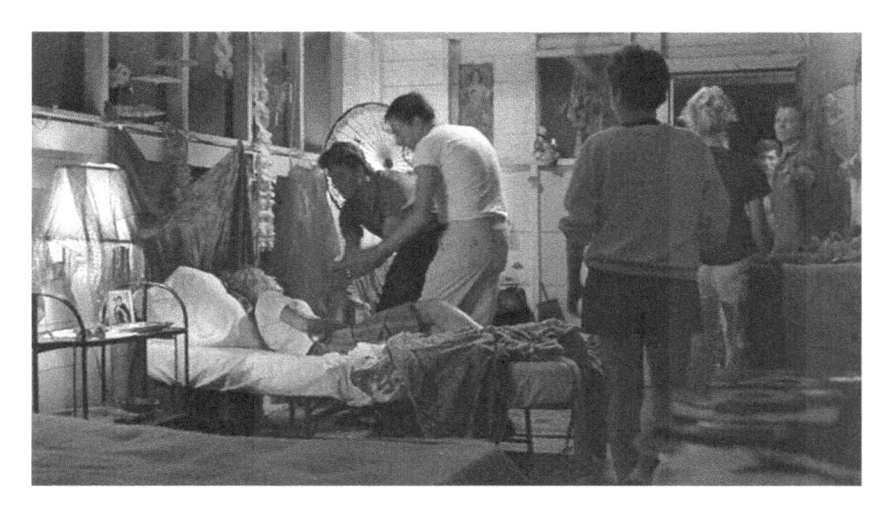

The sheets in Penny's pink-trimmed semi-teenage bedroom are soaked with the blood of the botched abortion; resourceful Baby has brought a "real" doctor to save her.

Even in the 1980s, there was some doubt as to the reality of such paragons as these New Men, who were caring, considerate, fashion-conscious, and, luckily for the women of the decade, nevertheless heterosexual.[17] Within the field of Cultural Studies, there was a suggestion that, if not "a gleam in the ad man's eye," there was certainly a relentless "cashing-in" around these images, and Rowena Chapman warned at the time that there was "something deeply suspicious about the enthusiasm with which the new man was taken up by the media, as he cloned and reproduced himself in the pages of glossy magazines and on celluloid."[18] There were undeniably changes in the portrayal of masculinity that were directly linked to new patterns of economic consumption, all analyzed by those who swiftly sought to make some sense of these new, potent, sexualized images of men.[19] But the writing on the *cinema* of the period does not usually locate film within this wider commercial context.

If the cinematic academy has ignored advertising, fashion, and magazine journalism, the writers within Cultural Studies whose work I reference within this essay have adopted a similarly neglectful attitude to cinema. In their writing there is, however, protracted discussion of the famous Levi's campaigns, which seem to feed directly into the mise-en-scène of *Dirty Dancing*. Yet they could not have exerted a direct influence, since the campaign was confined to Europe; in this case, the link between advertising and cinematic text seems, simply, to have been an example of cultural synchronicity.

Fifties Retro, Soul Soundtrack

> *I had this belief that if we went back to a time when jeans were at the heart of youth rebellion, when music was changing the world and the United States was at the centre of that revolution, then we could create a campaign that would be sexy, provocative and inspiring.*[20]

Here, the Levi's creative director explains the reasoning behind his 1980s campaign to "rebrand" Levi's. These words could be adapted to explain the success of the film; if we take this paragraph and substitute the word "film" for "campaign," we have what could be a mission statement for *Dirty Dancing*. Although not all those who worked on the film had the faith in their product that Hegarty palpably possessed, there were some involved who might feel a resonance here; Eleanor Bergstein, the film's writer and co-producer, is perhaps the most likely, since she based the story on her own memories of holidays in the Catskill Mountains. Significantly, she started this project by going through her carefully stored teenage vinyl collection and choosing particularly evocative songs.[21]

In 1985 and 1986, the years immediately preceding *Dirty Dancing* but following the success of *Grease*, Hegarty created two commercials for television: "Launderette" and "Bath." Hegarty selected the settings, the costuming, and, above all, the music for these two mini-narratives from what he saw as a "mythical time in American history."[22] The way to rebrand Levi's, Hegarty thought, was to place them within what seemed to be their original context. But he chose, too, to play fast and loose with historical accuracy; as in *Dirty Dancing*, there is much that is deliberately anachronistic.

Both commercials used songs from the 1960s. The first, which used Marvin Gaye's "I Heard It Through the Grapevine," saw young women in a launderette with "teased" hairstyles, plastic, pointed sunglasses,

Dressing and Undressing in Dirty Dancing

and neon socks, all intended to connote the Fifties. We even glimpse a G.I., an instantly recognizable Fifties figure, particularly after Elvis's well-publicized period of service in the American Army and his subsequent film, *G.I. Blues* (Norman Tuarog, 1960). This narrative is constructed around a striptease, performed within the launderette by model Nick Kamen. Under the fascinated eyes of his fellow patrons, he takes off all his clothes except for his boxer shorts and white socks. The camera lingers over his crotch as he undoes the fly-buttons of his Levi's, before placing them in one of the machines, thus ensuring that they "shrink-to-fit."

The second commercial used the Sam Cooke song "Wonderful World"; also referenced here was the mild narcissism and the film noir style of *American Gigolo* (Paul Schrader, 1980), through the careful use of Venetian blinds and the protagonist's visible pleasure in his own wardrobe (and his own body). Here, another photogenic young man adjusts his gelled hair and studies himself in the glass before sliding into a bathtub full of water while still wearing his Levi's. The camera pans along his body and then pulls back for a final overhead shot. There is, in both commercials, the same deliberate, ahistorical mix of music, dress styles, and modes of showcasing the male body that also characterizes *Dirty Dancing*.

These commercials increased the sale of Levi's by a figure never preceded nor matched in the history of advertising: an extraordinary 200 percent. The campaign actually had to be suspended, as supply could not keep pace with demand.[23] The songs used were re-released and were even more successful than on their first outings. In one final twist, retro boxer shorts instantly became the underwear of choice. This was pure chance, as Hegarty notes; jockey briefs were the bestselling male underpants in 1985, but the censor had decreed that these were too revealing.[24] Cultural critics of the time had a field day with the commercials.[25] In 1996 and 2001, Nixon and Cole were still debating their true erotic significance.[26] But the campaign, although significant in both commercial and iconic terms, has faded from public memory; *Dirty Dancing*, on the other hand, remains with us. It is time to examine the ways in which our heroine and her chosen initiator are costumed and presented and the reasoning behind the various decisions made in their dressing and, indeed, their *undressing*.

Dressing Baby, Undressing Johnny

Dirty Dancing did not set out specifically to build on the new masculinity, nor the seeming new power of young women. But the relationship between Baby and Johnny does reflect the changes of the 1980s, while costuming is key both to the working of the film and its enduring potency. Richard Dyer describes the cinematic conventions of falling in love within a heterosexual narrative: The man looks at the girl, who looks modestly down and away.[27] But here they are surely violated by Baby's "gaze" at Johnny. When Baby first sees Johnny, she is in the position of the classic male voyeur, lurking in the dark shadows of the restaurant to watch as Johnny makes his first dramatic entrance. He strides into the group of middle-class college boys wearing dark glasses and a tight T-shirt, his leather jacket slung insouciantly across his shoulders. Tim Edwards has recently suggested that Laura Mulvey's famous model has been "ruptured but not jettisoned."[28] There is certainly a challenge here, in Baby's "look" at Johnny; here, and again later in the staff quarters, she is seen open-mouthed. What provides the "challenge" is Baby's ability to initiate action.

She speedily discovers that his bad-boy garb paradoxically—and desirably—hides a New Man. He dons his James Dean outfit at particularly significant moments. In this early scene it is as a deliberate, working-class challenge, and he possibly uses it in this way again when they leave the sanctuary of his studio for the uncertainty of the rain-soaked countryside. He adopts this outfit as defiant armor for a third time when, disgraced and expelled, he tries to explain things to Dr. Houseman. The styling is self-consciously "bad," self-consciously retro.

At the start of the film, Baby herself wears loose, comfortable, and often unbecoming clothes. In the opening scene her ethnic blouse and long, cutoff denims are set against her sister Lisa's Ronettes' beehive, and her book on Third World poverty is carefully contrasted with her sister's anxious use of a hand mirror and hairbrush. When she first meets Johnny in person, on his own turf in the staff quarters, she is wearing a cotton dress, baggy cardigan, and flat moccasins—again in sharp contrast, but here to the young dancers whom she instantly envies.

Dressing and Undressing in Dirty Dancing

As she explores her own sexuality, she spends time not only with Johnny but with Penny, whom we first see wearing a bright red dress with voluminous swishing skirts, and to whom Baby first speaks when the older girl is wearing another ethnic blouse (this one, however, is diaphanous and pulled right down off the shoulders). Penny is invariably seen in bright colors; when she is rescued by Baby, Johnny, and Billy, she is in a short red dress that glitters with sequins, her black eyeliner smudged across her face. Though the color red is traditionally used within Hollywood costuming to signify brazen sexuality, this is undercut throughout by the visual suggestions of Penny's strange and charming mixture of knowledge and naïveté: the huge poster of France on her wall, the teenage quality of her decor, and the white ribbon shirring and white frothy petticoats of that very first red dress.

Baby changes her own style of dress, as the focus of her interest shifts from global poverty to sexual adventure. She ties up her shirts in front to reveal her taut midriff. This looks back to both Brigitte Bardot and Audrey Hepburn, who in the 1950s and 1960s both showcased this style; at the same time, it looks forward to the "crop tops" of the 1980s and 1990s. She already possesses striped Breton T-shirts,

In his natural habitat, among the other "dirty dancers," Johnny's formal shirt is open almost to the waist, thus allowing the gate-crashing Baby to admire his muscled chest.

which evoke both the androgynous chic of Coco Chanel and the class statements made by Pablo Picasso in his adoption of traditional fisherman's clothing (artisanal rather than "artistic"). She wears one of these when she goes to find out whether Robbie will help Penny. In reply, he holds up his copy of Ayn Rand's *The Fountainhead*, telling her "some people count, and some don't." The red-striped shirt inviolate, she pours cold water over Robbie's crotch, telling him "You make me sick. Stay away from me and stay away from my sister." But learning to dance means real sartorial change, reflecting the parallel discovery of her sexuality. She turns up for her first lesson with Johnny in a loose, checked shirt and neat jeans. We see, across the sequence of lessons, her swift adoption of skimpy vest tops, midriff-baring blouses, and two-piece outfits, while her shorts get progressively shorter.

But it is Johnny, not Baby, who is gradually disrobed as the narrative progresses. When she sees him in the off-limits staff quarters as leader of the "dirty dancers," he has come from work. Now his dress shirt is unbuttoned, his torso bared, his hair tousled—the designer *déshabillé* of 1980s fashion images. And if Baby changes her mode of dress, Johnny is *undressed* for much of the film. He wears a black undershirt and trousers for their rehearsals; again, in this particular

While Baby learns how to express her sexuality from a suitably red-clad Penny, the camera catches the gleaming arms of a watchful Johnny.

Dressing and Undressing in Dirty Dancing

We see Johnny's splendidly muscled back, Baby's attentive face.

undershirt with its cut-away back, he could have stepped straight out of a contemporary photo shoot, perhaps a Ritts advertising image for Armani or Valentino. Eventually we see him seated cross-legged, framed by the clothed limbs of Baby and Penny, his muscular arms seemingly oiled. His chest is bared for all their final rehearsals. As Johnny loses more and more of his clothes, it is his body that fills the frame and that attracts the close-up attention of the camera. We actually watch the very tensing of the muscles in his back; his face is sometimes lit so as to illuminate his cheekbones. By contrast, we see comparatively little of Baby's body, nor is her face the focus of the camera's attention in the same way.

The countryside sequence gives their simply clad, monochrome figures a timeless quality. In fact, the film's styling overall is in many ways now "timeless," for Baby's casual clothes have now become contemporary fashion staples, while her full-skirted frocks are revived again and again. Retro fashions for women, too, have an enduring appeal. Fashion seems trapped by the past; "second-hand" has been reincarnated as "vintage." In fact, the last truly forward-looking fashions were those of the mid-1960s. Parisian designer Pierre Cardin put short tunics over thick woolen tights in 1963; in 1964, his compatriot, André Courrèges, removed the thick tights and substituted futuristic ankle boots, thus heralding the era of the miniskirt. But by the late 1960s and early 1970s, Western designers were already looking either backwards to the 1930s or across the world to Asia for the ethnic styles that were first seen on the streets and then translated into couture. Fashion has never again looked forward; instead, the "look" of this film, the boat necks and swishing full-skirted frocks, makes recurrent appearances on the catwalks. A version of Baby's "look" has gone in and out of fashion, but has never disappeared.

"Otherness," Liberal Politics, Fantasies of Liberation

When Baby goes to confront her father after the disclosure of her sexual activities, she is back in simple cotton frock and cardigan, just as when she first heard the siren call of the soul music from the staff quarters. Now she can tell him that his liberal politics are severely limited; there can be no hint of "otherness" in the Houseman home. She tells him, too, that he has "lied" to her. We have already seen him boast of her academic accomplishments, and as she points out in this confrontation: "You told me everyone was equal and deserved a fair break, but you meant everyone who was like you."

So, what of the "otherness" I mentioned earlier? In the extended dance sequence in the finale, we see again those working-class dancers—including one black and one Latino couple—who so fascinated Baby when she first watched them dancing in the privacy of their quarters. Where, she had asked Billy, could they possibly have learned to dance like that? She had looked in awe at the buttocks, the thighs, the overt grinding; she was thrilled from the start by their overt physicality and triumphant otherness. Billy seemed bemused by her query, and could only say. "I don't know; kids are doing it in their basements back home."

Baby has no concept of these particular basements, but is determined to learn for herself what happens there. She, like Billy, can see that it is the antithesis of what we have seen on the main dance floor, "the home of the family fox-trot." Later during this first meeting, Johnny beckons to her, crooking his finger, and tries to show her how to grind, to sway, to move her hips and thighs—in fact, how to do a pelvic thrust. He lifts her across him and holds her between his thighs. He teaches her to dance at her own suggestion, and it is she who se-

Dressing and Undressing in Dirty Dancing 121

duces him. But having granted her wishes, Johnny is then banished, having given her the forbidden knowledge she wanted.

So she too must be chastened, and thus we see her donning genuine period underwear of the 1960s to replace the tactile Calvin Klein-like garments we glimpsed before. As she prepares for the last night celebration at Kellerman's, she is seen in stiff petticoats, rolling up nylon stockings—imprisoning herself. She has been relegated to seemingly restrictive dress and submissive behavior—put back in the corner. But when Johnny magically reappears, he not only places her center stage but brings behind him, like the Pied Piper, all of the socially excluded. The young dancers had been permitted to stand at the back in the semi-darkness and watch; now, empowered by Johnny, they are able to tempt the rich, stiff-bodied folks up out of their seats for some fun. And as Baby dances with Johnny, we see that her seemingly innocent pink dress is in fact light and fluid; the skirt is far more sensual in its movement than that of the stiff red frock she wore to dance onstage at the Sheldrake.

Johnny successfully brings the disenfranchised from the margins to the center, just as he takes Baby from her corner; she is now lifted high above his head in public. And Baby is not dressed in a way that she hopes is provocative, nor wearing borrowed lipstick as before; her

From the margins to the center: Johnny leads the successful invasion of the Dirty Dancers in their takeover of Kellerman's "last night."

sister had offered to do her hair but then stopped, saying, "You're prettier your way." Finally, her father acknowledges her success and his own defeat, telling her: "You looked wonderful out there." As Bergstein suggests: "Dancing in front of your parents? It's every little girl's dream."[29]

Conclusion

> *He's the really cool guy and you're just an ordinary girl, not pretty or well-dressed—but it's you he chooses. That's why we liked it then and why girls still like it now.*[30]

Some of my interviewees talked of replaying certain scenes again and again. Those who were young when the film first appeared talked of how they had quite literally *worn out* the video cassette, so that white flecks soon appeared on the tape. Surely the real secret of the film's longevity is its particular form of assurance for young women: conventional glamour is unnecessary, parents can be defeated, principles affirmed. The "cool" young man, punished and humiliated, nevertheless returns to acknowledge Baby's power, crooning publicly, "I owe it all to you." Even in 1987, when many were already asking if there re-

Baby, protected in her white T-shirt, leans back confidently against Johnny's bare, broad, muscular chest—echoes of the top-selling Athena poster of the 1980s.

ally was a New Man, the film showed the female audiences of the time that, yes, he did exist. Those who watched knew that he would come to rescue them from their own corner, and lift them safely skywards, high above parents, sisters, and rivals.

In this new millennium he is certainly lost to us, trampled underfoot by the "New Lads" of the 1990s and swept aside by narcissistic "metrosexuals"; he is now as mythical as the unicorn. But not in this diegesis, where he is immortal—and so it, too, lives on, moving from screen and video to DVD and now onto the stage. And most significantly, he is presented as accessible for the female viewer, however young and inexperienced. If Johnny is the boy who undresses in the launderette, who slides sexily into the bath, she can still watch him, and more—she may, seemingly, touch and possess him.

Notes

1. Stacy Gillis, Gillian Howie, and Rebecca Munford, *Third Wave Feminism: A Critical Exploration* (London: Palgrave Macmillan, 2004).
2. See Frank Mort, "Boys' Own? Masculinity, Style and Popular Culture" in *Male Order: Unwrapping Masculinity*, eds. Rowena Chapman and Jonathan Rutherford (London: Lawrence and Wishart, 1988), 193-225; Frank Mort, *Cultures of Consumption: Masculinities and Social Space in Late Twentieth-Century Britain* (London: Routledge, 1996); Rowena Chapman, "The Great Pretender: Variations on the New Man Theme" in *Male Order: Unwrapping Masculinity*, 225-249; Sean Nixon *Hard Looks: Masculinities, Spectatorship and Contemporary Consumption* (London: UCL Press, 1996); Tim Edwards, *Men in the Mirror: Men's Fashion, Masculinity and Consumer Society* (London: Cassell, 1997).
3. See Eve Kosofsky Sedgwick, *Epistemology of the Closet* (Berkeley: University of California Press, 1990) and Eve Kosofsky Sedgwick, *Tendencies* (London: Routledge, 1993).
4. See Mort, "Boys' Own," 193-225; Mort, *Cultures of Consumption*; Nixon, *Hard Looks*; Edwards, *Men in the Mirror*; and Shaun Cole, *Don We Now Our Gay Apparel: Gay Men's Dress in the Twentieth Century* (Oxford: Berg, 2000).
5. Frederic Jameson, *Postmodernism, or the Cultural Logic of Late Capitalism* (Durham, NC: Duke University Press, 1991).
6. Frederic Jameson, "Postmodernism, or the Cultural Logic of Late Capitalism," New Left Review 146 (1984), 53-92.
7. Cole, *Don We Now*, 170.
8. John Hegarty, *Hegarty on Advertising: Turning Imagination into Magic* (London: Thames and Hudson, 2011), 86.
9. My focus group interviews were conducted across a two-year period. I specifically selected three dozen women across a wide age range and from different socioeconomic backgrounds. I talked to those in their thirties and forties

who had watched *Dirty Dancing* on its release, and those in their teens and twenties who had, of course, seen it on DVD. Some of these younger women had also watched it at specially-organized screenings or on stage; all had seen it during "sleepovers." I found overall a uniformly positive response, a pattern of repeated group viewings, and an ability to recite much of the dialogue.

10 Richard Dyer, "Don't Look Now: The Instabilities of the Male Pin-up," *Screen* 23:3-4 (1982): 67.
11 Dyer, "Don't Look Now," 61.
12 Richard Armour's 1958 article in *Playboy* is cited in Steven Cohan, *Masked Men: Masculinity and the Movies in the Fifties* (Bloomington: Indiana University Press, 1997), 185.
13 Cohan, *Masked Men*, 164-201.
14 Yvonne Tasker, *Spectacular Bodies: Gender, Genre and the Action Cinema* (London: Routledge, 1993), 164.
15 Ibid., 165.
16 John Berger, *Ways of Seeing* (London: Penguin Books, 1972), 84.
17 Mort, "Boys' Own," 193.
18 Rowena Chapman, "The Great Pretender," 228.
19 See Mort, "Boys' Own," 200; Mort, *Cultures of Consumption*; Nixon, *Hard Looks*; and Edwards, *Men in the Mirror*.
20 Hegarty, *Hegary on Adverstising*, 176.
21 Bergstein explains this in her commentary for the DVD version of *Dirty Dancing* that was originally created for the Region 1 release and which is also available in the Region 2 version that was released in the same year.
22 Hegarty, *Hegarty on Advertising*, 177.
23 Ibid., 77.
24 Ibid.
25 Jonathan Rutherford, "Who's That Man?" in *Male Order: Unwrapping Masculinity*, eds. Rowena Chapman and Jonathan Rutherford (London: Lawrence and Wishart, 1988), 59; Mort, "Boys' Own," 198.
26 Nixon, *Hard Looks*, 119; Cole, *Don We Now*, 170.
27 Dyer, "Don't Look Now."
28 Tim Edwards, *The Function of Fashion* (London: Routledge, 2011), 142.
29 DVD commentary (see also note 21).
30 This was uttered by one of the interviewees in my focus group (see note 9).

II QUESTIONS OF RECEPTION

Introduction

SIÂN LINCOLN

If there is one thing that separates *Dirty Dancing* from many other so-called youth films of the same period, it is the film's enduring presence in popular culture since its release in 1987. As we explore throughout the collection, this presence is felt in a number of different ways, but perhaps most prominently in the audience's continued engagement with the text.

As a number of chapters in this book address, the film did not exactly receive rave reviews from film critics at the time of its release, despite its box office success; in fact, the film was consistently deplored as a "melodrama," a simple "fairytale romance," a film that by and large showed a weak engagement with the serious issues that it attempted to tackle (for example, abortion). Reviewers consistently questioned the film's plot, its politics, and its claims to be a feminist text, yet such negativity did not seem to prevail in the views and opinions of its audience, many of whom, both at the time and in more recent years, have celebrated it as quite the opposite. For instance, as one of the essays in this section shows, a large number of people found the film helpful in terms of dealing with their own problems. *Dirty Dancing* has also been praised as a film that tackles serious issues such as abortion head on and without patronizing its audience (especially its young female audience) and, importantly, as a film that treats young people—the film's key audience—as serious, rational human beings capable of making their own decisions and taking responsibility for their actions.

The film has undoubtedly retained its popularity, and this has been achieved largely through its continued dialog with its audience, both young and old. This dialog has been facilitated and enhanced in more recent years through the now ubiquitous use of social media, where the film can be discussed, dissected, and analyzed on fan websites and blogs and, even more commonly, on social networking sites such as Facebook. In this section of the book, a number of the chapters draw on data sourced from such sites, as well as from newspapers and other media texts, as evidence of the varying ways in which *Dirty Dancing* has meaning for its audience.

Chapter 7 examines the extent to which *Dirty Dancing* has been received as a feminist film. Following a discussion of a number of reviews that debated the film's feminist credentials, Hilary Radner examines the film's "ahistorical depiction of women's collective past" and argues that the 1987 depiction of 1963 removes from the equation second wave feminism and aligns itself with a view proposed by popular feminine culture, *neo-feminism*. Although neo-feminism appears to engage with some aspects of feminism, it is also compatible with ideas surrounding neo-liberalism, which, not surprisingly, makes any argument about the film as a feminist statement problematic.

Oliver Gruner, on the other hand, argues that the film's portrayal of abortion and female sexuality offered a politically progressive representation of issues that were still resonant in the 1980s. In chapter 8, he suggests that the film tried to intervene in very important 1980s debates about remembering the past and the factors that shape collective memories. However, the film's focus on politicized representations of private relationships and personal development was deemed by cultural custodians as apolitical, and therefore not worthy of serious consideration; instead, Gruner argues, films that focused on specific historical events and dealt with men's perspectives dominated the debates. Still, *Dirty Dancing* had the last laugh after it was rediscovered as an important political statement in more recent years, while its visibility in contemporary times has far surpassed the visibility of comparable, more historically specific films, such as *Platoon*.

The last two chapters of the section take questions of reception in two different directions. In chapter 9, my own essay, I examine the film's role as a rite-of-passage film for teenage girls. I argue that some of the actions taken by the main female character in the narrative (breaking away from a harmonious family life, taking risks, and especially standing up to a father who disapproves of her sexual partner) represent key actions taken by a large number of teenage girls during the course of their adolescence. Through an examination of women's responses on why they love *Dirty Dancing* in the film's fan reviews page on the Internet Movie Database, I argue that the film has stood to help generations of teenage girls navigate their own rites of passage, making the leap from adolescence to adulthood.

Gary Needham's chapter, on the other hand, provides a case study of the film's potential reception from a queer politics perspective. Commencing from the question of the kinds of pleasures that *Dirty Dancing* offers audiences, Needham argues that the film naturalizes heterosexuality. This is primarily achieved through an emphasis on the couples dancing and rules that reproduce ideological positions in which men and women occupy particular places. However, all is not lost for a queer reading of the film, as Johnny's "for-hire" services imply a history of "hustling" that on certain occasions threatens to detract from the naturalization of heterosexuality that the film serves.

"Questions of Reception" then, explores the film's historical reception and its potential reception among a variety of modern audiences.

7 DIRTY DANCING: FEMINISM, POSTFEMINISM, AND NEO-FEMINISM

HILARY RADNER

> *I was 13 years old when my mom took my little sister and me to see Dirty Dancing on a hot August afternoon in 1987. Years later, my mom would admit that she was slightly horrified to realize she'd taken her two young daughters to a movie that she thought was about dancing, but was really about class, feminism, sex, rape, and abortion.*
>
> —Melissa McEwan[1]

Melissa McEwan of the *Guardian* begins her tribute to Patrick Swayze in 2009 by recalling her adolescent experience of the film *Dirty Dancing*, referring to the female lead's character, Baby, as "the plucky star of my feminist awakening."[2] McEwan is not alone among women of her generation in attributing pro-feminist sentiments to the film;[3] notwithstanding, this perspective is not unanimous and was not necessarily expressed in initial reviews of the movie. Typically, Marjorie Baumgarten described the film in the *Austin Chronicle*, on the occasion of the film's re-release in 1997, as "a corny fairy tale about a princess who emerges from her protective isolation and, naturally, falls for a boy who spells 'big trouble.'"[4] Vincent Canby, writing for the *New York Times*, characterized the film in 1987 as "a nicely bittersweet genre movie,"[5] while Tart on loveshackbaby.net commented in 2009 that "Nobody wants to be reminded of the Jennifer Grey character in

Dirty Dancing. No modern, feminist, forward-thinking woman wants to be called 'baby' now do they?"[6]

Fairy Tale or Feminist Statement?

The problem that this film poses concerns the nature of feminism itself. In what ways can the film be termed feminist, particularly given that, as a prototypical Cinderella/ugly duckling story, it seems to confirm the very tenets that feminism worked so hard to interrogate and undermine: that a woman's fulfillment is best achieved in the arms of a man, a man who is sensitive yet knows how to "lead"? How does what was initially seen as a sentimental and perhaps touching "coming-of-age film," designed, in Vincent Canby's terms, to bridge the "culture generation gap" with regard to music and sex, come retrospectively (particularly with Patrick Swayze's death) to be understood as a belated "feminist call to arms"?[7]

The story recounts how "a pretty middle-class teen-ager," the heroine, "finds her adult identity in her first love affair."[8] Baby, the young Frances Houseman (Jennifer Grey), is a "strong-minded idealistic young woman" whose goal is to help the world.[9] Baby becomes involved with bad boy Johnny Castle (played by Patrick Swayze in his most famous role), a dance instructor at the middle-class resort Kellerman's where she and her family are vacationing. She assists his dancing partner Penny (Cynthia Rhodes) in obtaining a backstreet abortion after Penny is abandoned and derogated by the college man, Robbie (Max Cantor), who is, in fact, the father. Baby borrows money from her father (Jerry Orbach) to cover the costs and subsequently persuades him (he is a doctor) to treat Penny when her condition takes an expected turn for the worse. Though her father helps the unhappy Penny, reassuring her that she will still be able to bear children when the time is right, Baby must endure his disapproval (she is virtually ostracized by him) until he finally forgives her at the film's conclusion.

Despite this melodramatic subplot, the film's focus is on Baby's self-discovery at Johnny's knowing hands. A reviewer comments: "Patrick Swayze is the magical hunk that leads Baby to a sexual awakening."[10] Because Penny is unable to dance, Baby learns her routines in order to take her place in an upcoming performance with Johnny that is

A sexually fulfilled Frances (Jennifer Grey) with Johnny (Patrick Swayze) at the film's conclusion.

part of their obligation as the hired help, leading to further physical intimacies between the two protagonists. By the film's conclusion, Baby appears to have found her destiny in Johnny's arms; as a sexually experienced woman (thanks to Johnny), she is finally able to conquer her fears as a dancer and perform expertly as Johnny's partner. Aside from its focus on the concerns of a young female protagonist, the film's plot does not seem, at least initially, to merit its description as "feminist."

Indeed, those who characterize *Dirty Dancing* as feminist mention this dimension of the film, as does Melissa McEwen above, as something that they have realized retrospectively. Blogger Dave Weinfeld comments: "Bergstein [the film's screenwriter] said she has no problem with an eight-year-old seeing it and thinking it's simply a love story, as I'm sure many of the audience did when they first saw it many years ago. But upon repeated viewings (almost everyone in the audience could recite the lines verbatim), the powerful feminist message becomes clear."[11] The film's feminism was rarely apparent to fans in their initial viewing of the film, which usually took place when they were very young girls. Carrie Nelson explains: "As I have grown older, and as I have re-watched *Dirty Dancing* countless times, my feelings on the film have changed dramatically. I still love it, but now I love it for its strong political and feminist messages."[12] Those who see the film in the same light as Nelson tend to emphasize two aspects of the film: its heroine, who is described as "a strong, compelling female character who is true to herself, her beliefs and her desires,"[13] and the film's treatment of abortion, the feminism of which becomes apparent when they re-assess their understanding of their "past" viewings of the film in the context of the present.

While fans tend to emphasize the romantic dimension of the film, for many self-identified feminist critics the issue of abortion overshadows the sentimentality that marks the major plot line.[14] The abortion subplot provides a set of key motivations for the protagonist such that, though a potential sponsor put pressure on Bergstein to edit it out, she refused. Hoping to remind audiences of the important issues that she felt marked her experience of the period, she introduced "some things that you can't take out.... Not many people talked about it, except that we got a very, very big feminist audience."[15] Elsewhere, Irin Carmon reports that Bergstein incorporated the abortion subplot "back in the mid-1980s because she was afraid that *Roe v. Wade* would be overturned."[16] Indeed, in 2011, Jezebel sponsored a screening of *Dirty Dancing* "benefiting the New York Abortion Access Fund, and featuring a Q & A session with the film's screenwriter and co-producer, Eleanor Bergstein." Bloggers' responses, as well as the screening itself, testify to the continued and retrospective relevance of the film with regard to the abortion issue, one that was not critically highlighted at the time of the film's release.[17] In 1987, Alice McDermott, for example, merely described the film in the *New York Times* as one of a handful of movies that portray "teenagers of another time," and "treat their subjects with some seriousness."[18] In contrast, in 2007, Cath Clarke, in the *Guardian*, praised Bergstein's refusal to "buckle under pressure to edit [the backstreet-abortion storyline] out." Clarke singled out *Dirty Dancing* as one of two 1980s films (the other being *Fast Times at Ridgemont High*, [Amy Heckerling, 1982]) that suggest that, when it comes to the representation of abortion, "times have certainly changed," with the result that in contemporary Hollywood abortion is rarely portrayed or discussed on the big screen and certainly not without indicating "unfortunate side effects" with long-term psychological and ethical consequences.[19] Similarly, in 2010, Sarah Erdreich blogged on *Feminists for Choice*: "Over twenty years after *Dirty Dancing* was released,

Roe [v. Wade] is still the law, but films that present abortion in such a nuanced and realistic manner are very much the exception."[20]

While, the film's emphasis on the problems posed by unwanted pregnancies and abortion continues to inspire admiration among fans, especially those who "grew up" on the film, even naïve viewers may occasionally question the film's reproductive politics. One commenter responded to a posting entitled *"Dirty Dancing* and Abortion" as follows: "The thing I remember noticing about the movie as a teen was that even though it seemed perfectly clear to me what had happened to Penny, in 'that OTHER scene' Baby gets 'deflowered' and nothing is mentioned that might prevent the same thing happen [sic] to her. And this was supposed to be a *positive* experience."[21] As the comment above implies, the film tacitly positions the problem of an unwanted pregnancy as one that can be located in the past because today a young woman can easily "prevent" a pregnancy through various methods available to her. At the same time, online comments underline that the film does offer a compassionate depiction of abortion, in which the woman seeking an abortion was not demonized, with the primary concerns being her health and preserving her capacity to bear children at a future time rather than the ethical dilemma that might or might not inform her decision, a portrayal that is not necessarily available in current films. As "Emma" commented in 2009, *"Dirty Dancing* certainly did deal with abortion incredibly bravely, and it's depressing that things have gone so far backward since."[22]

A Past Without Feminism

Significantly, *Dirty Dancing* presents itself as a film about the past, locating its story during the summer of 1963. The film's screenwriter, Eleanor Bergstein, refers to the period as "The Last Summer of Liberalism," particularly with reference to what she calls "an upstairs and a downstairs." Because the film's story is situated in the past, the film avoids many of the complexities inherent in affirming sexual fulfillment as the path to adulthood and maturity, particularly in a period, the late 1980s, in which the need to encourage awareness about sexually transmitted diseases, including AIDS, was a growing and acute concern. As a result, its so-called feminism also seems about the past rather than the present, about what feminism was (or might have been) rather than what it might be today, accompanied by a certain slippage between various modes of representation, including historical, nostalgic and critical.

The film's ahistorical depiction of women's collective past is enhanced by its anachronistic use of fashion, of hairstyles, and of a popular soundtrack that has proven as enduring, if not more so, as the film itself. This soundtrack included actual "oldies" as well as new songs that re-created the musical style of an earlier time, such as "(I've Had) The Time of My Life" and "She's Like the Wind," the latter co-written and sung by Swayze himself. Jimmy Ienner, music consultant to Vestron, the company that produced *Dirty Dancing*, as well as executive producer for the soundtrack, commented: "I don't believe that anyone had the chutzpah to mix 31 years of music on a soundtrack quite the way we decided to do it."[23] Stephen Holden in the *New York Times*, pointing to the film's music, suggests that the film's "phenomenal success," which included two albums released in tandem with the film, "illustrates the potency of the movie's pop myth of a young woman's romantic awakening in an era remembered as carefree and golden."[24]

Bergstein herself comments on the sense of "pastness" that the film evokes. She includes it as an element that was part of her initial conception of the story, recalling the period and the place in which the film takes place with a pronounced nostalgia that softens her critique of the upstairs/downstairs social structure: "I didn't want to make it ugly and vulgar. . . . It was a world of grace and elegance and—yes—liberal values."[25] Bergstein invests this past with romance, but also presents the mores of the era as something that have been superseded, in particular in terms of what the *New York Times* described in 1987 as the "rigid class system" that governed the film's characters—which, according to Bergstein, made way for "radical action" after 1963.[26]

The presentation of the past as both idealized and outmoded enables the film to elide the passage of time between "then" (1963) and "now" (1987, the year in which the film was made); that is to say, to pass over the particular era in which gender roles were most publicly interrogated. In many ways, Frances, as the newly becoming woman of 1963, is arguably the feminine subject of the 1980s, one for whom self-realization and self-fulfillment, in particular sexual fulfillment, are unexamined rights, who has also been "cured" of her pesky reformist tendencies and prudish proto-feminism, and who thus avoids the stigma of feminism itself as well as the sustained interrogation of heterosexuality that inflected much of 1970s feminist thought. Feminism is relegated to the film's future past, the period after the film's conclusion but before the audience's viewing.

Not coincidentally, the film opens with a voiceover, a woman recalling her youth from a vantage point in which the social problems (and ethical certitudes) that produced the young "Baby" have been replaced by a wiser and more sober vision: "That was the summer of 1963 ... when everybody called me Baby and it didn't occur to me to mind.... That was before President Kennedy was shot ... before the Beatles came ... when I couldn't wait to join the Peace Corps and I thought I'd never find a guy as great as my dad." What is missing is in fact the time of "feminism," the period in which it was a very vocal political movement.

Feminism, on the one hand, might have taught Frances that she should "mind" if someone called her "Baby." On the other, feminism might also have sustained her interest in the study of economics and oppression. We see her reading and pondering a volume titled *The Plight of the Peasant,* representing her reformist ambitions and seriousness as a scholar. The voiceover recalls in lilting tones, "That was the summer we went to Kellerman's." The book does not return in later sequences, and the film's joyful concluding dance appears to signify the triumph of experience over education. Implicitly, then, the film dismisses Frances' "do-gooder" liberal ethos, even at times deriding it through other characters such as the resort owner's grandson, who hopes to volunteer as a Freedom Rider but is nothing more than a self-serving (and lewd) capitalist. Similarly, Baby's ideas about those less fortunate than her are challenged by Johnny and his friends, who know something about life that has as yet escaped her—represented by their ability (and her inability) to dance.

If Baby at the film's beginning wants to "change the world, not to fall in love with a lower-middle-class dance instructor," for Bergstein, this is not her dream—it is what her father wanted for her. The *New York Times* describes Baby's transformation: "The favored child, 'Daddy's girl,' had to stand on her own. Baby becomes Frances." Baby's perspective evolves, as does her sense of self. Before Johnny enters

A bookish Baby in the film's opening.

Baby's life, Bergstein explains: "Baby has grown up without ever 'living in the physical world,' as Wallace Stevens says."[27]

Dancing Like a Girl

The key to understanding the conversion that Frances Houseman undergoes lies in the idea of "living in the physical world," a concept that ties the film to the preoccupations of feminist theorists of the 1980s, most notably the philosopher Iris Marion Young, who wrote the influential article "Throwing Like a Girl: A Phenomenology of Feminine Body Comportment, Motility and Spatiality,"[28] arguably her most enduring contribution to feminist debates.[29] In the contexts of these debates, the centrality of Frances' experience, in particular her experience of the body as crucial to the film's conclusion, reflects the concerns of academic feminists like Young who, moving away from discussions of institutional and political reform, sought to understand the specificity of feminine experience and its embodiment.

Iris Marion Young's purpose is to describe "in a provisional way some of the basic modalities of feminine body comportment, manner of moving and relation in space."[30] Young, however, deliberately does not include, as part of her discussion, those experiences of the body that are most central to *Dirty Dancing*, what she calls "the modal-

Feminism, Postfeminism, and Neo-feminism

ities of a woman's experience of her body in its sexual being," and in "less task-oriented activities, such as dancing."[31] Dancing and sexual experience are at the heart of the film's appeal and, within its narrative, intimately connected. Fan Dawn Taylor blogs: "I love Baby's bravery ... she not only tells Johnny ... how she feels, but then takes the initiative and seduces him by asking him to dance."[32]

Frances' later decision to speak out and defend Johnny (and thus be true to herself), as well as her ability to take the lead sexually, critically influences fans' perception of her and Johnny as developing a relationship between equals. In film scholar David Shumway's words, "Baby is not only attracted to a working-class man, but willing to risk her reputation to help him."[33] The film's resolution, however, which brings the "new" Frances back into the family fold, where she is importantly again accepted by her father, depends on a further development: Johnny's willingness to defend Baby and to free her from the "corner" into which the family has attempted to place her. Johnny's support is crucial to Baby's independence, but also to her happy ending. Their relationship evolves around two significant experiences that they share: the first, Frances's initiation as a dancer; the second, her sexual awakening.

The limitations of Frances' dancing are signaled in various ways in the course of the film, testifying to a particular modality of experiencing the body and signifying her status as "girlish"; however, perhaps the most definitive example of how dance functions in this film revolves around the very dramatic lift that Johnny and Frances perform at the film's conclusion. Initially, Johnny attempts to teach Baby how to perform the lift by taking her down to the river. She must throw herself toward him so that he can lift her up above his head, an image that came to be indelibly associated with the film. The water provides an initial buffer that protects Baby should Johnny fail to catch her; however, for Johnny to catch her, she must initially throw herself into the air in certain and precise anticipation that his arms await her. She must project her body into both space and time. When she and Johnny perform together in a routine in which she stands in for Penny, Johnny's habitual partner, Frances is unable to perform the lift.

The failed lift corresponds to an important aspect of the restrictions in movement that Young sees as characterizing feminine bodily experience in everyday, ordinary activities. She notes: "Feminine

Baby performs the lift in the water.

Baby fluffs the lift on stage.

existence appears to posit an existential enclosure between herself and the space surrounding her, in such a way that the space that belongs to her and is available to her grasp and manipulation is constricted and the space beyond is not available to her movement." Young further specifies: "The timidity, immobility, and uncertainty that frequently characterize feminine movement project a limited space for the feminine 'I can.'"[34]

Frances performs the lift in the film's finale.

Though Frances worked hard to learn how to dance, this was not sufficient; her failure to perform the lift was not a result of her lack of technique, but of her inability to "act." Subsequently, however, she does act on her desire for Johnny. She invites him to dance, which leads to her first sexual experience. One of the film's major turning points, then, depends on the fact that Frances acts on her desire. When she is able to assume responsibility for her desire, she then also begins to change her relations to what Young calls "the modalities of feminine bodily existence" and moves toward the realization of her self as independent (expressed in the film's conclusion).

When, in the final scene, Frances successfully performs the lift with Johnny, this time exuding confident control, the film conveys that, at least within the realm of dance, Frances has overcome her initial training as a female to achieve a degree of what French philosopher Simone de Beauvoir called "transcendence."[35] That is to say, that within the dance, Frances is able to experience herself not as an object separate from her "self," but as an active and coherent agent capable of deliberate and coherent action, rather than, in Young's words, "a thing that exists as *looked at and acted upon*," what Beauvoir describes as "immanence."[36] Young explains that as women we are not prepared to "move out to master a world that belongs to us, a world constituted by our own intentions."[37] In successfully performing her lift, Frances overcomes a set of social conditions stipulating that a girl "learns actively to hamper her movements."[38] In the moment of the lift, she no longer exhibits the three primary characteristics that Young claims mark "feminine movement" and that have to varying degrees marred her performances as a dancer: "an *ambiguous transcendence*, an *inhibited intentionality* and a *discontinuous unity* with its surroundings."

Baby's happy ending is not an unalloyed victory. With Johnny's help, she moves out of the sequestered space in which her family had attempted to confine her. Johnny, in a kind of mini-revolution, returns to perform his last dance with Baby, though he has been fired and directed to leave Kellerman's. He pulls Baby from behind the table where she is sitting, uttering one of the film's most famous lines: "Nobody puts Baby in a corner." He drags her onstage, where they dance together in a performance that culminates with a moment of exaltation, expressed through the successful lift. The ambiguity of this moment derives from two very distinct factors. Baby's moment of transcendence is achieved through dance, a kind of movement deliberately excluded from Young's analysis. Secondly, the future of the couple remains uncertain: Will they remain together? Will Frances indeed enroll in the prestigious and intellectually demanding university course into which she has been accepted?

The answer to these questions revolves around understanding what dancing, and the dance that Frances and Johnny perform together, might mean. If dancing is the external representation of the couple's sexual relations, the film offers a very optimistic view of the possibilities for equality between men and women. Simone de Beauvoir, in *The Second Sex*, the volume reputed to have inaugurated second wave feminism, posits the conflict between a desire for independence and a desire to fulfill herself as a "sexed human being" as foundational to the condition of what she calls the "independent woman," by which she means the economically and professionally successful woman, torn between femininity and autonomy. In their final dance sequence, Frances and Johnny represent the idea of a perfect heterosexual union in which the problems that arise out of the inequalities between men's and women's conditions are resolved. Contemporary feminist theorist Toril Moi explains that, though Beauvoir allocated a privileged place to sexual relations between women, she remained convinced, unlike later feminist theorists, of the viability of heterosexuality. Moi comments: "Beauvoir stakes her sexual hopes on truly reciprocal sex with men," while at the same time signaling its difficulties.[39]

Beauvoir also claims that there is a certain category of women who are not subject to this contradictory pull of desires:

> There is one category of women to whom these remarks do not apply because their careers, far from harming the affirmation of their femininity, reinforce it; through artistic expression they seek to go beyond the very given they constitute: actresses, dancers and singers.... Their great advantage is that their professional successes contribute—as for males—to their sexual worth; by realising themselves as human beings, they accomplish themselves as women; they are not torn between contradictory aspirations.[40]

Similarly, it might be argued that the performer, but in particular the dancer, has a relationship to space and time that must transcend the limitations imposed as a rule on feminine modalities of movement—that the female performer is not simply exempt but, in fact, must overcome these modalities to become successful within her profession. From this perspective, Baby's access to a new modality of movement remains confined to a particular arena in which femininity is permitted a different status than that which it enjoys "off stage." The ambiguity of the film's ending, which leaves the audience guessing about the couple's future together, evokes a general uncertainty about how Frances' newfound and utopian identity, in which independence and sexuality are combined, will be maintained in the off-stage world.

Young herself specifically excludes what she calls "less task-oriented body activities, such as dancing," but also passes over activities, such as performance, that seem outside the realm of quotidian experience. Through her performance, heightened by the style and mode of dance that she adopts, Baby reproduces certain codes of glamor and femininity that are attuned with contemporary consumer constructions of identity. Susan Leigh Foster, a dance theorist who specifically addresses Young's observations, shifts the discussion to notions of performance and the ways in which the codified movements and standards of "glamour," "commodities and mediatized images" produce a "feminine corporeality" that "pins the bodies who participate in it" within in a new set of constraints that reproduce "the ... dislocated ambivalence of having to throw like a girl."[41] Along similar lines, Juliet McMains, a dance historian, describes competitive ballroom dancing as a "glamour addiction," in which the "overtly sexual" dimension of the dancers' interactions offers "an escapist route" of fantasies that obviate the need to address "the drudgeries and realities of life," at least temporarily.[42] American Studies scholar, David Shumway deems the film's conclusion "an exultant fantasy" that "gives the film a powerful note of hope that its historical framing should have prohibited," which counters the film's nostalgia. For Shumway, this element of fantasy "leaves the viewers with a feeling of political possibility"—linking his analysis to the belated feminism experienced by the film's now adult fans.[43]

Reassessing Feminism

The choice, then, to develop Baby's character and "coming of age" through her apprenticeship as a dancer has a number of significant consequences. Dance allows the film to stage a fantasy resolution in which both Johnny and Frances learn from each other and "lead" each other in new directions. Johnny teaches Frances to dance, but she encourages him to value himself, because she values him, and to stand up for himself and for her. Because, however, this utopianism is expressed through dance, and thus can only receive its full expression through art and performance, it remains a fantasy, one that sits safely within a set of conventions that allows artists and women special privileges. "lianhua" explains: "Being a romantic I'd like to imagine that they lived together in a long and harmonious relationship. But they might have been too different for that to work—although I'm sure they'd have always remained friends due to the respect that they had for each other."[44]

"lianhua" neatly expresses the film's conundrum: the genre requires that the lovers achieve that eternal romantic union, but the premise of their relationship by its very nature (their differences) makes this implausible. While the view proposed by "lianhua" is not idiosyncratic, in the many discussions of the film's conclusion, fans are divided. Bergstein was asked by a fan: "I'm wondering if in your mind you have any idea what happens to Johnny and Baby at the end of the movie?" She replied: "Sure I do.... But what you have in your mind is just as valid as what I have."[45] Alyssa Rosenberg, "culture blogger," goes further, explaining that the point of the movie does not lie in what happens to the couple subsequent to the film's conclusion because the movie is about Baby: "Johnny is the mirror in which Baby comes to see herself as a whole person. It matters that her vision of herself and her clarity about it last, not that she and Johnny get married."[46]

In its treatment of heterosexuality, the film predicts other late-1980s and early-1990s chick flicks like *Working Girl* (Mike Nichols, 1988), *When Harry Met Sally . . .* (Rob Reiner, 1989), and *Pretty Woman* (Garry Marshall, 1990), in which a woman's chastity no longer signals her virtue, with sexual experience and expertise replacing modesty as a sign of her value and sense of self. It looks forward to the blossoming of the chick flick and a subgenre that Charlotte Brunsdon has dubbed "postfeminist girly" films and that I have grouped under the term "neo-feminist cinema," which appear to engage in some aspects of feminism,[47] exhibiting many of the attributes that Rosalind Gill defines as constituting what she calls a "postfeminist sensibility," particularly with regard to its treatment of sexuality.[48]

I would like to argue something quite different, which is that, far from offering a postfeminist worldview that is, as such, a consequence of feminism, *Dirty Dancing* avoids second wave feminism in order to align itself with a view proposed by popular feminine culture—what I call neo-feminism. Writers such as Helen Gurley Brown in *Sex and the Single Girl*, published in 1962 (the year before the events depicted in *Dirty Dancing* took place), offered a vision of femininity that was compatible with neo-liberalism in which sexual fulfillment, a woman's status as a "sexed" being, became an important aspect of her identity.[49] The reclaiming of *Dirty Dancing* as feminist by fans today, then, highlights the near ubiquity of neo-feminism in contemporary culture as a stand-in for feminism itself.

On the one hand, this reclamation constitutes a belated negation of the earlier apology for feminism inherent in the phrase "I'm not a feminist, but . . . ."[50] *Dirty Dancing*, as a generally loved and re-watched film, one that has been an accepted part of contemporary girlhood for several decades, offers a vision of feminism for which no apology is necessary and, in a certain sense, makes feminists of the many women who have enjoyed the film, creating an inclusive definition of the term. On the other hand, the feminism of *Dirty Dancing* avoids the call to arms associated with the reformists of the second wave; rather, feminism, or more properly neo-feminism as incarnated by Baby/Frances, can be achieved through the work of individuals on themselves and thus is best understood as a program for self-improvement that aligns itself with neo-liberalism. Rosalind Gill observes that women, "required to work on and transform the self, to regulate every aspect of their conduct and to present their actions as freely chosen," may constitute neo-liberalism's "ideal subjects."[51] *Dirty Dancing* encourages women to embrace a philosophy that promotes "good looks," a toned body, and erotic expertise as the primary tools whereby the impediments of gender and class may be overcome in neo-liberal society.

In contrast, Simone de Beauvoir was adamant in asserting that significant and sustained reform (what the Russian Revolution had promised but failed to deliver) would be necessary to bring about the kinds of changes that would make possible equality between women and men.[52] Moi explains Beauvoir's position: "For genuine freedom to be possible, the social conditions of women's lives must be radically transformed."[53] Within the context of Beauvoir's perspective, engendering a discourse that understands *Dirty Dancing* as a feminist statement while remaining true to second wave feminism's original vision is difficult. Such an intellectual move recalls the position of Helen Gurley Brown in the 1970s when, as editor of *Cosmopolitan Magazine*, she was attacked by Kate Millet, who demanded that the magazine "undergo a transformation and begin to advocate for women." Brown riposted that "we were already a feminist book."[54] Positing *Dirty Dancing* as a feminist text relieves viewers from the obligation of revisiting the missing years, those years between 1963 and 1987 during which feminism appeared to offer a politically viable program of action to many women that was distinct from neo-feminism and the agendas proposed by the Helen Gurley Browns of the world.

To condemn *Dirty Dancing* as anti-feminist is too easy and perhaps overly pessimistic. These retrospective readings of the film reintroduce the label "feminist" as a term of approbation, giving voice to both the desire and need to resolve the issues—such as reproductive rights, a woman's relationship to her body, and the status of heterosexuality—raised by the second-wave feminists. This voice is not one that film scholars can afford to ignore if feminism is to remain a significant force in the field, a critical perspective from which to analyze and understand movies and the influence that they exert over women's ambitions, fantasies, and lives.

Notes

1. Melissa McEwan, "*Dirty Dancing*, Feminist Masterpiece," *Guardian*, September 16, 2009, http://www.guardian.co.uk/commentisfree/cifamerica/2009/sep/16/patrick-swayze-dirty-dancing-feminism. Accessed on October 1, 2011.
2. Ibid.
3. See, for example, Zosia Bielski, "*Dirty Dancing*: A Feminist Call to Arms?" *Globe and Mail*, September 17, 2009, http://www.theglobeandmail.com/life/family-and-relationships/dirty-dancing-a-feminist-call-to-arms/article1291826/. Accessed on October 1, 2011.
4. Marjorie Baumgarten, "Review of *Dirty Dancing*," *Austin Chronicle*, September 19, 1997.
5. Vincent Canby, "Film: 'Dirty Dancing,' a Catskills Romance in 1963," *New York Times,* August 21, 1987.
6. Tart, "Joan Osborne: Baby Love..., Crazy Baby..., Little Wild One," loveshackbaby.net, January 27, 2009, http://www.loveshackbaby.net/category/feminism/. Accessed on October 1, 2011.
7. Canby, "Film: 'Dirty Dancing.'"
8. Ibid.
9. Irin Carmon, "*Dirty Dancing* is the Greatest Movie of All Time," *Jezebel*, April 29, 2010, http://jezebel.com/5527079/dirty-dancing-is-the-greatest-movie-of-all-time. Accessed on October 1, 2011.
10. James May, "DVD Review: *Dirty Dancing*—Limited Keepsake Edition," Chud.com, September 9, 2010, http://www.chud.com/25208/dvd-review-dirty-dancing-limited-keepsake-edition/. Accessed on October 1, 2011.
11. Dave Weinfeld, "The Feminism of *Dirty Dancing*," *Ph.D. Octopus*, August 11, 2011, http://phdoctopus.com/2011/08/11/the-feminism-of-dirty-dancing/. Accessed on October 1, 2011.
12. Carrie Nelson, "An Interview with Eleanor Bergstein: On *Dirty Dancing*, Feminism and the Film Industry," *Gender Across Borders: A Global Feminist Blog*, May 25, 2010, http://www.genderacrossborders.com/2010/05/25/an-interview-with-eleanor-bergstein-on-dirty-dancing-feminism-and-the-film-industry/. Accessed on October 1, 2011.
13. Nelson, "An interview with Eleanor Bergstein."
14. See, for example, Anat Shenker-Osorio, "*Dirty Dancing* Moves to a Feminist Beat," *RH Reality Check,* September 22, 2009, http://www.rhrealitycheck.org/blog/2009/09/22/dirty-dancing-moves-feminist-beat. Accessed on October 1, 2011.
15. Eleanor Bergstein, quoted in Carrie Nelson, "An Interview with Eleanor Bergstein."

16 Irin Carmon, "*Dirty Dancing* is the Greatest Movie of All Time." Roe v. Wade (1973) refers to the US Supreme Court decision credited with legalizing abortion.
17 Ibid.
18 Alice McDermott, "Teen-Age Films: Love, Death and the Prom: Teen-Age Movies—Are They Cruising on Empty?," *New York Times*, August 16, 1987.
19 Cath Clarke, "Just Don't Say the A-word," *Guardian*, November 23, 2007.
20 Sarah Erdreich, "Abortion in Film," *Feminists for Choice*, July 12, 2010, http://feministsforchoice.com/abortion-in-film-dirty-dancing.htm. Accessed on October 1, 2011.
21 cjmr, August 4, 2007, comment on "*Dirty Dancing* and Abortion," Elizabeth Andrew.org, August 1, 2007, http://www.elizabethandrew.org/2007/08/dirty-dancing-and-abortion.html. Accessed on October 1, 2011.
22 Emma, September 23, 2009, comment on Anat Shenker-Osorio, "*Dirty Dancing* Moves to a Feminist Beat."
23 Jimmy Ienner, quoted in Stephen Holden, "The Pop Life: Musical Odyssey of 'Dirty Dancing,'" *New York Times*, December 9, 1987.
24 Stephen Holden, "Starless 'Dirty Dancing,'" *New York Times*, June 19, 1988.
25 Samuel G. Freedman, "'Dirty Dancing' Rocks to an Innocent Beat," *New York Times*, August 16, 2007.
26 Freedman, "'Dirty Dancing.'" Editors' note: see also Oliver Gruner's chapter in this volume.
27 Freedman, "'Dirty Dancing.'"
28 Iris Marion Young, "Throwing Like a Girl: A Phenomenology of Feminine Body Comportment, Motility, and Spatiality," in *Throwing like a Girl and Other Essays in Feminist Philosophy and Social Theory* (Bloomington and Indianapolis: Indiana University Press), 141-59.
29 Other feminist theorists concerned with the body include: Susan Bordo, Julia Kristeva, and Judith Butler.
30 Young, "Throwing," 143.
31 Young, "Throwing," 156.
32 Dawn Taylor, "Scenes We Love: *Dirty Dancing*," *Moviefone*, April 6, 2009, http://blog.moviefone.com/2009/04/06/scenes-we-love-dirty-dancing/. Accessed on October 1, 2011.
33 David Shumway, "Rock 'n' roll Sound Tracks and the Production of Nostalgia," *Cinema Journal* 38.2 (1999): 47.
34 Young, "Throwing," 151-52.
35 Ibid., 144.
36 Ibid., 150.
37 Ibid., 153.
38 Ibid., 154.
39 Toril Moi, *Simone de Beauvoir: The Making of an Intellectual Woman* (Cambridge, MA: Blackwell Publishers, 1994), 203.
40 Simone de Beauvoir, *Le deuxième sexe* (Paris: Éditions Gallimard, 1949). Translated by Constance Borde and Sheila Malovany Chevallier as *The Second Sex* (New York: Vintage, 2010), 757.

41 Susan Leigh Foster, "Throwing Life a Girl, Dancing Like a Feminist Philosopher," in *Dancing with Iris: The Philosophy of Iris Marion Young*, ed. Ann Ferguson, Mechtild Nagek (Oxford: Oxford University Press, 2009), 69-78.

42 Juliet McMains, quoted in Nona Willis-Aronowitz, "Permission to Follow: Interview with Juliet McMains," *PopMatters*, February 15, 2007, http://www.popmatters.com/pm/feature/permission-to-follow-interview-with-juliet-mcmains. Accessed on October 1, 2011.

43 Shumway, "Rock 'n' roll," 48.

44 lianhua, comment on "What happen [sic] with Baby and Johnny after the movie 'Dirty Dancing'?," *Yahoo! Answers UK & Ireland*, September 19, 2006, http://uk.answers.yahoo.com/question/index?qid=20060919153149AALckkx. Accessed on October 1, 2011.

45 Eleanor Bergstein, quoted in Esther Zukerman, "Eleanor Bergstein, Screenwriter, Talks *Dirty Dancing*," *The Village Voice*, August 10, 2011, http://blogs.villagevoice.com/runninscared/2011/08/dirty_dancing_eleanor_bergstein.php. Accessed on October 1, 2011.

46 Alyssa Rosenberg, "The Politics of the 'Dirty Dancing' Remake," Think Progress, August 11, 2011, http://thinkprogress.org/alyssa/2011/08/11/293006/the-politics-of-the-dirty-dancing-remake/. Accessed on October 1, 2011.

47 See Charlotte Brunsdon, "Post-feminism and the Shopping Film," in *Screen Tastes: Soap Opera to Satellite Dishes* (London: Routledge, 1997), 81-102; Hilary Radner, *Neo-Feminist Cinema: Girly Films, Chick Flicks and Consumer Culture* (New York: Routledge, 2011).

48 Rosalind Gill, *Gender and the Media* (Cambridge, UK: Polity Press, 2007), 255-59.

49 For a discussion of neo-feminism and the importance of Helen Gurley Brown, see Radner, *Neo-Feminist Cinema*, especially "Neo-Feminism and the Rise of the Single Girl," 6-25.

50 For a discussion of the term within contemporary feminine culture, see Elizabeth Stannard Gromisch, "I'm Not a Feminist, But . . . ," *Campus Progress*, June 10, 2009, http://www.campusprogress.org/articles/im_not_a_feminist_but. Accessed on October 1, 2011.

51 Rosalind Gill, "Postfeminist Media Culture, Elements of a Sensibility," *European Journal of Cultural Studies* 10.2 (2007): 164.

52 Beauvoir, *The Second Sex*, 776-77.

53 Moi, *Simone de Beauvoir*, 198.

54 Jennifer Scanlon, *Bad Girls Go Everywhere: The Life of Helen Gurley Brown* (New York: Oxford University Press, 2009), 180.

8 "THERE ARE A LOT OF THINGS ABOUT ME THAT AREN'T WHAT YOU THOUGHT": THE POLITICS OF *DIRTY DANCING*

OLIVER GRUNER

A police station on the outskirts of Chicago. Two teenagers sit on a couch in the foyer, and the young woman looks disdainfully at the young man, who is loudly cracking his knuckles. "Drugs?" he enquires. "No thank you, I'm straight," she spits back. "No, are you in here for drugs?" She is not. She is there to report a break-in at her house. The real cause of her irritation is, however, not the trespassing, but her absent brother, who is currently playing truant and, worse, getting away with it. Her companion offers some words of advice. "You should think less about your brother and more about yourself," he says. This sympathetic statement begins to quell her rage. Conflict quickly gives way to comity as the couple discuss emotional struggles and relationship woes. In the space of a few minutes, the young woman has not only found a kindred spirit, but also exits the police station on a wave of teenage epiphany, the one that goes: "Spend less time worrying about other people and just be yourself."

This saccharine-sweet moment is, unsurprisingly, taken from a movie—the hit teen pic *Ferris Bueller's Day Off* (John Hughes, 1986). A brief respite from the comic capers of the film's eponymous hero, the sequence features Charlie Sheen and Jennifer Grey, two actors about to achieve mass fame. By the time *Bueller's* reached cinemas in June 1986, Sheen was off shooting another youthful coming-of-age film in which he would take center stage, the Vietnam War drama *Platoon*

(Oliver Stone, 1986). In January of 1987, Grey was hired to star in *Dirty Dancing* (Emile Ardolino, 1987). Both films were set in the 1960s and explored several issues of political and historical import. On its release in December 1986, *Platoon* was widely hailed as the first Hollywood film to deal with the "real Vietnam" and was incorporated into large-scale public debates on the war's legacy for 1980s America.[1] *Dirty Dancing*, according to one of *Platoon*'s greatest celebrants, "might have been a decent movie, had it allowed itself to be about anything."[2] For film critic Roger Ebert and numerous other contemporaneous reviewers and commentators, *Dirty Dancing* was bereft of social significance, a piece of cliché-riddled bubblegum that placed "packaging ahead of ambition."[3]

The diverging critical fortunes of *Platoon* and *Dirty Dancing* are indicative of broader trends in popular reception and, subsequently, in academic writing on Hollywood representations of the 1960s. This essay will address what I believe to be a significant gap in historical film studies: the lack of attention paid to *Dirty Dancing*'s highly politicized narrative of the recent American past. *Platoon* is but one of several pictures set in the 1960s to have received enormous coverage in popular and scholarly writing. Films such as *Born on the Fourth of July* (Oliver Stone, 1989), *Mississippi Burning* (Alan Parker, 1988), *JFK* (Oliver Stone, 1991), *Malcolm X* (Spike Lee, 1992), and *Forrest Gump* (Robert Zemeckis, 1994) all inspired a firestorm of media debate and have since been the subject of in-depth academic analysis.[4] While *Dirty Dancing*'s politics have received some attention,[5] there is little evidence of its having stimulated the same intense historical dialogue as the other, male-centered films. In its representation of a young person's political and personal transformation against a 1960s backdrop, *Dirty Dancing* was in many ways a *Platoon* for women. Drawing on interviews with screenwriter Eleanor Bergstein, a 1985 draft script, and the finished film, I argue that *Dirty Dancing*'s narrative was developed to explicitly intervene in public debates on the legacy of the 1960s, and in particular the women's liberation movement. Then, turning to an analysis of the film's popular critical reception, I suggest reasons why *Dirty Dancing* did not achieve the same political impact as *Platoon*. Commentators' refusal to treat private relationships and female memories of the 1960s with the same reverence accorded to their male counterparts ensured that *Dirty Dancing* would be predominantly understood as a feel-good movie lacking in social or political value.

The Road to *Dirty Dancing*

Eleanor Bergstein has said that she conceived the basis of *Dirty Dancing* in 1980 while her first film script, *It's My Turn* (Claudia Weill, 1980), was in production.[6] The timing was apt, for the late 1970s and early 1980s saw an intensification of political conflicts over the meaning of the 1960s, or "Sixties" (the era was usually discussed more as a loose collection of events and movements than a neatly defined decade), for contemporary America. Phenomena such as the Vietnam War, the civil rights and feminist movements, and counterculture were sucked into high-profile debates as politically liberal and conservative commentators sought to shape public memory of the recent past.[7] Women's liberation became a particularly contentious issue. Conservative organizations such as the Moral Majority and the Heritage Foundation railed against feminism for destroying "traditional" family values and for contributing to the emergence of what Ronald Reagan and his political allies were fond of calling the "permissive society." What others saw as women's positive political and personal gains, achieved partly as a result of feminist activism in the late 1960s and early 1970s, were attacked for having taken women out of their "natural" environment: the home.[8] It has also been argued that popular culture was complicit in this onslaught against feminist gains. In the most well-known examination of the backlash, Susan Faludi shows how Eighties newspapers, magazines, films, and television programs portrayed feminism as a corrupting force, one that had led to a society full of career-obsessed, cold-hearted, infertile, emotionally crippled monsters.[9] In 1987, the year of *Dirty Dancing*'s release, Glenn Close played a character that Faludi argues to be the defining symbol of the conservative backlash; all the negative stereotypes the backlash had associated with women's independence coalesced in *Fatal Attraction*'s (Adrian Lyne, 1987) ruthless and psychologically unhinged female stalker, Alex Forrest.

Challenging this perceived backlash Bergstein promoted herself and her films as a liberal counterattack. Her first screenplay, *It's My Turn*, focused on a female mathematics professor and the struggles she faced in balancing her job and her love life. Bergstein informed *Newsweek* that she wrote *It's My Turn* because "I have never seen a film which honestly deals with a contemporary woman trying to put her life together."[10] Whether Bergstein had seen pictures of this sort or not, there were a number of films attempting to do something similar throughout the 1970s and into the 1980s. Karen Hollinger notes the existence of two strands of "New Women's film" that emerged in the 1970s: firstly, there was the "independent woman's film," in which a female character attempted to negotiate work and personal life without the support of a long-term spouse (*Alice Doesn't Live Here Anymore* [Martin Scorsese, 1974] and *An Unmarried Woman* [Paul Mazursky, 1978], for example); secondly, there was the "female friendship film," which examined the politics or, more often than not, simply the psychology of all-female alliances (e.g., *Julia* [Fred Zinnemann, 1977] and *Girlfriends* [Claudia Weill, 1978]).[11] Hollinger suggests that these films' political content is often contained by conventional tales of personal fulfilment. However, in dealing with independent women and female alliances the industry was nevertheless exploring "two issues initiated by the growth of the women's movement of this period."[12]

Within this context, *It's My Turn* might be viewed as an example of the independent woman's film. It focuses on a professional woman and the difficulties she encounters as she seeks to balance career and relationships. Will love or career choices prevail? We are left unsure whether the central protagonist, Kate (Jill Clayburgh), and her new love, Ben (Michael Douglas), will drop their old lives in order to be together. The only clue offered is a final message from Ben that he is "trying to redirect his flight," which, in the context of their relationship, suggests that he is giving up his old life and will fly to Chicago to be with Kate. If anything, it is Ben who has to make the compromise.

While *It's My Turn* was Bergstein's first attempt at exploring feminist issues on the big screen, she had already demonstrated an interest in dealing with similar themes in her 1973 novel *Advancing Paul Newman*. Since the ideas expressed in this novel anticipate those present in *Dirty Dancing*, it is worth briefly mentioning Bergstein's first significant contribution to the feminist debate. *Advancing Paul Newman* focuses on two young women, Kitsy and Ila, and their experiences of events such as civil rights marches, the assassination of John F. Kennedy, and the Vietnam War. It also revels in the liberated sexualities of its two central protagonists. Jumping backward and forward in time, the novel begins by, is interspersed with, and ends by detailing Kitsy and Ila's activism on behalf of anti-Vietnam War Senator Eugene McCarthy as he attempts to win the Democratic Party's nomination for 1968's presidential election. Perhaps because the narrative concludes in 1968, at about the time when large-scale feminist activism was just beginning to gain mass publicity,[13] *Advancing Paul Newman* makes no explicit reference to the women's liberation movement. Nevertheless, Bergstein explained that her female characters "are rejecting old roles, but they have no vocabulary by which they can understand they are doing so."[14] Such a notion could be just as easily applied to *Dirty Dancing*. This film addresses key feminist issues but does so in a historical context that avoids direct confrontation with late-1960s/early-1970s radical feminism. Instead, it transposes these issues onto a less contentious, or in popular parlance, more "innocent" time: the summer of 1963.

"The film couldn't have been set a few months earlier or later," stated Bergstein in an interview with the *New York Times*. "Because two months after the movie is over JFK is assassinated. Then the Beatles were on Ed Sullivan. And after that it's radical action."[15] *Dirty Dancing*'s period setting clearly was of immense importance to the screenwriter. Between 1985 and 1987, Bergstein added the now famous voiceover beginning: "That was the summer of 1963. . . ." *Dirty Dancing* was not the first film to utilize an early-1960s, pre-Kennedy assassination historical backdrop. It followed in a long line of commercially successful, youth-oriented pictures produced across the 1970s and 1980s. Films like *American Graffiti* (George Lucas, 1973), *Animal House* (John Landis, 1978), *The Wanderers* (Philip Kaufman, 1979), *The Outsiders* (Francis Ford Coppola, 1983), and *Peggy Sue Got Married* (Francis Ford Coppola, 1986) set all, or most, of their action at this time. In all these films, the historical period is suggested to be a turning point in the lives of each film's major protagonists. For good or for ill, things will never quite be the same again. In *Dirty Dancing*, 1963 is set up as a threshold. The addition of main protagonist Baby's "That was the summer before Kennedy was shot" voiceover is significant because it explicitly locates her narrative of personal transformation before the emergence of large-scale feminist activism. At the same time, however, *Dirty Dancing* anticipates many issues of importance to feminist campaigners of the late 1960s/early 1970s and beyond.

Baby's personal journey is predicated on her breaking away from the intense grip that her father, Dr. Jake Houseman, holds on her political beliefs and personal life. Dr. Houseman is the symbolic authority figure for both the Houseman family and middle-class American society more generally. When Baby begins to question his values she also is challenging what is represented in this film as broader social and political norms governing the behavior of women in the early 1960s. Early lines spoken by Baby and her father establish these two characters as the film's moral core. Dr. Houseman criticizes the recent use of police dogs during a civil rights protest. Baby follows this with a reference to "monks burning themselves in protest" in South Vietnam's American-backed Diem regime. However, Dr. Houseman, as is the case with many of the middle-class characters at Kellerman's, also holds rather conservative views towards women and the working classes.

Early in the film Baby is privy to the removal of camp owner Max Kellerman's moral authority. She overhears him demanding that his well-to-do waitstaff romance the guests' daughters—"even the dogs," as he bluntly puts it. At the same time, he orders working-class Johnny to keep his "hands off" the female guests. In the 1985 draft, Baby was not present during Kellerman's outburst, and is thus not provided with a rationale for wanting to break from this kind of sexism and middle-class snobbery.[16] The finished film, however, has Baby peering from the doorway. It is one of many instances where she witnesses firsthand the regressive politics lurking behind the holiday camp's liberal veneer.

Throughout the film, Baby becomes increasingly aware of her father and his friends' unwillingness to put abstract egalitarian ideas into practice. The sneering, snobbish, and thoroughly immoral college-boy waiter Robbie and the hideously avuncular Neil serve as representatives of the kinds of children Dr. Houseman's generation are actually raising. Robbie's "ask not what your waiter can do for you, but what you can do for your waiter" philosophy is the kind of selfish attitude towards life that Baby rejects. Neil is another caricature. He is a negative representation of the New Left man—he is to go on a civil rights Freedom Ride after all—whose political convictions are bound up with rather archaic views on masculinity. His insistence on asserting his authority over the camp's employees and over Baby provides a scathing indictment of the hypocrisy existing not just amongst older liberals but amongst a new generation of politically active young men who still equated "invigorated citizenship with masculinity, viewing it as a triumph over effeminacy."[17] As Sara Evans points out, part of the reason for the feminist movement's break from the 1960s New Left was the sexism that existed within its ranks.[18] The character of Neil was drastically altered between 1985 and 1987. In the 1985 draft, he was a more earnest and less condescending character who starts off attempting to endear himself to the working-class entertainment staff by joining their after-work activities and participating in their banter.[19] Neil's transformation into the patronizing brat with whom viewers of the finished film are familiar occurs only after he has been beaten up by one of the working-class characters; he is thus given a reason (of sorts) for becoming the "little boss man," as he is termed. None of this mitigating content remains in the version of *Dirty Dancing* that reached audiences, and Neil comes across as a wholly unsympathetic character. Robbie and Neil thus provide two negative stereotypes: the heartless individualist and the hypocritical activist.

Among the film's women, too, is a pantheon of undesirable characters. There is Baby's sister, Lisa, who cannot countenance love as anything more than a pathway to marriage and social status. Then there is the girls' mother, Marjorie Houseman, the "typical" housewife: domesticated, loyal to her husband, and devoted to her children. Her binary opposite is found in the form of Vivian Pressman, the cheating shrew. A number of script changes, particularly with respect to Vivian—who was going to be presented in a more sympathetic light (the 1985 draft paints her initially as a bubbly, affable, and artistic friend of Marjorie)—suggest that female characters were simplified during script development.[20] They became less complete individuals than stock representatives, intended merely to act as foils to Baby and her process of personal development.

Indeed, *Dirty Dancing* plays with ideas of femininity and female identity throughout. Such a concern is immediately illuminated in the opening credit sequence. Not mentioned in the 1985 draft but present in the finished film, this sequence features a sepia-tinted montage of dirty dancers. The backing music is African-American girl group the Ronettes' "Be My Baby." Susan Douglas argues that "in the early 1960s, pop music became the one area of popular culture in which adolescent female voices could be clearly heard."[21] Articulating female desires and anxieties in a far more direct manner than was common at the time, groups such as The Ronettes and The Shirelles helped teenage girls to come to terms with their own hopes, desires, and sexuality.[22] The eventual inclusion of this opening sequence therefore sets up an important aspect of *Dirty Dancing*'s historical representation: popular music as liberator. Shumway argues that the music used in the film "evokes the subversive or transgressive experience with which rock 'n' roll was associated."[23] It is the musical equivalent of the dancing itself, offering Baby an escape from the confines placed upon her by the family, and, more generally, by middle-class mores.

It is clear from the 1985 draft that music was always going to act as a non-diegetic commentary on Baby's personal development. There is what Bergstein refers to as "Clean Teen" songs like "'Goin to the Chapel'"[24] that emphasize the safe, middle-class girlhood enjoyed initially by Baby and her sister, Lisa. This musical style is equated with repression and emotionlessness. Then there is "Johnny's Music," the raw, soulful sounds of songs like "Do You Love Me" and "Wild Thing."[25] Bergstein associated this music with vitality and liberation. Baby's romantic relationship with Johnny is accompanied by various songs. For example, when she enters the entertainment staff's quarters for the first time, she is greeted by a blast of "Do You Love Me." She begins dancing with Johnny, and the accompanying screen direction states, "a new Baby is being born before our eyes."[26] In many ways, the soul tracks played in *Dirty Dancing* serve as the other side of the more literal (at least vocally) rebellion of the revived early-1960s American folk music scene. Singers such as Joan Baez, Phil Ochs, and Bob Dylan were at this time challenging overtly the political establishment through the lyrics of their songs. Their music was, however, missing the visceral kick and sexual aggression of Johnny's soul music. Baby is already in possession of the outward-looking liberal politics of these folk singers; the soul music facilitates her turn inward.

Baby's personal struggles are further emphasized through her relationship with the two men in her life: Dr. Houseman and Johnny. Immediately after she admits that she is involved romantically with Johnny, Baby demands that her father face up to his hypocrisy. "You told me you wanted me to change the world," she says to him during the climax of their argument. "But you meant by becoming a lawyer or an economist and marrying someone from Harvard." Dr. Houseman had wanted to mold Baby in his own image; she was to change the world, but not herself. These two characters had been at loggerheads ever since she had revealed that his money had paid for Penny's abortion. With regard to *Dirty Dancing*'s abortion subplot, Bergstein has said that her intention was "to show a generation of girls who have grown up post-*Roe* what could happen without legal safeguards."[27] She first inserted the abortion subplot in 1985 because she was worried that *Roe vs. Wade* was in danger of being overturned.[28] Given the high-profile public conflicts over abortion rights raging in the 1980s, its inclusion indicates an attempt to inject the film with serious subject matter and to engage with political debate. As we will see, however, contemporaneous commentators tended to view it as an all-too-convenient plot device and of little political consequence.

In direct contrast to Dr. Houseman, who seems intent on maintaining authority over his daughter, Johnny is invested in Baby's personal maturation. For much of the film, it is Baby who takes the lead in the relationship. Johnny may teach her the dance steps, but she instigates the romance. The estimation in which Johnny holds Baby rises throughout the film. His referring to "Frances" as opposed to "Baby" during the final scene acts as a symbolic assertion that Baby has grown up, has become her own woman. Bergstein tellingly cut a line of dialogue in the 1985 draft following the couple's first sexual encounter that would have weakened the narrative greatly. When Baby informs Johnny that her real name is Frances, in the 1985 draft, Johnny replies, "Frances? . . .That's a real grown-up name. But you're still Baby to me."[29] Removing the final part of this statement curbs what might be construed as quite a patronizing assertion of authority on Johnny's part, paving the way for the film's conclusion.

Dirty Dancing's final scene witnesses both the consummation of Baby's personal narrative and her reunion with her father. Baby no longer simply parrots her father's political rhetoric but instead reveals its limitations and stands up to his hypocrisy. Her sabbatical from middle-class society, and by extension the oppressive expectations placed upon "good" middle-class female behavior, allow her to develop her own political and ethical code. Furthermore, and contrary to conservative discourse, her disruption of the family unit and independent behavior does not end up destroying familial relations. She is welcomed back into the family a changed woman who is similarly capable of changing other people's political and social outlooks. Taking Baby's lead, the final dance sees previously staid and stolid men and women come together in a collective expression of social and sexual freedom. Of course, this could be seen as an overly Utopian ending, and it was certainly criticized by many public commentators.[30] Nevertheless, *Dirty Dancing* did provide enough political and cultural touchstones to at least indicate an attempt to inspire serious dialogue and debate on several issues of importance. Contemporaneous reception indicates, however, that this attempt was largely unsuccessful.

"Have the Time of Your Life": Critical Reception

Dirty Dancing was in many ways *Platoon* for women. Its representation of feminist issues and its narrative stressing a young protagonist's political coming-of-age offered plenty of subject matter for a political debate. *Dirty Dancing* did not, however, become a catalyst for public remembrance in the way that *Platoon* had done. The debate surrounding *Dirty Dancing* exemplified the manner in which feminism and women's memories of the Sixties had, to some extent, been evacuated of political significance. For example, Susan Douglas argues that the 1980s saw numerous attempts on the part of the advertising industry to court the "liberated woman." Ads for cosmetics, clothes, and exercise equipment tipped their hats to the feminist movement while at the same time erasing its political agency. "Women's liberation metamorphosed into female narcissism," argues Douglas.[31] Individuality and self-empowerment were reduced to improving one's appearance and having a good time. While arguing that this became more pronounced in the 1990s, Yvonne Tasker and Diane Negra note the emergence in the 1980s of discourses that they attribute to a "postfeminist" culture that "works in part to incorporate, assume, or naturalize aspects of feminism" and to "commodify feminism via the figure of woman as empowered consumer."[32] One might link such sentiments to *Dirty Dancing*'s famous promotional tagline, "Have the time of your life"—an apolitical appeal to individual desires. The theatrical poster in particular did not include any evidence of the film's political or historical content. It featured Swayze and Grey dancing against a plain white background. The emphasis on romance and the absence of any historical context suggests the film to be less about real issues and important events than about personal wish-fulfilment, or having "the time of your life." And, a few dissenting voices notwithstanding, critical reception followed suit, ignoring Dirty Dancing's politicized narrative of the recent American past.

The Christian Science Monitor lamented the film's "overcooked melodrama."[33] New York magazine thought Dirty Dancing "sweet and rich and a bit runny around the edges."[34] Other film critics felt that the film should never have strived for social commentary in the first place. The Wall Street Journal suggested that the "movie is at its weakest when it elaborates on its 'serious' theme—that the revolution in dancing will soon spread to every facet of society."[35] This separation of Dirty Dancing from politics was facilitated by way of the words used to describe the film. The term "melodrama" was accompanied by semantically "feminine" adjectives like "sweet" and "coy."[36] Other commentators associated the film with extreme emotionalism. "Drop into a shopping-mall multiplex and listen," announced Newsweek. "There are pockets of people reciting the lines along with the actors."[37] One audience member, who apparently had seen the film twenty-five times, was described as being in a state of "Dirty Denial." Another was quoted as stating: "I see the movie instead of eating"; yet another audience member apparently commented that the film was "the first girls' porno ever made."[38] Such word choices as "addiction," "denial," and "porno" suggest that a kind of extreme emotional attachment, if not hysteria, surrounded the film's release. Dirty Dancing's impact on women, as discussed in this article, was to shatter their self-control. These were not the sobering reports of a film helping people to come to terms with political and personal struggles, but the ravings of viewers steered by their uncontrollable libidos. This Newsweek article also suggests that Dirty Dancing did not appeal solely to teenagers, but to older women as well. The woman in a state of "dirty denial" was 45 years old; others were described as young professionals: writers, finance managers, etc. They were all associated with a kind of extended adolescence, a release of hormonal energy usually associated with teenage girls. While I do not wish to evacuate the fun from a film to which many people do seem to have reacted positively, it is notable that this was considered the only newsworthy element of *Dirty Dancing*'s public impact. Whereas *Platoon* acted as a canvas on which sober reflections on the Sixties and on growing up at this time were written large, *Dirty Dancing* was reported as having an infantilizing effect on women. *Platoon*'s media coverage spoke of a long-lasting, emotional, therapeutic relationship between film and viewer; *Dirty Dancing* was reported to be the cinematic equivalent of a one-night stand. Or, as *New York* reviewer David Denby announced: "To women I'd say, you may enjoy *Dirty Dancing*, but you'll hate yourself in the morning."[39]

Not all reviews were quite so negative about *Dirty Dancing*'s attempts to engage with history and politics. Some found in the film a metaphorical potency. "The filmmakers use dirty dancing as a hint of what is almost palpably around the corner in the America of 1963," wrote Sheila Benson in the *Los Angeles Times*. Around the corner was "change of a radical, sweeping, all-pervasive nature."[40] Benson was one of the foremost critics to promote the film as an attempt at least to grapple with serious historical issues.[41] In an article in which she reflected upon her own baby boom childhood, writer Alice McDermott noted approvingly that *Dirty Dancing* was "among the few current films that treat their [teenage] subjects with some seriousness."[42] Other critics found in the film at least an attempt at political commentary. Molly Haskell wrote in *Vogue* that *Dirty Dancing* "is a conventional film" but one with "a deliciously subversive core." Haskell argued that, although the film eventually ends with a rather staid gesture toward reconciliation, the earlier representation of Baby's "unleashed sexuality" is in itself a "declaration of independence."[43] That Haskell could dismiss the ending as contrived yet still find some kind of progressive possibility in its political representation suggests one way in which other viewers may have understood the film. As George Lipsitz argues, "as long as ruptures and closures accompany each other within media texts, at least the possibility of oppositional readings remains alive."[44] The scenes and lines of dialogue recalled by viewers, like those upon which they place special significance, are liable to change. While *Dirty Dancing*'s ending may have been considered contrived and excessively Utopian, it does not mean that the subversive potential in other scenes and sequences was completely denigrated or erased.

But these critics' efforts notwithstanding, *Dirty Dancing* failed to enter political debate to any significant degree. Even the controversial abortion subplot was dismissed as a distraction. When reviewers referenced this subplot, it was usually in a very brief sentence. "Penny conveniently gets pregnant so she can have an abortion and therefore be unable to perform at a neighboring resort," wrote one.[45] Vincent Canby also devoted one sentence to "a really quite awful subplot about Penny's abortion, financed by money that Baby has borrowed from her conventionally liberal doctor-father."[46] Generally, no one was willing to discuss the abortion, and rarely mentioned any of the film's other political issues.

Indeed, it would not be until several years after its initial reception that the abortion subplot gained credence in journalistic discourse. In 1997, *USA Today* noted that the film was in many ways subversive; it "[broke] the rules" by not punishing "a character for getting an illegal abortion." The same article refers to screenwriter Eleanor Bergstein's claims that feminist activists such as Gloria Steinem approved of *Dirty Dancing*'s political outlook.[47] A decade later, Cath Clarke of the *Guardian* favourably compared the abortion subplots present in films like *Dirty Dancing* and *Fast Times at Ridgemont High* (Amy Heckerling, 1983) to contemporary (2000s) Hollywood's unwillingness to mention "the A-word," let alone suggest that a character has had one.[48] Whether investing films such as these with a progressive ideological outlook indicates an attempt to challenge standard views on 1980s Hollywood—so often dismissed as an era of conservative "Reaganite entertainment"—or speaks more to a desire on the part of younger journalists (those born a generation after baby boomer critics such as Roger Ebert, David Denby, and others) to "rehabilitate" the movies of their youth is debatable. But as the recent spate of online blogs and newspaper articles attest, a generation after *Dirty Dancing*'s theatrical release, the film has enjoyed its own political awakening.[49]

Conclusion

Dirty Dancing was produced and received within political and cultural debates where feminism was the subject of conflict and contestation. By way of certain creative decisions and script changes, screenwriter Eleanor Bergstein infused Baby's personal narrative with a political dimension. Baby's challenge to the hypocrisy and blatant sexism of her father's generation of older liberals and to that of younger left-wing activists (represented by the character of Neil) shows her adopting principles and philosophies associated with the feminist movement (even if she does so in 1963, several years before the emergence of large-scale feminist activism). Nevertheless, a widespread unwillingness to treat Baby's transformation as anything but wish fulfillment and fodder for personal/sexual desires meant that *Dirty Dancing*'s political representation initially received little coverage in the public sphere. This reading was influenced by broader discourses in which feminism frequently found itself either being attacked outright as a negative social phenomenon or re-configured, in Tasker and Negra's words, as "empowered consumption."

The suggestion that *Dirty Dancing* embodied mindless and disposable entertainment is all the more ironic given that this film, in terms of its cultural profile, has gone from strength to strength. Its success on VHS and DVD and the constant *Dirty Dancing* revival screenings at cinemas indicate that it has had at least as long a lasting impact as films like *Platoon*, *JFK*, and *Forrest Gump*. That political commentators did not incorporate *Dirty Dancing* into their debates to the same extent as they did the other three may say as much about what they considered "important" historical subject matter as it did about the films' textual content. Male-centered narratives and pictures dealing with prominent public figures tend to be ascribed a gravitas that films dealing with private relationships, no matter how political, fail to achieve. Nevertheless, the film's enduring popularity and its recent critical re-evaluation indicate a newfound feeling that, to paraphrase Baby, there is a lot more to *Dirty Dancing* than was initially thought.

Notes

Author's Note: I would like to thank Richard Nowell, Peter Krämer, Mark Jancovich, Yannis Tzioumakis, Siân Lincoln, and Maggie Gruner for their helpful comments and advice on various drafts of this essay.

1 See, for example, Judy Lee Kinney, "Gardens of Stone, Platoon *and* Hamburger Hill: *Ritual and Remembrance*," in *Inventing Vietnam: The War in Film and Television*, ed. Michael Anderegg (Philadelphia: Temple University Press, 1991), 153–65.

2. Roger Ebert, "*Dirty Dancing*," *Chicago Sun-Times*, August 21, 1987, http://roger ebert.suntimes.com/apps/pbcs.dll/article?AID=/19870821/REVIEWS/708210301/1023. Accessed May 2010.
3. Ibid.
4. See Robert Burgoyne, *Film Nation: Hollywood Looks at US History* (London: University of Minneapolis Press, 1997), 57-119; Robert A. Rosenstone, "JFK: Historical Fact/Historical Film," *American Historical Review* 97.2 (1992): 506-511.
5. See Chris Jordan, *Movies and the Reagan Presidency: Success and Ethics* (Westport, CT and London: Praeger, 2003), 111-118; David Shumway, "Rock 'n' Roll Sound Tracks and the Production of Nostalgia," *Cinema Journal* 38.2 (Winter 1999): 45.
6. Eleanor Bergstein, "Best of Times, Worst of Times," *The Sunday Times*, September 21, 2008, http://entertainment.timesonline.co.uk/tol/arts_and_enter tainment/film/article4772857.ece. Accessed May 2010.
7. Daniel Marcus, *Happy Days and Wonder Years: The Fifties and Sixties in Contemporary Cultural Politics* (New Brunswick, NJ: Rutgers University Press, 2004).
8. See Susan Faludi, *Backlash: The Undeclared War Against American Women* (New York: Crown Publishers, 1991); Philip Jenkins, *Decade of Nightmares: The End of the Sixties and the Making of Eighties America* (Oxford: Oxford University Press, 2006), 85-89.
9. Faludi, *Backlash*.
10. Jack Knoll, "Little Fantasies," *Newsweek*, November 3, 1980, 90.
11. Karen Hollinger, *In the Company of Women: Contemporary Female Friendship Films* (Minneapolis: University of Minnesota Press, 1998), 9.
12. Ibid., 2.
13. Alice Echols, "Nothing Distant About It: Women's Liberation and Sixties Radicalism," in *The Sixties: From Memory to History*, ed. David Farber (Chapel Hill: The University of North Carolina Press, 1994), 149-174.
14. Wendy Martin, "Eleanor Bergstein, Novelist," *Women's Studies* 2 (1974): 96. Editors' note: see also Radner's essay in this volume.
15. Samuel G. Freedman, "*Dirty Dancing* Rocks to an Innocent Beat," *New York Times*, August 16, 1987, H19.
16. Eleanor Bergstein, *Dirty Dancing*, second draft, September 23, 1985, 5 (available for consultation at the Margaret Herrick Library, Los Angeles).
17. Doug Rossinow, *The Politics of Authenticity: Liberalism, Christianity and the New Left In America* (New York: Columbia University Press, 1998), 17.
18. Sara M. Evans, *Personal Politics: The Roots of Women's Liberation in the Civil Rights Movement and the New Left* (New York: Random House, 1979).
19. Bergstein, *Dirty Dancing*, 58.
20. Ibid., 8, 78.
21. Susan Douglas, *Where the Girls Are: Growing Up Female with the Mass Media* (London: Penguin, 1994), 87.
22. Ibid., 83-98.
23. Shumway, "Rock 'n' Roll," 46.

24 Bergstein, *Dirty Dancing*, 10. Although Bergstein's script uses the title "Goin to the Chapel," she is actually referring to the well-known song "Chapel of Love" by the Dixie Cups.
25 Ibid., 4.
26 Ibid., 23.
27 Cath Clarke, "Just Don't Say the A-Word," *Guardian*, November 23, 2007, http://www.guardian.co.uk/film/2007/nov/23/1. Accessed May 2010.
28 Irin Carmon, "*Dirty Dancing* is the Greatest Movie of All Time," *Jezebel: Celebrity, Sex, Fashion for Women* http://jezebel.com/5527079/dirty-dancing-is-the-greatest-movie-of-all-time. Accessed May 2010. *Roe vs. Wade* refers to the 1973 US Supreme Court decision which ruled that a woman's choice to have an abortion was a constitutional right.
29 Bergstein, *Dirty Dancing*, 80.
30 See, for example, Helen Knode, "Father Knows Best," *LA Weekly*, September 4, 1987, 43.
31 Douglas, *Where the Girls Are*, 246.
32 Yvonne Tasker and Diane Negra, *Interrogating Post-Feminism: Gender and the Politics of Popular Culture* (Durham and London: Duke University Press, 2007), 2. Editors' note: see also Radner's essay in this volume.
33 David Sterritt, "*Dirty Dancing*: A Second Look at a Big Box-Office Hit," *Christian Science Monitor*, November 19, 1987, 24.
34 David Denby, "The Princess and the Peon," *New York*, September 7, 1987, 60.
35 Julie Salamon, "On Film: Borsch Belt Princess Hot to Cha Cha Cha," *Wall Street Journal*, September 3, 1987, 16.
36 See Vincent Canby, "*Dirty Dancing*: A Catskills Romance in 1963," *New York Times*, August 21, 1987, C3; Salamon, "On Film," 16.
37 Charles Leershen and Tessa Namuth, "Getting Down and Dirty," *Newsweek*, December 21, 1987, 63.
38 Ibid.
39 Denby, "The Princess," 60.
40 Sheila Benson, "*Dirty Dancing* Takes a Big Step Toward Being Very Smart and Funny," *Los Angeles Times*, August 21, 1987, F11.
41 Benson, "Two Attempts at Social Comment Hit the Mark," *Los Angeles Times*, August 23, 1987, 39–40.
42 Alice McDermott, "Teen-Age Films: Love, Death and the Prom," *New York Times*, August 16, 1987, B1.
43 Molly Haskell, "What's New/What's Coming," *Vogue*, August 1987.
44 George Lipsitz, *Time Passages: Collective Memory and American Popular Culture* (Minneapolis: University of Minnesota Press, 1990), 94.
45 Salamon, "On Film," 16.
46 Canby, "*Dirty Dancing*," C3.
47 Susan Wloszczyna, "*Dirty Dancing*: Can It Still Generate Steam?," *USA Today*, August 15, 1997, 7D.
48 Clarke, "A-word."
49 See, for example, Carmon, "*Dirty Dancing* Is the Greatest Movie of All Time"; Bergstein, "Best of Times, Worst of Times."

9 "YOU DON'T OWN ME!": *DIRTY DANCING* AS TEENAGE RITE-OF-PASSAGE FILM

SIÂN LINCOLN

I have seen this movie over 5000 times and that is no lie. The first time that I seen it [sic] I was swept away with the dancing but most over all with the developing love of Johnny and Baby. The movie was amazing and now almost 20 years later I still make sure to have a Dirty Dancing *Night once a week.*[1]

I *Heart* Dirty Dancing

In 1987, the year of *Dirty Dancing*'s theatrical release, I was thirteen years old. I had just recently moved for the fourth time in the space of five years and had found myself yet again in a position where I had to settle in a new town and make new friends. To make matters worse, I had just hit my teenage years, and I did not like them very much. I was not really that good at being a teenager. There are a lot of memories about those early teen years that I care to forget, but the first time that I saw *Dirty Dancing* was not one of them. I did not see the film in the cinema; I am not really sure why, but on reflection this was probably because I was a bit too young to go on my own or with friends. But given that the film was, among other things, about a girl losing her virginity, this was definitely one to watch alone in one's bedroom or with close female friends—certainly away from the parental gaze.

A few months after its theatrical release I finally watched it on VHS. And not only did I see the film, I also organized a sleepover with a number of my school friends so that we could all experience it together and then spend the entire night talking about it. We had heard so much about the film, it having been a hot topic on the school playground for months, and were so excited to be finally watching it. I even bought a new nightdress for the occasion. So on a Friday night five of my friends and I excitedly prepared for the "screening" on my parents' television. With duvets out, nightwear on, and fizzy drinks and sweets at the ready, we watched the film. I instantly fell in love with it, not least because of the presence of Patrick Swayze who, for me, played the "bad boy" role perfectly (and whom I found so physically attractive). But I also loved the music, the clothing, the film's retro aesthetic, and of course the love story between Johnny and Baby. I distinctly remember us girls practically screaming when at the end of the film Johnny comes back to dance with Baby and he utters the immortal line "nobody puts Baby in a corner." I'm not sure how many times we rewound that scene that night, but it was plenty.

I am by no means alone in having such memorable experiences of watching the film; indeed, despite its being almost twenty-five years old, it still has a continuing attraction and an appeal, particularly for women. So why is *Dirty Dancing* significant to women, even in contemporary popular culture? I would like to argue that as a rite-of-passage film that portrays a young girl's journey from adolescence toward maturity over a three-week summer vacation, *Dirty Dancing* acts as a microcosm of what readily occurs in the life of the average young woman during those transitional years. In this respect, the film could be perceived as a valuable resource for young girls who are able to identify in it relatable experiences and apply them to their own situations and emerging biographies. This is because this rite-of-passage film contains a wealth of smaller and clearly identifiable rite-of-passage moments that young girls commonly encounter during their teen years, including experiencing a holiday romance, falling for an older guy, losing your virginity, defying your parents and questioning their integrity, rethinking and redefining family relationships and dynamics, finding yourself, and becoming a mature individual. Even seemingly more trivial rites of passage, such as applying makeup for the first time and wearing outfits that flaunt your body, are at the core of some of the film's scenes, underscoring further the significance of transition from adolescence to maturity. For this reason, and as my discussion will also demonstrate, *Dirty Dancing* has helped many young women act in the "real" world; has taught them how to make particular decisions and how to deal with important problems (at least for young people); has given a lot of young girls hope for a better future, irrespective of the nature of their individual circumstances; and has generally provided a life-affirming scenario that has resonated with large numbers of (although not exclusively with) young women around the world—and all this within the context of an extremely entertaining popular film.

To demonstrate how the film has come to occupy this unique position in women's cultural biographies (even compared to other famous, similarly themed films such as *Grease* [Randal Kleiser, 1978] and *Pretty in Pink* [Howard Deutch, 1986]), I start my discussion from the concept of young people's "emerging biographies" and the role that media texts can play in shaping them.[2] Songs, films, television shows, and many other media texts, which tend to be consumed in young people's private spaces, are often utilized by young people in their efforts to deal with particular circumstances during their difficult teenage years. In this respect, some of these texts acquire particular significance in young people's emerging cultural biographies, and *Dirty Dancing* certainly falls into this category of "helpful" media texts. I then move on to examine some of the reasons why *Dirty Dancing* has become so significant in young women's biographies and argue that the film subtly puts forth an image of a young woman who questions the normative structures nested in her middle-class upbringing, which without a doubt strikes a chord with many women's teenage experiences. This questioning primarily takes the form of rebelling against the authority of the young protagonist's father, around which a significant number of rite-of-passage moments presented in the film coalesce. It is Baby's responses to these moments that provide touch points for young women on how to deal with their own, similar scenarios. This is especially the case as Baby's responses prove effective enough to succeed in receiving her father's acceptance as she moves toward womanhood. Importantly, this success has been achieved on her own terms and through acting upon her sexual impulses, and it is the combination of these two factors that holds a fascination for many of the film's legions of female fans—and could potentially explain the film's continuous presence in popular culture even twenty-five years after its release.

To support this series of arguments further, I will provide some evidence from reviews or comments on the film offered by fans in the review pages of the Internet Movie Database (IMDb). Specifically, after examining the 100 most recent reviews of the film that were posted by the database users within the space of six and a half years (between May 2005 and November 2011), I demonstrate that there is a significant percentage (15 out of 100 users) who clearly discuss the film as a rite of passage, one that often spoke to their individual circumstances and taught them how to deal with the "real" problems they had to face at various points in their lives. As one such reviewer put it: "Sure, it's not perfect. Sure, some lines could be considered 'clichéd,' and the movie's not that unpredictable. But, it's my life. Literally."[3]

"Some People Count and Some People Don't": Youth Culture, Media Practices, and "Emerging Biographies"

Young people engage with media content both in the public and in the private domain. For teenagers in particular, watching films or television, as well as consuming other media texts such as magazines, often takes place in a private space, especially in their bedrooms. This is a space where a young person can be away from the parental gaze, often away from siblings and, if not completely alone, then just in the presence of a select group of friends. In some of the classic youth-cultures literature that explores the notion of a "bedroom culture,"[4] consuming media texts becomes almost by default a solitary practice because it is an exercise in identity formation and exploration. Consuming such texts can result in experimenting with hairstyles, clothing, and makeup (often in order to imitate the latest styles and fashions), while in the case of girls magazines reading the letters in the advice column is a way of obtaining information about one's own dreads and fears.[5] There are also certain media texts, such as particular types of films, that are considered embarrassing to watch with one's parents, while even popular programs such as soap operas, despite targeting family viewing, will contain scenes of a romantic or sexual nature that are awkward to watch with the rest of the family. Hence, teenagers will opt to watch in the privacy of their bedrooms, either on television or on a laptop. Finally, teenagers might opt to engage in solitary media practices not only because they do not want to share their experiences with other family members, but also because it is considered an important part of growing up and of "coming of age."

In his analysis of adolescents' media use in private spaces, Reed Larson argues that solitary media practices "cultivate a newly discovered private self" and allow the exploration of "numerous possible selves."[6] When watching a film on their own, young people can rewind particular scenes and watch them over and over again, they can watch the film repeatedly, and they may even experience the film as part of their sexual development, masturbating over particular aspects of it or over particular characters and creating fantasy worlds based around them. No matter how the film is watched, the experience is individual, and for Larson this is a crucial aspect of young people's solitary media practices as part of their emerging sense of self, of their biographies, and of authenticating their identities.

Furthermore, according to Larson solitary media use enables young people to engage with a text to an extent that they can use it as a means through which they can deal with particular feelings or emotions. As he puts it, "in searching for a private sense of who they are, [young people] frequently draw on very public packaged images, often drawn from the media."[7] In this respect, while things may not make sense to them in their experiences of "real life" in the home or at school, young people can relate to the content of particular media texts—the lyrics of a song or the plot of a film/the characters constructed within it. These texts are then used as "helpful" reference points in young people's understanding the experiences that they are dealing with in their own lives.

There are specific films that are adopted by young people as "emblems" of their teenage experiences and identities, and *Dirty Dancing* is undoubtedly one of them. It is a film that many young people, and especially young women, have watched numerous times over a number of years, both as a solitary activity and as a collective pursuit with friends or, later in their lives, with family. So why is this the case? What is it about *Dirty Dancing* that makes it such an important film in many people's, and particularly young women's, emerging biographies? As the following section suggests, two important reasons are that the film encourages young women to question norms, especially when these are represented by the often pre-determined and limiting options available to them as they enter adulthood, and that it provides a number of significant rite-of-passage moments to which young people can refer in an attempt to understand their own lives. The connective tissue that brings all these moments together is rebellion against patriarchal authority, arguably the ultimate rite of passage in a young woman's biography and the focal point of the film's narrative. There comes a time when father does not necessarily know best.

"Everybody Called Me Baby and It Didn't Occur to Me to Mind": *Dirty Dancing* and Rites of Passage

Dirty Dancing can be considered "emblematic" in women's rite-of-passage biographies because it is essentially about that pivotal moment when a girl becomes a woman: when she moves from sexual innocence to experience, when she begins to question the family structure within which she has been brought up, and when she perhaps questions some of that ideology within which she has to that date lived her life. And while in its entirety the film serves as a teenage fantasy exemplar of the summer romance and falling in love with the "wrong" (but very attractive) guy, it does so in a way that does not resemble the saccharine nature of other teenage fantasy films such as *Grease*. Instead, the multiple rite-of-passage elements on which the film is built (and which I discuss in some detail below) bear a certain affinity for many young women, reflecting upon aspects of their own coming-of-age experiences. This is especially important as in recent years an increasing number of young women have been delaying entering adulthood, irrespective of whether they have passed the age when they are legally considered adults.

Specifically, as Kearney has argued, the period of women's lives known as "youth" has in contemporary Western society become "extended."[8] As young women hurtle toward their adult years, the pursuit of continued youthfulness persists, represented, for example, through the delay of traditional transitions such as settling down with a partner and having a family. This extended period of youth, Kearney continues, provides women with additional time to continue to explore their identities. As she puts it, "Girls are menstruating at younger ages and many women are forming committed relationships and having children much later in life, if at all. This situation has provided girls with a much longer period to experiment with a variety of identities, lifestyles, and interests, including those that take them beyond the realms of domesticity and heterosexual relationships."[9] Whether in their late teens or as young adults, this increasing number of women is presented with a predetermined pattern of transitions that, in the Western world, has traditionally followed the linear structure of education-work-marriage-family.[10] *Dirty Dancing* is a film that teases— if not outright supports—the idea of diversion from this historically established pattern of transitions. What the spectator witnesses in the film is Baby's departure from a period of adolescent innocence and naivety to a world of sexual exploration and a diversion from her broader life plans to go to college, study the politics of underdeveloped countries, and join the Peace Corps—in other words, a diversion from what was perceived as normative for many middle-class young women in early-1960s America. Indeed, while Baby's parents, who are quite traditional in their hopes and desires for their daughter, have been encouraging her intellectual concerns and her pairing with Max Kellerman's grandson Neil (whom Baby is very clearly not interested in)—a hotel owner heir with good educational prospects and, no doubt, a secure future ahead of him ("quite a catch," as he self-proclaims)—Baby seems to be willing to put indefinitely on hold her plans to go to college and start a family in order to explore her sexuality and identity. In this respect, despite the fact that she is still a teenager, her potential decision to extend her adolescence artificially by not entering (normative) adulthood—the end of the film does not make clear what the heroine will do next—is bound to have struck a chord in terms of the problems faced by young adults, too.

The inconclusive end to the film provides the backdrop for another important reason why *Dirty Dancing* is perceived as such a key text in young women's emerging biographies: namely, its unmitigated support of rebellion against patriarchal authority through the realization of sexual desire. Indeed, the love story as a rite of passage in *Dirty Dancing* is inextricably linked to the frictions that emerge in Baby's relationship with her father.[11] That relationship is established as a very close one from the outset through Baby's voiceover, which states that during those years of her life she thought that she would "never find a guy as great as [her] dad." In this respect, the narrative anticipates the breakup of this relationship as the turning point that will propel the young protagonist's move to adulthood and therefore to a clear character transformation by the end of the film. This breakup as rite of passage can be encapsulated in the phrase "you don't own me," a phrase that a number of Baby's defiant actions and verbal exchanges with her father suggest and that is also underscored by the titular song by the Blow Monkeys that is heard in one of the film's sequences.

The first cracks in the father-daughter relationship appear when Baby starts experiencing a number of smaller rite-of-passage moments that inevitably put her on a collision course with her father: going where she is not supposed to go (the staff quarters), lying to her family in order to spend time practicing with Johnny for the dance, and lying to her father in order to help her new "friends." However, the first actual showdown between Dr. Houseman and his daughter takes place after a classic act of parental defiance through the seemingly ordinary teenage pursuit of applying makeup (by no means ordinary for Baby, who seems to shun such vanities). In her enduring quest to do well by others, Baby agrees to replace Johnny's professional dance partner, Penny, in a "make or break" feature at the neighboring Sheldrake hotel. To perform her number, Baby is required to dress in the traditional ballroom costume that is by definition flamboyant, comprising a fuchsia pink dress with a plunging neckline, silver ballroom shoes, hair pinned back into a chignon, heavy, stage-friendly makeup, and glitzy jewelry. Far removed from her everyday attire, Baby looks completely transformed, but in a very artificial manner; she almost looks more like a caricature of a ballroom dancer than a real one. On seeing this professional makeup on his daughter, Dr. Houseman begins to understand that Baby is involved with the "wrong crowd" and more specifically with Johnny; the makeup that is alien to Baby in the context of the Sheldrake is alien to her father in the context of their family life and signifies, probably for the first time, that perhaps Baby is changing. Not surprisingly, Dr. Houseman orders his daughter to take her makeup off before her mother sees it, attempting to reverse this change, to bring back the Baby he knows, loves, and trusts and wipe away the performance face that has been painted on for the attentions of another man. It is clear then that even the simplest rite-of-passage moment—applying makeup for the first time—becomes a sign of rebellion against patriarchal authority (which, predictably, causes her father's anger).

Following this initial act of rebellion and in the condensed period of three weeks that Baby and her family are at Kellerman's, she experiences many of the rite-of-passage moments that the average girl experiences over the course of her teenage years. She has embarked on a relationship with her first love; has upset members of her family in undertaking a relationship that is for them, and particularly for her father, with the wrong man; has continued it in secret anyway; has had sex; and has, arguably, ended a relationship. At the same time, she has begun to question the extent to which her parents are actually right about things, often challenging certain orthodoxies, especially the extent to which her only option is the traditional, linear move through "college-work-marriage-family." For all those reasons, it is not surprising that Baby is such an important role model for so many young women and that *Dirty Dancing* is such a significant film in their emerging biographies.

However, the ultimate triumph of the film does not so much lay in the fact that its main character challenges patriarchal authority but that she succeeds so convincingly in her efforts. The narrative of *Dirty Dancing* is remarkable in the ways in which it represents in a positive light the acquisition of sexual experiences by its teenage female protagonist while at the same time refusing to place her completely under a new patriarchal regime once she starts escaping from her father's control. This can be seen specifically in the otherwise fulfilling and happy end of the film, which nonetheless refuses to confirm whether Baby and Johnny's union is temporary or permanent. Indeed, their earlier declarations to each other that they will "never be sorry" seem to point to the fact that this is very much a summer romance, with neither of them likely to pursue a relationship beyond Baby's three weeks at the holiday camp. This could also explain why Baby does not want to let her father know about her romance—it is not a serious enough relationship for the girl to formally introduce her boyfriend to her father. In this sense, the film's ending seems to be particularly empowering for women—and not just within the context of the conservative early 1960s when the film takes place—as it seems to suggest that it's OK to have a holiday romance and to have sex with a man you have known only very briefly and with whom you don't intend to engage in a serious relationship. And if this is not a strong enough message, Dr. Houseman's final approval of his daughter after the last dance comes part and parcel with his approval of Johnny, a clearly older man who repeatedly has had sex with his teenage daughter during their stay at Kellerman's. In this respect, the film arguably goes even further than endorsing casual sex to suggest that it is fine for young women to embrace their sexual desires, as these tend to represent a much clearer point of orientation than anything else during these uncertain and transitional years of their lives—a radical position for a US film, even one coming from the independent film sector.

Dirty Dancing, then, presents much more than a young woman who engages in a series of important rite-of-passage moments. It presents a winner! Baby's diversions from the norm and her acts of rebellion against her father's wishes not only go unpunished but are rewarded: She gets Johnny and the acceptance on the part of her father that she is becoming an adult. And even if her triumph is seemingly undermined by the narrative's refusal to point specifically and explicitly toward a "happily ever after" future (will she still go to college, the Peace Corps, and from there to a predictable middle-class marriage and family? Or will she eschew all these to be with Johnny? She might even take some additional time off and extend her youth in order to assess her options and make the best decision for herself, as an increasingly large number of young people have been doing in recent years), Baby has succeeded in becoming her own person. She's done this by breaking the rules forced upon her, and for that reason she stands as the personification of a freedom that young women dream of during their transitions from adolescence to adulthood. In this respect, *Dirty Dancing* is an invaluable resource and an extremely helpful text, as it offers female audiences hope for a future the way they might dream of it, and this can be seen in many of the comments and reviews of the film on the Internet Movie Database.

"[It] Made Me Feel Like A Winner!!" *Dirty Dancing* as a "Helpful" Text

> [The film] reflect[s] very well on the problem that a 17-year-old girl faces in the Sixties and shows that every problem comes with a

> solution! And in her case with help from her dad! It made me think a lot about my life and how to deal with my own problem and overcome it! Made me feel like a winner!![12]

In a recent *Guardian* article about the auditions for the forthcoming *Dirty Dancing* UK tour, Journalist Zoe Williams ponders why women of a particular age (for example, those who were teenagers at the time of the film's release) were, and continue to be, such huge fans of *Dirty Dancing*, citing its "rite of passage" status as one of the reasons. Her view is worth citing in some length:

> Women born between 1970 and 1980 are obsessed with this film. I have a theory about this. I stole it off a friend who is into Freudian psychoanalysis: the whole theme, the eponymous dirty dancing, is sublimated sexual energy, that much is obvious. That memorable moment when Swayze finally manages to heave, sorry, lift Jennifer Grey off the ground … is a metaphor for losing your virginity. And it's clearly a female-crafted metaphor, proceeding not with a clear narrative urgency, as straight as a die to the irreducible explosion, but rather, with mis-starts and damp squibs and dance routines that don't go right because both people weren't doing the right thing at the right time and didn't have the right feelings for each other.[13]

As mentioned earlier, the continuing significance of *Dirty Dancing* for many people, especially young women, is because its narrative is constructed around those very experiences that many women have in their teenage years like falling in love for the first time, losing one's virginity, and challenging family ideologies. The experience of one's first love is rarely like the happily-ever-after scenario that tends to characterise the boy-meets-girl film and, indeed, as Williams states above, those romantic encounters are more likely to be characterized by false starts, uneasiness, clumsiness, and naivety; not being experienced enough to be able to assess whether the boy or girl one has feelings for are reciprocated and whether these feelings should be acted upon. Indeed, in observing users' comments on IMDb it was obvious that the film resonated with many women's rite-of-passage years, not just in terms of their questions about sex but more generally about being able to deal with the problems and pressures of entering adulthood. Arguably, the main quality of *Dirty Dancing* for the fifteen or so reviewers who wrote specifically about the film's impact on their lives was the notion of empowerment and the ability of the film to inspire them to hope for a better future, as the following quotations clearly suggest:

> *Dirty Dancing* portrays the trials and tribulations that every girl faces while growing up and becoming her own person. Although this movie is predictable in its conclusion, I personally love watching it whenever possible. I highly suggest it for any young girl dreaming of what she will become as she grows up.[14]

> For me it's about following your dreams, OK so Baby didn't exactly follow hers but she found new and exciting things to explore and she had new dreams to for-fill [sic] and she did it! GO BABY your [sic] beautiful girl!!![15]

Indeed, for one woman the film's ability to inspire was life-changing:

> Not only did I enjoy watching this film over and over again with wishful thinking and dreaming, I actually made some of my thoughts and dreams develop into reality by dancing more often myself (which is great aerobics, by the way). *Dirty Dancing* inspires a zest for living and empowers one to action. When a film grips you and motivates to make dreams come true, it is an excellent film that did its job of stirring your soul and mind to make fantasy a reality in your life.[16]

Of course, the film did not succeed in empowering all women to the extent identified in the above comments, but for many it helped them cope with difficult moments in their lives. Indeed, the film's ability to "teach" young girls how to behave in specific situations, how to handle things and understand and manage change in their lives, was an equally prominent theme of empowerment and inspiration in the reviews:

> You rarely see female characters who are motivated primarily by lust and it is a nice change. I also think the movie captures very well what

it is like to be a teenager coping with issues of class and of having [her] ideals suddenly come up against reality.[17]

Baby was well reserved young girl [sic].... This movie is one of my favorite movies. It teaches young individual [sic] how to be mature and follow their hearts.[18]

One of the movies [sic] themes is you sometimes have to take risks to find true happiness.[19]

But even for viewers who were not prepared to admit that *Dirty Dancing* helped them actively to deal with specific rite-of-passage situations, the simple fact that the film managed to capture what they saw as their experience or desires was enough to become a key text in their emerging biographies:

You can only really enjoy Jennifer Grey here. Her acting was spot on. Her subtle glances have me rolling, but deeper they're very true to her character. It's what a lot of us go through.[20]

It's not about the dance, I still wonder why do they call it "dirty dancing" cause I didn't see anything dirty in it. It's about a moments [sic] in our lives, moments that anyone experienced or ... not.[21]

A love story that all of us wish we could live (at least if you're female), this is a movie that you want to watch over and over again.[22]

Although there are other elements that link the film to the lives of the viewers, such as the loss of innocence and, perhaps, a longing for that time prior to its loss (especially by older women fans[23]), the triptych of capturing the rites of passage, teaching young women how to navigate those difficult moments, and offering inspiration and empowerment for the future seem to be at the very core of women's engagement with the film. In this respect, *Dirty Dancing* seems to go much further than the average American film for young people: It is taken seriously (and therefore not dismissed as entertainment) and becomes a major reference point both during the emerging and later moments of their cultural biographies.

Conclusion: Hitting Home: Referencing Rites of Passage in Everyday Teenage Life

While a large number of other IMDb commentators did not discuss directly the impact of the film on their lives or cited the music and dancing and the love story as the key reasons why they love the film, the sheer enthusiasm with which the vast majority of reviewers wrote their comments does suggest that *Dirty Dancing* is a film that has, at some point in their lives, spoken to them as a coming-of-age text. As I argue in the opening of this chapter, *Dirty Dancing* is in many ways unique compared to its contemporaries because it is a rite-of-passage film within which a number of smaller rite-of-passage moments are subtly embedded. Through the young protagonist Baby, who is holidaying at Kellerman's with her family, the film manages to present a microcosm of the rites of passage that a young girl experiences over the course of her teenage years in the space of three weeks. In achieving this, not only does the film become important in women's emerging cultural biographies, but it is also a text that female fans relate to in accordance with their own experiences of having been a teenager and as they moved toward an adult life of maturity and independence.

Dirty Dancing is not a romanticized version of the experiences of one's first love, but rather encapsulates those turbulent teenage moments, their ups and downs, stops and starts. The holiday romance is celebrated and, even more importantly, the young female protagonist is accepted by her audience, without judgment, for the choices that she makes, no matter how progressive they may sound. These choices compromise many of the stable elements of an adolescent girl's life, namely the relationship with her parents and siblings, as well as her sexuality, elements that clearly mark her move toward independence and adulthood. And while the context of the narrative may not be so familiar to young women today, the rites of passage through which the narrative is constructed are still the same. Even in a world of new media whereby communication is primarily electronic through social networking sites, instant messaging, texting, tweeting, and so on, the trials and tribulations of experiencing one's first love rarely change. For this reason, *Dirty Dancing* is passed down from generation to generation, making the experience of watching the film for those who first saw it in the cinema in 1987 a whole new experience all over again.

Notes

1. Mallorysauntcher, "The Best Movie I Have Ever Seen" in the Internet Movie Database, July 23, 2006, http://www.imdb.com/title/tt0092890/reviews?start=80. Accessed on November 1, 2011.
2. Reed Larson, "Secrets in the Bedroom: Adolescents' Private Use of Media," *Journal of Youth and Adolescence* 24.5 (1995), 535-49.
3. Thesar-2, "Each Dance Is the Time of My Life" in the Internet Movie Database, February 6, 2011, http://www.imdb.com/title/tt0092890/reviews?start=40. Accessed on November 9, 2011.
4. See, for instance, Angela McRobbie, *Feminism and Youth Culture from Jackie to Just Seventeen* (London: Macmillan Press, 1991).
5. See Elizabeth Frazer, "Teenage Girls Reading *Jackie*," *Media, Culture, Society* 9.7 (1987): 407-42; McRobbie, *Feminism and Youth Culture*.
6. Larson, "Secrets," 535.
7. Ibid., 536.
8. Mary Celeste Kearney, "Girlfriends and Girl Power: Female Adolescence in Contemporary U.S. Cinema," in *Sugar, Spice and Everything Nice: Cinemas of Girlhood*, eds. Frances Gateward and Murray Pomerance (Detroit: Wayne State University Press, 2002).
9. Kearney, "Girlfriends," 129.
10. On the subject of transitions for young women, see Andy Furlong and Fred Cartmel, *Young People and Social Change: New Perspectives* (Buckingham: Open University Press, 2006); Ken Roberts, *Youth in Transition: Eastern Europe and the West* (Basingstoke: Palgrave MacMillan, 2008); and Marc Molgat "Do Transitions and Social Structures Matter? How 'Emerging Adults' Define Themselves as Adults," *Journal of Youth Studies* 10.5 (2007): 495-516.
11. Editors' note: see also Jeffers-McDonald's essay in this volume.
12. foisy_2003, "Viva! *Dirty Dancing!*" in the Internet Movie Database, October 30, 2006, http://www.imdb.com/title/tt0092890/reviews?start=70. Accessed on November 1, 2011. Capitalization and spelling standardized for clarity.
13. Zoe Williams, "*Dirty Dancing*: It's Not Just About Sex," *Guardian*, May 7, 2011, http://www.guardian.co.uk/stage/2011/may/07/dirty-dancing-musical-not-just-about-sex. Accessed on October 20, 2011.
14. amhuss, "*Dirty Dancing*" in the Internet Movie Database, September 29, 2008, http://www.imdb.com/title/tt0092890/reviews?start=50. Accessed on November 1, 2011.
15. I_love_bopeep, "Romance Is Blissful If Your [sic] in Love" in the Internet Movie Database, January 2, 2007, http://www.imdb.com/title/tt0092890/reviews?start=70. Accessed on November 1, 2011.
16. dustyshoes2003, "Empowers and Inspires" in the Internet Movie Database, January 2, 2008, http://www.imdb.com/title/tt0092890/reviews?start=50. Accessed on November 1, 2011.
17. weissgang, "Female Sexual Desire—On Screen" in the Internet Movie Database, http://www.imdb.com/title/tt0092890/reviews?start=20. Accessed on November 1, 2011.

18　labreshah, "A Teenage Love Affair" in the Internet Movie Database, April 8, 2009, http://www.imdb.com/title/tt0092890/reviews?start=40. Accessed on November 1, 2011.
19　MAUREEN, "Enjoyable and Nostalgic" in the Internet Movie Database, October 19, 2005, http://www.imdb.com/title/tt0092890/reviews?start=90. Accessed on November 1, 2011.
20　Thesar-2, "Each Dance."
21　dacoroman, "My Favorite Movie . . . Ever" in the Internet Movie Database, July 12, 2006, http://www.imdb.com/title/tt0092890/reviews?start=80. Accessed on November 1, 2011.
22　angelgirl21788, "A coming-of-age story sure to spark a love. . . ." in the Internet Movie Database, October 8, 2005, http://www.imdb.com/title/tt0092890/reviews?start=10. Accessed on November 1, 2011.
23　See, for instance, "Somehow watching the making and the story behind *Dirty Dancing* made me long for my childhood days as a thirteen year old. . . . I watch it fondly now with all the awkwardness of Baby's first days and her first true love with Patrick Swayze as heart throb, Johnny Castle." sylviastel@aol.com, "Dirty Dancing Coming to Broadway for It's [sic] 20th anniversary!" in the Internet Movie Database, June 24, 2004, http://www.imdb.com/title/tt0092890/reviews. Accessed on July 27, 2012.

10 HETEROS AND HUSTLERS: STRAIGHTNESS AND DIRTINESS IN *DIRTY DANCING*

GARY NEEDHAM

Introduction: The (Dis)Pleasures of *Dirty Dancing*

Coming from a position enlightened by thinking critically queer, one can argue that the dirtiness of *Dirty Dancing* is straight people lifting the lid on their repression. It is also, in a less direct way, a coming-of-age story about female independence, freedom, and rebellion, and is perhaps also an attempt to look at Fifties conservatism through the prism of Reagan's America. I know it is not a film that is intended to speak to me the way others have probably argued that it speaks to them, which is perhaps why my initial thought for this chapter, based on the memory of seeing the film on video as a teenager in the 1980s, was about *not* having the time of my life. Perhaps this film, in which dancing "produces" heterosexuality, taps into the childhood anxiety of being forced by teachers to ask girls to be your partner at the school Christmas dance—a feat of compulsory heterosexuality.[1] Always last to be picked were me—the sissy—and the fat girl, which might explain my long-standing preference for *Hairspray* (John Waters, 1988) over *Dirty Dancing*. The title of the song "(I've Had) The Time of My Life" can also be perceived as a self-reflexive gesture in terms of how one ought to feel for having seen the movie; however, never have I felt so unmoved, while others around me were clearly being taken to a special place.

Dirty Dancing would never have had such a lasting appeal if the latter statement did not have some truth to it, because for a seemingly very large percentage of the people who have seen it the film is assuredly life-affirming. My own resistance to Dirty Dancing is partly because I find it "too straight," to the point of convincing myself that it is anathema to the pleasures I usually expect from the films I choose to watch. As someone situated so clearly on the "outside" of the text, I have the opportunity to develop a critical vantage point that can help me observe how heterosexuality is constructed: as effortless, naturalized, and transcendent. The weight of the symbolism in the lift performed in the final dance yokes many ideas about bodies, gender, sexuality, and feeling that I shall examine in due course. As I will argue, Dirty Dancing uses dance effectively to tell us not only what heterosexuality and romantic love might look like, but what it might *feel* like. The concept of being "dirty" becomes a means to express a raunchier form of heterosexual courtship dancing, with moves that evoke a freedom to put the "sex" in heterosexuality. Dirty Dancing makes heterosexuality exciting and literally uplifting in ways that secure a rather robust ideological sentiment that renders heterosexuality the most natural feeling and the most rightful way of representing love and desire in mainstream cinema.[2]

The power of Dirty Dancing, this chapter will suggest, lies in its ability to divert any thoughts of sexuality being something cultural, and thus something inherently constructed and ideological, even when it is dirty and licentious. One of the aims of this chapter is to interrogate the straightness of Dirty Dancing, especially the way straightness is located and performed in the dancing sequences of the film. However, all is not lost and closed down to a straight reading of the film's dirty politics. In my re-viewing of Dirty Dancing, a rather overlooked aspect of the film piqued my queer interest and perhaps may be considered the alternative angle (and one that might complement feminist critics' interest in the abortion subplot[3]). This aspect is the fact that Johnny, the film's male lead, is presented on a few occasions as more or less a hustler, a man for sale. Johnny may not be the fully blown (pun intended) male prostitute of American hustler cinema, but the textual evidence is there, and I will take the opportunity to make this case in detail and with relish. In this respect, this chapter is also about how sexuality is "sold" to audiences in different ways:

on the one hand, the up-front heterosexual pleasures of dancing as an ideological force to be reckoned with, and on the other, the way in which Johnny is himself a commodity that is up for sale, feeding our "Hungry Eyes" (as the song goes), and whose style and rebellious iconography taps into a hidden history of visual codes regarding male hustling.[4] There is something far more dirty to be uncovered than the film's relentless close-ups of pelvic undulation.

The Heteros

Straight from the moment we experience *Dirty Dancing*'s credit sequence, it is already doing some work in the service of ideology through dance, music, and the body. The black-and-white, grainy, slow-motion images of dancing couples stitched to the sound of the Ronettes' "Be My Baby" (1963) captures the ecstasy and the intimacy of couples-based dancing. The credits also refer to a later scene when Baby first encounters the dirty dancing that takes place in the "no guests beyond this point" staff quarters over the white bridge. The place where the dirty dancing is located is hidden away because it is about sexuality and sexual expression. Although there are many white couples, several others are clearly from different ethnic backgrounds, which, given the racial politics in the early-1960s America in which the film is set, provides a topos of progressive politics as opposed to the conservatism taking place on the other side of the bridge. In this respect, the staff quarters ought to remain away from the public eye, while the actual place where the dancing takes place, in its clandestine tone, is reminiscent of the pre-liberation underground gay bars—another context in which sexuality and dancing remained secretive and away from the public eye.

In both the credit sequence and the later scene when, through Baby's guidance, we finally enter the staff quarters, we see men and women dancing together in a mode of bodily conduct that complements each other. This form of dancing, which is sometimes referred to as "vertical sex," speaks volumes about how gender and sexuality (and in this case, race) are interlinked through dance. The dancing in *Dirty Dancing* maybe construed as dirtier, more liberating and capricious than the staid waltz and fox-trot that are performed on the main dance floor, but nonetheless all the dancing in *Dirty Dancing*,

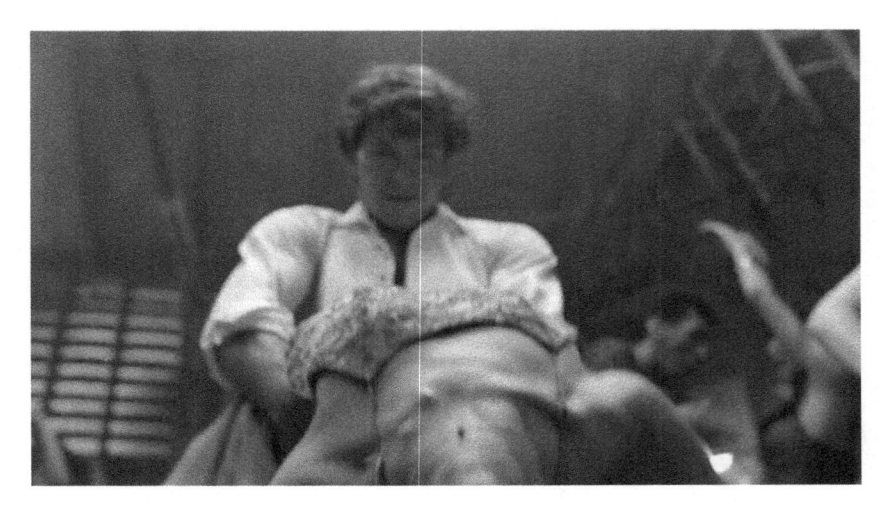

"Vertical Sex" in *Dirty Dancing*

even when it is at its dirtiest and most Latin-inspired, is structured around the complementary pairing of women and men's bodies. As I will discuss shortly, couple-dancing has a long-established history that goes back to the eighteenth century and was central to the way gender was deployed in relation to the development of heterosexuality as a new type of identity.[5] *Dirty Dancing* cannot escape this legacy, even if it does offer us choreographed "dry humping."

Dance is of course a non-verbal form of communication, and Angela McRobbie's often-cited article on dancing refers to it is a "way of speaking through the body" while also being a signifier of "a sexual ritual, a form of self-expression."[6] The dirty dancing in the film is also a position that speaks against the conservatism of the parents and their moral panic sentiments about dancing as a means toward loosening the morals of the young in a similar fashion to the film *Footloose* (Herbert Ross, 1984). Johnny Castle is the vector of dancing's sexual ills, it would seem. Julie Malnig, in her in analysis of dancing in the 1910s, talks about the way that, historically, "protests against social dance have typically focused on apprehensions of sexual promiscuity and lower-class rebellion."[7] From the narrative perspective of the parents and the conservative Kellerman staff, the dirty dancing often pairs with rebellion and is associated with a lower-class echelon. On the other hand, sexual promiscuity, which dirty dancing and Johnny's teachings seem to promote, stands to corrupt white, middle-class, Jewish daughters like Baby. Malnig also goes on to say: "Invariably, the arguments always come back to fears of (and for) the feminine: that the dancing would wreak havoc on the morals and sexual development of women and girls, threaten their roles as keepers of the domestic sanctity of home and hearth, or tempt their susceptible sexual natures."[8]

In "speaking through the body," *Dirty Dancing* presents the trajectory of Johnny and Baby's relationship through dance: The better they work/dance together, the more they become emotionally involved, while dance also stands in here for freedom, sex, and, in Baby's case, sexual awakening. The dirtier the dancing gets, the more we are convinced that Baby and Johnny are made for each other, and the more we get the impression of Baby's being liberated from the infantilization of her name. On the other hand, their dancing also achieves Johnny's "taming" and his introduction into the sphere of respectability. Johnny and Baby do not really need to speak about how they feel, but they do that anyway, since we know that through the dancing, right up to the moment when she is finally lifted in the air, she cannot feel any higher than when she gives herself over to Johnny's support; elevation and elation become one and the same as she is lifted up like a trophy.

As a form of non-verbal communication, dance uses the body to produce and express cultural ideas about gender and sexuality, and the dancing in *Dirty Dancing* is no less a form of courtship and couple-making than the dancing it deems to be not so dirty. No matter what shape the dancing takes in the film, it is ultimately about bringing together opposite genders, promoting a form of mutual (gender) exclusivity, and finding a way to articulate the joy of heterosexuality, both conservative and rebellious, through the bodily movement of women and men. In short, the kind of dancing we see, both dirty and non-dirty, are all the same ritualized expressions of heterosexuality made material. Dancing here makes heterosexuality both meaningful and material, because it seems so natural that men and women effortlessly seem to complement one another, whether they nimble across the floor to the fox-trot or offer up some kind of sexual gyration.

Dirty Dancing's representations of dancing belong to a longer history in which dancing was a form of courtship ritual that brought young men and women into initial physical contact with one another. In the film, it is dancing that brings Johnny and Baby together; it produces their coupledom, it sexually awakens Baby and tames Johnny's rebellion and feelings of inadequacy, it transcends class difference, and, rather problematically, it ends up defining Baby and Johnny's role within a traditional gender system. After the final dance there is an outrageously patriarchal moment when Baby's father actually "passes" Baby into the care of Johnny as if she were property owned and relinquished between men. Any potential threat of sexual immorality or gendered impropriety suggested by the dancing is resolved firmly by this closing scene. However, it is no coincidence that this scene follows the major dance at the end in which the very movement of Baby and Johnny, their place within the logic of dancing together, has already cemented the idea that the man leads and the woman follows. Baby throws herself back, arching her back, and puts her trust in Johnny that he will be there to "support" her body from falling backwards. Such scenes of movement are so gendered that I challenge the reader to imagine the bodies in reverse, in which Johnny falls back with his body fully arched and with Baby supporting him. While it is doubtful she could lift him in the air, she could nonetheless support him if he willingly put his body into her trust, at which point she might be the one to do the "supporting" instead. But that is not how dancing, dirty or clean, works. Even at its most raunchy and dirtiest, the dancing is ultimately heteronormative. Even when they are embracing outside the dance, Johnny always stands behind Baby, holding her in his care, and not the other way around.

The heteronormativity of couples-based dancing has become a fixation of reality television programs like *Strictly Come Dancing* (BBC, 2004–) and *Dancing With the Stars* (ABC, 2005–), which are organized around the success not just of dancing technique but also of how well-matched the dancing partners are, how right they look together.[9] In another dancing reality show, *So You Think You Can Dance* (Fox, 2005–), the heteronormativity of couples dancing was tested when two men appeared as contestants in the ballroom category. They are introduced coming out of a men's public toilet in their identical sparkly outfits to the sound of The Weather Girls' "It's Raining Men," in a scene that manages to allude to both cottaging and disco simultaneously. They perform their audition dancing the samba, one sweeping the other around the floor, which often appears as a ghastly spectacle of badly judged camp performance. However, campiness was not "the problem" compared to the judges' homophobic outbursts, in which it was observed that two men dancing as a couple is literally beyond logic and imagination. Heterosexuality is so deeply embedded and hegemonic when it comes to the logic of dancing that a couple "must" always be composed of a man and woman. It is also why disco and house music were so liberating and important to gay people, because you could dance by yourself and partner with the music. Some of the judges' comments in *So You Think You Can Dance* are very instructive in this case: "I don't really know what to say"; "You probably alienate a lot of our audience"; "I'm really one of these people who likes to see guys be guys and girls be girls"; "I'm confused because I see you're both sometimes being the female role"; "I'm confused in terms of the classical form"; and, the ultimate insult: "I'd both like [sic] to see you dancing with a girl."

The commonsense assumptions behind such judging, and the debt owed by *Dirty Dancing,* can be traced back to the history of European dance since the eighteenth century. Dancing was introduced as an ordered social ritual that was heavily rule-bound, especially in relation to gender and the roles of leading and following.[10] The rules and what one learns from dance is a tradition that is often passed on from one generation to the next and arguably brings together the eighteenth century debutante with the school Christmas dance, the reality TV dance shows, the Hollywood film musical, and the more recent, phenomenally successful *High School Musical* franchise (2005-2010). There is a sense of continuity in the production of gendered identity in terms of how men and women relate to one another through bodily movement and ritual, and when that is challenged and transgressed it appears wrong and queer. It so powerfully ingrained that even to me it just does not look right.

In the history of European dancing, the origin of couples-based dancing like the waltz was rooted in the "creation of a good moral citizen" who would behave in a way that was appropriate to his or her gender and class.[11] Learning the rules of the dance was equated to learning the rules of social conduct: Men lead and women follow, the body remains poised and in control, women are to be picked and judged, and so on. Dance as a social activity was then a first point of bodily contact between young women and men, and the rules of who leads and who follows are suggestive of many other social and cultural discrepancies that have perpetuated inequality between genders. Furthermore, European dance was organized around a system of physical support in which the woman's body relies on the man to both support and lead her. In this respect, the first dances of the debutante established rules of support and dependency upon which it was assumed that women had to rely on and trust men. The efficacy of this logic is that it defines the role of women in dancing as depending on the male partner and never being in a "lead" position. Despite the centuries between the eighteenth century European ballroom tradition and *Dirty Dancing*'s appropriation of Latin American dance influences (the lower center of bodily gravity in the hips and pelvis), one can see how the bodies are still organized in such a way, to the extent that Baby is often dependent on Johnny for support (and which, of course, is expressed most obviously in the iconic lift at the end of the film). Dancing is merely another expression that performs and reproduces structures of dependency based on unequal power relations. So while *Dirty Dancing* is a modern film about modern dance, the movement bears the traces of a much older tradition based on women's physical dependency as a prelude to other types of dependency that

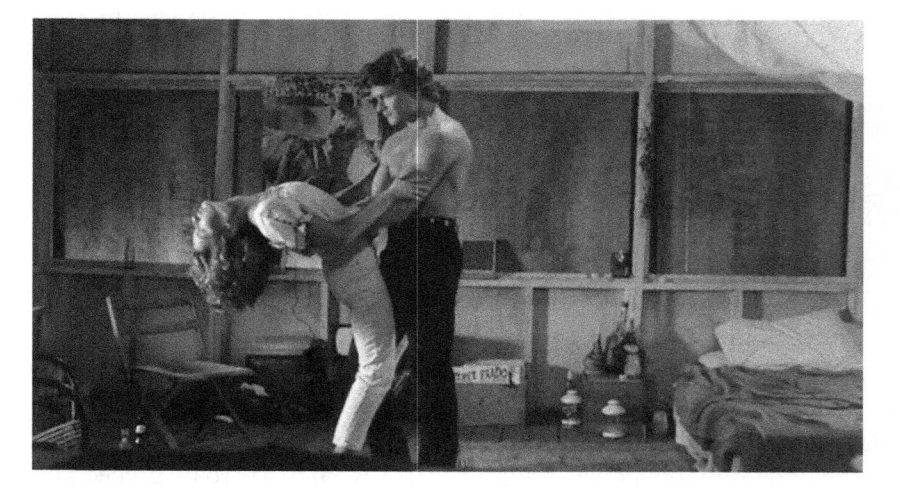

"Structures of Support"

might follow or be expected of her identity (for instance, financial support). This is why the final dance is tagged by the scene in which Baby's father literally passes her over into Johnny's safe keeping.

The Hustler

There are many unanswered questions about sex and sexuality in *Dirty Dancing*. This is partly because a lot of it takes place offscreen, is dealt with in rather coy fashion, or is elided from the narrative. Despite the side profiles of those crotch-grinding close-ups, for a dancing that is meant to be so dirty that it has to remain hidden up in the staff quarters, there are no visible erections in those tight dancing pants. The film has to be commended for even including a major subplot on abortion and thus highlighting indirectly the presence of recreational sex. However, the abortion that follows it and the pain and misery it causes Penny and her young friends are more reminiscent of cautionary sex education features and classroom films such as *The Road to Ruin* (Norton S. Parker, 1928) and *Street Corner* (Albert H. Kelly, 1949) than an affirmation of any pleasures involved in sex.[12] Sex without love and pre-marital sex are part of a specter that haunts the film and are very much associated with the practices of the young people at the staff quarters. One could even argue that the iconic white bridge that separates the guests and the staff at Kellerman's is the road to Sodom itself; it does literally lead Baby, melon in hand, to a scene of bacchanalian excess, nothing short of orgiastic in its impression, while later in the film the same bridge functions as a location of release from all sexual tension and pent up desire as Baby, in high-cut denim shorts, lets herself go, dancing away with wild abandon in the famous "Wipe Out" montage sequence.

While *Dirty Dancing* evokes the *Romeo and Juliet* plotting of lovers from conflicting worlds, the film also gravitates to a seedier plot that one might call the "*Emmanuelle* plot" as homage to Just Jaeckin's extremely commercially successful 1974 soft-core feature. In that plot, a young woman, who more often than not is sexually repressed, is sexually awakened by a more experienced man. However, *Dirty Dancing* is no *Emmanuelle*, as most of the sex in the former is indirect and worked out through the dancing, which clearly stands in for the sexual journey that we do not see on screen. This is despite the fact that our first glimpse of the dirty dancing in the staff quarters is tantamount to an orgy that takes place in a secluded area and under subdued red lighting. Of course, there is sex in the film, including many post-coital moments with Baby and Johnny tucked up in bed discussing his background and the status of their own relationship. There is also a quick moment of sex "in the act," which is witnessed by Baby's sister, Lisa, and involves one of the film's female characters that we are expected to pass judgment upon: older woman Vivian Pressman. While in contemporary parlance Vivian would be called a "cougar" and her engagement in sexual activities with younger men would arguably cause less shock, in the 1960s milieu of the Kellerman resort and the 1980s exhibition of the film in Reagan's America, Vivian is rendered both tragic (for wanting sex) and desperate (to have it). This is certainly justified by the element of shock that the audience is set up to experience when Lisa catches her in the act.

However, the sex that interests me the most in this chapter is Johnny's, specifically whether or not anyone is paying Johnny for his services. As an audience, we have certainly paid to see Swayze with his top off prancing around in black stretch pants. This hustling aspect should not be a revelation, since there are two minor scenes in the film that suggest otherwise, while throughout *Dirty Dancing* he plays nothing short of a tease for those both onscreen and the audience offscreen. At the very least, *Dirty Dancing* suggests that Johnny has been used or allowed himself to be used for the purpose of someone else's sexual gratification. Even the name "Johnny" refers to the hustling trade, for a "john" is the hustler's client, as well as a common alias for hustlers themselves, who often adopted all-American, generic names.[13]

In one of these hustling scenes we see Johnny approached by Vivian Pressman's husband at his poker table. Moe Pressman is going to be busy playing cards all evening, and he hands Johnny a wad of cash to make sure that his wife gets some "extra dancing lessons," as he calls it. One can almost see the quotation marks around the line of dialogue "extra dancing lessons," which is rich in innuendo but also suggestive of the fact that Johnny's services have been bought up regularly by this specific patron of Kellerman's for his attention-seeking wife. How many other women get those extra dancing lessons, one wonders? The narrative is certainly not subtle about the fact that

Johnny's services can be bought. This scene is also important because Johnny rejects Pressman's offer to keep Vivian busy because he is now "going steady" with Baby. She has made a better man of him by rescuing him from vice, and he is now prepared to reject much-needed cash for the benefit of a life grounded in respectability.

Vivian is an interesting character who is treated rather unfairly in the movie. She is portrayed as jealous of Baby and, more generally, of all the younger women at Kellerman's. Interestingly, when she is caught in bed with Robbie by Lisa—a scene that stands as the film's only legitimate sex scene, since the rest is all foreplay, heavy petting, and postcoitus—she is straddling a man half her age, which demonstrates clearly her ability to "lead" in an environment where all women are learning how to "be led," in dancing as well as in life more generally. Vivian is at one point referred to as a "Bungalow Bunny," precisely at the moment when she partakes in a salacious mambo embrace with Johnny. "Bungalow Bunny" is the label given to older women who stay all week at Kellerman's while their husbands only stay on weekends. In this early mambo dancing scene, Johnny is clearly set up as "entertainment" for the older ladies, a label also attached to him in one of the film's opening scenes when Kellerman himself calls him "entertainment staff" and dictates to him what he can and cannot do under that designation. Of course, Johnny is also "entertainment" for the audience, both in terms of his dancing skills, as a spectacle to be enjoyed, and as the male lead in the film's narrative.

The scene where Moe Pressman is procuring Johnny's "dancing lessons" also refers to an earlier scene when Baby asks him how many women he has used before her. Johnny replies that he is the one who was used and not the other way around. Such a reversal speaks of Johnny's passivity, evoking clearly the idea that he is up for grabs as the semi-tragic hustler, as the one who has been sexually mistreated. Despite his bravado and cocksure attitude, Johnny has no qualms about confessing that he has been used by other women, which within the romantic plotting helps make him seem vulnerable, adorable, and ready to be rescued by the respectable, middle-class Jewish girl. The exact way he has been used by all these women is veiled in the narrative, but again there are hints that he has been paid for contact with his body. Indeed, if not directly for sexual services or romantic companionship, Johnny is getting paid by Kellerman to "entertain" the resort's guests, and the film seems to comment on that when, toward the end, Kellerman's grandson Neil asks Baby to ensure that she is getting her money's worth of Johnny services. In this scene, Neil almost walks in on them teasing each other in Johnny's studio, and they have to pretend that Baby had hired Johnny to give her dance lessons. Johnny is always for sale, and there for more than just dancing—dirty or otherwise.

This particular subplot might have been less apparent to myself had it not been for the way that Johnny's clothes and overall style gesture toward the iconography of the "bad boy" and the male hustler that was a fairly dominant image in American postwar gay subculture, and which was even brought to public attention in *Time* magazine in 1964.[14] The infamous exposé in *Time*, called "Homosexuality in America," introduced mainstream America to the underground culture and dress codes of gay sexuality through a series of photographs and captions. In this exposé, one of the captioned photographs reads, "a San Francisco gay bar run for and by homosexuals is crowded with patrons who wear leather jackets, make a show of masculinity and scorn effeminate members of their world."[15] This fact stood in contradistinction to the commonsense assumption in the 1960s that all gay men were effeminate, fluffy-jumper-wearing sissies and instead could look like the dangerous hood on the street corner.

Johnny Castle: rebel and hustler.

Heteros and Hustlers: Straightness and Dirtiness 195

In fact, I was alerted to the homoerotic dimension of this plot detail from the very first moment in which we are introduced to Johnny, with his black leather jacket slung over the shoulder, tight t-shirt with rolled up sleeves, and black jeans, the stock-in-trade look of the hustler so endlessly documented in postwar gay literature and film, both underground and mainstream.[16]

Furthermore, this is an iconography that extends beyond the male hustler and underground cinema and draws upon 1950s youth culture to include numerous figures of rebellion, macho posturing, and lawlessness: juvenile delinquents, rockers, and greasers like the Jets and Sharks from another well-known musical, *West Side Story* (Robert Wise and Jerome Robbins, 1961). *Dirty Dancing* has plenty of these bad-boy hustler types performing in the background in various states of sexiness and undress. For instance, in the scene at the staff quarters, while Baby looks on in awe, the camera moves about the room and reveals a number of young men with the hustler look: tight white t-shirts with sleeves rolled up to reveal the bicep, greased back quiffs, beer bottles from which they are slugging. And just to the right of the frame when Johnny arrives there is someone topless and perspiring.

The hustler was an important outlaw figure in the 1960s, much like Johnny and his uneasy fit within the 1960s milieu that the Kellerman's resort represents in *Dirty Dancing*. For Michael Moon, the hustler was

Background homoeroticism in *Dirty Dancing* (enlarged detail).

"Background hustler" in a scene from *Dirty Dancing*.

a central figure that "served as a major trope for a crisis in 'American manhood,'"[17] and is similar to what Leerom Medovoi calls the "Bad Boy" in the context of 1950s rebel discourses.[18] Indeed, Johnny is often taciturn, nonchalant, and introspective, with his feelings for Baby originally ambivalent and with no real interest in acknowledging her presence early on in the film. Baby's eventual conquest of "the Castle," of Johnny's feelings, is also an attempt to resolve his disaffected manhood, especially as one of the film's final messages is that she made him a better man and not more of a bad boy. To put it in other words, she saved him from what the widespread crisis in postwar masculinity typified by disaffected male stars like James Dean and Montgomery Clift.[19] The crisis had been created by instabilities in gender following WWII, the emergence of a politics of identity on the cusp of the feminism and civil rights movements, cold war paranoia, and the failure of the 1950s to live up to the patriarchal *Father Knows Best* (CBS, 1954–1960) suburban ideal.

The leather boys, with their upturned "stiff" collars, are icons of rebelliousness and of living dangerously. Danger is more often than not sexually charged and appealing and finds homoerotic expression in body language, hairdos, tattoos, and sartorial style.[20] Style and clothing are important to queer reception, especially when films do not speak about homosexuality directly. A black leather jacket can sometimes say more than words, and historically the item functioned as a signifier of gayness or hustler availability.[21] The iconography of the hustler has been treated at length in Barry Reay's *New York Hustlers*, which provides ample photographic evidence of "the look," often drawn from the Kinsey archives, of the sartorial style of hustlers to which Johnny so clearly conforms when in his leather jacket, t-shirt, and black jeans look.[22] However, just like with the issue of sex, which is treated coyly and takes place in-between scenes, Johnny's bad-boy styling in *Dirty Dancing* never goes far enough to become threatening or narratively significant. There does not seem to be real commitment to the delinquent look, with his Folsom-style quiff being a bit floppy and lacking in "edge" compared to the bad-boy looks of Johnny Depp in *Cry-Baby* (John Waters, 1990) or Elvis in *Jailhouse Rock* (Richard Thorpe, 1957) and *King Creole* (Michael Curtiz, 1958). Still, on the few occasions that Johnny's image becomes prominent it does refer to social rebellion as much as it does to sexual lawlessness. This look is best typified in Hollywood cinema by James Dean in *Rebel Without a Cause* (Nicholas Ray, 1955) and Marlon Brando in *The Wild One* (Laszlo Benedek, 1953). Indeed, one could argue that Swayze's Johnny is an attempt to channel Dean and Brando's "emotionally vulnerable" qualities with his "disaffected inner isolation, and eroticized sensitivity,"[23] and the scenes where the otherwise self-assured Johnny confesses his exploitation by women certainly help to construct him in the image of the two 1950s Hollywood stars.

Dirty Dancing is clearly not a hustler movie compared, for instance, to *Andy Warhol's Flesh* (Paul Morrissey, 1968) and *Midnight Cowboy* (John Schlesinger, 1969). It is not even comparable to *American Gigolo* (Paul Schrader, 1980), despite the fact that Schrader's film works hard to deny the queer history of male prostitution in much the same way *Dirty Dancing* works to avoid the pitfalls of homoeroticism, despite the presence of a plethora of homoerotic elements. Although I am aware of the fact that I am stretching the limits of interpretation here, I also want to open up the possibility of reading Johnny against this history and iconography of hustling that is caught between the "soft eroticism" of delinquency[24] and the "hidden cultural history of gay erotics centered around men in musicals."[25] Johnny's look is neither a wardrobe accident nor a product of period verisimilitude.[26] Through reference to Johnny as "entertainment," through the "extra dancing lessons" that Pressman is happy to pay for to ensure his wife is kept satisfied, and through his emotional realization that he has been used by women, the film points to a sexual traffic, in which Johnny is something that can be bought and used, that is generally hidden from the narrative surface.

Conclusion

The "dirtiness" of *Dirty Dancing* is overrated to me, but that may depend on the perspectives one brings to the film and on the ways in which identity affects reception and interpretation. What a close analysis of *Dirty Dancing* does reveal is the nature of sex and sexuality in American popular cinema as something fairly fluid and dynamic, in the sense that one cannot assume that any popular film is entirely straight or entirely queer and that conservative impulses may be challenged by other facets that, for many audiences, remain hidden and obscure. What I hope I offered here were two perspectives that open up the questions of sexuality and its intersection with other issues in the film: on the one hand, dancing and the normalization of heterosexuality and, on the other hand, hidden narratives of male prostitution and codes of homosexual style and subculture. Sex is part of the financial and cultural economy of American cinema because it is exciting and arousing, especially when it is displaced onto good music, performance, and costume—in other words, kept at a safe distance from direct expression. Sex is both visible and invisible in *Dirty Dancing*, both obvious and subtle. But no matter how "dirty" the dancing gets, it does not seem to be able to transgress its being a regulatory system of gendered pairings. However, as I hope to have revealed in the latter half of this chapter, there is something else dirty about *Dirty Dancing*, and it is not the dancing.

Notes

1 The term "compulsory heterosexuality" comes from Adrienne Rich's often reprinted "Compulsory Heterosexuality and Lesbian Existence," originally written in 1980 and which can now be found in Henry Abelove, David Halperin, and Michel Aina Barale, eds., *The Lesbian and Gay Studies Reader* (London and New York: Routledge, 1993).

2 On heterosexuality as a cultural form, see Chrys Ingraham, ed., *Thinking Straight: The Power, Promise, and Paradox of Heterosexuality* (New York: Routledge, 2004); and Jonathon Ned Katz, *The Invention of Heterosexuality* (Chicago: Chicago University Press, 2007). On heterosexuality and the cinema, see Sean Griffin, ed., *Hetero* (New York: State University of New York Press, 2009). On heterosexuality and the film musical, see Richard Dyer, "I Seem to Find the Happiness I Seek," in *Dance, Gender and Culture*, ed. Helen Thomas (London: Macmillan, 1993).

3 See, for instance, Irene Carmon, "*Dirty Dancing* Is the Greatest Movie of All Time," *Jezebel*, http://jezebel.com/5527079/dirty-dancing-is-the-greatest-movie-of-all-time. Accessed on October 20, 2011.

4 These codes, which are similar, if not conflated, with visual codes of rebellion, include posture, hairstyle, clothing, and the overall sartorial look. For a more detailed analysis of these codes, see Barry Reay, *New York Hustlers: Masculinity and Sex in Modern America*. (Manchester: Manchester University Press, 2011), as well as other books that document the homoeroticism of rebellion and hustler life, such as Karlheinz Weinburger, *Rebel Youth* (New York: Rizzoli, 2011).

5 See Julie Malnig, ed., *Ballroom, Boogie, Shimmy Sham, Shake: A Social and Popular Dance Reader* (Chicago: University of Illinois Press, 2009).

6 Angela McRobbie, "Dance Narratives and Fantasies of Achievement," in *Meaning in Motion: New Cultural Studies of Dance*, ed. Jane C. Desmond (Durham: Duke University Press, 1997), 211.

7 Julie Malnig, "Apaches, Tangos, and other Indecencies: Women, Dance, and New York Nightlife of the 1910s," in *Ballroom, Boogie*, 73.

8 Ibid.

9 Perhaps not surprisingly, a similar reality TV program based on *Dirty Dancing* made its appearance in 2007: *Dirty Dancing: The Time of Your Life* (Living TV). Taking place in one of the locations where the film was shot, the show is about pairing professional dancers with amateurs and choosing the best and worst couple. The show lasted for two seasons.

10 See the two collections on the social and gendered aspects of dance, one edited by Julie Malnig (note 5) and the other by Helen Thomas (note 2).

11 Ibid.

12 On sex education films (including abortion themes), see Robert Eberwein, *Sex Ed: Film, Video, and The Framework of Desire* (New Brunswick, NJ: Rutgers University Press, 1997); Ken Smith, *Mental Hygiene: Better Living Through Classroom Films* (New York: Blast Books, 1999); and Susan K. Freeman, *Sex Goes to School: Girls and Sex Education Before 1960* (Chicago: University of Illinois Press, 2008).

13 Reay, *New York Hustlers*.

14 Paul Welch, "Homosexuality in America," *Time*, June 26, 1964.

15 Ibid.

16 See Juan A. Suarez, *Bike Boys, Drag Queens, and Superstars: Avant-Garde, Mass Culture, and Gay Identites in the 1960s Underground Cinema* (Bloomington: Indiana University Press, 1996); and Reay, "Hustler Hustled," in *New York*

Hustlers. Gay fiction that also describes the hustler in detail includes James Barr, *The Occasional Man* (Toronto: Swan, 1966); and John Rechy, *City of Night* (New York: Grove Press, 1963).

17 Michael Moon, *A Small Boy and Others: Imitation and Initiation in American Culture from Henry James to Andy Warhol* (Durham: Duke University Press, 1998), 13.

18 Leerom Medovoi, *Rebels: Youth and the Cold War Origins of Identity* (Durham: Duke University Press, 2005).

19 See Steve Cohan, *Masked Men: Masculinity and the Movies in the Fifties* (Bloomington: Indiana University Press, 1997); and Amy Lawrence, *The Passion of Montgomery Clift* (Berkeley: University of California Press, 2010).

20 See Sam Steward, *An Obscene Diary: The Visual World of Sam Steward* (Hanover, NH: Elysium Press, 2010); Don DeCeccho, Michael Williams, and Phil Andros, eds., *Bad Boys and Tough Tattoos* (New York: Routledge, 1990); and the seminal work of gay artist Tom of Finland collected in *Tom of Finland: The Art of Pleasure* (Cologne: Taschen, 2004).

21 Shaun Cole, *Don We Now Our Gay Apparel: Gay Men's Dress in the Twentieth Century* (London: Berg Publishers, 2000).

22 Reay, *New York Hustlers*.

23 Medovoi, *Rebels*, 169.

24 Medovoi, *Rebels*, 191.

25 Alexander Doty, *Making Things Perfectly Queer: Interpreting Mass Culture* (Minneapolis: University of Minnesota Press, 1993), 10.

26 Editors' note: for a discussion of Johnny's costume, see also Pamela Church Gibson's essay in this volume.

III THE PRODUCTION OF NOSTALGIA

Introduction

SIÂN LINCOLN

If one were to ask *Dirty Dancing* fans what it is about the film that they find particularly appealing, their response is likely to be one that in some way draws on its nostalgic elements. From the soundtrack to the film's politics, *Dirty Dancing* is a text within which elements of decades past and present are reproduced for nostalgic effect.

As the chapters in this section demonstrate, the nostalgia of the film emerges primarily through a series of what can be described as "recollections": recollections of the writer, recollections of past decades, and audiences' own personal recollections.

First, the recollections of the film's writer, Eleanor Bergstein, are evident throughout *Dirty Dancing*, as she admits that the film draws on her own teenage experiences in the 1950s and 1960s when she herself was a dancer and working her way through college. For Bergstein, 1963, the year in which the film is set, represents a pivotal period in America's political, social, and cultural history, a country on the cusp of radical political and social change. As Bergstein herself proclaims, *Dirty Dancing* could not have been situated either a few months earlier or later than the summer of 1963; "after that it was radical action."

Second, and aligned to this critical moment, the film is about recollections of the 1950s and 1960s as well as the social and political realities of the 1970s and 1980s, through which, as the following chapters explore, we can meaningfully engage with the past and the present.

References to the "Fifties" and "Sixties" specifically hone in on what Osgerby refers to as "the coming of age and the loss of innocence" that typified the optimism of the 1950s and early 1960s, which saw an idealized representation of teen cultures and lifestyles as carefree, explorative, and innocent but which, as Bergstein notes above, hung critically in the balance as the political, social, and cultural landscape significantly reconfigured.

Finally, *Dirty Dancing*'s nostalgic elements are drawn from the audiences' personal recollections of the film, be they through their reminiscences of their own teenage experiences in the decades within which the film is set, their experiences of watching the film for the first time in the late 1980s, or through specific elements of the film such as its soundtrack, its fashion, or its "retro" aesthetic (with "retro" being loosely defined as being in reference to the 1950s, 1960s, or even 1980s if the film is being watched in the 2010s) that evoke particular memories and feelings.

As the following chapters demonstrate, "nostalgia" in *Dirty Dancing* is packaged and repackaged in a number of ways, many of which further reinforce the film's rather unique contribution to popular culture and highlight the seemingly relentless marketing opportunities it continues to present for audiences of all ages.

"The Production of Nostalgia" contains three essays that examine the important and multi-faceted issue of nostalgia that is so intricately linked to the film. In chapter 11, Bill Osgerby explores the recurring mythological reconstruction of the early 1960s as an era of "lost innocence" in a number of coming-of-age movies, including *Dirty Dancing*. Although the fictionalized (re)constructions of idealized teen lives and cultures of the past usually evoke nostalgia for an era that never really existed, these accounts are not necessarily regressive. Some films, Osgerby argues, have managed to introduce conflict into nostalgia by presenting it as problematic and contradictory, and *Dirty Dancing* represents a prime example of this trend through its emphasis on gender, class, and ethnic conflict. In this respect, the film does not necessarily imitate a dead style but actively mobilizes a mythical past in meaningful ways in the cultures of the present.

In chapter 12, Claire Molloy discusses two forms of nostalgia associated with the film. One is the film's recreation of a mythical and idealized past, and the second, more reflexive form tracks the original emotional effects of the film, especially when audiences revisit it at a later stage in their lives. Music is central in the creation of both of these forms of nostalgia, and Molloy argues that repeated viewings of the film "trigger a flood of impressions that illuminate moments from one's history with unexpected vividness." This is especially true for young audiences who saw the film in its original context and who could not engage in any nostalgia for the 1960s. Coming back to the film in later years, these audiences experience the film "as nostalgia" rather than as a "nostalgia film," especially as both the 1960s and the 1980s songs in the film are rendered nostalgic from a 21st century vantage point.

In the last chapter of this section, Tim McNelis argues that the effect of anachronistic music in a film can only be understood through a close examination of its context. While contemporary songs in *Dirty Dancing* are quite noticeable as such, McNelis argues that they would be perceived as more disruptive if the entire film, like many period films, did not contain many other anachronistic elements and modern re-interpretations of the historical period. In addition, he states that the film's audiovisual evocation of nostalgia is strengthened by the presence of retro musical elements in the new songs, which are also performed by artists whose careers began not long after the time in which the film is set. In this respect, the film manages to integrate the 1980s with the 1960s in an almost seamless and very effective way, and therefore is able to appeal to both older and younger demographics at the same time.

No discussion of the film would be complete without giving attention to issues surrounding nostalgia. This section, "Questions of Nostalgia," explores the many facets of this term within the context of *Dirty Dancing*.

11 "(I'VE HAD) THE TIME OF MY LIFE": ROMANTIC NOSTALGIA AND THE EARLY 1960S

BILL OSGERBY

"That Was the Summer of 1963..."

As the Ronettes belt out Phil Spector's 1963 hit "Be My Baby," the opening credits to *Dirty Dancing* (1987) root the film in a wistful look back to a past immersed in passion and promise. The mood is underscored by a series of rose-tinted, slow-motion images of teenage couples dancing, lost in sensuality, as the soundtrack gives way to an announcement by radio DJ Bruce Morrow. Famous as "Cousin Brucie," Morrow was a huge hit on New York's WABC station, where his teen-oriented evening shift became a fixture in the lives of East Coast youngsters as it charted the shockwaves of the early-1960s pop explosion. "Hi everyone, this is your Cousin Brucie," enthuses Morrow. "Whoa! Our summer romances are in full bloom and everybody, but everybody's in love. So cousins, here's a great song from the Four Seasons." And the soundtrack segues to another 1960s teen classic, "Big Girls Don't Cry."

As the song continues, the film's action begins. Beside her precocious sister, Frances "Baby" Houseman (Jennifer Grey) sits in the back of their father's car as it speeds through the Catskill Mountains toward Kellerman's, the family's vacation resort. The sense of affectionate reminiscence resurfaces as a voiceover from an older Frances reflects on this moment in her youth, casting it as a time of innocence and optimism, and a point on the cusp of momentous change: "That was the summer of 1963, when everyone called me 'Baby' and it didn't occur to me to mind. That was before President Kennedy was shot, before the Beatles came, when I couldn't wait to join the Peace Corps, and I thought I'd never find a guy as great as my dad. That was the summer we went to Kellerman's...."

Of course, many factors contributed to the film's popularity. Alongside *Flashdance* (Adrian Lyne, 1983), *Staying Alive* (Sylvester Stallone, 1983), and *Footloose* (Herbert Ross, 1984), *Dirty Dancing* was one of a slew of dance musicals that successfully followed in the box office footsteps of *Saturday Night Fever* (John Badham, 1977). The film's soundtrack was also a solid asset. With a rough 80-to-20-percent mix between oldies and new material, the score of *Dirty Dancing* had broad appeal, and it held down the top spot in *Billboard*'s album chart for nine consecutive weeks while the movie's theme, "(I've Had) The Time of My Life," topped the US singles chart. But the nostalgic recreation of the early 1960s in *Dirty Dancing* was also crucial to the film's appeal; one critic noted on its release how the movie "stands as a metaphor for America in the summer of 1963—orderly, prosperous, bursting with good intentions, a sort of Yiddish-inflected Camelot."[1]

Dirty Dancing was not alone in its rosy nostalgia. Throughout the 1970s and 1980s, American youth culture of the late 1950s and early 1960s was recreated in numerous movies, including *American Graffiti* (George Lucas, 1973), *Animal House* (John Landis, 1978), *Big Wednesday* (John Milius, 1978), *Grease* (Randall Kleiser, 1978), *More American Graffiti* (Bill L. Norton, 1979), *The Wanderers* (Philip Kaufman, 1979), *Grease 2* (Patricia Birch, 1982), *Porky's* (Bob Clark, 1982), *Baby, It's You* (John Sayles, 1983), and *The Big Chill* (Lawrence Kasdan, 1983). Similar themes also surfaced on TV. Most obviously, from 1974 to 1984, the ABC sitcom *Happy Days* presented an idealized vision of teen life in America from the mid-1950s to the mid-1960s and, in turn, spawned further retro comedy series *Laverne & Shirley* (ABC, 1976-83) and *Joanie Loves Chachi* (ABC, 1982-83).

This chapter explores the appeal of the nostalgic recreation of teen culture of the late 1950s and early 1960s. It considers the centrality of coming-of-age themes to nostalgic teen films and the way these leitmotifs gave the genre particular appeal during the late 1970s and early 1980s—a period when the culture and ideals of a romanticized past offered a fresh-faced, more optimistic contrast to a seemingly uncertain and despondent present. The chapter also considers critiques that deride "nostalgic" popular culture as necessarily conservative or "regressive." Against theorists such as Fredric Jameson, who malign nostalgic representations of the past as effacing and commodifying history, reducing it to "the glossy qualities of the image,"[2] I will argue that nostalgia is always conflicted and contradictory. Moreover, as films such as *Dirty Dancing* weave their way through nostalgia's morass of tensions and ambiguities, they offer a way of meaningfully engaging with history and offer valuable insights into the relationship between the past and the present.

Teenage Eden: Coming of Age, Loss of Innocence, and the Early 1960s

In essence, *Dirty Dancing* is a coming-of-age or rite-of-passage movie.[3] As Lesley Speed argues, the nostalgic, rite-of-passage teen film is a distinctive genre in American cinema's treatment of adolescence. According to Speed, the narratives of such films often depict the protagonist's experience of trauma as the catalyst for his or her development and the acquisition of greater maturity, which is "equated with greater understanding of past events, and a new capacity to face the future."[4]

Rather than trauma, however, the heart of *Dirty Dancing's* rites of passage lies in a blossoming sense of self and the realization of desire. At the Catskills resort, Baby finds herself fascinated by the "underground" culture of the hotel's young staff, who let loose in vibrant, hip-grinding dances late into the night, out of sight of the staid, middle-class guests who look on them as little more than anonymous servants. Baby soon falls in love with dashing dance instructor Johnny (Patrick Swayze), whose "bad boy" reputation—emphasized (predictably) by his black, leather motorcycle jacket—not only fuels her desire, but raises her father's conservative ire, especially after Baby volunteers to replace Johnny's dance partner in a big show at the nearby Sheldrake Hotel. As Timothy Shary observes, Baby finds individuality through her developing dance expertise, and "her eventual mastery of dance techniques through Johnny's training becomes her ascension to sexualized womanhood, literally and figuratively."[5] After learning both dance and lovemaking from Johnny, and in defiance of her father, Baby debuts at the Kellerman's end-of-season extravaganza, where she proves to her family that her hard work has paid off; and, as Johnny dances while looking up at her onstage, she "achieves the visible heights of adoration and confidence that her previous lifestyle could never have allowed for."[6]

Clearly, the film's nostalgia is being framed in terms of romance and optimism. But according to Speed there is also an underlying conservatism to the nostalgic teen movie. Basing her argument on an analysis of *American Graffiti* and *Stand By Me* (Rob Reiner, 1986), she argues that such films are framed by "a retrospective, and potentially conservative, adult perspective."[7] This is achieved, Speed suggests, through the use of particular formal devices. Most obviously, she argues, the use of a nostalgic voiceover—a feature common to retrospective rite-of-passage movies—serves to situate events in the past and emphasize a subjective, adult point of view. In *Stand By Me*, for example, the voiceover of a middle-aged man recalls an adventure from his adolescence, and this, Speed argues, works to reconstruct a teenage past in the light of an authoritative, adult perspective.

The final documentation of characters' biographies is, according to Speed, a similar strategy of containment. The first noted teen film to deploy this device was *American Graffiti*. Directed by George Lucas, the film is a chronicle of one night's events for a group of Californian high school graduates in 1962. The narrative encompasses a series of interwoven vignettes as the characters drive around town hanging out and listening to the radio, the story ending on a note of disillusionment as an impromptu car race ends in a fatal crash. Prior to the end credits, an onscreen epilogue catalogues the characters' achievements in later life—one is killed by a drunk driver in 1964, one is reported missing in action in the Vietnam War, one becomes an insurance agent, and one settles in Canada and becomes a writer. This coda, Speed suggests, works as a moralistic revision of youth from a privileged, post-teenage viewpoint, and imposes an adult narrational authority on the experiences and expressions of adolescence. From this angle, then, nostalgic teen films can be seen as essentially "conservative in their preoccupation with the past and in their containment of youth culture through the imposition of an adult perspective."[8]

The nostalgic teen film, however, boasts a greater range of potential meanings than this account acknowledges. For example, Speed herself notes how the comedy *Animal House,* directed by John Landis, uses formal devices similar to those employed in *American Graffiti,* but reverses their sombre and moralistic tone. Set in 1962 and based on Chris Miller's humorous stories about his college experiences (originally published in *National Lampoon* magazine), *Animal House* portrays the wacky antics of a group of fraternity misfits as they run up against their straight-laced peers and the university administration. Like *American Graffiti,* the film concludes with an epilogue charting the protagonists' later lives, but this time the device is used to comedic effect. The fraternity jokers go on to supremely improbable careers—one becomes a US Senator, another becomes a gynecologist in Beverly Hills—while their nemesis, the clean-cut campus bully, meets an ignominious end—"killed in Vietnam by his own troops."

In her account of Hollywood's representations of girlhood, Sarah Hentges, like Speed, argues that many of the mythologies of coming-of-age movies work to reinforce structures of power and privilege. In mainstream cinema, she argues, coming-of-age for young women invariably equates not simply to finding oneself or overcoming adversity but more often to "conforming to adult standards or dominant mainstream expectations."[9] Nevertheless, Hentges also recognizes the degree of space and possibility that exists within many narratives. "In some cases," she observes, the spaces in the films "offer little power," but in others the possibilities "offer more powerful rites of passage, and even empowerment."[10] For instance, while Hentges says relatively little about *Dirty Dancing* specifically, she highlights the way dance acts not simply as a means toward a sexual and social awakening for Baby, but also as an avenue for her intellectual and political development as she recognizes and analyzes the class dynamics of the Kellerman's resort.[11]

In fact, *Dirty Dancing* exemplifies Hentges's "spaces" and "possibilities" more than she allows. While the film's story is explicitly told as a recollection and begins with a nostalgic voiceover, its narrative remains relatively open-ended. There is no morality-laden voiceover at the film's conclusion, and it includes no epilogue à la *American Graffiti*. Instead, *Dirty Dancing* effaces narrative closure. In the closing scene, Johnny returns to the resort after having been unjustly fired. Gate-crashing the hotel's big show, he pulls Baby onstage ("Nobody puts Baby in a corner!") and the pair deliver a stunning dance performance to "(I've Had) The Time of My Life." The routine culminates in Baby's triumphant completion of a difficult lift sequence for the first time. The duo are met with exultant applause and cheers from the crowd, while Baby's father sheepishly concedes he misjudged Johnny and looks on his daughter with pride and admiration ("You looked wonderful out there!"). The film ends as the dance sequence continues. The hotel playhouse is transformed into a throbbing nightclub and everyone—the young resort staff, the middle-aged patrons, and even Max Kellerman (Jack Weston), the curmudgeonly hotel owner—dances together blissfully. So, while *Dirty Dancing* concludes with the romantic pairing of Baby and Johnny, it still sidesteps Hollywood convention. As David Shumway observes, by ending with the dance routine the film effectively frames the couple's romance as a summer fling and, rather than "living happily-ever-after," their relationship and future lives are left open.[12] Moreover, while the concluding production number is clearly an idealized fantasy, it still "gives the film a powerful note of hope ... [that] could be read not as an ideological diversion but as progressive in that it leaves viewers with a feeling of political possibility."[13]

Shumway also notes the inherent contradiction between the storyline of *Dirty Dancing* and the film's elements of nostalgic melancholy. The message of the film's narrative, Shumway argues, seems to be that individual commitment can make a difference and that the world is full of social and political possibilities. Baby plans to study "the economics of underdeveloped countries" at college and enter the Peace Corps, while her father tells Max Kellerman that "Baby's gonna change the world." Moreover, the development of Baby's dancing talent under Johnny's tutelage parallels not only her sexual maturation but also her growing social awareness and, sickened by the artificiality and arrogance of the wealthy resort guests, she finds she has greater sympathy for the working-class hotel staff and tries to resolve their personal dilemmas. As Shumway observes, however, this optimistic storyline sits somewhat uneasily alongside *Dirty Dancing*'s wistful mise-en-scène, which, he argues, encourages a sense of loss "not only of innocence but of a particular time and place," so that values such as social justice are effectively framed as "an illusion of innocent youth."[14] Indeed, the commemoration of lost innocence and the ephemerality of idealist values are themes deliberately central to the film. *Dirty Dancing* is set during the late 1950s and early 1960s, when its scriptwriter and co-producer, Eleanor Bergstein, was herself competing in "dirty dancing" contests and was working her way through college as a dance teacher. And, as Bergstein later recalled, in writing the film's screenplay she wanted *Dirty Dancing* to be "a celebration of the time in your life when you could believe that a kind of earnest, liberal action could remake the world in your own image": "The film couldn't have been set a few months earlier or later. . . . It was the summer of the Peace Corps and the summer of the 'I Have a Dream' speech. It was like the summer of liberalism. Because two months after the movie is over, J.F.K. is assassinated. And two months after that the Beatles are on the 'Ed Sullivan Show.' And after that, it's radical action."[15]

The relationship between coming of age and a melancholic loss of innocence so central to *Dirty Dancing* is common to nostalgic recreations of the early 1960s. Promoted with the tagline "Where Were You in '62?," for example, *American Graffiti* is shot-through with a sense of lost innocence. Loosely based on George Lucas's own experiences of growing up in the early 1960s, the film presents snapshots of youngsters passing from the carefree days of a teenage summer into the worldly realities of adulthood. Cruising the strip for a final night before he leaves for college, Curt (Richard Dreyfuss) glimpses a beautiful blonde girl in a white Ford Thunderbird who mouths "I love you" before speeding out of sight. Curt's desperate search for the mysterious blonde is emblematic of his desire for the world beyond the horizon, and his various encounters during the evening—such as being inducted into a greaser gang in which he has no interest— demonstrate how he has outgrown his youth. The sense of a lost, youthful innocence is underscored by a scene near the film's conclusion in which Curt stumbles upon legendary DJ Wolfman Jack, whose radio broadcasts have punctuated the film's narrative. Wolfman is described by Dale Pollock as "a delightful enigma to his listeners; they couldn't tell if he was black or white, thirty or seventy, human or animal. . . . He was the outlaw of the airwaves, the secret friend of a million anonymous listeners."[16] But in reality, the mysterious DJ turns out to be disappointingly mundane. Wandering into Wolfman's studio, Curt discovers that he is just an ordinary-looking guy, sitting in a control room, slurping popsicles. And, in a poignant exchange omitted from the movie's final cut, a disillusioned Curt says, "Gee, I've known you all my life, but you're not at all what I expected." To which Wolfman ruefully replies, "You'll find that applies to a lot of people."

A similar trope underpins *Big Wednesday*. Based around surfing (a huge teenage craze during the early 1960s), the film was co-written and directed by John Milius and is loosely based on his own experience of growing up around Malibu Beach. But, as Joan Ormrod argues, *Big Wednesday* "is more than just a film about surfing, it is an evocation of American society's hopes, fears and conflicts between 1962 and 1974."[17] The film tells the story of three young buddies with a passion for surfing, tracing their lives from the summer of 1962, through their efforts to dodge the draft in 1965, to the end of their innocence in 1968 when one of their friends is killed in Vietnam. The friends reunite six years later on the day of a lifetime—"Big Wednesday"— when the cleanest, most transcendent swell is approaching the shore. The trio conquer the waves, but a new generation of surfers steal the day, showing that times have clearly changed and the era of innocence is forever gone. Like *Dirty Dancing* and *American Graffiti*, *Big Wednesday* presents an idealized version of teen culture during the late 1950s and early 1960s as a metaphor for the "innocence" of American society on the point of its turbulent coming-of-age amid political assassination, social conflict, and the tragedies of the Vietnam War.

"The Cool Generation": *Dirty Dancing* and the Myth of 1960s Youth

In harking back to an early 1960s Eden of teenage innocence, *Dirty Dancing*, *American Graffiti*, and *Big Wednesday* are constituent in a broader set of discourses. As Christine Sprengler suggests, this period occupies a privileged position in American popular culture. Distinguishing between the 1950s and "the Fifties," Sprengler argues that, while the former denotes the actual decade that followed 1950, the latter can be seen as the mythic, nostalgic construction of an era that stretches to 1963, ending sharply with Kennedy's death.[18] And it is "the Fifties," Sprengler contends, that have become enshrined across the American media as a mythic "golden age," to the extent that the era now virtually defines the evocation and experience of nostalgia.

In reality, this period was characterized by flux and fragmentation in American public and private life. Certainly, the era was characterized by high levels of economic growth and a consumer boom, but the global tensions of the Cold War, shifting gender and generational identities, and the rise of civil rights activism contributed to a climate of social stress and apprehension. In spite of this, Sprengler borrows from Thomas Hine to argue that,[19] across contemporary popular culture, "the Fifties" have been recreated as a moment of optimism and security, a time when America celebrated "confidence in the future, the excitement of the present" and "the ability of the 'average' family to share in the bounty of a prosperous time."[20] And, in *Dirty Dancing*, the middle-class Housemans—with their stylish car, comfortable holiday resort, and chirpy daughters—clearly epitomize this mythology.

As Sprengler explains, the nostalgic "Fifties" myth was partly molded by social, economic, and political forces operating during the era itself. Throughout the 1950s and early 1960s, advertisers and media industries made an intensive effort to mythologize the period as a spectacle of unprecedented prosperity and material abundance. Sprengler highlights the important role of television in this process. Domestic sitcoms such as *The Adventures of Ozzie and Harriet* (ABC, 1952–66), *Father Knows Best* (CBS and NBC, 1954–60), and *The Donna Reed Show* (ABC, 1958–66) showcased the morality and prosperity of the "average" American family, so that TV became "a key site where conspicuous consumption was made visible in its presentation of a model of appropriate consumer behavior which elevated people's consciousness of commodities, enhancing their desirability and reinforcing their various symbolic meanings."[21] Though not discussed by Sprengler, youth culture and its media manifestations also played a major role in the creation of the "Fifties" myth.

After 1945, the American youth market underwent spectacular expansion. The growth was partly a consequence of demographic trends, with wartime increases in the birthrate and a postwar "baby boom" that escalated the US teen population from 10 million to 15 million during the 1950s, eventually hitting a peak of 20 million by 1970. A postwar expansion of education, meanwhile, further accentuated the profile of youth as a distinct generational cohort.[22] However, the vital stimulus to the youth market was economic. Although full-time youth employment declined after the Second World War, a significant rise in youth spending was sustained by a combination of part-time work and parental allowances; some estimates suggest that young Americans' average weekly income rose from just over $2 in 1944 to around $10 by 1958.[23] During the early 1950s, however, media representations of youth were dominated by menacing images of criminality. James Gilbert argues that widespread concerns about delinquency served as "a symbolic focus for wider anxieties in a period of rapid and disorienting change," with fears of youth crime articulating "a vaguely formulated but gnawing sense of social disintegration."[24] By the end of the decade, however, more positive images of youth were coming to the fore.

During the late 1950s and early 1960s, young people were portrayed (celebrated even) as an invigorating and inspiring social force. John Hellman, for example, shows how ideals of "youth" were powerfully mobilized by JFK in both his public persona and in his optimistic vision of America's "New Frontier."[25] But commercial interests were also central to the upbeat "rebranding" of youth. As Gilbert argues, the positive social responses to young people during the late 1950s and early 1960s were "derived from a further extension of the market economy in American cultural life."[26] With the growing profitability of the teen market, the media and consumer industries fêted young people as never before, and "The Cool Generation" (as it was dubbed by George Gallup and Evan Hill in 1961) was enshrined as the signifier of a newly prosperous age of freedom and fun.[27] Here, Kirse May argues, images of Californian youth culture were in the forefront. During the early 1960s, the Golden State—home to surfing, hot rods, and pop groups such as the Beach Boys—set the pace for America's "New Frontier" in teenage leisure, pleasure, and good living. As media images of monstrous delinquents slipped into the background, they were superseded by archetypes of "well-behaved, well-meaning, middle-class teenagers" as films, TV series, and pop records all "packaged California's kids as a beautiful and wholesome generation living it up on the coast."[28]

Nostalgic teen films at once celebrate this myth and lament its passing. They hark back to a time of innocent hopes, a time when teenage culture stood for excitement, fun, and progress. Indeed, the

Californian motif identified by May is a central feature of both *Big Wednesday* (with its homage to surfing) and *American Graffiti* (with its paean to hot rods cruising up and down the strip). *Dirty Dancing* may lack the West Coast setting, but it trades in similar images suggesting an idealized teenage lifestyle of carefree kicks. Recurring contrasts, for example, are drawn between the torrid exhilaration of the parties held by the young resort staff and the lackluster entertainment preferred by the aging guests—wig shows, genteel putting competitions, and merengue classes in the gazebo. Moreover, Johnny, the sexy dance instructor, is juxtaposed against creepy Neil Kellerman (Lonny Price), grandson of the resort owner. Johnny is an icon of youthful vigor; self-assured and a bit dangerous, he dresses in a tight t-shirt, leather jacket, and dark shades. Neil, meanwhile, is prematurely middle-aged. Favoring lifeless suits or (at his most adventurous) chino slacks and studying hotel management at college, Neil is irretrievably stuck in Squaresville.

The 1950s and 1960s teen ideals at the heart of films like *Dirty Dancing*, then, are partly shaped by mythologies generated during the era itself. But, as Keith Booker argues, the social, economic, and political realities of America during the 1970s and 1980s also rendered society prone to nostalgia for the myths of "the Fifties."[29] At that moment, the

"Self-assured and a touch dangerous": Johnny as the archetypal young man of the mythic Fifties America

past offered precisely what society seemed to lack or have lost. So, at a time of economic recession, oil crises, and stagflation, "the Fifties" were revered for their apparent prosperity and stability. At the cinema, this veneration was played out in such films as the sci-fi adventure *Back to the Future* (Robert Zemeckis)—the biggest-grossing movie of 1985—which saw bullied, lower-middle-class teenager Marty McFly (Michael J. Fox) travel back in time to 1955, where he accidentally reconfigures history so that, on returning to the 1980s, his life has been transformed into the essence of confident, upper-middle-class success.

Politically, the 1950s and early 1960s also seemed to represent a worthier, more admirable contrast to the 1980s. In the wake of Vietnam and Watergate, contemporary governments seemed woefully immoral compared to the benevolent paternalism signified by Eisenhower or, especially, the honest idealism embodied by JFK. But there was also a personal dimension to nostalgia for "the Fifties." The adults of the 1970s and 1980s had themselves been part of the "mythic" teenage generation and could wistfully look back to the halcyon days of their youth. And, as Sprengler observes, their longings were well served, "thanks in part to their own efforts in film, television, manufacturing and publishing—efforts which made the visual landscape of their childhood available to others."[30] Indicative were *American Graffiti*, *Big Wednesday*, and *Dirty Dancing*, all of which were, at least partly, nostalgic autobiographies.

"Do You Love Me?": The Controversies of Nostalgia

During the 1980s, cultural critics often judged the "nostalgic" turn in popular culture negatively. This was partly a response to the way nostalgia for "the Fifties" was habitually enlisted in the service of right-wing political agendas, but it also stemmed from a conviction that nostalgic aesthetics are in themselves inherently conservative. In this respect, the ideas of Fredric Jameson were especially influential. Focusing on *American Graffiti*, Jameson argued that the movie inaugurated "a new aesthetic discourse"—the "nostalgia film"—which was intrinsically reactionary in the way it represented the past through superficial stereotypes rather than engaging with history in any meaningful way.[31] From this perspective, nostalgia films such as *American Graffiti* and the neo-noir *Body Heat* (Lawrence Kasdan, 1981) "render the 'past' through stylistic connotation, conveying 'pastness' by the glossy qualities of the image, and 1930s-ness or 1950s-ness by the attributes of fashion."[32]

According to Jameson, then, while modernist forms of art once provided audiences with a meaningful access to history, the postmodern nostalgia film recalls nothing more than a superficial impression of the past through an aesthetic style dominated by fashion, style, and surface. And, while Jameson does not discuss *Dirty Dancing* directly, it is hard to imagine him cheering on Johnny and Baby as they wow the Kellerman's crowd with their sizzling dance moves. Instead, it is more likely that the film's evocation of "the summer of 1963" through an emphasis on music, dance, and style would be derided by Jameson as a woeful example of the way nostalgia films appropriate the past and refract it "through the iron law of fashion change and the emergent ideology of the generation."[33]

Other theorists, however, have challenged Jameson's scathing viewpoint. Notably, Linda Hutcheon contests the assumption that it is possible to engage with an "authentic" history, a history that exists somehow outside or independent of its cultural referents. As she explains, "there is no directly and accessible past 'real' for us today: we can only know—and construct—the past through its traces, its representations."[34] In these terms, then, there is no "real" summer of 1963 waiting to be discovered, only cultural constructions of the moment; rather than living "in a perpetual present" as Jameson claims, nostalgia films are "if anything, obsessed with history and how we can know the past today."[35]

Paul Grainge and Vera Dika both take this discussion further, exploring the way nostalgic representations can be instructive about the ways in which the past is used in the present. Grainge analyzes the way black-and-white images are used in magazines, advertising, films, and TV "to establish and [make] legitimate particular kinds of memory in cultural life,"[36] arguing that Jameson fails to recognize either the way audiences actively negotiate the meaning of such representations or the way that "meaningful narratives of history or cultural memory can be produced through the recycling and/or hybridization of past styles."[37] Dika, meanwhile, argues that the nostalgia film is much more conflicted in the way it reworks the past than that for which Jameson allows. In the drama *Last Exit to Brooklyn* (Uli Edel, 1989), for example,

Dika argues that there are pronounced frictions between the film's depiction of a visually recognizable "Fifties" and its narrative, which "foregrounds the ills of the 1950s."[38] According to Dika, these tensions shatter the viewer's expectations and force recognition that "the Fifties" are a fabricated construct. The nostalgia film therefore "does not necessarily return uncritically to the past" but undertakes this return "to address both the past and the images that have produced it."[39]

Dirty Dancing is also complex and conflicted, and much more than a mere glossy, "stylistic connotation" of the summer of 1963. Indeed, Shumway highlights the way the film uses music to deliberately disrupt its own carefully constructed frame. The familiar hits at the beginning of the film ("Be My Baby" and "Big Girls Don't Cry") certainly evoke a sense of nostalgia for the period but, Shumway argues, many of the other featured songs "seem to be in the service of another agenda besides the production of nostalgia."[40] For example, Shumway suggests that the black rhythm and blues records that Johnny and his friends dance to—the Contours' "Do You Love Me?" and Maurice Williams and the Zodiacs' "Stay"—were unlikely to have been readily familiar to the 1987 audience and, portrayed as sexually liberating and transgressive, they "serve the film's overtly liberal agenda."[41] Dirty Dancing also contains songs that were newly composed for the film and that are distinctly anachronistic in their style of production, most obviously "(I've Had) The Time of My Life," featured in the film's dance finale. As Shumway notes, the track is sung by former Righteous Brother Bill Medley and is reminiscent of the 1960s hits Phil Spector produced for the Righteous Brothers such as "You've Lost That Lovin' Feeling" or Ike and Tina Turner's "River Deep, Mountain High." Yet the song's production style is clearly that of the 1980s, and the triumphant combination of the song and the fiery dance routine "seem designed to make us forget the very temporality that the film earlier insisted upon."[42]

Dirty Dancing, then, is a rite-of-passage teen film that both celebrates and mourns the myths of the early 1960s. But its use of nostalgia and historical allusion amount to more than what Jameson would dismiss as a depthless "imitation of dead styles."[43] As John Storey argues, the re-animation of historical aesthetics is a practice of active cultural enterprise in which media forms of the past are commandeered and employed in meaningful ways in the lived cultures of the present.[44] In these terms, *Dirty Dancing* can be seen as a site of expressive processes of appropriation, bricolage, and intertextuality in which the sounds and styles of the past are reconfigured and mobilized in ways that have cultural resonance for the present. Indeed, this partly accounts for the film's enduring popularity. *Dirty Dancing* is not a simple, superficial mimic of the summer of 1963; instead, its synthesis of diverse visual and aural aesthetics gives it multiple layers of meaning that have allowed it to circulate through successive cultural and political contexts, becoming a locus for the formation and expression of a wide variety of ideals, identities, and pleasures.

Notes

1. Samuel D. Freedman, "*Dirty Dancing* Rocks to an Innocent Beat," *New York Times*, August 16, 1987.
2. Fredric Jameson, *Postmodernism, or the Cultural Logic of Late Capitalism* (Durham: Duke University Press, 1991), 19.
3. Editors' note: see also Lincoln's essay in this volume.
4. Lesley Speed, "Tuesday's Gone: The Nostalgic Teen Film," *Journal of Popular Film and Television* 26.1 (Spring 1998): 25.
5. Timothy Shary, *Generation Multiplex: The Image of Youth in Contemporary American Cinema* (Austin: University of Texas Press, 2002), 91.
6. Ibid.
7. Speed, "Tuesday," 30.
8. Ibid.
9. Sarah Hentges, *Pictures of Girlhood: Modern Female Adolescence on Film* (Jefferson, NC: McFarland, 2006), 60.
10. Ibid., 101.
11. Ibid., 78.
12. David Shumway, "Rock 'n' Roll Sound Tracks and the Production of Nostalgia," *Cinema Journal* 38. 2 (Winter 1999): 47.
13. Ibid., 48.
14. Ibid., 47.
15. Bergstein was cited in Serge Denisoff and William Romanowski, *Risky Business: Rock in Film* (New Brunswick: Transaction, 1991), 261-62.
16. Dale Pollock, *Skywalking: The Life and Films of George Lucas* (New York: Harmony Books, 1983), 32.
17. Joan Ormrod, "'Just the Lemon Next to the Pie': Apocalypse, History and the Limits of Myth in *Big Wednesday* (1978)," *Scope: An Online Journal of Film & TV Studies*, http://www.scope.nottingham.ac.uk/article.php?issue=1&id=6. Accessed on August 25, 2011.
18. Christine Sprengler, *Screening Nostalgia: Populuxe Props and Technicolor Aesthetics in Contemporary American Film* (New York: Beghahn, 2009), 39.

19 Thomas Hine, *Populuxe* (New York: MFJ Books, 1986).
20 Sprengler, *Screening Nostalgia*, 42.
21 Ibid., 49.
22 John Modell, *Into One's Own: From Youth to Adulthood in the United States 1920-1975* (Berkeley: University of California Press, 1989), 225-26.
23 Dwight Macdonald, "A Caste, A Culture, A Market," *New Yorker* (November 22, 1958): 60.
24 James Gilbert, *A Cycle of Outrage: America's Reaction to the Juvenile Delinquent in the 1950s* (Oxford: Oxford University Press, 1986), 77.
25 John Hellmann, *The Kennedy Obsession: The American Myth of JFK* (New York: Columbia University Press, 1997), 105.
26 Gilbert, *A Cycle*, 214.
27 George Gallup and Evan Hill, "Youth: The Cool Generation," *Saturday Evening Post* (December 23, 1961): 63.
28 Kirse Granat May, *Golden State, Golden Youth: The California Image in Popular Culture, 1955-1966* (Chapel Hill: University of North Carolina Press, 2002), 119.
29 Keith Booker, *Postmodern Hollywood: What's New in Film and Why It Makes Us Feel So Strange* (London: Praeger, 2007), 65.
30 Sprengler, *Screening Nostalgia*, 48.
31 Jameson, *Postmodernism*, 18.
32 Ibid., 19.
33 Ibid.
34 Linda Hutcheon, *The Politics of Postmodernism* (London: Routledge, 1989), 109,
35 Ibid.
36 Paul Grainge, *Monochrome Memories: Nostalgia and Style in Retro America* (London: Praeger, 2002), 3.
37 Ibid., 6.
38 Vera Dika, *Recycled Culture in Contemporary Art and Film: The Uses of Nostalgia* (Cambridge: Cambridge University Press, 2003), 142.
39 Ibid., 155.
40 Shumway, "Rock 'n' Roll," 45.
41 Ibid.
42 Ibid., 48.
43 Fredric Jameson, "Postmodernism, or the Cultural Logic of Late Capitalism," *New Left Review* 146 (1984): 65.
44 John Storey, "The Sixties in the Nineties: Pastiche or Hyperconsciousness?," in *Action TV: Tough Guys, Smooth Operators and Foxy Chicks*, eds. Bill Osgerby and Anna Gough-Yates (London: Routledge, 2001), 247.

12 "IT'S A FEELING; A HEARTBEAT": NOSTALGIA, MUSIC, AND AFFECT IN *DIRTY DANCING*

CLAIRE MOLLOY

Reviews of *Dirty Dancing* at the time of its release criticized the film's thin plot, one-dimensional characters, derivative narrative, dialogue clichés, indulgent dance sequences, and emotional excesses. In spite of critical reviews, the film was phenomenally successful, and it is notable that fans comment that they can return to *Dirty Dancing* multiple times without the film's affective dimension being diminished. Barbara Klinger argues that, in viewing a favorite text multiple times, "such returns are often strongly motivated by a desire to recapture and to understand the emotions the film initially elicited."[1] For many viewers, although not all, the pleasures of re-experiencing the text are tied to a desire to not only reactivate but also to enhance the film's original affective dimension by invoking personal recollections; in this regard, music is absolutely central. Often remarking that the film is timeless, *Dirty Dancing* fans claim that multiple viewings of the film not only enhance its emotional effects but that the soundtrack is a key element of its continuous appeal.[2]

Dirty Dancing used period songs that were unfamiliar to many of the original core audience of the time, contemporary songs that were cross-marketed as part of the synergistic strategy of the film, and classical Hollywood scoring techniques. The fusion of past and present musical references knowingly eschewed any claims to historical accuracy, undercut the film's period authenticity, and, aurally at least, disrupted its depiction of the past.³ In short, *Dirty Dancing*'s timelessness was conveyed through the deployment of codes that evoked a sense of past entangled with a cultural present.

Watching the film again in the 2000s, the original contemporary cultural references have become dated. Setting aside definitional problems associated with "nostalgia films" for a moment, *Dirty Dancing* is now both a 1960s and a 1980s nostalgia movie. The film offers viewers who first saw *Dirty Dancing* in their adolescence pleasures derived from personal nostalgia, and this return to a film from one's youth can be situated within a larger set of re-watching practices that have clear economic benefits for media industries. Whether during the initial theatrical release or when a film is distributed through ancillary markets, repeat viewing is a profitable activity that is acknowledged within the film revenue cycle and also reflected in the practices of re-issuing and re-releasing, as well as in the value placed on film libraries.⁴ In the case of *Dirty Dancing*, the film and the soundtrack have been re-released in various formats and special editions, and this re-packaging presents an interesting opportunity to consider how nostalgia, music, and repeat viewings intersect.⁵ I begin the chapter with a discussion of the practices of repeat viewing as they have been conceived within scholarly debates before moving on to consider the relationship between music and narrative. This chapter discusses personal recollection and considers how music activates forms of nostalgia that are specific to the pleasures of repeat viewings of *Dirty Dancing*.

Repeat Viewing

Repeat film-viewing has long been associated with cult film fandom and arthouse cinema-going.⁶ Within recent scholarship on cult movies, repeated dedicated viewing of a particular film has been aligned with alternative viewing practices that have their roots in the midnight movie scene that grew out of New York in the 1960s. In their discussion of midnight movies, Ernest Mathijs and Jamie Sexton propose that repeat audiences once looked for "'underground' thrills, and gusts of revelations—often aided by illegal substances."⁷ The activity of repeat film-viewing was thus allied with 1960s counterculture and, in the next decade, with alternative cinema exhibition of films that were distinguished from the mainstream by their "generic and aesthetic radicalism."[8] Writing about cult movie-viewing in more general terms, Janet Staiger argues that it is "a particularly visible form of fandom."[9] Cult texts, she suggests, are "texts to which people wish to initiate others," and by way of example Staiger notes that "these initiation texts may be classic movies such as *Casablanca, Gone With the Wind,* or *The Sound of Music*."[10] In this sense, then, "cult film" is elastic enough to accommodate *Dirty Dancing* on the basis of the repeat-viewing practices of the film's fans.[11] Furthermore, initiation to a text is particularly salient to a discussion of *Dirty Dancing*, where repeat viewing occurs in the context of the intergenerational transfer of cultural capital, with one generation introducing the next to the film.[12]

However, practices of repeat film-consumption are by no means confined to cult fandom and, as Richard Maltby points out, repeat theatrical attendance has figured in the financial planning of blockbuster movies since the 1980s.[13] Repeat viewing also figures prominently in Justin Wyatt's discussion of the high-concept film from the 1970s onwards. In his analysis of films such as *Saturday Night Fever* (John Badham, 1977), *Flashdance* (Adrian Lyne, 1983), and *Grease* (Randall Kleiser, 1978), the latter of which bears many similarities to *Dirty Dancing* not least because of its mixing of period and contemporary music designed to attract both youth and older audience segments, Wyatt argues that "the strong connections between high-concept, marketing and music—the cross-fertilization of marketing efforts and their inseparability from the film—encourage an endless consumption of the high-concept films."[14] For Wyatt, narrative simplicity coupled with marketing through music that had broad audience appeal were key factors in the growth of the repeat viewing phenomenon. *Dirty Dancing* shares high-concept characteristics with films such as *Flashdance,* which pioneered the music video tie-in and the use of simple but striking imagery in its marketing.[15] In the case of *Dirty Dancing,* the film poster used a single image of Patrick Swayze and Jennifer Grey in an intimate dance moment, while the iconic "lift image" that appeared multiple times in the film was integrated into the music video for one of the contemporary tracks, "(I've Had) The Time of My Life."

If the integration of music and marketing have been crucial to building a repeat attendance, which in turn has accounted for the theatrical successes of high-concept films in the 1980s, it has been developments in domestic technology that have advanced the phenomenon of multiple viewings in other ways, particularly in the diversification of modes of film-viewing that developed during the 1980s through the mass market penetration of home video (which in the US reached fifty percent by 1987, the year of *Dirty Dancing*'s release).[16] Although widely regarded as a time-shifting technology in relation to television viewing, by 1986 home video accounted for greater revenues for the majors than theatrical releases by a large margin. As Maltby recounts, the domestic box office had shrunk from 80 percent in 1980 to 25 percent of the studios' overall revenue by 1992. In comparison, video rentals in 1990 accounted for $8.4 billion, a figure almost double that of total box office grosses for the same year.[17]

Home video altered film consumption patterns, giving rise to the popularization of repeat viewing as a private experience. Particular moments from a film could be endlessly experienced, favorite segments rewound and replayed according to the whims and desires of the viewer.[18] According to Henry Jenkins, the VCR facilitated particular viewing strategies that distinguish between general viewers and fans. Jenkins writes, "The social institutions of fandom . . . encourage and facilitate the rereading of prized texts," but he also notes that repeat viewing "threatens to exhaust the narrative's emotional hold on the viewer, to wear out the material so that it may be enjoyed a little less the next time."[19] This view assumes that fans engage in repeat viewing for reasons of interpretation: to deepen understanding, identify gaps and details, and find opportunities for textual elaborations. A text must therefore become, over time, "more productive of personal meanings . . . to sustain the intense emotional experience [the viewer] enjoyed when viewing it the first time."[20]

Practices of intensive re-watching for the purposes of uncovering new or previously unnoticed meanings or details are relatively easy to align with complex narratives, puzzle films, and DVD technologies.[21] Indeed, Thomas Elsaesser refers to complex narratives as "DVD-enabled movies" that demand or "repay multiple viewings."[22] Nicholas Rombes also places emphasis on technology to facilitate the normalization of what were previously considered alternative or excessive viewing practices, remarking that "DVD introduced the idea that traditional mono-directional, or sequential cinema, was just one component of the moving image experience, and that repeat watching was not only acceptable but was almost required."[23] Yet, in the case of a film such as *Dirty Dancing*, which has a straightforward plot and archetypal characters, there is a distinct lack of ambiguity or complexity; rather than seeking to expand on or find additional layers of meaning, repeat viewing of the film may instead offer other pleasures.[24]

Barbara Klinger argues that "chick flicks," a category to which she assigns *Dirty Dancing*, tend to blend feminism and romance, and she argues that repeat viewing "amounts to a kind of ritual anchoring of female subjectivity in normative standards of gender."[25] At the same time, though, repeat viewing of romance narratives is empowering in the sense that viewers take control of their affective states and, Klinger proposes, "the pleasure in reading lies both in identification with a character who is cherished and in the feeling of self-sufficiency achieved by choosing a text that will unfailingly raise spirits."[26] A third reason for repeat viewings Klinger identifies is nostalgia, and she notes that re-watching a film can be "like reencountering popular songs" in the sense that both can "trigger a flood of impressions that illuminate moments from one's history with unexpected vividness."[27] What, then, of a film such as *Dirty Dancing*, which combines popular songs (which in themselves can evoke personal memories) with the pleasures derived from the emotional familiarity of re-experiencing a romance narrative? Music clearly plays a key role in the production of nostalgia for a mythical and idealized past, as well as a reflexive form of nostalgia for the "original" emotional effects of a film when considered within the context of repeat viewings. Ian Inglis proposes that when film and popular music combine to depict a collective public past and evoke personal memories, the synthesis of past events and particular songs is "an extraordinarily potent device through which the practice of nostalgia is activated."[28] It is to these intersecting affective dimensions of the film and its music that this chapter now turns.

Music and Narrative

Dirty Dancing is set at a particular historical moment that has been invested with its own mythology by late-twentieth-century American cinema and that has, in turn, been part of the structuring of collective public memories of the past.[29] In this regard, *Dirty Dancing* fits with Phil Drake's typology of "Hollywood cinema's activation of the past" as a "retro film," one that "mobilizes particular codes that have come to connote a past sensibility as it is selectively remembered in the present (i.e., "the seventies" or "the sixties") as a structure of feeling."[30] The "feel" of an historical period is marshalled by the fusion of codes that evoke and mix pastness with the present; whilst Drake focuses on retro style in films with a contemporary setting, the broader terms of his observation remain useful when it comes to *Dirty Dancing*, which brings elements of a cultural present to a film set in a selectively remembered past.

Dirty Dancing is set at the end of an era. To be more precise, the film is set in 1963 and at the axis of change, the brink of a transforming social, cultural, political, and moral climate, as it has been remembered by cinema. For this reason, *Dirty Dancing* can be grouped with other films that have soundtracks from the 1950s and 1960s, such as *American Graffiti* (George Lucas, 1973), *The Wanderers* (Philip Kaufman, 1979), *Diner* (Barry Levinson, 1982), and *Stand By Me* (Rob Reiner, 1986), all of which are set within an idealized rock 'n' roll era of 1959 to 1963. Indeed, the extent to which this period is romanticized by cinema is reflected in the trailer for *The Wanderers*, which begins with a voiceover that states: "We now know that the 1950s ended in 1963. The fall of '63 was the end of an era." Echoing this nostalgia for the same period in an interview about *American Graffiti* and talking about the impact of his personal experiences on the film's depiction of 1962, George Lucas noted: "in one year you had a President that a lot of kids admired, were proud of; you had a certain kind of rock 'n' roll music; a certain kind of country where you could believe in things."[31] *Dirty Dancing* takes up the same era-memorialization in the opening scene, where Baby's voiceover pinpoints the political and cultural specificity of the time and informs us, "That was the summer of 1963, when everybody called me Baby and it didn't occur to me to mind. That was before President Kennedy was shot, before the Beatles came, when I couldn't wait to join the Peace Corps, and I thought I'd never find a guy as great as my Dad. That was the summer we went to Kellerman's."

The period setting, 1963, re-imagined as a transformative moment in history, provides a compelling backdrop for the coming-of-age story. In *Dirty Dancing*, the sexual awareness that signals the loss of Baby Houseman's childhood and her resulting passage into adulthood structures the narrative trajectory, and Baby's transformation is metonymically connected to the loss of the political and social certainties of the time. By the end of the film, "Baby" is granted an adult identity as "Frances" Houseman; middle-class life and social status have been exposed as dull, hollow aspirations; the older generation is revealed to be out of touch with, even confused by, cultural changes they cannot comprehend; and loss of faith in 1950s paternalism is paralleled by the breakdown of Baby's relationship with her father. From the point where her bond with Johnny starts to blossom and the sexual relationship begins, Baby's trust in her father is undermined, and we follow the inevitable transfer of her desire for the "ideal man" from father to bad boy.

The songs in *Dirty Dancing* reinforce this coming-of-age narrative, and the story of transition and transformation uses music to punctuate important plot points, reveal characters' emotional states, and foreshadow narrative developments. Thus, *Dirty Dancing* integrates period songs for reasons of diegetic verisimilitude and so that they can undertake crucial narrative functions. For instance, the exposition in the opening scene is accompanied by the falsetto tones of "Big Girls Don't Cry," a hit for Frankie Valli and the Four Seasons in November 1962, which initially plays on a radio. Although it is unclear as the scene progresses whether the track is diegetic or not, the presence of a period song at the beginning of the film illustrates the obvious relation between setting and music, which serves to indicate time and place. The radio, and later in the film, record players, provide realistic motivation for the music, which in turn supports the textual construction of a time period that is associated with a cultural and political innocence that is eclipsed by the Beatles, counterculture, the Kennedy assassination, and Vietnam. Lyrically, "Big Girls Don't Cry" foreshadows Baby's loss of childhood and the breakdown of her relationship with her father, which is constructed as contiguous with the more general loss of innocence precipitated by political and social changes after 1963.

In *Dirty Dancing*, much the same as in *American Graffiti, The Wanderers, Diner,* and *Stand By Me*, the characters look toward an imminent and uncertain future and find some degree of assurance in the music of the time, which is brought to the fore and explicitly claimed as cultural capital within the narrative. In *Diner,* Shrevie's encyclopedic knowledge of popular music is central to the adolescent identity to which he clings, while the supplanting of "real" rock 'n' roll by surfer music or the songs that reflected 1960s counterculture is lamented by the John Milner character in *American Graffiti* and Richie Gennaro in *The Wanderers*. In *Dirty Dancing,* the diegetic music is generational and class-specific: wealthy, middle-class parents dance to ballroom music, while the working-class youth dance "dirty"—something we are informed that the kids are doing "in the basements back home"—to R&B tracks such as "Do You Love Me" by the Contours, "Love Man" by Otis Redding, and Maurice Williams and the Zodiacs' "Stay." Inasmuch as each of the period songs works to evoke a particular time, the music also alludes to the distinctions that structure the narrative. Cultural differences in music and dance are aligned with social differences. Baby is a Jewish, middle-class girl, the daughter of a doctor with an already-mapped-out future; Johnny is the dance instructor who lives from job to job. Thus, while the wealthy, repressed parents do the mambo and take ballroom dancing instruction, in darkened rooms late at night grinding dance movements are performed to the strains of R&B, which is constructed from the title sequence onwards as the music of libidinous transgression; the soundtrack thus also provides important erotic and romantic identifications.[32]

Although I have drawn comparisons here with *American Graffiti, The Wanderers, Diner,* and *Stand By Me, Dirty Dancing,* of course, differed from these films in that it mixed contemporary and period songs. In this regard, Anahid Kassabian points out that "the kind of meanings perceivers produce in relation to *Dirty Dancing* ... depend heavily on age and class, both generally and particularly in relation to the soundtrack."[33] As one of the few contemporary songs in *Dirty Dancing,* "(I've Had) the Time of My Life," was getting radio airplay at the time of the film's release, the track was "already available to teen audiences for romantic identification."[34] The contemporary music, not just the period songs, was available to viewers prior to their seeing the film, and thus the tracks had the opportunity to accumulate meanings and affects in advance. In turn, this meant that the combination of songs could address the emotions and memories of different audiences simultaneously, leading Kassabian to note that, in the case of *Dirty Dancing*, "the identifications it conditioned opened onto perceivers' relationships to the songs, but carefully tracked their attachments toward the coming-of-age narrative."[35] The process she identifies can be usefully illustrated in two connected dance instruction montages in the film. During the first sequence, we see Johnny Castle's black leather, Cuban-heeled shoes and Baby Houseman's white lace-up canvas plimsolls, tightly-framed. The energetic driving instrumental "Wipe Out" by the Surfaris structures this first montage in which Johnny teaches Baby to dance. His voiceover instructs the audience and Baby that "the steps aren't enough. *Feel* the music." The scene cuts to a long shot of Baby, who has shed her inhibitions and begins to dance with abandonment and mock sensuality on the footbridge. She dances out of frame, "Wipe Out" fades, and the sequence cuts to Johnny telling Baby, "It's not on the one. It's not the mambo. It's a feeling; a heartbeat." Holding her hand to his chest, he tells Baby to close her eyes and to feel the beat of his heart. At the same time, the instrumental opening to "Hungry Eyes" signals the change in the emotional register of the film. The song foreshadows the intimacy to come and reshapes the relationship between Baby and Johnny, while the montage of shots describes Baby's progression from awkward, naïve girl to sexually aware woman.

In the "heartbeat" scene, the tutor/pupil relationship shifts from dance instruction to sexual initiation. Johnny's direction to "feel the music" has been interpreted by Baby through her exaggerated display of provocative movements on the footbridge. Her immature understanding of sexuality is now given an emotional context, a license to "feel," and the rhythm of the music and its corporeal expression through dance is equated to the beat of Johnny's heart. The "heartbeat" scene connects the two montage sections, which condense Baby's dance instruction and sexual awakening and bridge the historically accurate "Wipe Out" with the contemporaneous "Hungry Eyes." The abrupt fade-out that occurs partway through the third drum solo break of "Wipe Out" signals the equally rapid change of mood from Baby's frustration and subsequent abandonment of her reserved demeanor, which are unified by the percussive emphasis of the track, to "Hungry Eyes," a slow rock ballad, the lyrics of which then also direct the new emotional tone. "Hungry Eyes" accompanies the serious, intense, hard work of the dance training, as well as underlining Baby's sexual awareness and the burgeoning eroticism of her relationship with Johnny. However, the shift in tempo and mood from childhood, identified with "Wipe Out," to the maturity signalled by "Hungry Eyes," is eased by the stress placed on rhythm through the dialogue in the linking scene where Johnny describes the beat of his heart as "gu-gun, gu-gun," and both he and Baby tap it out in time. This cues the (albeit extremely short) drum intro to "Hungry Eyes," the instrumental opening over which Johnny then proceeds to count, and he and Baby begin to move in time to the rhythm.

Conclusion

Although some reference is made of the politics of the time, *Dirty Dancing* is more concerned with referencing America's cultural past, primarily the music and, to a lesser extent, the fashion and other aspects of the material culture. The film's pastness is not recreated in loving detail, as would be the case in an historical reconstruction; instead, *Dirty Dancing* blends the visual and sonic styles of the 1960s and the 1980s as much as it fuses the morality of both eras. The film's treatment of Penny's abortion, Baby and Johnny's relationship, Johnny's numerous sexual encounters with married women (which are only spoken about and never witnessed), and the salacious moves of dirty dancing are suspended somewhere between a strict, albeit simplified, 1950s moral code imposed by narrative necessity and a later, liberal moral climate. In the same way, the cultural references of the different eras mingle, and 1980s hairstyles, music, and clothes are woven into the visual and sonic fabric of the film's mise-en-scène.

The pastness *Dirty Dancing* re-creates is characteristic of what Fredric Jameson has identified as that of the postmodern nostalgia film, which combines the surfaces (the atmospheric and stylistic contours of different eras), recycles past cinematic styles, and plunders older film plots as pastiche. In his consideration of what constitutes a nostalgia film, Jameson offers a taxonomy that is able to accommodate a wide range of films from *American Graffiti* to *Star Wars* (George Lucas, 1977), on the basis that the classification includes films that "reinvent a picture of the past in its lived totality," metonymical nostalgia films that recreate "the feel and shape of characteristic art objects of an older period," and those films that are located somewhere in-between.[36] However, the affective dimension of nostalgia films is unequal, and Jameson suggests that audiences will differ markedly in their experience. By way of example, he suggests that *Star Wars*, a metonymical nostalgia film, reinvents the Saturday afternoon serial for an adult audience, who experience it as a form of pastiche. He argues that *Star Wars* is "a complex object in which on some first level children and adolescents can take the adventures straight, whilst the adult public is able to gratify a deeper and more properly nostalgic desire to return to that older period and to live its strange old aesthetic artifacts through once again."[37]

This reading of *Star Wars* as a nostalgia film may however be locked into the temporal coordinates of Jameson's own writing and experience; moreover, the approach does not acknowledge other viewing experiences, and takes as its default the single cinema viewing. In this regard, Jameson is, of course, far from alone, despite the phenomenon of repeat film-viewings being the basis of key revenue streams for media industries. What Jameson does do, though, is acknowledge that the nostalgia film is not universally experienced, and this in itself is a particularly important point. At the time of its release, the 1960s and 1980s music used in *Dirty Dancing* functioned to evoke personal recollections, nostalgia, and identifications for different audiences. The core audience—the first "home video" generation—who were teenagers in the 1980s did not view *Dirty Dancing* as reactivating previous experiences evoked by the film's setting; instead, the period songs evoked "a fiction of a shared past."[38] What, then, of the audience who returns to the film to re-experience it as nostalgia later in life? For those who watched *Dirty Dancing* in adolescence and returned to the film as adults, repeat-viewing practices are heavily enmeshed with personal nostalgia for the memory of the original viewing contexts. Moreover, the music of an imagined, shared past (the songs from the 1960s) is entwined with the recollections of an actual, experienced past (the 1980s) in a revised form of nostalgia that differentiates the "film as nostalgia" in the context of repeat viewings from its classification as a "nostalgia film" in the sense that Jameson discusses.

In an attempt to delimit the various ways in which nostalgia can be defined, David Shumway offers a useful distinction between personal nostalgia and commodified nostalgia, which, he proposes, are linked. Personal nostalgia, he writes, "is the subjective experience of an emotional state or consciousness of longing for one's own past" while "commodified nostalgia involves the revival by the culture industry of certain fashions and styles of a particular past era."[39] Personal nostalgia and commodified nostalgia function together, and the songs used in *Dirty Dancing* did indeed serve to amplify the affective dimension of the film in that they were already assigned with meanings prior to the film's having been viewed—an outcome of successful cross-marketing strategies, music video, and radio play. In returning to the film, repeat viewings serve to reactivate personal nostalgia, although the distinctions between 1980s and 1960s music in the mode of contemporary and nostalgia songs are erased to the extent that *all* the music in the film is rendered nostalgic. A trend toward revisiting the material culture and aesthetics of the 1980s in the 2000s, of which both the practices of repeat viewing and even this book are a part, involves a complicated layering of nostalgia and affect. What *Dirty Dancing* demonstrates is that the tendency for songs to become intrinsically woven into personal recollections outside of the film experience continues to enhance the romantic and erotic identifications evoked by the music when re-watching.

Notes

1 Barbara Klinger, "The Art Film, Affect and the Female Viewer: *The Piano* Revisited," *Screen* 47.1 (Spring 2006): 19.
2 See fan interviews in Sue Tabashnik, *The Fans' Story: How the Movie "Dirty Dancing" Captured the Hearts of Millions* (Parker, CO: Outskirts Press), 1, 73–74, 81, 151, 152, 163, and 198. In her book, Tabashnik interviews fans who have seen the film multiple times and asks them what they like about *Dirty Dancing* and why they re-watch it. Reviews on the Internet Movie Database website also confirm that the soundtrack is a crucial aspect of the film's continuous appeal. Many of those fans who offer positive reviews of the film and claim to have seen it multiple times note specifically that the "soundtrack," "music," or "songs" are central to their enjoyment of *Dirty Dancing* (Internet Movie Database at http://www.imdb.com/title/tt0092890/reviews?count=352&start=0. Accessed on July 12, 2011).
3 One can add to this other material references to the 1980s in the form of hairstyles, makeup, and elements of costume.
4 For a comprehensive description of the film revenue cycle, see Jeffrey Ulin, *The Business of Media Distribution: Monetizing Film, TV and Video Content in an Online World* (Oxford: Focal Press, 2011), 1–47.

5 For example, in 2007 *Dirty Dancing* was released on Blu-ray, the *Dirty Dancing 20th Anniversary Collector's Edition* was released on DVD, and a two-disc anniversary *Scratch & Sniff Watermelon Edition* was also made available; *Dirty Dancing: The Ultimate Girls' Night In Collector's Edition* was released as a DVD boxset in 2008; and *Dirty Dancing Keepsake Edition* was released as a double-play Blu-ray and DVD set in 2010.

6 Janet Staiger, "The Cultural Productions of *A Clockwork Orange*," in *Stanley Kubrick's A Clockwork Orange*, ed. Stuart McDougal (Cambridge: Cambridge University Press, 2003), 54.

7 Ernest Mathijs and Jamie Sexton, *Cult Cinema* (Chichester and Oxford: Wiley-Blackwell, 2011), 14.

8 Ibid.

9 Janet Staiger, *Media Receptions Studies* (New York: New York University Press, 2005), 125.

10 Ibid.

11 The aim here is not to argue for *Dirty Dancing* to be admitted to the canon(s) of "cult film," a term which is beset with definitional problems from the outset. Rather, that the activities associated with cult fandom (particularly around devotion and excess) map onto the repeat viewing practices of *Dirty Dancing* fans and suggest that the pleasures of re-watching the film are multiple and diverse. Indeed, the difficulties in arguing for *Dirty Dancing* as a cult film are numerous. For example, in a symposium on cult movies published in *Cineaste*, I. Q. Hunter problematizes the cult film by asking, "[W]hat is the difference between a cultist and a fan; how many people make up a cult (I'm very keen on the remake of *Stepford Wives*—am I completely mad and alone?); and why are cult films usually associated with male tastes (*Withnail and I* and *Fight Club* are cult movies, so why not *Titanic* or *Dirty Dancing*)?" (I.Q. Hunter, "Cult Film: A Critical Symposium (Web Edition)," *Cineaste* 34.1, 2008, at http://www.cineaste.com/articles/cult-film-a-critical-symposium. Accessed on July 12, 2011.

12 Interviews with fans in *The Fan's Love Story: How the Movie "Dirty Dancing" Captured the Hearts of Millions* reveal that initiation to the text is regarded as an important bonding experience between parent and child. When asked whether they would continue to re-watch *Dirty Dancing*, it is notable that fans who were also parents said that they had to watch the film again for the specific reason of sharing the experience with their child or because repeat viewing was now being initiated by their child (Tabashnik, *The Fans' Story*, 73-162). Salient to this is David Shumway's point that "music in these films secures a bond between consumer and product while also arousing a feeling of generational belonging in the audience" (David Shumway, "Rock 'n' Roll Sound Tracks and the Production of Nostalgia," *Cinema Journal* 38.2 (Winter 1999): 37).

13 Richard Maltby, *Hollywood Cinema*, 2nd Edition (Oxford: Blackwell, 2003), 633.

14 Justin Wyatt, *High Concept: Movies and Marketing in Hollywood*, 4th Edition (Austin: University of Texas Press, 2003), 145.

15 A discussion of *Dirty Dancing* and the high-concept film is considered in detail in Yannis Tzioumakis, "High Concept Independence or the First Example of 'Indiewood'? The Curious Case of *Dirty Dancing*," unpublished paper, Society for Cinema and Media Studies Conference, New Orleans, March 16-20, 2011.
16 Maltby, *Hollywood Cinema*, 193.
17 Ibid.
18 In the case of *Dirty Dancing* and other films which utilized pop songs, domestic video allowed consumers to re-watch films in ways that more closely paralleled the practices of listening to music and replaying favorite songs from the soundtrack album.
19 Henry Jenkins, *Textual Poachers: Television Fans and Participatory Culture* (London: Routledge, 1992), 71, 74.
20 Jenkins, *Textual Poachers*, 75.
21 For a discussion of complex narratives and repeat viewing, see Claire Molloy, *Memento* (Edinburgh: Edinburgh University Press, 2010), 45-85.
22 Thomas Elsaesser, "The Mind-Game Film," in *Puzzle Films: Complex Storytelling in Contemporary Cinema*, ed. Warren Buckland (Oxford: Wiley-Blackwell, 2009), 38-9.
23 Nicholas Rombes, *New Punk Cinema* (Edinburgh: Edinburgh University Press, 2005), 97.
24 The Internet Movie Database discussion boards do suggest that the film retains some levels of ambiguity for fans who discuss "rationales" for relationships, particularly those between Baby and Johnny and Baby's father and Johnny. Questions about relationships within the film tend to be points of discussion for fans rather than dominant reasons for re-watching, as would be the case in, for instance, a puzzle film. I am therefore making a distinction here between films which repay multiple viewings by revealing additional layers of meaning and those that offer affective pleasures.
25 Barbara Klinger, *Beyond the Multiplex: Cinema, New Technologies, and the Home* (Berkeley: University of California Press, 2006), 170.
26 Ibid., 172.
27 Ibid., 174.
28 Ian Inglis, "The Act You've Known for All These Years: Telling the Tale of the Beatles," in *Popular Music and Film*, ed. Ian Inglis (London: Wallflower, 2003), 86.
29 Editors' note: see also Gruner's essay in this volume.
30 Phil Drake, "'Mortgaged to Music': New Retro Music in 1990s Hollywood Cinema," in *Memory and Popular Film*, ed. Paul Grainge (Manchester: University of Manchester Press, 2003), 188.
31 Sally Kline, ed., *George Lucas: Interviews* (Jackson: University Press of Mississippi, 1999), 22-23.
32 Editors' note: see also Richard Dyer's essay in this volume.
33 Anahid Kassabian, *Hearing Film: Tracking Identifications in Contemporary Hollywood Film Music* (New York: Routledge, 2001), 89.
34 Ibid., 79.

35 Ibid.
36 Fredric Jameson, *The Cultural Turn: Selected Writings on the Postmodern, 1983–1998* (London and New York: Verso, 1998), 9.
37 Ibid., 8.
38 Shumway, "Rock 'n' Roll," 40.
39 Ibid., 39.

13 DANCING IN THE NOSTALGIA FACTORY: ANACHRONISTIC MUSIC IN *DIRTY DANCING*

TIM MCNELIS

If you were to ask any fan of *Dirty Dancing* what he or she liked about the film, you would likely receive an answer that includes some mention of the film's score.[1] Likewise, those who dislike the film could probably still tell you something about its highly successful soundtrack album—perhaps the names of the hit singles, or the fact that it contains "period music." R. Serge Denisoff and George Plasketes explain that "the soundtrack was number one [on the *Billboard* 200] for eighteen weeks, only surpassed by *Saturday Night Fever's* twenty-four-week stay, keeping both Michael Jackson and Bruce Springsteen out of the coveted spot."[2] Furthermore, the single "(I've Had) The Time of My Life," released two months prior to the film, failed to sell until after the film's release, when the soundtrack album sold a million copies in five weeks.[3] But why did a score containing period music, composed score, and anachronistic 1980s pop songs work at all in a film set in 1963, let alone become so popular? In the following chapter, I will argue that the anachronism of songs is not in itself an overriding factor in the determination of meaning in *Dirty Dancing*. While anachronistic songs may disrupt the musically motivated nostalgia typical of many period films, it is the context within which a song is placed in any film that affects the role the song's anachronism plays. Elements such as film and music genre, association of songs with characters, music's relationship with the diegesis, and the audience's knowledge of performers can determine in different ways how musical anachronism can work in the film. As I will demonstrate, *Dirty Dancing*'s musical anachronism is part of a larger picture that involves a lack of concern, on the one hand, for realistic audiovisual representation and, on the other, for historical accuracy. In this respect, musical anachronism becomes one more strategy for the filmmakers to represent a specific time in the past in a way that feels as contemporary as possible.

Nostalgia and Anachronism in Film Scores of the 1970s and 1980s

David R. Shumway discusses two types of nostalgia intimately linked with film music: "personal nostalgia," which is a "longing for one's own past," and "commodified nostalgia," which "involves the revival by the culture industry of certain fashions and styles of a particular past era."[4] For Shumway, commodified nostalgia can work on those who have no personal memory of a period or event, and "music is the most important ingredient in the production of the affect of nostalgia or the recollection of such affective experience in the viewer."[5] As many scholars have asserted, popular songs in films are particularly good at triggering memories and associations in individuals.[6] For Jeff Smith, "the perpetually changing fads and fashions of popular music furnish a kind of built-in obsolescence to the idiom, which in turn imparts a certain historical specificity to individual styles, performers, and songs."[7] This is why popular music is so useful for establishing time period, location, and a variety of character traits.

By the time of *Dirty Dancing*'s release, there was no shortage of films spewing nostalgia for the 1950s and 1960s, and all of these films relied heavily on popular music to establish this nostalgia. Arguably, the template for song use in these films was *American Graffiti* (George Lucas, 1973). While other films did not follow *American Graffiti*'s strict song-per-scene structure, they did adopt similar audiovisual strategies. Smith describes George Lucas' intentions for the film's unique song placement: "Each of the film's planned forty-eight scenes would run about two and a half minutes, or the length of a popular song.... The song-per-scene strategy kept the story constantly moving."[8] The inclusion of full pop songs gradually developed into standard practice, becoming particularly important for cross-promotion or "synergy" in the age of MTV. For Shumway, *American Graffiti* is "a prime example of the postmodern image-society, in which images are supposed to replace any more substantial understanding of past or present."[9] However, Shumway is careful to clarify that not all nostalgia films are de facto politically conservative.

Other films borrowed stylistic traits from *American Graffiti* to create nostalgia, but did so in a manner that further complicated concepts of genre. While many of these films focused on young characters (and were often marketed to young audiences), they were not usually teen films in any strict sense. The precise incorporation of music and its predominance in the films also brought elements of musicals to the mix. Some films, such as *Grease* (Randal Kleiser, 1978), were obviously musicals, while others, like *The Big Chill* (Lawrence Kasdan, 1983) and *Peggy Sue Got Married* (Francis Ford Coppola, 1986), were not; music plays such a strong narrative role in these films, though, that they share certain affinities with musicals.

Some youth films set in the present, such as *Footloose* (Herbert Ross, 1984), also contained nostalgic elements. While *Footloose* is a dance *and* teen film set in the present, its central struggle—teens battling against a ban on dancing in a small town—seems to be nostalgic for both the rock 'n' roll rebellion of the 1950s and the real struggles against socioeconomic inequalities of the 1960s, which were, in the Reagan era, often framed as past struggles no longer relevant in a country where, with a little hard work, anyone could achieve "The American Dream." A considerable vein of nostalgia also ran through teen films written and/or directed by John Hughes in the 1980s, despite their often modern scores full of British pop songs. In *Pretty in Pink* (written by Hughes but directed by Howard Deutch, 1986), for example, Iona (Annie Potts), who runs a record outlet and is somewhat older than the film's teen protagonists, reminisces about her high school prom and professes a love for *The Big Chill*. Furthermore, two other films written by Hughes, *Sixteen Candles* (John Hughes, 1984) and *Some Kind of Wonderful* (Howard Deutch, 1987), were named after songs originally released in 1958 and 1961, respectively.

Other films from this period contain anachronistic songs that disrupt potential nostalgia. *Baby, It's You* (John Sayles, 1983), set in 1967, contains both period music and Bruce Springsteen songs from the 1970s. The Springsteen songs in this film are associated with Albert "Sheik" Capadilupo (Vincent Spano). This pairing emphasizes themes of working-class New Jersey life that are present in the songs and reflect the character's own background.[10] Another film that uses anachronistic music in a slightly different way is *Eddie and the Cruisers* (Martin Davidson, 1983), set in 1983 but with significant flashbacks to the early 1960s. In this film, the music of fictitious rock star Eddie Wilson (Michael Paré) and his band is actually performed by John Cafferty and the Beaver Brown Band. Rather than resembling early 1960s rock 'n' roll music, however, the songs sound like Bruce Springsteen tributes—a musical choice likely influenced by commercial concerns. The makers of these two films consciously avoided making straight period films designed to evoke nostalgia.

It was into this audiovisual milieu of nostalgic representations and play with anachronistic music that *Dirty Dancing* was released in 1987. Incorporating various film genres and periods of music with a contemporary audiovisual aesthetic, *Dirty Dancing* was not at all unusual among its peers. In the remainder of this chapter, I shall discuss the score of *Dirty Dancing* in greater depth and consider how specific contexts within the film alter the implications of period and anachronistic songs, although both classes of songs tend to mix well within the overall audiovisual strategies of the film.

Period Songs and Audiovisual Relationships in *Dirty Dancing*

Dirty Dancing's score is made up of "period" soul and pop from 1956–1969, contemporary pop, original composed score, Latin American dance music, and jazz. The mix of musical styles and periods and the relationships between the songs and the diegesis problematize ideas of verisimilitude and historical accuracy. This makes more sense when one considers *Dirty Dancing* from various generic frameworks, such as that of a musical, a teen film, or, as Lesley Vize insists, as a dance film.[11] With regard to the film's mixed score, Vize states that, "while not possessing the same degree of 'historical realism' as *Saturday Night Fever*, [*Dirty Dancing*] attempted to portray dialogically the cultural contours of [1963]."[12] She goes on to argue that the centrality of music and dance to the film makes its representation of the past more effective, stating "the *affect* of music and dance accentuates the effect."[13]

The first song heard during the opening title sequence of *Dirty Dancing* is "Be My Baby," performed by The Ronettes (1963) and produced by Phil Spector. "Be My Baby" plays as young couples of various races and ethnic backgrounds, who appear throughout the film as staff of Kellerman's Mountain House, "dirty dance" in a black-and-white, stylized, slow-motion sequence. The distinctive, echoing drum beat of the song starts over a black screen that soon opens upwards, like a curtain being raised, to reveal the first dancers with the words "A Vestron Pictures Presentation" in hot pink, in a font that would now be considered quintessentially '80s. Opening title sequences are often the place where the audiovisual style of a film is established and the relationships between music and other narrative elements are given meaning. Much of this happens within the first thirty seconds of *Dirty Dancing*. The fullness of sound (courtesy of Phil Spector's trademark "Wall of Sound") and recognizability of the distinctive drumming immediately draw the audience into the film. But the artificial framing of the film is suggested by the opening curtain effect and slow motion dancing. Furthermore, while the music and visual appearance of the dancers may suggest 1963, the title font and audiovisual production are certainly 1987. And, in fact, the hairstyles and clothing of the dancers are modern representations of a stylized reproduction of the past rather than "authentic" period costumes. The slow-motion dancing, combined with the high volume of the music and lack of any other sound, seems to prioritize the song. At full speed, "Be My Baby" carries a greater sense of urgency than the protracted dancing; in addition, the lyrics of the female vocals set up the central romance of the film from a female perspective. Furthermore, as Shumway states, "if we accept Susan Douglas's argument—that early 1960s girl-group music helped teenaged girls of the period value and accept their own sexuality—we can understand such songs as early instances of enunciation from such a point of view."[14] Finally, the song contains a rhythm played by castanets, a percussion instrument typically associated with some forms of flamenco for Western audiences. For those who notice the song's allusion to flamenco dance, the castanets can evoke the marginalization and struggle of *Gitanos*, thereby foreshadowing the segregation of the film's dirty dancers and the class-based prejudice that is central to the plot.[15]

In the audio commentary of the 20th Anniversary Edition DVD, writer/co-producer Eleanor Bergstein explains that the opening title sequence was added to foreshadow later events in the film.[16] Bergstein says she separated the film's period music into "clean teen" and "dirty dancing"; these two categories represent Baby (Jennifer Grey) before and after her multi-faceted awakening (sexual, class, and otherwise). In Bergstein's view, this sequence prepared audiences for the later dirty dancing scenes by which they would otherwise have been shocked. Female musical agency,[17] (racialized) class struggle, musical prominence, "inaccurate" representation of period, ensemble dancing, and artificial framing are all established during the opening title sequence.

At the end of the opening titles, another framing device appears to ease the audience into the film proper. As "Be My Baby" fades out, the voice of Bruce "Cousin Brucie" Morrow, a radio DJ, enthusiastically announces that summer romances are in bloom and introduces the next song by The Four Seasons. As the slow-motion dancers fade to black, the drum intro of "Big Girls Don't Cry" is heard. An otherwise obtrusive and abrupt cut from a black screen to a highway is given aural motivation by its synchronization with the entry of enthusiastic falsetto vocals on the word "big." The score then moves into what Bergstein describes as "clean teen" territory, contrasting with the song and dance that precede it. As the song plays, Baby's voiceover reminisces about that summer as the Houseman family drive toward Kellerman's resort. Anahid Kassabian suggests that this "sequence establishes the meaning of white sixties music in the film: it is innocent, nostalgic, hearkening back to a prepubescent peace of mind."[18] This opposes the connotations of African American music established in the opening titles: sexual awakening, class struggle, experienced (as opposed to naïve) youth, and agency.

The volume of "Big Girls Don't Cry" lowers during Baby's voiceover,[19] but when she is not speaking it stays as high as it was when the exterior of the car was first seen on the highway. At this point, the song's position is ambiguous. The source does not seem to be the car's radio because the volume was not lower on the establishing shot of the car, and when Baby hugs her father, Jack (Jerry Orbach), his lips move as if he is speaking but he makes no sound. The sound of the car's engine is audible, though, and what is more confounding is that, with a cut to the exterior of the car pulling into Kellerman's, the volume drops and the sound quality is such that the car's radio now seems to be the source of the song. The music even stops when Jack turns off the car.

The audiovisual relationships established during the two sequences discussed above continue throughout the film, but the score is further complicated by the addition of anachronistic music. However, considering the lack of concern with realistic audiovisual presentation already described, anachronism becomes but one more unrealistic element in the mix, which supports the film's strategy of presenting the period setting with a contemporary inflection. In the following section, I shall consider the role of such music in the film and the effect it has on the overall audiovisual meaning. I will also examine how anachronistic songs are manipulated and worked into the diegesis in a manner similar to those songs already discussed.

Anachronistic Songs—More Than Meets the Ear?

The effect of anachronistic music on a scene largely depends on relationships between music, diegesis, and narrative, as well as audience expectations.[20] As David Butler points out, even classical Hollywood scoring would technically be anachronistic in films set in a time before this type of score existed, but its ubiquity generally goes unnoticed by audiences because it is used to guide emotions rather than denote place or time.[21] The genre of the music is also of great importance. If an anachronistic popular song functions as dramatic score, and the genre does not diverge greatly from period songs in the film, then the song's presence may not be as disruptive. And, as Butler notes, whether or not music is identified as anachronistic also depends on the audience's knowledge of the music.[22]

Butler identifies other functions of anachronistic music in film, and many of these are functions typically served by popular songs regardless of the type of film or period, such as giving information about characters' emotional states and providing commentary, which is sometimes ironic, on actions and situations.[23] Likewise, William Johnson identifies the humorous function of older music in a future scenario: "When Stanley Kubrick, at the end of *Dr. Strangelove*, sets the image of a nuclear explosion to Vera Lynn's singing of 'We'll Meet

Again' he is accomplishing more than a verbal joke: by superimposing World War II on World War III he is reminding the audience, as they laugh, that the latter will not lend itself to nostalgia so well as the former."[24] This perception of anachronism complicates a definition centered on new music in a past-set film. The success of audiovisual humor in this instance is based on the song's cultural association with a specific time *and* place/event. Robynn J. Stilwell describes a different type of musical anachronism used to communicate certain ideas to a contemporary audience in *Sense and Sensibility* (Ang Lee, 1995): "As portrayed in the film, Brandon's musicality is anachronistic, but is used to communicate his suitability as a mate for Marianne effectively to a modern audience; a male amateur musician—particularly a military man like Brandon—would never play a keyboard instrument, as it was too closely identified with feminine accomplishment. He is much more likely to have played a violin or flute."[25] While this example deals with instrumental performance rather than film score, it nevertheless illustrates how modern musical connotations are sometimes needed to communicate ideas to contemporary audiences, even at the expense of historical accuracy.

In the following discussion of anachronistic songs in *Dirty Dancing*, I will mainly focus on pop/rock songs rather than the Latin American dance songs, many of which were composed for the film and still sound somewhat dated but could be perceived as contemporary to the film's setting. Despite the attention typically given to "Hungry Eyes" and "(I've Had) The Time of My Life," there are plenty of anachronistic songs in the film, the first of which is heard quite early on (0:13:13). "Where Are You Tonight?" is performed by Tom Johnston, guitarist and singer of the Doobie Brothers. This 1980s take on 1950s/1960s R&B is the first song heard emanating from the dirty dancing shack on top of the hill as Baby encounters Billy (Neal Jones) carrying watermelons. The quality of sound and low volume of the music make the song's source clear. This song's presence in the film is barely memorable, not only because of the low volume, but also because of what comes next. After "Where Are You Tonight?" ends, "Do You Love Me?" begins, and this is the song to which Baby is first exposed to the dirty dancers. Because of its imitative style, low volume, and position immediately preceding a very memorable scene, the anachronism of "Where Are You Tonight?" is much more subtle than later and better-known songs in the film and does not necessarily prevent the song from fitting into the diegetic world of the early 1960s. This case clearly shows how genre, volume, and placement in relation to other songs and narrative events can dampen the impact of a song's anachronism.

The next anachronistic song is "Hungry Eyes," performed by Eric Carmen and written by Franke Previte and John DeNicola (0:34:34). Eric Carmen had some hits with 1970s power pop band The Raspberries and as a solo artist, and he wrote the music for "Almost Paradise" from *Footloose*. Thus, like Tom Johnston, Carmen had an established career before this song. "Hungry Eyes" functions as source score as Johnny and Penny (Cynthia Rhodes) teach Baby the dance steps so she can replace Penny in the annual Sheldrake Hotel performance. The song starts as dramatic score—it is clear that Baby and Johnny are dancing to a completely different song. However, "Hungry Eyes" becomes source score as lyrical content and changes in volume seem to match onscreen events. At one point during the sequence, Penny moves the needle back to the beginning of a record. The visible record is not heard, but when she places the needle on the record, the volume of "Hungry Eyes" jumps up. This rise in volume also corresponds with the end of Johnny's dance instructions, and thus no longer needs to underscore dialogue, but the synchronization of the needle and the jump in volume is too obvious to ignore. The first lyrical articulation of action occurs when Baby looks up at Johnny just as the chorus hits the words "hungry eyes." Similarly, the lyrics "Now I've got you in my sights" are heard when Johnny is watching Baby and Penny dance with each other. Another lyrical match occurs when Johnny smiles and nods at Baby with the words "Now did I take you by surprise?" When the idea of Baby taking Penny's place was first proposed, Johnny did not believe that Baby could learn so quickly, and he now realizes he was wrong. Baby has also taken Johnny by surprise in the respect that he is developing feelings for her.

As Vize asserts, throughout the "Hungry Eyes" sequence, "we have seen Baby transformed from a virginal girl to a sexually aware young woman."[26] Vize also suggests that "the introduction of the soul-based saxophone ... complements their new physical closeness, and is suggestive of sexual intimacy," which connects with her later comments on the relationship between classic soul music and heterosexual romance and sexuality.[27] Likewise, the roughness of Eric Carmen's voice at points throughout the song also draws on these connotations. The timbre of Carmen's voice and the parallel gritty timbre of the saxophone, and their similarity to 1960s soul music, serve to create a consistency of style with the film's period songs. This kind of use may dampen the shock of the anachronistic songs, but it also questions the very concept of musical anachronism, breaking down the clear distinction between anachronistic and period music.

Other anachronistic songs in the film continue to problematize thinking about music in such terms. "Overload," performed by Zappacosta, is contemporary, traditionally masculine blues-rock (0:38:32). This song is heard as dramatic score, commenting on Johnny's aggressive masculinity as he breaks his car window to retrieve the keys locked inside. As if to emphasize this point, Baby playfully screams, "You're wild!" to Johnny as he drives in the next scene. "Overload" serves functions typical of pop songs in cinema and does not have a source in the diegesis. Equally important, its position as the next piece of music after "Hungry Eyes" provides some continuity that could ease the shock of the anachronism, although the status of "Overload" as dramatic score makes its overall anachronism less of a problem to audiences familiar with similar uses of current pop songs in contemporary films.

Another song that complicates the concept of anachronistic music is the contemporary cover of "You Don't Own Me" by British new-wave band The Blow Monkeys (1:08:14). The song is source music, as evidenced by the Cousin Brucie banter preceding it and the low volume/quality of sound suggesting emanation from a radio. Originally released by Lesley Gore in 1964, this song was a strong declaration of independence for a woman to sing at that time, and it has a history of re-appropriation too long to discuss in this chapter. This version, sung by a man with a "queer" voice at odds with other music in the film, belongs in a lineage of covers of "You Don't Own Me" by Dusty Springfield, Joan Jett, and Klaus Nomi, among others. It is therefore odd that the song clearly comments on Johnny's class struggle as he beats up Robbie (Max Cantor), one of the wealthy college students who works as a waiter and who earlier impregnated and then abandoned Penny. The song's incongruent underscoring of a very masculine fight scene serves to tone down or re-appropriate the testosterone in some way, and it also supports Vize's claim for the possibility of queer readings of the film.[28] Perhaps more important for the purposes of this chapter, the song's status as a cover of a well-known song originally released in the 1960s makes it stand out less as anachronistic music, once again ensuring that it fits comfortably within the overall audiovisual aesthetic of the film despite its classification as source music.

"Yes," performed by Merry Clayton, is the only anachronistic song in the film performed by an African American singer (1:12:09). Clayton, another music industry veteran, sang backing vocals on The Rolling Stones' "Gimme Shelter" and songs of other artists, as well as having a solo singing and acting career. In this instance, the song's anachronism is flaunted. "Yes," a now dated-sounding 1980s R&B/soul song, starts after Baby's sister, Lisa (Jane Brucker), tells her she is going to sleep with Robbie that night. After Baby's half-hearted attempt to stop her sister as she walks away, the song starts and bridges a cut to Lisa, now in a nice dress and makeup, strutting confidently to Robbie's cabin. The brashness of the singer's assertion that "we're gonna make love, gonna be tonight" clearly reflects Lisa's intentions. But once Lisa reaches the cabin and opens the door, she finds Robbie making love with an older woman who propositioned Johnny in the previous scene. After a cut to the couple looking shocked in bed, there is a cut to Lisa accompanied by the lyrics "everything can't be anticipated."

This scene is played for laughs, with the unabashed anachronism of the keyboards and production of the song underlining Lisa's role in the film—she is a more traditional and shallow girl than Baby, only concerned with her appearance and attractiveness. The song's anachronism further emphasizes Lisa's disinterest in politics and social problems by distancing her from the current sociocultural issues with which Baby is so concerned. This is re-enforced when the music bridges a cut to a 45-rpm record on a turntable in Johnny's room. The needle reaches the end of the groove, and the music stops mid-song when the needle lifts. However, this seems more like a visual justification for a change of music than an actual suggestion that the record is the source of "Yes." A new record then falls onto the turntable: "In the Still of the Night." This more "authentic" music brings the audience back to the serious romance and historically relevant concerns of Baby and Johnny. In this case, historical accuracy is sacrificed in service of creating humor by employing a contemporary pop song at a high volume to structure the scene and comment on characters and events. This task is made easier because the music has no source in the diegesis, and the film returns to the period music seamlessly through the cut to the record player, ensuring that even examples of more blatant anachronisms are well-regulated within the film's overall representational strategies.

The next anachronistic song in the film, "She's Like the Wind" (1:19:59), is dramatic score but has a close connection to Baby and Johnny. This song, which is performed by Patrick Swayze and features Wendy Fraser, is a soft rock ballad that has no source in the diegesis, but its volume is manipulated to allow dialogue to be heard as with previous songs. "She's Like the Wind" plays as Johnny and Baby say their goodbyes after Johnny loses his job for sleeping with Baby. While the song's lyrics and style bring romantic connotations to the scene, the dialogue is actually rather awkward and not terribly intimate. Although the characters do not express love for one another, the song seems insistent on adding romance to the primarily physical relationship that has developed between them. The song rises in volume to emphasize Johnny's car speeding away and bridges a cut to Baby staring wistfully off into the distance, accompanied by a saxophone solo that is more subdued and yet not dissimilar to the one in "Hungry Eyes." Although the lyrics about feelings of insecurity and inferiority are sung by a man, specifically Patrick Swayze, the song's placement situates it in relation to Baby's feelings about Johnny. Therefore, as is typical, the male character rambles while the female pines. Baby's contemplative pose in this scene could represent a reflection on becoming an individual with different views from her father, but the song steers the reading of Baby's inner state toward the romantic and sentimental. And of course, Swayze's aural presence helps even this song integrate well with the rest of the score.

The film's final anachronistic song, "(I've Had) The Time of My Life" (1:26:46), has the most problematic relationship with the diegesis and, arguably, renders the whole consideration of anachronistic music moot. This pop/soul/dance hybrid is again performed by industry veterans—Bill Medley, formerly of The Righteous Brothers, and Jennifer Warnes, who, among other things, sang "Up Where We Belong," a duet with Joe Cocker from *An Officer and a Gentleman* (Taylor Hackford, 1982). Like "Hungry Eyes," this song was written by Franke Previte and John DeNicola, but with the addition of Donald Markowitz. "(I've Had) The Time of My Life" has perhaps the strongest ties, both sonically and with regard to its performers, to the period songs in the film's score, making an otherwise clearly anachronistic song also fit perfectly within the film's stylized version of the past. Medley's vocal style throughout the song has a rough timbre that approximates classic soul singers more than any of the other new songs in the film, and there is, once again, a raspy saxophone solo.

A different arrangement of "(I've Had) The Time of My Life" is heard earlier in the film in the form of instrumental dramatic score. This plays when Baby overhears Max Kellerman (Jack Weston) telling the wait staff there are "two kinds of help," thus making Baby aware of the class divisions and inequality amongst staff (0:05:41). This version is heard again when Baby and Johnny are practicing lifts in the lake (0:42:16). Once again, the music underscores an important event in Baby's maturation. She does the lift briefly but successfully in the water, proving that she finally trusts Johnny. "(I've Had) The Time of My Life" thus becomes a leitmotif signifying Baby's coming of age. This arrangement of the song also prepares the audience for the later occurrence of the full-length, overtly anachronistic version.

The fully formed song plays during the final dance sequence, when Johnny returns despite having been fired. In this sequence, the leitmotivic status of the song is further enforced—Baby finally breaks free of her parents to become her own woman. Any chronological concerns are dismissed immediately as Billy is shown putting the 45 on a turntable; "(I've Had) The Time of My Life" is clearly source music from the start (1:26:46). At first, Johnny and Baby simply do parts of the routine they prepared for the earlier Sheldrake Hotel performance, although this time Baby appears much more relaxed, confident, and competent.

Lyrically, the song's first chorus corresponds with a pause in the dance when Baby and Johnny hold each other close and look longingly into each other's eyes. The second chorus occurs when Baby finally does the lift successfully. Before the lift, however, Johnny jumps from the stage into the aisle on a brass hit, and brings the other staff into an obviously pre-choreographed dance routine that makes no sense in what appears to be an impromptu performance. In the DVD commentary, Bergstein insists the dance did not come out of nowhere, but rather that the staff can be seen practicing it in the background during a couple of scenes.[29] While this is true, it is very difficult to spot without Bergstein's guidance. The dance sequence gets progressively less realistic from this point onwards, and, paradoxically, the musical choice seems to make more sense. After Baby and Johnny do the lift, the dancing staff coax audience members into dancing, and soon everyone, including Max Kellerman and Baby's parents, is dancing. Perplexingly, Kellerman's band director, Tito Suarez (Charles "Honi" Coles), is shown directing his swing band, who play along with the song. Max then asks Tito, "You have sheet music on this stuff?" Max's unfamiliarity with this type of music humorously highlights the song's anachronism. Near the end of this sequence there is a cut to a close-up of Baby and Johnny that corresponds with a subdued chorus. Johnny, almost begrudgingly, mouths the words of the song, finally getting enthusiastic as Bill Medley barks, "And I owe it all to you!" Baby laughs after this, almost echoing what the audience is likely to think is an absurd revelation of the song's unrealistic placement.

Regarding this sequence, Markus Rheindorf suggests that the song and action extend into the non-diegetic space of the audience,[30] while Shumway argues that the film should be understood as a backstage musical, and that while no unmotivated singing occurs, the combination of new songs with some dance numbers "may be seen to heighten their unreality."[31] He goes on to suggest that "in this move, *Dirty Dancing* seems to break its own carefully constructed frame, to move from the 'reality' of another time to become an explicit movie fantasy."[32] I would argue, however, that the film's period frame is not very carefully constructed at all with regard to reality or historical accuracy. As I have shown throughout this chapter, the film audiovisually crosses the permeable period film frame on many occasions. I do, however, agree with Shumway's assertion that the film's anachronistic songs "might be read as disrupting the nostalgia effect," although this likely applies to some songs more than others.[33]

Conclusion

While one should never dismiss a film's score as being purely commercially driven, it is safe to assume that soundtrack sales were

Anachronistic Music in Dirty Dancing

a major motivation for the musical choices in *Dirty Dancing*. Andrew Goodwin states that in the 1980s the movie industry was increasingly using popular songs to target youth, "with films such as *Flashdance*, *Pretty in Pink*, and *Dirty Dancing*. Such soundtracks often yielded promotional clips that simultaneously advertised a song, a film, and perhaps a soundtrack album."[34] Smith goes so far as to assert that "MTV's target audience was essentially the same demographic sought by film producers during this period."[35] The music videos for "Hungry Eyes," "(I've Had) The Time of My Life," and "She's Like the Wind" are included in the 20th Anniversary DVD set, and all three of these videos feature a combination of the singers lip-synching in non-performance scenarios and footage from the film. MTV insisted the recording artist be featured in at least 50% of each video after accusations that it was providing free advertising with videos such as "Maniac" from *Flashdance*, which was completely made up of footage from the film.[36] Thus, having a song performed by a film's star on the soundtrack allows for a video that features the actor throughout. This is the case for the "She's Like the Wind" video, which features Patrick Swayze throughout as both Johnny, with a "duck's ass" haircut in scenes from the film, and Patrick, with a "mullet" to connect with the contemporary teen audience. Despite the fact that a video was made for "Yes" (with footage from the film, a retro-60s aesthetic, and dancing couples), this video is not included on the 20th Anniversary DVD.

For Kassabian, "*Dirty Dancing* is a teen film, pitched to a teen audience to whom the music of the early 1960s would not necessarily speak.... [It] uses today's music in a yesterday-set film to connect today's youth with yesterday's youth."[37] As I have argued throughout this chapter, however, *Dirty Dancing* is a mixed-genre film, and while definitely targeting a teen audience, the appeal to adults is just as strong. Although my assertion seems somewhat obvious with regard to the film's period setting and songs, it also applies to the newly recorded songs. First, although older actors playing teenagers was more commonplace in the 1980s than it is today, the stars of *Dirty Dancing* were well beyond their teenage years—Jennifer Grey was 27, and Patrick Swayze (whose character was somewhat older in the film) was 35. In addition, the singers of the film's newly recorded songs were almost all in their mid-30s or older, and some had recorded music as early as the 1960s.

Musically, the newly recorded songs also have links to the past. Such elements as raspy saxophone solos and rough, soul-inspired vocals, as well as the updated soul of "Yes" and R&B of "Where Are You Tonight?," produced an affinity between these songs and the old songs, even if the new songs had distinctly modern production. The film would have been quite different, for instance, if multiple synth-pop or rap tracks were included in the score. Thus, the original soundtrack album, which contained seven anachronistic songs (including the Blow Monkeys' "You Don't Own Me") and five period songs, held a strong appeal for both younger and older audiences despite the majority of new songs. In this respect, the generalization that young audiences would not also appreciate the soul classics on the album is problematic.

While the anachronistic use of songs is central to a discussion of the music in *Dirty Dancing*, the issue goes far beyond purely chronological concerns. A song's placement, volume, history, and relationship with the diegesis all affect the reading of a film's audiovisual moment. In addition, meaning is created by multiple occurrences of a song in a film, character engagement with playback technology, mise-en-scène of the audiovisual event, and employment of film genre conventions in relation to music. Despite *Dirty Dancing* being a nostalgia film and a period film, it is, just as importantly, an audiovisual production distinctly of its time.

Notes

1. I use "score" to refer to the overall music of the film and not just the original composed score.
2. R. Serge Denisoff and George Plasketes, "Synergy in 1980s Film and Music: Formula for Success or Industry Mythology," *Film History* 4.3 (1990): 264.
3. Ibid.
4. David R. Shumway, "Rock 'n' Roll Sound Tracks and the Production of Nostalgia," *Cinema Journal* 38.2 (1999): 39.
5. Ibid., 40.
6. See, for example, Jeff Smith, *The Sounds of Commerce: Marketing Popular Film Music* (New York: Columbia University Press, 1998), 154-185; Shumway, "Rock 'n' Roll," 40; Anahid Kassabian, *Hearing Film: Tracking Identifications in Contemporary Hollywood Film Music* (New York: Routledge, 2001); Ian Garwood, "Must you Remember This? Orchestrating the 'Standard' Pop Song in *Sleepless in Seattle*," in *Movie Music: The Film Reader*, ed. Kay Dickinson (Lon-

don: Routledge, 2003), 107-117; and Faye Woods, "Nostalgia, Music and the Television Past Revisited in American Dreams," *Music, Sound, and the Moving Image* 2.1 (2008): 27-50.
7. Smith, *The Sounds of Commerce*, 165.
8. Ibid., 174.
9. Shumway, "Rock 'n' Roll," 42.
10. Shumway (Ibid., 45) suggests these anachronistic songs work because "in *Baby, It's You* popular records often function more like classic film scores, serving to augment the emotional character of the scenes."
11. Lesley Vize, "Music and the Body in Dance Film," in *Popular Music and Film*, ed. Ian Inglis (London: Wallflower Press, 2003), 22-38.
12. Ibid., 34-35.
13. Ibid., 35.
14. Shumway, "Rock 'n' Roll," 46-47.
15. Flamenco originated from the urban *Gitanos* or Gypsies of Andalusia, and its lyrical themes reflect a history of persecution by Spanish authorities and general outsider status in mainstream Spanish culture. For more information on the cultural context of flamenco, see Peter Manuel, "Andalusian, Gypsy, and Class Identity in the Contemporary Flamenco Complex," *Ethnomusicology* 33.1 (1989): 47-65.
16. Eleanor Bergstein commentary in "Special Features,". *Dirty Dancing 20th Anniversary Edition*, dir. Emile Ardolino (Lions Gate Home Entertainment, 2007, Region 2 DVD) 0:00:40-0:02:07.
17. For my development of the concept of "musical agency," see Timothy McNelis, *Popular Music, Identity, and Musical Agency in U.S. Youth Films* (PhD thesis, University of Liverpool, 2010).
18. Kassabian, *Hearing Film*, 77.
19. The fact that Baby's voiceover is done by Jennifer Grey rather than someone older further problematizes the film's period framing.
20. Rather than the more common "diegetic" and "non-diegetic" music, I shall be using Kassabian's (*Hearing Film*, 43-45) terminology. "Source music" and "dramatic scoring" roughly correspond to "diegetic" and "non-diegetic," respectively. "Source scoring," Kassabian states, is "music that falls between diegetic and nondiegetic music.... Source scoring combines aspects of source music and dramatic scoring in terms of both its relationship to the film's narrative world and its coincidence with the onscreen events."
21. David Butler, "The Days Do Not End: Film Music, Time and Bernard Herrmann," *Film Studies* 9 (Winter 2006): 53.
22. Ibid.
23. Ibid., 52-57.
24. William Johnson, "Face the Music," *Film Quarterly* 22. 4 (1969): 7.
25. Robynn J. Stilwell, "Sense & Sensibility: Form, Genre, and Function in the Film Score," *Acta Musicologica* 72.2 (2000): 220.
26. Vize, "Music and the Body in Dance Film," 32.
27. Ibid., 32, 36.
28. Ibid., 36-37.

29 Bergstein, 20th Anniversary DVD commentary.
30 Markus Rheindorf, "The Multiple Modes of *Dirty Dancing*: A Cultural Studies Approach to Multimodal Discourse Analysis," in *Perspectives on Multimodality*, eds. Eija Ventola, Cassily Charles, and Martin Kaltenbacher (Amsterdam: John Benjamins, 2004), 150.
31 Shumway, "Rock 'n' Roll," 48.
32 Ibid.
33 Ibid., 45.
34 Andrew Goodwin, *Dancing in the Distraction Factory: Music Television and Popular Culture* (London: Routledge, 1993), 38.
35 Smith, *The Sounds of Commerce*, 200.
36 Ibid., 201.
37 Kassabian, *Hearing Film*, 77.

IV BEYOND THE FILM

BIBLIOGRAPHY

Introduction

YANNIS TZIOUMAKIS

"Beyond the Film," the fourth and final section of this volume, examines aspects of other manifestations of *Dirty Dancing*. Since its release in 1987, a proliferation of other texts have derived from *Dirty Dancing* following its unexpected commercial success in theatres. Some of these derivatives, like a spin-off television show with the same title, disappeared quickly and without a trace; others, however, especially its stage adaptation, *Dirty Dancing: The Classic Story on Stage*, have found great commercial success and helped enhance the popularity of the film while also solidifying its appeal as a prime example of entertainment for female demographics. Not surprisingly, this increasing visibility brought with it a new demand for merchandising associated with the film (and the stage adaptation) and for licensing its logo to a large number of products, turning *Dirty Dancing* into an extremely lucrative franchise.

"Beyond the Film," then, aims to examine certain aspects of *Dirty Dancing*'s significant afterlife. Given that this afterlife extends outside the medium of film, the chapters in this section originate not only from the area of film studies but also from theater studies, offering two very different perspectives on the reasons behind the popularity of the film, (some of) the other texts it has inspired, and especially its stage adaptation.

In chapter 14, Amanda Howell examines the history of the *Dirty Dancing* franchise, focusing on both the early efforts by Vestron immediately following the film's theatrical success and the more recent, successful franchising by Lionsgate. Howell's discussion makes the interesting proposition that franchising efforts tended to be successful when the result allowed audiences to "relive the movie with the music" rather than when it tried to expand, reinvent, or remake the film. This potentially explains why the various copyright-holding companies behind *Dirty Dancing* have always made the film available in every single home entertainment format, helping the original story and music become the "essence" of the property. One wonders whether the newly announced remake will fare well if the music and other important narrative elements are changed.

In chapter 15, Millie Taylor focuses on *Dirty Dancing: The Classic Story on Stage* and argues that the audience's live experience of the show cannot be separated from their experience of the film. This is because audiences are not seeing the live show alone, but are also enjoying the re-enactment of the film, especially as the use of projection in the show brings the experience of film into the live performance. The conflation of the present experience with past memory, Taylor argues, creates in this case a new composite that stimulates imagination, memory, witnessing, and presence in an intense mix of the personal and the communal, which goes a long way to explain the great success of the show.

Finally, in the last essay of this volume, George Rodosthenous examines the ways in which *Dirty Dancing* has re-negotiated the place of sensual dancing within the canon of musical theater through a celebration of the male body—the male "dirty dancing body" in this case. Commencing from a discussion of recent shifts in the public perception of male dancers, who are now habitually perceived as muscular athletes, Rodosthenous moves to discuss the role of Johnny Castle's muscular body in the *Dirty Dancing* stage show and suggests that its function is to help create "the ultimate teenage girl fantasy," which could also explain why the audiences for the show have been primarily women who love to see this fantasy recreated for their benefit. Given that most musicals tend to have a "fantasy scene" where the protagonists express their innermost feelings, emotions, and dreams, and *Dirty Dancing* does not have any such scene in its story, it is Johnny Castle's dancing body, Rodosthenous suggests, that becomes the vehicle for the articulation of this fantasy through his physique, his style, and his alluring, irresistible demeanor.

Dirty Dancing, then, does translate from screen to stage, with the latter sharing a similar success to the original film. And typically, unlike with many other similar stage adaptations (for example *Footloose* and the recently adapted *Ghost*), fans of *Dirty Dancing* have embraced the live production with relish, seeing it as yet another opportunity to lose themselves and indulge in the love story of Baby and Johnny all over again.

14 A DANCE FILM WITH LEGS: THE *DIRTY DANCING* FRANCHISE

AMANDA HOWELL

Anyone with a *Dirty Dancing* fan to shop for has plenty of options. Of course, there are multiple versions of the film and soundtrack—most recently, the remastered *Limited Keepsake Edition* (2010) DVD and Blu-ray of the film and the *20th Anniversary Edition* (2007) of the soundtrack. Need something more adventurous? How about the "*Dirty Dancing* Weekend" at Mountain Lake Hotel in Virginia, one of the film locations? A more affordable option that likewise offers the opportunity to enjoy film and music-oriented trivia, singing, dancing, and role-playing is the *Dirty Dancing* board game. In keeping with the spirit of the film, even losers can win if they get up and dance, as "players who answer incorrectly get a chance to move ahead if they are willing to strut their stuff."[1] Retro-themed clothing offers a different sort of identificatory experience with the film and its characters; how about a faux vintage tee from Cold Crush that cheekily asserts "Johnny Castle taught me all my moves?"[2] Or a genuine vintage *Dirty Dancing* gown by Fantasy Formals, licensed by Vestron in 1987 and now sold as a collectible? Such items highlight the ongoing cultural relevance of *Dirty Dancing* and offer the opportunity to reengage with the film. Their popularity confirms that—as *Billboard* observed when the *Dirty Dancing* soundtrack unexpectedly captured and held number one on the album chart all through the Christmas season of 1987—"*Dirty Dancing* ... still has legs."[3]

The ready availability and familiarity of such film-oriented merchandise also signals the ubiquity of the film franchise in contemporary culture, where the line between "shopping and entertainment" is now routinely blurred.[4] Many film franchises are planned ahead of time to allow Hollywood studios to increase profits from core assets; in such cases, companies effectively work backward from an already-popular commercial property—such as the Disney theme-park ride "Pirates of the Caribbean"—to put that experience on screen. By contrast, there are those franchises that emerge more spontaneously, in response to the popularity of a film whose fans—to quote track five of the soundtrack album—want to "stay, just a little bit longer." And so it is in the case of *Dirty Dancing*; but, just like those movie campaigns based on properties like rides, TV shows, and comic book characters, its franchise likewise exemplifies the industrial strategy of synergy and is informed by the shape of the US and global film industries after 1975.

Movies at the Mall: Franchises, Synergy, and New Hollywood

Franchises in which characters or entire fictional worlds are licensed for distribution across different media have a long history in US filmmaking: Frank L. Baum's Oz book series prompted stage and screen adaptations and had its own film-manufacturing company in the 1910s; Felix the Cat sauntered out of comic strips into silent films and onto a variety of merchandise in the 1920s; and Tarzan swung out of a newspaper serial into books, and thereafter into the MGM jungle adventures of the 1930s.[5] But like blockbuster films, such franchises were the exception rather than the rule in early US cinema and studio-era Hollywood. After 1975 this changed, following a series of mergers that consolidated industries such as music, film, and publishing into conglomerates designed to profit from collaborative arrangements, or "synergies," among different media. Conglomeration, combined with the emergence of new technologies and delivery systems during the 1970s and 1980s, effectively transformed US filmmaking.

The character of film entertainment as reinvented by New Hollywood, with the central role of the franchise and cross-media synergies that are so much a part of the history of *Dirty Dancing*, can be summed up by two major hits of 1977: *Star Wars* (George Lucas) and *Saturday*

Night Fever (John Badham). *Star Wars* was the top box office hit of the decade and currently is still second only to *Gone with the Wind* (Victor Fleming, 1939) in adjusted domestic grosses.[6] A prime example of the "high-cost, high-tech, high-stakes blockbuster," *Star Wars* is symptomatic of the way New Hollywood moved beyond the standalone film and instead produced "multi-purpose entertainment machines."[7] *Star Wars* was—and is—not so much a discrete textual object in these terms, but the theatrical jumping-off point for its franchise, in which an ever-expanding universe continues to be explored more than thirty years later in sequels, prequels, and a bewildering array of film-themed merchandise. The aesthetic character of the first *Star Wars* film lent itself to this treatment, with its "toyetic" qualities,[8] as well as its combination of simple plot and densely-textured mise-en-scène that quoted multiple genres from Hollywood's cinematic past. By combining the old with the new, nostalgia, and innovation, it achieved a cross-generational appeal that—as in the case of *Dirty Dancing*—has contributed to its longevity as a franchise.

Saturday Night Fever was, in contrast to *Star Wars*, a relatively low-budget film produced by music, TV, and film impresario Robert Stigwood, who designed the project to capitalize on the disco craze, rather in the manner of Sam Katzman's jukebox musicals of the 1950s. The film was an unexpected hit, out-performing the expectations of distributor Paramount—who passed on the opportunity to share in the Polygram soundtrack, a decision based on industry wisdom that "soundtracks just didn't sell."[9] The success of *Saturday Night Fever* and its soundtrack album by the Bee Gees permanently changed Hollywood's attitude, as the soundtrack effectively marketed the film, with 850,000 albums sold prior to film's release. Whereas *Star Wars* exemplifies the financial possibilities offered by the franchise—with its 30-year stream of video and DVD re-issues, new films, novelizations, toys, and games—*Saturday Night Fever* demonstrated the possibilities offered by the reconfigured industrial environment of American filmmaking, with its striking use of cross-media promotion and the extraordinary success of its music. Both films epitomize New Hollywood as it evolved in the late 1970s, especially in the way that they capitalized on the commercial opportunities offered by multi-media conglomerates. In these terms, they serve as exemplars of the conditions that made the *Dirty Dancing* franchise possible. They also serve as counter-examples that highlight its difference in terms of the way that the *Dirty Dancing* franchise has developed.

In the decade that followed the successes of *Star Wars* and *Saturday Night Fever*, New Hollywood continued to transform itself and its products, especially through new delivery systems such as video, laser discs, and pay cable television. Films now had multiple windows of exhibition following their initial theatrical release, and among these home video became the most significant, its popularity a global phenomenon by the mid-1980s. By the end of the decade, film "ceased to be primarily a theatrical medium, based in celluloid" as "movies took their place as one 'software' stream among the others."[10] At the time *Dirty Dancing* was released in 1987, "revenues from video outpaced those from theatrical box office"; and yet, because the most profitable videos were those films that performed well theatrically, there were "strong synergies" between theatrical and video markets "that provided a rationale for the exhibition sector's expansion beginning in mid-decade."[11]

The theatrical exhibition space that typified New Hollywood was the mall multiplex. With as many as 18 screens in the mega-multiplex, these theaters offered moviegoers a "smorgasbord" of films to choose from, while allowing exhibitors to share in shopping malls' "economies of scale."[12] But most significantly, in terms of franchising and cross-media synergies, the multiplex also put movies and moviegoers in convenient proximity to various types of ancillary products. This positioning of theatrical exhibition is particularly relevant to the film and music synergies that have fueled the ongoing success of *Dirty Dancing*. As Jay Lasker, president of Motown Records from 1980-1987, observed: "After the movie, when you're all pumped up, you can walk two doors down to the record store to buy the album."[13]

Girls' Dreams: The Unexpected Successes of *Dirty Dancing* and Its Music

The rapid expansion of ancillary markets in the New Hollywood period, especially home video sales and rentals, increased audience demand for movies; as a consequence, in the 1980s new opportunities opened for indie film production and distribution. Although many indie films never got distribution or went straight to video without theatrical release, independent companies like Miramax, New World, and Vestron nevertheless gave independent filmmakers unprecedented access to audiences, effectively diversifying a marketplace otherwise dominated by the New Hollywood blockbuster. Among these independently produced films were various genres aimed at youth audiences: slasher horror, high school comedies, coming-of-age dramas, and dance films. In this industrial context, scriptwriter and co-producer Eleanor Bergstein, after a decade of attempting to find a company interested in her semi-autobiographical story of music, dance, and female coming-of-age, finally got the chance to put *Dirty Dancing* on screen. David Denby of *New York* magazine, like a number of other reviewers in 1987, dismissed the resultant film as "cheese," but also admitted that it hit a chord with audiences and was perhaps likewise symptomatic of a—long overdue—shift in youth cinema. "After several decades of boys' dreams," Denby observed, "we are now beginning to get girls' dreams."[14]

Dirty Dancing was the first feature by Vestron Pictures, a subsidiary of home video pioneer Vestron Video. Made for a mere $6 million, *Dirty Dancing* made $10 million from the US theatrical box office in its first ten days. Ranked eleventh at the box office for 1987, the film has to date grossed over $200 million worldwide.[15] The success of both the movie and its music exceeded the wildest hopes of both Vestron and its soundtrack distributor RCA. Particularly in the success of its albums and singles, *Dirty Dancing* was a film that confirmed the viability of the 1980s strategy of synergy. More specifically, its success—where other films failed in their attempt to invoke the cross-media magic of *Saturday Night Fever,* whereby "movies + soundtrack + video = $$$"[16]— demonstrated what a creative and highly integrated use of music could accomplish even for a low-budget indie film. As *Billboard* summed up the surprise success of the *Dirty Dancing* soundtrack: "While everyone was watching to see whether Michael Jackson or Bruce Springsteen would be No. 1, this modest soundtrack came out of left field to pass them both on the chart. The fact that the album doesn't feature any superstar names didn't seem to matter."[17] The *Dirty Dancing* album topped the charts for eighteen weeks: released in August, it hit number one on November 14, and stayed there until January 15, 1988; it returned to the top again on March 12, staying until May 13, its renewed popularity apparently prompted by the release of a follow-up album, *More Dirty Dancing*, on the first of March. In an "industry first,"[18] the sequel soon joined the original soundtrack in the top ten. As a soundtrack LP, *Dirty Dancing* ranked second only to *Saturday Night Fever*'s twenty-four-week stay at number one.

The path to soundtrack success was different for *Dirty Dancing*, however, than it had been for *Saturday Night Fever*. Whereas producer Stigwood used the Bee Gees' soundtrack to market the film—capitalizing on the group's comeback success of the previous year with *Children of the World*, a platinum album in 1976—in the case of *Dirty Dancing*, it was the movie that sold the music. Following the pattern set by *Saturday Night Fever*, the Bill Medley and Jennifer Warnes' duet "(I've Had) The Time of My Life" was released in June 1987, with the expectation that the film's release would be boosted by a hit single. But the single did not move up the charts until after *Dirty Dancing* was finally released in late August. As a consequence of the single's poor reception, RCA was taken by surprise when the film opened and moviegoers rushed to purchase the soundtrack album. The label, hoping to sell perhaps 300,000 to 500,000 units, had pressed only 50,000 initially; the limited supply caused "stock problems all across the country."[19] As one Chicago retailer commented in regard to the way demand for the album outstripped availability, "When you see a [soundtrack] record happen before the label knows it, you know it had to be the movie."[20] The *Dirty Dancing* album sold a million copies within five weeks of the film's release, reaching 3x multi-platinum by the end of 1987 and 10x multi-platinum by the end of 1988.[21] Retailers noted the soundtrack's broad following, which encompassed "lots of 12-to 15-year-old kids and lots of 40-plus adults." They also noted, perhaps not surprisingly, that, among the younger buyers at least, females predominated, or guys "buying for a girl."[22]

The reason for the album's cross-generational appeal seems clear. In its use of late-1950s and early-1960s pop/R&B crossover hits, it continued a baby-boomer nostalgia trend that began in the 1970s with films such as *American Graffiti* (George Lucas, 1973) and continued into the 1980s with *The Big Chill* (Lawrence Kasdan, 1983). But in contrast to the megastars that populated *The Big Chill* soundtrack, *Dirty Dancing* used hits by lesser-known acts and "one hit wonders" such as Mickey & Sylvia's "Love is Strange" (1956), Maurice Williams and The Zodiacs' "Stay" (1961), and Bruce Channel's "Hey! Baby" (1961). But the most innovative quality of the soundtrack was its mix of old and new. "I don't believe that anyone had the chutzpah to mix 31 years of music on a soundtrack quite the way we decided to do it," said the executive producer of the album, Jimmy Ienner. "It was an experiment, with the music designed to match the personalities of the characters. Johnny the hero's music tended more toward sexy soul, while Baby's music which was more pop and Latin I would call 'white bread.'"[23]

In addition to the way the film soundtrack followed—and modified—the nostalgia trend, the particular musical choices also reflected the highly personal origins of the film and its character as an exercise in music-driven memory and fantasy. Just as George Lucas had done with the *American Graffiti* script before her, Bergstein drafted scenes while listening to her personal record collection: "Music is what I started with before I wrote," she says. "I went to my old 33s and 45s and I put together the track of all the songs . . . and dreamed my way through it and wrote against it."[24] But, while Lucas claims that with *American Graffiti* he "could take almost any song and put it on almost any scene and it would work . . . they just sort of meshed, no matter how you threw them together," Bergstein, by contrast, emphasizes the specificity of her musical choices in terms of rhythm, melody, and meaning: "If you have written a scene . . . and always imagined it in your heart and soul to that [song] it is just not going to work when you do something else."[25] In these terms, the film/music synergies that *Dirty Dancing* made so profitable can be understood not merely as an industrial strategy but likewise as a particular method of audiovisual storytelling in which dialogue and mise-en-scène are fully synthesized with pre-recorded popular music. Rob Buziak, president of RCA, notes the importance of an "emotional link" between music and other filmic elements, saying, you "can't just wallpaper a film with songs—there has to be some connection."[26] That the *Dirty Dancing* soundtrack was—and is—successful in these terms is demonstrated by its extraordinary sales record, and also by the level of demand for a follow-up to the first soundtrack album. Ienner reported receiving "tons of requests" from fans wanting the music not included in the first album and concluded that, in regard to the success of the film, the soundtrack, and its sequel, *More Dirty Dancing*, they had "simply hit an emotional chord": the *Dirty Dancing* franchise was successful because the "music, the dance, and the fantasy all worked."[27]

(Re)Living the Dream: The *Dirty Dancing* Franchise Continues

Dirty Dancing continued to work for its audiences. In February 1988, while the film was still playing in hundreds of theaters in the US, its videocassette became the "most rented tape in the nation" and sold more than 375,000 units by the first week of March.[28] The total revenue from the US video release was $40 million by the end of 1988.[29] In June 1990, the *Wall Street Journal* ranked *Dirty Dancing* third on its list of "All-Time Top Rental Titles," with 62.6 million rentals; and, as of 1997, videotapes of the film were still selling "about 40,000 copies a month."[30]

Prompted by the continued fervor of *Dirty Dancing* fans, in the summer of 1988, concert promoter David Fishof launched *Dirty Dancing: the Concert Tour* in North America, with a troupe of twenty Dirty Dancers, including four of the original cast, as well as musical performers Bill Medley, Eric Carmen, Merry Clayton, and the newly reunited Contours. The tour kicked off in May on Memorial Day weekend in the Catskill Mountains of New York and played "its swan song" at the Minnesota State Fair in September 1988.[31] To capitalize on the global popularity of the film, after the US tour the show split into two troupes, one of which headed for Australia, the other to Europe, Japan, and Mexico. The tour was promoted by Rowe's video jukeboxes in cooperation with RCA, Rowe's airing the four *Dirty Dancing* videos along with local concert tour information; music channel VH-1 also promoted the "family-oriented" tour by featuring the *Dirty Dancing* videos and a vintage clip of the Four Seasons' "Big Girls Don't Cry" on high rotation throughout the summer of 1988.[32]

The show was non-narrative, a musical revue designed to be "one big dance party," during which a few concert-goers were always invited onstage to dance with the troupe.[33] It included the music from the *Dirty Dancing* and *More Dirty Dancing* albums, plus additional songs. Referencing the film's resort setting, its master of ceremonies—in the manner of Kellerman's social director—used a megaphone to announce the acts, which were loosely structured around key scenes from the film: Baby learning the mambo, Baby mastering a lift. It was a show that—according to its performers and promoters—drew a multi-generational audience: "Mothers go to the concerts with their daughters," Fishof observed, "but the daughters sit in the front row and the mothers sit in the back." Bill Medley summed up the mix, saying, "It's our music, but it's the kids' movie."[34] According to Fishof, it was a lucrative show, the US leg alone generating ticket sales of $30 million by August 1988.[35] But many reviews were lukewarm at best: The *New York Times* dismissed its sold-out Radio City Music Hall appearances as a "dispirited exercise in quick exploitation."[36] Even those reviewers who offered more positive responses tended to regard the enthusiasm of its audiences with an air of bemusement: "How much mileage can you get out of strutting, bumping, and grinding?"[37]

Plenty, apparently—provided that it offers audiences the opportunity to relive their pleasure in the original film and its music. When Vestron announced the simultaneous release of the video and LP of "*Dirty Dancing*: Live in Concert" just in time for Christmas 1988, the company estimated the total of "consumer expenditures" for the entire franchise to be more than $400 million to date.[38] The concert tour, for all the lukewarm or negative reviews it garnered, appeared to work for its audiences, who, according to all accounts, were highly enthusiastic and interactive. In these terms, the tour's success perhaps had less to do with its particular quality of spectacle or performance than the way it acknowledged and provided the opportunity to celebrate shared enthusiasm for the film, its music, and dance. By contrast, attempts to explore further or expand the world of *Dirty Dancing* in the same way as the *Star Wars* franchise, by pushing the temporal and spatial boundaries of its fictional universe, were not so successful.

For instance, the popularity of the *Dirty Dancing* film, music, and tour encouraged Vestron Television to launch a TV series; but the half-hour romantic comedy aimed at young audiences was short-lived. First aired on Saturday 29, October 1988 at 8pm on CBS, the series' title sequence recalls the opening of the film in its use of black and white images of dancers; over these images, the hit single "(I've Had) The Time of My Life" plays as its theme music. The setting of the series is the same as that of the film—a resort called Kellerman's—with some changes in the characters and a whole new cast: "Baby" Kellerman (Melora Hardin) is the daughter of its owner Max (McLean Stevenson); she falls for fresh-faced "bad boy" dance instructor Johnny Castle (Patrick Cassidy). The storylines focused on the tension between "two headstrong young people from different backgrounds who work together" and offered plenty of opportunities for dances created by original *Dirty Dancing* choreographer, Kenny Ortega.[39] Despite its efforts to be true to the original premise while expanding its fiction, the series dropped steadily in the ratings and was canceled in January 1989.

There was a similarly lackluster outcome for the film sequel to *Dirty Dancing*. The possibility of a sequel was under discussion as early as 1988 and continued as the rights to *Dirty Dancing* passed from company to company during a series of mergers and takeovers in the 1990s and 2000s: Vestron Pictures' failure led to its takeover by LIVE Entertainment in 1991, a production and distribution company renamed Artisan Entertainment in 1998; Artisan, after some years of expansion, was acquired by Lions Gate (now commonly called Lionsgate) in 2003. As of 1997, there had been numerous scripts, all of which, according to Patrick Swayze, managed to "miss the boat entirely."[40] In 2004, Lionsgate finally released *Dirty Dancing 2: Havana Nights* (Guy Ferland). Rather than a conventional prequel or sequel, *Havana Nights* re-located the *Dirty Dancing* story to a different time and place. Like *Dirty Dancing*, it is a semi-autobiographical tale, based on the story of Hollywood choreographer JoAnn Jansen, the film's co-producer. *Havana Nights* also resembles *Dirty Dancing* in its temporal location on the cusp of major social and political change. When Jansen was in her teens in 1958, she moved from St. Louis to Havana and fell for a Cuban working at the hotel where she lived with her parents. Her romance ended when she and her family fled Cuba in the wake of revolution.[41] Made for what in 2004 was a relatively modest budget of $25 million, the film is painstakingly accurate in its 1950s costumes and settings, while its music, like that of *Dirty Dancing*, blends the old and the anachronistically new. After brainy Katey Miller (Romola Garai) falls for charming young waiter Javier (Diego Luna), they dance to a contemporary mix of hip-hop and salsa against the backdrop of vintage Havana settings. Despite the parallels between *Havana Nights* and *Dirty Dancing*—including a cameo by Patrick Swayze as a dance teacher—the film's worldwide box office gross was less than $28 million.[42]

Lionsgate's more recent attempts at *Dirty Dancing*-centered original television programming for US and UK markets fared somewhat better. In 2006, Lionsgate Television announced a new, eight-episode reality show called *Dirty Dancing: Live the Dream*, to air on American cable channel WEtv. Set in a lodge-style resort, the series featured thirty young women competing for the chance to perform onstage, and focused on personal interactions between them and their six male dance instructors; each contestant had to persuade her teacher—and the judges—that she was good enough to continue. While the US version of the reality program only ran one season, the UK version, *Dirty Dancing: The Time of Your Life*, launched in conjunction with the twentieth anniversary of *Dirty Dancing* and featuring a somewhat different format, was more successful and continued for a second series in 2008. The UK version featured sixteen contestants, eight men and eight women, who auditioned for the roles. While the US series focused on the competitive spirit of its female contestants, this version endeavored to play on the relationship between Baby and Johnny by matching eight novice females with eight experienced male dancers. The series was filmed at Mountain Lake in Virginia, and the original assistant choreographer on *Dirty Dancing*, Miranda Garrison, was a judge.[43]

Considering the relative success—and failure—of these attempts to expand or further explore the world of *Dirty Dancing*, it appears that its franchise, unlike those blockbuster franchises like *Star Wars*, is only profitable to the extent that it works on principles of repetition and proximity, allowing fans to reengage with or get closer to the film, its music, and its dance. In these terms, growth patterns of the franchise support the truth of what RCA president Bob Buziak identified as the cause of *Dirty Dancing*'s initial triumph: its "emotional windows" that made people want to "relive the movie with the music."[44] Viewed in these terms, even the "garish, jerry-built revue" that was *Dirty Dancing: The Concert Tour* of 1988 offered this opportunity to its audiences,[45] in a way that the various television shows and the attempted film remake did not.

In contrast to these less successful attempts to expand the franchise in new narrative directions, the original film continued to make money in new formats, as it passed the milestones of its tenth and twentieth anniversaries. Timed to coincide with its twenty-five-city theatrical rerelease, LIVE Entertainment released *Dirty Dancing* on DVD for the first time in 1997. In 2004, Lionsgate released the *Ultimate Dirty Dancing* DVD along with the newly-remastered *Ultimate Dirty Dancing* soundtrack as lead-ins to the theatrical release of *Havana*

Nights.[46] While *Havana Nights* was not a notable success, both DVD versions of the film and the soundtrack rerelease were. The *Ultimate Dirty Dancing* soundtrack "zapped to the top of the chart as soon as it was released in April and sold more than 600,000 copies."[47] In 2006, it went 2x platinum, and in 2010 it was still in the top twenty—ranked eleventh—for soundtrack compilation albums.[48] As for the film on DVD, in 2005, John Feltheimer, head of Lionsgate Entertainment, told his investors that the studio still shipped approximately 110,000 copies of *Dirty Dancing* to retailers each month; and, as of 2007, when the new *Dirty Dancing: 20th Anniversary Edition* DVD was released, more than 10 million DVD copies of *Dirty Dancing* had been sold in total.[49]

Since the lackluster showing of *Havana Nights*, Lionsgate has engaged in a variety of projects designed to capitalize upon the steady popularity of the original 1987 film and its music, including a range of merchandise. In 2006, a line of retro 1980s-style t-shirts was aimed, according to *Women's Wear Daily*, at the "fanatical and the fashionable alike."[50] In 2007, Codemasters released the *Dirty Dancing* video game. In 2008, the *Dirty Dancing: Official Dance Workout* DVD gave fans the opportunity to combine dancercise with the music and moves from the film, to "Get fit and have the time of your life!"[51] And, also in 2008, Lionsgate licensed a line of baby apparel from Urban Smalls emblazoned with the now iconic quote, "Nobody puts Baby in a corner."[52] But by far the most significant development in the *Dirty Dancing* franchise in the twenty-first century has been the global success of *Dirty Dancing: The Classic Story on Stage*, which had its world premiere in Sydney in 2004.

With *Dirty Dancing: The Classic Story on Stage*, the franchise found a new way to address the desires of its audience. Eleanor Bergstein's analysis of the *Dirty Dancing* fans who watch the film "over and over and over" offers insight into the popularity of the stage production, as well as the shape taken by the franchise as a whole. She says, "I began to believe that they were not watching because they wanted to look at [the film] so much as they ... wanted to be there while the story was happening." As audiences of the stage production, fans are given the opportunity to be "more present," as Bergstein puts it, for the fiction, rather than taking the voyeuristic role assigned to the film spectator.[53] A show that literally has fans dancing in the aisles, *Dirty Dancing: The Classic Story on Stage* was sold out in Australia and Germany, and its run in London's West End broke previous records for live theater box office. At its North American premiere in Toronto, it broke records again, selling $1.9 million in tickets on the first day.[54] Its success has had follow-up effects for ancillary revenue. For instance, following the London success of the stage production in 2008, 400,000 units of the *Dirty Dancing: The Ultimate Girls' Night In Collector's Edition* DVD were sold, "the biggest-selling special edition in UK's history."[55] More pertinently, the continued success of *Dirty Dancing: The Classic Story on Stage* confirms the remarkable longevity of the franchise—a franchise that is effectively made up of a single film and its music.

Conclusion

As the first official spin-off in the *Star Wars* franchise—the disastrous *Star Wars Holiday Special* that aired on CBS in 1978—made clear decades ago, even the most lucrative media franchises are somewhat hit-or-miss in their development. In the case of *Dirty Dancing*, the pattern of its hits and misses is evocative. Fans of the film have embraced numerous rereleases of both the film and soundtrack and their adaptation from screen to stage, but have resisted any attempt to substantively re-formulate or expand upon the original film. Less-than-successful attempts to replicate the film's success—by retelling it in a different time and place, by transplanting its gender dynamic and focus on dance to different generic contexts—point to there being something else at work in the original film than its much-commented-upon formulaic qualities. So, at the same time the shape of the *Dirty Dancing* franchise says a good deal about the industrial context that produced it, it also reflects—and raises questions about— the nature of the entertainment it offers and the audience it attracts. In its particular mix of music and dance, its narrative focus on the creation of the romantic couple via wish-fulfilment scenarios where an audience member becomes a performer, it taps into many of the same pleasures long provided by the Hollywood musical. And its eclectic mix of 1950s, 1960s, and 1980s pop offers contemporary viewers multiple layers of musical nostalgia. But perhaps most significant is its ability to use its specific mix of music and dance to strike an emotional chord, particularly—but not exclusively—with its female audiences. In these terms, the film's ongoing popularity and cultural relevance point to the idea that "girls' dreams" do have a place in American cinema, especially when they can also form the basis for franchised entertainment.

Notes

1. Mountain Lake Hotel is located in Pembroke, Virginia (http://www.mountainlakehotel.com); the *Dirty Dancing* board game is produced by University Games Corporation (http://ugames.com/ugitem.asp?itemno=01794).
2. JEM sportswear's Cold Crush by Awake brand designed the t-shirts, plus a line of sleepwear to celebrate the film's 20th anniversary; their availability online and at Target stores was timed to coincide with the film's theatrical re-release in May 2007. "Lionsgate and National CineMedia's Fathom to Bring Baby Out of the Corner and Back Onto the Big Screen" (http://www.prnewswire.com/news-releases/lionsgate-and-national-cinemedias-fathom-to-bring-baby-out-of-the-corner-and-back-onto-the-big-screen-to-celebrate-20-years-of-dirty-dancing-58678637.html).
3. Ken Terry, "'Dirty Dancing': Giant Killer Still Has Legs," *Billboard*, January 16, 1988, 3.
4. Thomas Schatz, "The Return of the Hollywood Studio System," in *Conglomerates in the Media.*, ed. Eric Barnouw et al. (New York: The New Press, 1997), 73-106.
5. Jason Scott, "The Character-Oriented Franchise: Promotion and Exploitation of Pre-sold Characters in American Film, 1913-1950," in *Cultural Borrowings: Appropriation, Reworking, Transformation*, ed. Iain Robert Smith (Nottingham: *Scope: An Online Journal of Film and Television Studies*, 2009). http://www.scope.nottingham.ac.uk/cultborr/Cult_borr_ebook.pdf#page=46. Accessed on October 1, 2011.
6. http://www.boxofficemojo.com/alltime/adjusted.htm. Accessed on October 1, 2011.
7. Thomas Schatz, 'The New Hollywood,' in *Film Theory Goes to the Movies*, ed. Jim Collins et. al. (New York: Routledge, 1993), 9, 10.
8. A term Jack Valenti uses to describe a film that acts as a "platform to other markets." Quoted in Noel King, "'The Last Good Time We Ever Had': Remembering the New Hollywood Cinema," in *The Last Great American Picture Show: New Hollywood Cinema in the 1970s*, ed. Alexander Horwath et. al. (Amsterdam: Amsterdam University Press, 2004), 28.
9. R. Serge Denisoff and William D. Romanowski, *Risky Business: Rock in Film* (New Brunswick, NJ: Transaction Publishers, 1991), 222.
10. Stephen Prince, *A New Pot of Gold: Hollywood Under the Electronic Rainbow, 1980-1989* (Berkeley: University of California Press, 2000), 2, 3.
11. Prince, *Pot of Gold*, 97.
12. Barbara Stones, "Modern Times," in *Moviegoing in America: A Sourcebook in the History of Film Exhibition*, ed. Gregory Albert Waller (Malden, MA: Blackwell, 2002), 297.

13 Richard Zoglin, "Show Business: Hollywood Catches the Rock Beat," *Time*, March 24, 1984, at http://www.time.com/time/magazine/article/0,9171, 921657,00.html. Accessed on October 1, 2011.

14 David Denby, "The Princess and the Peon," *New York* magazine, September 7, 1987, 60.

15 For details of U.S. and international box office, see http://www.imdb.com/ title/tt0092890/business and http://www.boxofficemojo.com/movies/?id= dirtydancing.htm. Accessed on October 1, 2011. Editors' note: see also Wasser's essay in this volume.

16 R. Serge Denisoff and George Plasketes, "Synergy in 1980s Film and Music: Formula for Success or Industry Mythology?," *Film History* 4.3 (1990): 257.

17 Paul Grein, "1987—The Year in Music & Video," *Billboard*, December 26, 1987, Y-15.

18 Jon Bowermaster, "The 'Dirty Dancing' Music Man," *Premiere*, August 1988, 90.

19 Bowermaster, "Music Man," 92.

20 Terry, "Giant Killer," 67.

21 See Bowermater, "Music Man," 92; and Recording Industry Association of America database http://www.riaa.com/goldandplatinumdata.php?content _selector=gold-platinum-searchable-database. Accessed on October 1, 2011.

22 Terry, "Giant Killer," 67.

23 Stephen Holden, "The Pop Life," *New York Times*, December 9, 1987, C33.

24 *Dirty Dancing* commentary, *20th Anniversary Edition Dirty Dancing*, dir. Emile Ardolino, 1987 (Lionsgate DVD, 2007, Region 4).

25 See George Lucas, *George Lucas Interviews*, ed. Sally Kline (Jackson, MS: University Press Mississippi, 1999), 40; and Eleanor Bergstein, DVD commentary.

26 Bowermaster, "Music Man," 92.

27 See Bruce Haring, "RCA Releases 'More Dirty Dancing' Demand Seen for 2nd Soundtrack," *Billboard*, March 12, 1988, 67; and Bowermaster, "Music Man," 92.

28 See Bruce Westbrook, "'Dirty Dancing' Still a Hit on Video and in Theaters," *Houston Chronicle*, February 9, 1988, http://search.proquest.com.libraryproxy .griffith.edu.au/docview/295575442?accountid=14543v. Accessed on October 1, 2011; and Laura Landro, "Vestron Inc. Posts $14.4 Million Loss for Fourth Quarter," *Wall Street Journal*, March 8, 1988, 40.

29 Frederick Wasser, *Veni, Vidi, Video: The Hollywood Empire and the VCR* (Austin: University of Texas Press, 2001), 174.

30 See Richard Turner, "Movie Studios Produce Uneven Picture with Efforts to Win More Video Buyers," *Wall Street Journal*, June 6, 1990, B1; and Ann Kolson, "Fairy Tale Without An Ending," *New York Times*, August 17, 1997, 2: 11.

31 Jon Bream, "'Dirty Dancing' Tour Ends on a High Note," *Star Tribune*, September 5, 1988, 3.

32 See Denisoff and Romanowski, *Risky*, 272; and Peter Malbin, "Talent in Action: *Dirty Dancing*—The Concert Tour," *Billboard*, July 16, 1988, 28.

33 See Jim Bessman, "Medley, Carmen Set for Summer—*Dirty Dancing* Tour To Roll," *Billboard*, April 30, 1988, 19, 31; and John Horn, "'Dirty Dancing' the

Tour," *Orange County Register,* June 19, 1988, http://search.proquest.com.libraryproxy.griffith.edu.au/docview/272159610?accountid=14543. Accessed on October 1, 2011.

34 See Susan Spillman, "Ageless Amusement: Family Fun Isn't Just For Kids Anymore," *USA Today,* August 1, 1988, http://search.proquest.com.libraryproxy.griffith.edu.au/docview/306099077?accountid=14543. Accessed on October 1, 2011; and Horn, "Tour."

35 Guy Aoki, "How Fishof Became Prime Chaperon for 'Dirty Dancing' Tour," *Los Angeles Times,* August 12, 1988, http://articles.latimes.com/1988-08-12/entertainment/ca-357_1_dirty-dancing. Accessed on October 1, 2011.

36 See Stephen Holden, "Starless 'Dirty Dancing,'" *New York Times,* July 19, 1988, http://www.nytimes.com/1988/06/19/arts/reviews-music-starless-dirty-dancing.html?scp=1&sq=&st=nyt. Accessed on October 1, 2011; and Tama Janowitz, "What the Hell is a *Dirty Dancing Concert Tour,*" *Spin,* August 1988, 27–28.

37 David Stearns, "'Dirty' Tour: Not Quite the Time of Your Life," *USA Today,* June 16, 1988, 4.

38 Tom Spain, "Pepsi's Paramount Parade," *The Washington Post,* December 8, 1988, http://search.proquest.com.libraryproxy.griffith.edu.au/docview/307127342?accountid=14543. Accessed on October 1, 2011.

39 John Carmody, "The TV Column," *The Washington Post,* May 27, 1988, http://search.proquest.com.libraryproxy.griffith.edu.au/docview/306992508?accountid=14543. Accessed on October 1, 2011.

40 Kolson, "Fairy Tale," 18.

41 Valerie Gladstone, "Dance—The Catskills Meet Castro: 'Dirty Dancing' in Cuba," *New York Times,* February 22, 2004, 2, 31.

42 http://boxofficemojo.com/movies/?id=dirtydancing2.htm. Accessed on October 1, 2011.

43 See "Q4 2006 Lionsgate Entertainment Earnings Conference Call," *Fair Disclosure Wire,* June 15, 2006, http://search.proquest.com.libraryproxy.griffith.edu.au/abicomplete/docview/466911457/130551C689D7D39E1EC/16?accountid=14543. Accessed on October 1, 2011; Lindsay Key, "Highlights from the 'Dirty Dancing' Reality Show," *The Roanoke Times,* November 27, 2007, http://www.roanoke.com/extra/wb/140043. Accessed on October 1, 2011; and Lindsay Key, "British Reality TV Series Returns to Mountain Lake," *McClatchy-Tribune Business News,* May 31, 2008, http://search.proquest.com.libraryproxy.griffith.edu.au/docview/465013994?accountid=14543. Accessed on October 1, 2011.

44 Jean Rosenbluth, "Spotlight: Soundtracks," *Billboard,* July 16, 1988, S1.

45 Holden, "Starless."

46 Daniel Frankel, "Musical Accompaniment for Two Artisan Special Editions," *Video Business,* November 3, 2003, http://search.proquest.com.libraryproxy.griffith.edu.au/docview/223903332?accountid=14543. Accessed on October 1, 2011.

47 Alan Jones, "Charts 2004—Year-End Charts: Compilations," *Music Week,* January 22, 2005, 22, http://search.proquest.com.libraryproxy.griffith.edu

.au/abicomplete/docview/232248183/1305924A5151DF3AA96/24?accoun tid=14543. Accessed on October 1, 2011.
48 See "Upfront: BPI Awards," *Music Week*, November 4, 2006, 23, http://search.proquest.com.libraryproxy.griffith.edu.au/abicomplete/docview/232159057/1305924A5151DF3AA96/7?accountid=14543. Accessed on October 1, 2011; and Alan Jones, "Charts Noughties: The Rise and Fall," *Music Week*, January 30, 2010, 18.
49 See Joshua Chaffin, "There Is Gold in the Silver Screen's Archives," *Financial Times*, April 5, 2005, 14; and Emiliana Sandoval, "Five Things About 'Dirty Dancing,'" *McClatchy-Tribune Business News*, April 26, 2007, http://search.proquest.com.libraryproxy.griffith.edu.au/docview/464267112?accountid=14543. Accessed on October 1, 2011.
50 Elizabeth Thurman, "Jean Therapy: Clean Feminine Looks In Soft Fabrics Replace Denim as the Dominant Trend in the Market," *Women's Wear Daily*, August 14, 2006, 12.
51 See http://dirtydancingworkout.com. Accessed on October 1, 2011.
52 "Urban Smalls Baby Apparel Lands Famous *Dirty Dancing* Quote," *Global License*, September 26, 2008, http://www.licensemag.com/licensemag/Entertainment/Urban-Smalls-Baby-Apparel-Lands-Famous-iDirty-Danc/ArticleStandard/Article/detail/553706. Accessed on October 1, 2011.
53 See DVD commentary, "Special Features," 9; and "The Classic Story on Stage," Eleanor Bergstein interview (see also note 24).
54 See Meredith Goldstein, "The Audience Has Been Ready for Years—Tickets Fly for 'Dirty Dancing' On Stage," *Boston Globe*, January 29, 2009, http://search.proquest.com.libraryproxy.griffith.edu.au/docview/405143096/130595804AA5B71F05/2?accountid=14543. Accessed on October 1, 2011; and Brian Johnson, "'Dirty Dancing' Just Got Dirtier," *Maclean's*, May 21, 2007, 72.
55 "Event Brief of Q3: 2008 Lions Gate Entertainment Earnings Conference Call—Final," *Fair Disclosure Wire*, February 12, 2008, http://search.proquest.com.libraryproxy.griffith.edu.au/docview/466227621?accountid=14543. Accessed on October 1, 2011.

15 FROM SCREEN TO STAGE: *DIRTY DANCING* LIVE

MILLIE TAYLOR

I saw the live stage show based on the film of *Dirty Dancing* on a Saturday in May 2010 and again in April 2011. It had opened in Australia in 2004 and transferred to London's West End in 2006. On the occasions I saw the show the theater was filled with a rapturous audience consisting predominantly of women and including a number of bachelorette parties. The audience was lively, cheerful, and often vocal in its appreciation of the performance in general, but particularly of the dancing bodies and any sensual or sexual moments. It felt like a party, and one in which the audience was eager to participate; many joined in with the words of famous lines that all appeared to know, especially "Nobody puts Baby in a corner." But why were we all paying West End prices to attend that performance when the film is readily available and very well known? The reviews of the London show address the key themes that will be explored in this chapter: the popularity of a reproduction of the film onstage, despite the notable absence of its stars; the deliberate attempt to mimic the film and so draw on nostalgic associations; the double-reading of the film through the theatrical performance; the opportunity to feel the immediacy and danger of live dance performance; and the energy generated as performers and audiences are affected by each others' participation in the event.

The *Mail Online* records that in November 2006, "DD is a sellout, even though this is a weekday matinee. I judge the audience is

95 percent female and 5 percent men, who are either manacled to their women or here by mistake."¹ The company manager reported to that same reviewer that "the ladies arrive, buy their merchandise ... and by the time they are in the auditorium they are wearing it." In this respect the show might be considered comparable to the cult musical *The Rocky Horror Show*, for which audiences arrive dressed in the costumes of their favorite characters, join in with lines that they know from the film version, and sing and dance to their favorite numbers. As the *Mail Online* reviewer notes—though she doesn't enjoy the evening—"And we scream. We scream at these people in a fictional hotel in a fictional past. We scream at Johnny. We scream at the watermelon."²

There is no doubt the show is extremely popular. Many of the reviewers acknowledge that this musical took a record-breaking amount in advance ticket sales. On April 13, 2006, it had taken more than £3m in advance sales³; on October 25, 2006, when it opened, Lyn Gardner reported a £12m advance,⁴ which Dominic Cavendish related to a staggering 260,000 tickets sold before opening night⁵; and, by November 1, 2006, the *Mail Online* reported that the box office had "already taken £15 million." So, as Dominic Cavendish concluded, "You can accuse director James Powell of a lack of imagination or just providing great customer service."⁶

The story of *Dirty Dancing* allows people to connect to it and respond in personal ways. In many respects the story is uplifting and transformational. It tells of a rite of passage to adulthood with which many people can identify, and in this way it is like a fairy story in which the untried youngster enters new territory (the woods of fairy tales equates to the staff camp at Kellerman's). There Baby is tested; she triumphs and returns to a new phase of life—dancing into adulthood. Like a fairy story, then, it envisages the transformational moment that can be recreated and revisited throughout life. This is what the *Mail Online* reviewer perceived after interviewing a number of audience members about why they were at the stage show. She concluded that "It's all their teenage fairy tales on a stage and on a T-shirt—The Search for Love, Duckling into Swan, Forsaking Father for Lover, Growing Up and The Eternal Summer of Love. DD is another chapter in the search for the idealised past that never was; a curtsy to the love that never happened but should have, could have."⁷

From Screen to Stage: Dirty Dancing Live   283

The nostalgic feel is also stressed by Alastair Macaulay, writing in the *Financial Times*, who discusses the show as a dance metaphor for sex: "Dirty-type dancing is contrasted with vivid accounts of rumba, fox-trot, quickstep, tango, and waltz—all patently the sexually romantic dances of yesteryear."[8] Emma Brockes, writing in the *Guardian*, describes how the stage show calls up a series of nostalgic recreations: of the film (made in 1987); of the era when the film was set (1963); and of the time when each audience member first saw the film. "In its latest incarnation as a stage show, it will therefore benefit from a double-whammy of nostalgia: for the age of innocence in which it takes place, and for the state of innocence in which most people first saw it, as children."[9] A narrative of utopian transformation and nostalgia is clearly present as much in the stage show as in the film it evokes, but the double-reading of the film through the live experience of the stage show is one of the features that I will return to below.

The attempt to recreate the film as accurately as possible is one of the main sources of disquiet for the reviewers. Lyn Gardner in the *Guardian* suggests that audiences "might not be disappointed if what they are looking for is a straightforward frame-by-frame recreation of the movie experience, because that is pretty well what is on offer here in an evening which is less full-blown musical and more a play with a musical soundtrack."[10] Charles Spencer in the *Telegraph* sums up his experience of a later recasting of the show as follows: "There's no mistaking the energy and talent on stage, but the show so slavishly attempts to recreate the film that it never establishes a theatrical life and rhythm of its own."[11] Dominic Cavendish records that the appeal might not reach his male psyche, but "whatever cynical metropolitan males may think of it, the producers have made sure not to risk losing that army of ardent supporters: in all key respects, the stage version is a carbon-copy of the film."[12] The writer, Eleanor Bergstein, who adapted her own screenplay for the stage, argues that "The show has everything from the film and more."[13] A contextual civil rights subplot is foregrounded in the stage show, though it still feels like an unimportant aside. As Alastair Macaulay comments, "we can believe here that DD is part of what expands the consciousness of our serious 17-year-old heroine, Baby, along with news of Martin Luther King."[14]

One of the few differences from the film is that many of the songs are sung live. Also, the audience is addressed directly by singers and by Kellerman's entertainment manager, who encourages them to join in with games, though there is no real interaction. For the most part, however, as identified by the reviewers, the look of the stage show aims to imitate the film. The set incorporates a revolving platform so that the many short scenes of the film can transform fluidly into each other. The design incorporates screens so that filmed backdrops can recreate the filmic imagery and (perhaps) reference the medium of the original. Film is used to create atmospheric background, to re-create outdoor scenes (the lake and the wheat field), and in dance scenes to increase the action and energy by doubling the number of dancers through projections immediately behind the dancers. In direction and design, in the costumes, the body language, the physicality, and the use of key scenes, this show is designed to be a reminder of the film. Scenes and sets such as dancing on the log, Baby dancing up the steps, the famous lift being practiced in the lake (created using lighting and a projection onto a gauze front-cloth through which the actors are lit), the huts, and the ballroom are all re-created to evoke a memory of the film.

So if we can all see the movie version as often as we want, and this is a faithful evocation of the film, why do audiences want to see the film re-created live onstage by different actors? What is the function of a stage version of a successful music/dance film?

Ghosting the Film

My experience of the live show, the comments of the reviewers above, and the comments from people sitting near me suggest that the live experience is not one that is separate from the filmed experience. Rather, the two are melded together in a complex blend in which the stage show is not always deemed successful. Nevertheless, audiences are not simply seeing the live show, but are enjoying a re-enactment of the film that allows them simultaneously to relive the film and playfully to acknowledge the differences. This is encouraged by scenic re-creation through the use of projection in the show, bringing the experience of film into the live performance, but mostly it is encouraged by the marked similarities in plot and script. There were cheers at particularly famous lines from the film; "Nobody puts Baby in a corner" brought the second-largest cheer of the evening. This was only exceeded by the moment the overhead lift was achieved and held, a feat that was greeted with cheering and rapturous applause.

The experience of watching a stage show made famous on film and consciously revisited onstage is one in which the viewer is conflating both the present experience and the past memory to create a new composite that is neither one nor the other, but both. The stage show is a blend of memory and experience that the audience creates. The layers of intertextual association and nostalgia generated as a result of the imagery or memory of the 1960s, the 1980s music and context for the film, subsequent viewings of the film, and the contagious experience of the live performance, create a reading that feeds into a new identification with the live performance.

Marvin Carlson argues that "every play is a memory play" because the relationships between theater and cultural memory are so deep,[15] and that "the dynamic of recycling is deeply embedded in the process of theatrical reception."[16] Within performance this may include quotation, reference to other works, or the presence of star performers, but it also includes the theater's, and particularly the musical theater's, re-use of familiar narrative materials. In this case, it is the coming-of-age love story, in which lovers from different sides of the tracks, established through their different musical and physical languages, come together through dancing together. So music and dance articulate similarity and difference in the narrative. These signs are understood, since theater encourages "a simultaneous experience of something previously experienced and of something being offered in the present that is both the same and different, which can only be fully appreciated by a kind of doubleness of perception in the audience."[17]

This is clearly the way in which audiences perceive the narrative. They know the story from the film, but also from other narratives through which the film narrative was always already familiar. And although Swayze and Grey are not present, there is a sense that audiences are almost in their presence through this evocation. Most importantly, Johnny and Baby are present. So there are degrees of familiarity and multiple nostalgic experiences alongside an immediate presence.

The ability of audiences to negotiate different realities has been explained recently in neuroscience as "conceptual blending." Gilles Fauconnier and Mark Turner demonstrate that all learning and thinking consists of blends of metaphors based on bodily experiences, which are continually blended together into an increasingly rich structure.[18] Bruce McConachie and Elizabeth Hart apply this work to theater when they argue that "actors engage in conceptual blending to play a role," and that actors and audiences "together create a fourth 'mental space,' which is distinct from the perception of themselves in real time-space."[19]

Within this fourth space, information from the inputs of the actors and spectators, along with generic and remembered information, are "blended together to create perceptions that are distinct from all the inputs."[20] Audiences select the blend of information they choose to construct into meaning, which will include different balances between awareness of narratives and meta-narratives, genre expectations, vocal stereotypes, other audience members, characters, and performers, and many other performances. In this case, the reading will contain both the film and live performances alongside many other intertextual associations. It will contain Jennifer Grey and Hannah Vassallo, Patrick Swayze and Johnny Wright, as well as Johnny Castle and Frances "Baby" Houseman.[21] While all performances invite spectators to move between various blends, all performances involve active cognition, and all stage performances involve spectator recognition of theatrical framing, this performance takes that to an extreme by the active evocation of the ghosted, absent other.

A cognitive approach suggests that, when presented with a network of spaces or images, the audience processes the images, maintaining a blend so that interpretation and response are playful and continually in flux. Amy Cook refers to Gilles Fauconnier to suggest that "while any particular blend might vary from individual to individual, the network of spaces prompted in a given situation is more powerful as a process in flux, a series of variables, than simply a final blend."[22] This might be interpreted in relation to *Dirty Dancing* to suggest that in the course of the performance the blend of images from film and live performance will continually alter the potential meanings of previously presented images. At the same time, the individual will continue to respond to the full range of images and materials, performances and atmospheres, blending them according to personal choice within context. Memories of naïve teenage foolishness and infatuation are incorporated, for example, in the watermelon moment. Furthermore, what blending theory suggests is that extraordinarily complex information is assimilated using more of the brain but no more time. It is possible that some people might find that the more textured performance, that consciously taps into layers of memory and experience, that activates more parts of the brain and increases the intensity of the brain activity, could also produce a greater sense of pleasure.

Long before the recent discoveries in neuroscience, Roland Barthes theorized in relation to language that "the logic regulating a text is not comprehensive ... but metonymic; the activity of associations, contiguities, carryings-over coincides with a liberation of symbolic energy."[23] The text is plural, not simply in that it has several meanings, but in that it is irreducible, an explosion or dissemination. He suggests that "the plural of the Text depends ... not on the ambiguity of its contents but on what might be called the *stereographic plurality* of its weave of signifiers." This plurality is "woven entirely with citations, references, echoes, cultural languages ... which cut across it through and through in a vast stereophony."[24] He suggests that such a text is playful, and that the reader plays twice over in reproducing it both as an inner mimesis and in the musical sense of playing.[25] Such a text, he argues, is "bound to *jouissance,* that is to a pleasure without separation.... [T]he text is that space where no language has a hold over any other, where language circulates."[26]

Barthes' theorizing refers only to language and not to performance; nevertheless, it is possible that he and others have predicted in theory processes that have now been observed in scientific experiments. The idea of a circularity of language can be read alongside the idea of a playful performance text whose images and meanings actively recall earlier performances. This process suggests that the way meanings are interpreted in a performance can be plural and simultaneous rather than individual and separate, and that the process of recognizing and assimilating this plurality can be pleasurable and playful.

The result of this multiplicity is that audiences are aware simultaneously of the plot, the characters with whom they might empathize, the performers in their roles, the theater space, and the references to political, social, or entertaining identities and realities. So the performance of *Dirty Dancing* adds layers to the film text that result from the identities of performers and the theatricality of performance.

Experiencing the Performance

The theatrical performance is not simply a blending of the memory of the film with the live performance and other nostalgic moments, however. It is also a living event in which a narrative is re-created. This is experienced by the audience, whose empathy is activated within the mirror neuron system. The perception of music, dance, and other behaviors, intentions, or emotions is conducted through an embodied response to those gestures in which the perceiver's brain mirrors the movements or gestures of the performer. This is the result of the activation of the mirror neuron system (MNS) in the pre-motor cortex of the brain through which audiences' brains mirror the gestural activities they observe.[27] Such mirroring derives from basic learning instincts; children learn through imitation and mirroring, and most early learning relies on copying.[28] This remains a feature of skills acquisition in humans throughout our lives.

Physical gestures are related to emotions and feelings through the connections of mind and body.[29] Observed emotions or physical actions are physically embodied in the observer through the MNS. These two findings, the combination of relationship of gesture to emotion and its physical embodiment in observers, when taken together suggest something for audiences. Simply observing physical gestures that associate to emotions (as the physical act of crying might be associated with sadness) also activates in the observer both the physical gesture and the emotions and memories attached to that physicality. Audiences can perceive, and, in fact, feel intended emotions, and thus extrapolate meaning.[30] The emotional understanding is interpreted and responded to in a way appropriate to the cultural environment, but every time a gesture activates the brain and a similar response is generated the stronger the connection becomes—so repetition strengthens the emotional response.[31] Through this process, audiences rehearse multiple roles because they can, for the short time of the performance, experience the identity of the characters.[32] So, as almost suggested by the *Mail Online* reviewer, for the time of the performance the audience is experiencing what it is like to be Johnny and Baby, and is rehearsing or revisiting the experience of falling in love.

Bruce McConachie concludes that in the theater, where empathy is encouraged, "imitation and embodiment tend to be heightened."[33]

The film is likely to activate the same empathetic responses through observation of acted emotions, but the live performance has a much greater degree of closeness to those emotions as a result of physical presence, and it draws on the memory of the emotions attached to the film, thus doubling the emotional attachment. In addition, audience members respond to each others' responses, and that collective response feeds back to the stage in a circular contagion. This is not an absolute cause and effect, but cultural factors set up pre-conditions for a series of responses that audience members enact. Thus, in watching the film audiences might experience moments of dance, music, and narrative transformation and feel the emotional presence of other audience members. In the theater, those resonances and identifications are amplified and fed back by the contagion of the shared experience with the performers and the circularity of response between audience and performers.

Musical theater inspires and encourages participation from audiences to a degree that is rare in cinema, despite the fact that both types of audiences partake in a communal experience. It is rare for cinema audiences to speak or to applaud, and even rarer for audiences to dance in the theater at the end of a film (with the notable exception of cult films like *The Rocky Horror Picture Show*),[34] but most of the audience was dancing during the final number of the stage production. The energy produced by the interaction between stage and auditorium is a two-way exchange that has been referred to by Erika Fischer-Lichte as the "feedback loop" of performance[35] and related by Jill Dolan to the "event exchange" that creates the transformative potential of live performance.[36] This is different from the cinematic certainty that is unaffected by audience response.

Performers comment on "good" and "bad" audiences, and to some extent this can be the result of less focused performances or performers having had a bad day. However, there is an experience for performers of the audience—perceived as a homogenous group—and their response to that particular performance. This is communicated through silence as much as sound, through concentrated attention or raucous laughter, but the aural and physical communication that suggests attention and engagement is the result of an emotional connection between audience and performers, and is created partly through the mirror neuron system.

Dirty Dancing for All

Music, singing, and most importantly in this case, dancing are also experienced by audiences through the MNS. An experience of witnessing and live presence is activated by the flamboyant dancing and difficult lifts that the dancers undertake. Audiences acknowledge the difficulty of the task and the potential for failure with awe because they are aware it is live. The experience of the live event draws forth acknowledgement of authenticity in dance and song; the performers are performing it here and now. This creates a particular type of tension because of the vulnerability of the performers, which is then released as the moment of tension passes, often into applause or laughter in praise of the technique or expertise on display. Such moments can be the result of high notes at the end of a song, but, although some of the songs are sung live and produce these emotions, in this case these moments are predominantly felt as a result of dance moves: pirouettes, acrobatic leaps, and, of course, lifts. The audience is aware from the plot of the film that some dance moves are difficult—after all that is a key aspect of the narrative. Once Baby has accomplished the difficult task of learning to dance, and more specifically achieved the balance and trust for the overhead lift, she will have moved into adulthood and claimed her utopian ending. In the stage show, that overhead lift has to be performed live, adding to the sense of expectation, danger, and, finally, achievement. It is also the case that performing the lift is probably outside the ability and experience of most audience members, making its achievement perhaps even more worthy of applause.

It is not only the narrative of overcoming difficulty that causes audiences to experience this type of tension and release. Many of the company dance numbers contain lifts and high energy moments in which the same experience of bearing witness to the veracity of the live event, its authenticity and its difficulty, is apparent in the applause generated. The technique and energy required are acknowledged with awe; the pace and pulse of the music and the sexuality and pure hard work of the dancers produces corresponding excitement and energy in the audience. But that assumes audiences are affected by the difficulty, energy, and excitement of particular movements, and if they have never danced that assumption might be considered problematic. However, cognitive science is also applied by researchers to dance and music to begin to understand how audiences perceive such moments of performance.

Since the mid-1990s, a number of experiments have been undertaken that suggest that when audiences are watching dance they experience the dance mimetically, as though they are undertaking the movement themselves.[37] Empathy or mirroring is augmented by expertise in the skill concerned; an expert dancer will have a stronger response to a dance gesture than a non-dancer, but there will still be a response.[38] Similar work has been done in relation to the effects music can have on audiences. Istvan Molnar-Szakacs and Kate Overy claim that "Music has a unique ability to trigger memories, awaken emotions and to intensify our social experiences,"[39] and Smith et al. have identified the role of sub-vocalization in the way listeners respond to melody (and consequently to the sung voice) by effectively singing along in their heads.[40]

Another recent study undertaken by Corinne Jola et al. investigated brain activity when dance was performed with and without music.[41] The team found increased synchronization across spectators in areas of the brain that process audiovisual stimuli. They concluded that, at least as far as the study went, audience responses to an audiovisual stimulation were more likely to be similar than to either stimulus alone. It is possible in light of this to speculate that the combination of narrative with song and dance might result in increased brain activity in certain parts of the brain, and that there is likely to be a greater level of synchrony, or similarity, in the response to a dance musical than to either dance or music alone.[42] In conjunction with the contagion of shared experience described above, this is likely to activate a stronger emotion in the audience than might be activated when watching alone.

The effect of doing something together, whether watching a performance or performing in it, if it is done well, can be to activate the reward areas of the brain.[43] So, in addition to the responses described above, the social cohesion observed among the dancers is likely to activate the reward areas of the dancers' brains, which might be the cause of the adrenaline high experienced by many performers. The social cohesion of watching and responding to the performance together is likely to activate reward areas in the brains of the audience members, though perhaps not to the same extent. All this suggests that audiences who are excited by and interact with a live performance are likely to create a spiraling contagion of emotion and energy if they are enjoying the performance, and that dance and music contribute to the triggering and development of this spiral.

Victor Turner's notion of "spontaneous communitas" describes a similar response. He describes it as the experience of a group of compatible people who together experience "a flash of lucid mutual understanding on the existential level, when they feel that all problems . . . could be resolved, whether emotional or cognitive, if only the group . . . could sustain its intersubjective illumination. This illumination may succumb to the dry light of the next day's disjunction, the application of singular and personal reason to the 'glory' of communal understanding."[44] The memory of the experience of communitas can lead avid fans to replicate the event by repeated attendance at the performance. Of course, this type of response can be triggered within other group situations, and it can be resisted, but the theater space offers a safe location in which to indulge in the pleasure of having one's emotions manipulated before returning to the real. Moreover, the awareness of these effects does begin to account for the engagement and participation of audience members with the live version of *Dirty Dancing*, which is extremely popular even though it is not critically acclaimed.

New intertextual associations are created in experiencing the film narrative in its new context, but more importantly audience members become part of a group and can share in the momentary transcendent experience of communitas. The participation in the event led from the stage by Kellerman's entertainment organizer and through the direct address by the singers further extends the feeling of group identity. The audience is encouraged from the stage to participate, which, when conformed to, leads to greater feelings of engagement and pleasure.

This could be regarded as hopelessly utopian—and clearly the plot is exactly that—but the utopianism of live performance is not based on the plot alone. Rather, it is based on the coming together of groups of people who form a community in their responses to a performance. The activation of that community around bodies of music, narratives, or dancing bodies leads to a sense of identification and reinforcement. The experience of entrainment is enhanced by the audiovisual connections of narrative and number, dancer, singer, story, and song. So music and dance, live presence and nostalgia are linked, and the combination provides access to moments of transcendence and pleasure.

Conclusion

What this chapter argues is that there are ways in which the live experience of *Dirty Dancing* is an ontologically different experience from watching the film. There are many similarities with the communal experience and emotional connection achieved when watching the film, but there are also differences resulting from the involvement with and danger of live action and the spiraling of energy between audience and performers. The stage show of *Dirty Dancing* functions on many levels, levels that audiences read and blend as they choose. The stereophony or multiplicity of the associations created both within and without the text allows the audience to be entertained. The cliché of musical theater making audiences laugh and cry in a cathartic excess is enacted here through an excessive, dynamic range. Moreover, the audiovisual combination produces synchrony in interpretation that allows audiences to experience the pleasure of bonding even as individual interpretation offers different blends of the plural, libidinal, and dynamic text. This combination of stereographic plurality, libidinal excess, and dynamic range might begin to account for the ability of the stage show to continue to attract audiences.

Understanding of cognitive processes begins to account for experiences that have been theorized in the past. The mirror neuron system is activated so that audiences do not simply watch the performance, but sing, dance, and re-enact the experience, empathetically connecting to the emotions of the performer/characters in a contagious spiral of response. This, of course, also depends on the skill of the performers and the quality of the performance. However, through conceptual blending the experience of watching a stage show made famous on film and deliberately revisited onstage is one in which the viewer is conflating both the present experience and the past memory to create a new composite that is neither one nor the other, but both, stimulating imagination, memory, witnessing, and presence in an intense and heady mix of the personal and the communal. The stage show is a deliberate evocation of the film, but the experience is much, much more.

Notes

1. "My Night of *Dirty Dancing* (But No, I didn't Have The Time Of My Life)," *Mail Online*, November 1, 2006, http://www.dailymail.co.uk/tvshowbiz/article-413825/My-Night-Dirty-Dancing-I-didnt-The-Time-Of-My-Life.html. Accessed on April 2011.
2. Ibid.
3. "*Dirty Dancing* Is Box Office Hit," *Mail Online*, April 13, 2006, http://www.dailymail.co.uk/tvshowbiz/article-382954/Dirty-Dancing-box-office-hit.html. Accessed April 2011.
4. Lyn Gardner, "Dirty Dancing," *Guardian*, October 25, 2006.
5. Dominic Cavendish, "A Chick Flick Live on Stage," *Telegraph*, October 26, 2006, http://www.telegraph.co.uk/culture/theatre/drama/3656126/A-chick-flick-live-on-stage.html. Accessed April 2011.
6. Ibid.
7. "My Night of *Dirty Dancing*."
8. Alistair Macaulay, "Dirty Dancing, Aldwych Theatre, London," *Financial Times*, October 25, 2006.
9. Emma Brockes, "The Time of Our Lives—Revisited,'" *Guardian*, April 13, 2006.
10. Gardner, "Dirty Dancing."
11. Charles Spencer, "*Dirty Dancing* at the Aldwych Theatre, Review," *The Telegraph*, April 21, 2010, http://www.telegraph.co.uk/journalists/charles-spencer/7615576/Dirty-Dancing-at-the-Aldwych-Theatre-review.html.
12. Cavendish, "A Chick Flick Live on Stage."
13. Quoted in "*Dirty Dancing* is Box Office Hit."
14. Macaulay, "Dirty Dancing."
15. Marvin Carlson, *The Haunted Stage: The Theatre as Memory Machine* (Ann Arbor: University of Michigan Press, 2001), 2.
16. Ibid., 35.
17. Ibid., 51.
18. Gilles Fauconnier and Mark Turner, *The Way We Think* (New York: Basic Books, 2002), cover note.
19. Bruce McConachie and F. Elizabeth Hart, "Introduction," in *Performance and Cognition*, ed. Bruce McConachie and F. Elizabeth Hart (London and New York: Routledge, 2006), 20.
20. Ibid., 19.
21. Vassallo and Wright were the actors who played the parts of Baby and Johnny in the stage production I saw at the Aldwych Theatre, London, in 2010 and 2011.

22 Amy Cook, "Interplay: The Method and Potential of a Cognitive Scientific Approach to Theatre," *Theatre Journal* 59.4 (2007): 584.
23 Roland Barthes, "From Work to Text," in *Image, Music Text*, trans. Stephen Heath (London: Fontana Press, 1977), 158.
24 Ibid., 159-60.
25 Ibid., 162.
26 Ibid., 164.
27 V. Gallese, "Embodied Simulation: From Mirror Neuron Systems to Interpersonal Relations," *Novartis Foundation Symposium* 278 (2007): 3-12.
28 Elizabeth Tolbert, "Untying the Music/Language Knot," in *Music, Sensation, and Sensuality*, ed. Linda Austern (New York and London: Routledge, 2002), 87.
29 Antonio Damasio, *The Feeling of What Happens: Body, Emotion and the Making of Consciousness* (London: Vintage, 2000).
30 V. Gazzola, L. Azziz-Zadeh, and C. Keysers, "Empathy and the Somatotopic Auditory Mirror System in Humans," *Current Biology* 16.18 (2006): 802-04.
31 Christian Keysers, "From Mirror Neurons to Kinaesthetic Empathy," *Kinaesthetic Empathy: Concepts and Contexts* (Keynote Presentation, Manchester University, April 22-23, 2010).
32 Susan Foster, "Dancing with the 'Mind's Muscles': A Brief History of Kinesthesia and Empathy," *Kinaesthetic Empathy: Concepts and Contexts* (Keynote Presentation Manchester University, April 22-23, 2010).
33 Bruce McConachie, "Falsifiable Theories for Theatre and Performance Studies," *Theatre Journal* 59.4 (2007): 563.
34 Youth audiences also danced in theaters during the credits of *Blackboard Jungle* when Bill Hayley and the Comets' "Rock around the Clock" was playing in 1955, for example; but such moments are the exception and may have other causes.
35 Erika Fischer-Lichte, *The Transformative Power of Performance: A New Aesthetics* (London and New York: Routledge, 2008).
36 Jill Dolan, *Utopia in Performance: Finding Hope at the Theatre* (Ann Arbor: University of Michigan Press, 2005).
37 An Arts and Humanities Research Council (AHRC) funded research project, "Watching Dance: Kinaesthetic Empathy" is in the process of exploring the experience and impact of watching dance and attempting to identify its social and affective consequences. For more information about this project, visit http://www.watchingdance.org/index.php. As part of that project, a conference, *Kinaesthetic Empathy: Concepts and Contexts*, was held at Manchester University (April 22-23, 2010).
38 See Marie-Hélène Grosbras, Corinne Jola, Anna Kuppuswamy, and Frank Pollick, "Enhanced Cortical Excitability Induced by Watching Dance in Empathic and Visually Experienced Dance Spectators," *Kinaesthetic Empathy: Concepts and Contexts* (Poster Presentation, Manchester University, April 22-3, 2010); and Beatriz Calvo-Merino et al., "Action Observation and Acquired Motor Skills: An fMRI Study with Expert Dancers," *Cerebral Cortex* 15, (2005): 1243-49.

39 Istvan Molnar-Szakacs and Kate Overy, "Music and Mirror Neurons: From Motion to 'e'motion," *Social Cognitive and Affective Neuroscience* 1.3 (2006): 235–41.
40 J. D. Smith, M. Wilson, and D. Reisberg, "The Role of Subvocalisation in Auditory Imagery," *Neuropsychologia* 33 (1995): 1433–54.
41 Corinne Jola, Marie-Hélène Grosbras, and Frank Pollick, "Dance With or Without Music: Does the Brain Care?" *Kinaesthetic Empathy: Concepts and Contexts* (Poster Presentation, Manchester University, April 22–23, 2010).
42 Personal communication at *Kinaesthetic Empathy: Concepts and Contexts* (Manchester University, April 22–23, 2010).
43 See Tai-Chen Rabinowitch, Ian Cross, and Pamela Burnard, "Musical Group Interaction and Empathy—A Mutual Cognitive Pathway?," *Kinaesthetic Empathy: Concepts and Contexts* (Manchester University, April 22–23, 2010); and Keysers, "From Mirror Neurons to Kinaesthetic Empathy."
44 Victor Turner, *From Ritual to Theatre* (New York, 1982), 49.

16 *DIRTY DANCING* AND ITS STAGE JUKEBOX DANSICAL ADAPTATION: THE DANCING MALE IN A TEENAGE FEMALE FANTASY OF DESIRE AND SENSUALITY

GEORGE RODOSTHENOUS

Introduction

The iconic "teen dance movie"[1] *Dirty Dancing* (Emile Ardolino, 1987) renegotiated sensual dancing and its positioning within the Western dancing canon by celebrating the male body in relation to its female counterpart. Amy Nicholson suggests that *Dirty Dancing* celebrates "fun, freedom, flirting. The eponymous dirty dancers of this movie are the free-spirited staff of Kellerman's holiday resort—a far cry from Jennifer Grey's lead Baby's staid family, and the escape from childhood-adolescence she has been searching for. Through meeting Patrick Swayze's heartthrob Johnny Castle, she encounters a new world and ends the film a different person—and in the corner no more."[2] *Dirty Dancing* empowered women and allowed them to go on journeys of self-discovery, maturity, and liberation. According to Lyn Gardner, the film "gave a generation of young women permission to get in touch with their own bodies and sexual desire."[3]

Its stage adaptation, *Dirty Dancing: The Classic Story on Stage* (2004),[4] is sometimes wrongly marketed as a stage musical when, in fact, there is too little sung musical material in the work for it to qualify for such a genre classification.[5] Gardner remarks that it is "an evening which is less full-blown musical and more a play with a musical soundtrack."[6] And admittedly, the work's genre falls closer to the genre of the dansical.[7] The book of the jukebox dansical is kept nearly identical to the one of the film. Eleanor Bergstein, the main source of inspiration behind this meta-theatrical dansical, explains that live dancing onstage has

> a sense of danger and contagious achievement. Our story allows us to approach dance in the theatre in a new way. For many of our characters, dance is how they make meaning in their lives, and so the dancing in our show comes out of story and finds its power in individual expression and discovery. Kate Champion's original choreography uses the movements of everyday life ... each performer is usually following out an individual personal line, rather than the traditional unison dancing of much musical theatre.[8]

Traditionally, musicals tend to have dream sequences that allow the protagonists to express their dreams and desires through song and dance. "Dream sequences (either as flashbacks or flash-forwards) interrupt the action and give us a 'what-if'/alternative scenario in the form of a fantasy-based vision."[9] In *Dirty Dancing*, Baby is having her teenage revolution, and Johnny Castle, a dance instructor at the summer camp, acts as a catalyst to her journey of discovery and maturity. And since *Dirty Dancing: The Classic Story on Stage* does not include a dream sequence, I will be proposing that the *whole* stage adaptation functions as an extended dream sequence: a female teenage fantasy. In this chapter, I will examine the male dancer in relation to the visual representations of the "dirty dancing body" on stage. This will provide a context for a discussion of the male dance instructor and his place within the female teenage fantasy. Specifically, the chapter will present how the male lead is used to facilitate this self-discovery through the medium of dance. The empowerment of Baby (and the female audience that Gardner highlighted) is mediated by Johnny's masculine dancing, which makes for a not-as-straightforward experience in terms of women getting in touch with their own bodies. The dynamics of Johnny's dancing masculinity will be analyzed within the framework of this jukebox dansical. Furthermore, the dance rehearsal/lesson will be re-contextualized as a space for romance involving the dance instructor and his student, and the stage adaptation's treatment of the act of dancing as erotic foreplay will be compared to "grinding" and sexualized dancing.[10] This will be explored as a means to sexual fulfillment and the way the audiences observe this in a voyeuristic manner. The chapter will conclude with some observations about the actual audience demographic of the work, the critical reception, and the impact of its 2006 London production.

"You Are Better Than Fred Astaire": Men Can Dance!

Mennesson writes that "[d]uring the nineteenth century, professional artistic dancing was prohibited for men, who were relegated to the rank of *porteur* (a man who lifts and carries the ballerina) to glorify female dancers."[11] However, in the early twentieth century, new dancers (e.g., Isadora Duncan, Serge De Diaghilev) "who had broken away from the gender norms dictated by trends in academic and institutional circles, helped to promote the development of professional dancing careers for men."[12] This presents us with an interesting gap from the male point of view of why dance became so female-focused as ballet became codified, reinforced by the wealth of material that has men as the primary focus of courtly dance prior to this time. Since the dance masters designed and invented the dance technique, female ballerinas were still controlled by the masters. The latter used women to show the craft and attract an audience. The women were their muses and were also used as "bodies on display"; evident are multiple layers of control, vulnerability, and codification of the body as other than human.

Ideas of masculinity seemed to undergo a substantial shift in the early twentieth century, even when set alongside attempts by Diaghilev, who was also working toward reinstating the potential of the male dancer. Working with an astute intelligence to modernize performance in his terms, Diaghilev had dance as only part of his agenda. His use of the exotic and the fantastic had the ability to tread the boundary between homosexual and heterosexual sensuality. And if we trace the development of the male dancer even later in the twentieth century, we will see that there were some remarkable examples of male dancers who excelled before the 1990s, such as Nijinsky, Nureyev, Kelly, Astaire, and Travolta. Since the 1990s, we have seen another shift in perceptions, engagements, and expectations from the male dancer, and as I observe in my 2007 essay on *Billy Elliot: The Musical*, the male ballet dancer has been re-invented in the theatre canon. Matthew Bourne is partly responsible for this new trend of presenting the male dancer on stage, changing the popular assumptions that dancing as a masculine activity is a suspect phenomenon. Companies like DV8 and Lloyd Newson have blurred the boundaries between the classical male ballet dancer and the "new" male dancer. These works erotised and homo-erotised the male body, giving it a new political status.[13]

Television shows in the US such as Fox's *So You Think You Can Dance* (2005-) and ABC's *Dancing with the Stars* (2005-), and in the UK such as BBC's *Strictly Come Dancing* (2004-) and Sky1's *Got to Dance* (2010-), as well as the film and musical *Billy Elliot*, are partly responsible for the change of attitudes toward male dancers.

Strong muscular dancers with their strong physical presence are compared and equated to athletes, and this is now generally regarded as a more acceptable behavior and casting decision.[14] The male lead in *Dirty Dancing* has recontextualized the male dancer and has provided a new role model for younger generations (both male and female). In the London production, Josef Brown (from the original Australian cast, and "a strapping mass of muscle" according to Paul Taylor[15]), his successor Johnny Wright, and their understudies have all performed the role of Johnny Castle. They all had the "Ghost" of Patrick Swayze's iconic performance haunting them; for Wright, however, this was an inspirational moment. *Dirty Dancing* was iconic to him because Patrick Swayze, and that sort of masculine, sexy role that he portrayed, made him feel that "it was cool to dance," coming full circle twenty years later when he was asked to play the role that got him started dancing.[16] This presents an important shift in public perceptions regarding male dancers; even as recently as the 1980s, the male dancer was not entirely taken seriously as a respectable occupation for men. Fisher and Shay comment on the homophobia, effeminophobia, and choreophobia that characterized the reception of male dancers: "Although Swayze's character ... was a confident heterosexual presented as a muscular hunk, the theme of class difference, emphasized by him being a 'hired dancer' patronized by an upper-class clientele, harked back to an era of class prejudice based on choreophobia and economic realities."[17]

Dance at the summer resort is initially presented as a pastime, as entertainment. Men are depicted as being useless at it, following the well-existing stereotype that "men cannot dance." All the waiters are well-educated college students and have strict instructions on how to behave with the rich daughters. They are matched with them, they have to entertain them, but not get them into trouble. For a cynic, this suggests that their function is purely to be glorified male escorts for the rich "daddy's girls." For Baby's father, his daughter, whom he *still* calls "Baby," is precious. "Our Baby is going to change the world," he announces proudly.[18] Within this summer resort environment, the presence of the working-class dance instructor, Johnny Castle, is a catalyst for Baby's journey to maturity. In his earlier scenes when he is dancing on his own (just before the dance lessons that Baby starts taking to replace Penny), his solo dancing has a "wild horse" quality: rough, untamed, imposing. It is a self-indulgent number that he is practicing in front of the mirror, like a new Narcissus flirting with his reflection in the water. His athletic body is on display, and with raised arms he is (ironically) miming to the song "Baby, You Are the One." It is an exhibition of strength, energy, and masculinity.

In recent years, a number of academics examined the aversion of young males to dance.[19] Writing about a group of young Australian boys, Michael Gard demonstrated that

> when it came to dance, almost all boys expressed negative feelings about ballet and more modern forms of stage dancing. The issue here seemed to be what the body signified when it moved in particular ways.... While a small number of boys expressed interest in learning to dance, the rest ranged from ambivalence to contempt ... among those who expressed some interest in dance, most thought it would not be something they could do during physical education classes because they assumed other boys would refuse to participate.[20]

In *Dirty Dancing*, however, the lead young girl finds dancing to be something noble, attractive, and glamorous, while she instantly admires the male dancing body. In her first dance lesson, Baby, in a moment of surprise, flatters Johnny by comparing him to Sammy Davis, Jr., and later exclaiming that "You are a good teacher!" There are no prejudices here about male dancers. After all, he is a muscular, sporty, heterosexual man and the girls at the summer resort regard him as "better than Fred Astaire".

According to Cohan, Fred Astaire was responsible for a "new styling of masculinity."[21] This new style, which was both athletic *and* balletic at the same time, was reinforced by Gene Kelly and followed through in a new fashion by John Travolta. Patrick Swayze, and his portrayal of Johnny Castle, develops this further. For the cynics, again, in the narrative he functions as just another male gigolo; he is there to fulfill the female fantasy: the element that completes the summer romance equation.

The Dance Lesson/Rehearsal as a Space for Summer Romance: The Amateur Falling in Love with the (Un)Professional

Susan Russell, in her controversial article "The Performance of Discipline," links the work of the actor and producer to the one described in Foucault's *Discipline and Punish*[22] and claims that the only thing that the performers can do is create "an image of energized hyperreality, and this image must be maintained by corporate checks and balances in order to stabilize financial return. But how can artists maintain such enforced 'discipline'? What is the infrastructure of this form of performance that makes 'discipline' the tool of the producer instead of the actor?"[23] How are the bodies trained for the performance? These questions could provide one with the opportunity to view the bodies separated from the actual persons—a commodification of muscle.

Like in most backstage musicals, *Dirty Dancing* provides us with the opportunity to get a glimpse of the process. It gives us access to the backstage and even the rehearsal space. In the case of *Dirty Dancing*, the dance rehearsal becomes the physical space for summer romance. When I watched the 8 o'clock performance on a Friday night in May 2011, I was fully aware that it was the sixth show of the week and the second performance of that evening. I am not suggesting, in any way, that the bodies of the performers looked tired. However, at the back of my mind I was intrigued about how the body performs this daily reproduction of a product that was created to please its (mostly) female-targeted audience. The body has been trained/ disciplined to perform eight times a week in an attempt to provide a kind of freshness every single time.

In *Dirty Dancing,* part of this discipline is dramatized and shown throughout the work, especially in the scenes where Johnny and his female dance partner Penny Johnson try to teach Baby the dance sequence for the competition. The instructors encourage her to concentrate:

JOHNNY: Don't put your heel down. Don't put your heel down. Stay on the toe.
BABY: I didn't.
JOHNNY: The steps aren't enough, feel the music.

The rehearsal space is transformed into a romantic *ménage à trois* where Johnny is dancing with the two females. The traditional territorialization and expected jealousy are omitted here, because the steps for the competition *must* be taught—in other words, the show must go on.

The scene is constructed gently to serve its romantic narrative, and, unlike in most *ménages à trois,* the first meeting of the three is not painful but has a welcoming feel to it. The female instructor ensures, with the accompaniment of the song "Hungry Eyes," that the technical aspect of the choreography is transferred from body to body, while the male instructor stresses the importance of focusing the energy on the dancing partner's eyes. The three undulating bodies are moving in harmony to the music, and this unifying proximity and physicality allow the audience's imagination to be "aroused." The choreography allows them to see the sensualized movement through their own life context. For the heterosexual male audience, this love triangle could perhaps be an erotic fantasy come true. For the heterosexual female audience, the triangle might work on the level of another kind of fantasy, the fantasy that the freedom of dancing provides and its romantic associations: inviting a new, young, "uninitiated" understudy to join the ritual of performance. This rite of passage, this unavoidable reality, is sensualized and glamorized here. Dancing becomes a catalyst for Baby's repressed emotions and the facilitator for her liberation. The music is used in a filmic way to set the mood and to help the diegesis reinforce the movement through the episodes and scene changes, combining the aural and visual senses. What is ironic is that the male teacher has to follow the steps of the iconic Patrick Swayze in an attempt to evoke, like a "faithful" understudy, the original nostalgic feel that Swayze has offered the millions of fans already.

When the dance lesson becomes a duet, the meta-theatricality of the dance lesson/rehearsal raises questions about the teaching space and the (un)professional relationship of the dance teacher and his student. The dance teacher (leader) becomes her platonic adviser, working on the duet for the competition that, as expected, involved a series of lifts. Burt wrote extensively about the role of duets and lifts between males and females, and he claims that

> Duets signify social relations. The actual practice of partnering and lifting is one which requires a high degree of skill and co-operation between the male and the female dancer, but the extent to which the spectator is made aware of this varies between one duet and another, and between styles and traditions. Some signify hierarchies of dominance and subordination, others suggest more egalitarian relations.... The male dancer's active roles ... can compensate for, or repress, the way in which he is the erotic object of either a spectator's or another dancer's gaze.[24]

It would be useful to discuss the stage semiotics at work both in the film and the stage version to portray Johnny's dominance and representation of masculinity. Johnny's vest allows for the muscled arms of the dance teacher to be constantly on display. The arms demonstrate strength and masculine energy—values traditionally linked to manual labor. The dangerous intimacy of the duet, instead of creating discomfort in the "aroused" audience, creates a kind of liberation, a romantic apotheosis of repressed feeling. When Johnny says, "Again, concentrate," the audience, together with the overwhelmed Baby, are placed back into the dance studio and reminded of the work that needs to be done.

Mary Louise Adams claims that dancing for men is an "arena of physical exertion and toughness. Male dancers, it seems, need to advertise their bodily hardness."[25] The protagonist's six-pack functions as a living proof of the fact that he is, indeed, an athletic dancer—a constant reminder that dancing is like sport. And in this kind of discipline, practice makes perfect. The consequent rehearsals change locations (moving to an outside space and leading to the well-known lake scene) and involve increasingly fewer pieces of clothing, making each touch on the bare flesh possible to misinterpret as a sensual touch. The summer romance, at least on Baby's behalf, has begun.

The dance rehearsal/lesson is now being transformed into erotic foreplay. The ethics of the dance instructor and his teenage dance student is an area that is not touched upon in either the film or the stage version. One could examine Johnny's conduct from two angles, namely, whether his function in the narrative is to be the male teacher or, controversially, the male escort—a male gigolo to fulfill the young girl's fantasy. As for Baby's role, it is equally difficult to pinpoint whether her fantasy was to be a dancer or to use dancing as a catalyst for romance. In this respect, it is not easy to distinguish whether Johnny is unprofessional or a true professional. However, the discussion of how dance is used as sexual foreplay needs to be linked to our discussion of the male protagonist and his positioning within the narrative structure of the piece.

Dance as Erotic Foreplay: A Guide to the Kama Sutra's Sexual Positions and a Perfect Real Plastic Doll for Baby to Play With

Throughout *Dirty Dancing*, two kinds of dancing are juxtaposed: on the one hand, there is traditional ballroom dancing, which is a rather conventional form with very smiley male partners, camp choreography, and effeminate moves, and which sometimes verges on a mannered, grotesque feel. Ballroom dancing allows heterosexual men to lead with effeminate moves and alternate between masculine and feminine states of physicality. During the ballroom sequences, the men are mostly *porteurs* for the women. The music is familiar to the audience: Dusty Springfield, Everly Brothers, etc. The men seem to be indifferent and cold, while their dancing feels like a pre-learned sequence, nearly robotic and soulless. But the songs are not sung here, they are just danced to, which creates a peculiar form of the dansical genre. And when an older character sings the well-known song "Besame Mucho," this provides a comic interlude. It also reminds us that the older body is unfit for dancing. Dancing is thus restricted only to the young, virile bodies.

In the staff quarters, however, the dancing to the mambo music is rough, dynamic, and the men are using their hips in an aggressive, predatory manner. There are no smiles here; it feels more professional, serious—an exhibition of strength and accuracy. It is an opportunity for the virile young men to prove that they are bursting with (sexual) energy. The moves are suggestive, and the female pelvic area is often in the male partner's face, hinting to the activity of cunnilingus. As Philips wrote, the "sensual hip swaying, high leg kicking, pulsating and grinding comes alive in the vibrant party scenes.... Couples partner dance, bodies melt together, swirl and sway."[26] The intensity and control of the dancing appear to be effortless. It takes practice and skill to dance in this environment; it is strictly for "professionals"—no "amateur" guests are allowed in this world of dance seduction. The dances move from the sensual to the erotic, and to the sexual; this evidently changes as the piece progresses: different drives direct the potential interpretation/s of the plot.

Emilyn Claid made a valid discovery on seductiveness by stating that seduction

> has signified a variety of elements relevant to sexual desire without being the sexual act itself. Seduction has also suggested a narrative, a subject who seduces and an object who is seduced, a linear story familiar to most sexual scenarios, with a goal of conquest.... Letting go of these interpretations of seduction—but not forgetting the act of desiring—seductiveness is re-figured as a play of desires and meanings between performers and spectators. Seduction, like ambiguity, becomes an embodied practice.[27]

There is no ambiguity in the dancing in the staff quarters. The moves are explicit, suggestive, and violent. The choreography allows for plenty of gyrations amongst the male and female dancers. The act of dancing, the close proximity of the bodies and the libidinous rhythms are the main drivers here. The hands of the men touch every part of their female partners' bodies; there are no forbidden areas. In some of the acrobatic choreography, as I mentioned earlier, the female pelvic area is elevated up to the male partners' mouths. There are jumps; it seems that the girls are in heat, raising their dresses and skirts and whipping them across their partners' legs sharply. Backsides thrust backwards on high heels that speak only of availability. It is all about display: performing "flirtation," displaying the act of dancing as "erotic seduction." One could read this as accepted cultural practice, but having underneath it an instinctual display with a sexual purpose.

The dancers' erotic moves on stage could be paralleled to the Kama Sutra's athletic sexual positions. The male pelvic area gyrates on the female backside and frontal female pelvic area. The whole movement has an edgy, eroticized, gymnastic quality to it. The male partner seems to simulate penetration when standing behind the female, and this is reversed when the female stands behind the male. Paul Taylor reports that "[a]ll the trademark movements of their mambo-ing—the erotically arched backs, the showy lifts, the fingers trailing down the arm that is sexily cupping a face, etc.—are executed with a raunchy, amused sensuousness."[28]

The flexibility required by the performers is evident throughout the dance sequences, and when the combinations involve two men together, it seems like a fiery competition. Williams also playfully observes that

> the eponymous dirty dancing, is sublimated sexual energy, that much is obvious. That memorable moment when Swayze finally manages to heave, sorry, lift Jennifer Grey off the ground ... is a metaphor for losing your virginity. And it's clearly a female-crafted metaphor, proceeding not with a clear narrative urgency, as straight as a die to the irreducible explosion, but rather, with mis-starts and damp squibs and dance routines that don't go right because both people weren't doing the right thing at the right time and didn't have the right feelings for each other.[29]

When Johnny teaches Baby the movement of the pelvic dance, for her, it is a freedom from the norm: a journey to sensuality, a loss of innocence. The elements of the dance sequence itself (rhythm, space, dynamics) as set against the context of the scene give us the reading of simulated sex. Shelly Ronen writes in a parallel, yet significant, in-depth discussion about "grinding" at college parties that 'it is a kind of sexual act that carries significant, socially constructed meaning and may influence behavior in other settings."[30] Her analysis of sexualized dancing insinuates that "the sexualized nature of the dancing, and accompanying explicit gestures" lead to a "hookup," which "can mean any sort of sexual encounter from kissing to intercourse ...

[grinding] is a public manifestation of contemporary heterosexual scripts."[31] This claim can be also applied to the treatment of dance in *Dirty Dancing* and its overall narrative.

The actual sexualization of the dance routine allows dance to function as erotic foreplay, which does later lead to full sexual intercourse. The audience, as voyeurs from the stalls, are watching this action happen live in front of their eyes. This proves Judith Lynne Hanna's suggestion (in her richly extensive study on dance and sexuality) that dance has often been seen as "'immoral' sexuality . . . a source of power."[32] Just before the interval, after Baby shouts "Dance with me," a new explosive sequence unfolds. Her female pelvic area is rubbing on Johnny's left leg, and then his top is removed. We have a sequence of what feels like two consequent rejections of Johnny's sexual advances and then Baby's acceptance of his flirtatious offerings. Dance is treated like a sex simulation. The male dancer finally fulfills his purpose in the teenage fantasy dansical. He becomes Baby's romantic partner. The removal of their clothes, the touch, and the whole erotic ritual are not dissimilar from softcore porn renditions of similar narratives. This has led Benedict Nightingale to enthuse that "dancing isn't almost as good as sex. No, sex is almost as good as dancing."[33] Act II starts with a postcoital scene, *the* naked-in-bed scene (essential in every love-play since Shakespeare's *Romeo and Juliet*). The man's body is so "perfect" it looks like plastic: a "perfect plastic doll" for Baby to play with.

"Not Enough Dirty Dancing": A Teenage Female Fantasy for Women Only?

In *Dirty Dancing: The Classic Story on Stage,* there is a definite absence of a dream sequence, which, as I discussed earlier, presents a peculiar unorthodoxy when it comes to the musical genre. The producers wanted the stage adaptation to stay as close to the original as possible. Since dream sequences are traditionally famous for their dancing, we can read *Dirty Dancing* on stage as an *extended* dream sequence: a teenage female fantasy.

Nostalgic films of the genre have a strong impact on their audiences when they first come out because of their "evocation of nostalgia . . . emotional and time-specific connotations . . . and an ever-present popular song soundtrack."[34] In *Dirty Dancing*, the men are simply peripheral to the narrative, and the main catalyst is the journey of the young female lead and her experience of "living the moment." I would have to agree with Woods that "*Dirty Dancing* held a certain nostalgia for the youth of [her] parents' generation. However, younger audiences may also enjoy these texts primarily through their processing of the 'emotional realism' of the truths of teenage life."[35]

The initial critical responses to the stage adaptation were rather mixed. When Gardner complained that "there are a lot of boring bits and not half enough dancing. Or at least not enough dirty dancing,"[36] one wonders whether the structure of the work suffers mainly because of its close and faithful reproduction of the film. Gardner even advised readers that "if you want to see really sexy dancing it's on display in *Guys and Dolls* just down the road, which incidentally just happens to star Patrick Swayze."[37] Dominic Cavendish wonders further whether one "can accuse director James Powell of a lack of imagination or just providing great customer service."[38] And in one of the even more negative reviews, Paul Taylor of *The Independent* joked that he was "already at work on a spin-off. It's called Filthy Flower-Arranging and follows the fortunes of a vicar's daughter, new to the village, who notices that there's a hunk from the wrong side of the tracks working in the florist's and that this guy really knows where to stick his dahlias. Her snobbish father disapproves but soon the young couple are practicing flower-arrangement like there's no tomorrow in secret for a local competition."[39]

Still, the show drew thousands of (mostly) female audiences every night who were attracted to the work's nostalgic feel and that sense of freedom. According to marketing specialist Guy Chapman, the audience demographic included "[t]wenty-five percent of people buying a ticket [that] have never booked with that theatre before—so it's not people who go to *Mamma Mia!* or *The Sound of Music*. It's the Take That/Kylie crossover, it's basically the pop audience...women born between 1970 and 1980 are obsessed with this film."[40] While Mark Shenton, in his review of the first UK tour, reveals that "some sections of the audience actually booed when [Paul-Michael Jones as Johnny] puts his trousers back on after one scene played just in his underwear. It's that kind of show, for that kind of audience."[41] The question that remains unanswered is whether the paying audience cares about the actual content of the work, since the impact of the thrill of re-experiencing their favorite nostalgic film adapted for the stage is so significant.

The last dance—with its volcanic eruption of feelings betraying Baby's years of repressed artistic energy—is inspiring. It causes "crowd *arousal* in the psychological sense, to include conditions that range from excitement, exhilaration and ... ecstasy."[42]—at least, for the female part of the audience who can really associate with that ecstasy. Johnny's and Baby's dancing becomes a symbol of freedom from social, class, and parental restrictions. It reminds us of the final scene of another iconic dance movie, *Saturday Night Fever* (John Badham, 1977); Johnny Castle, as the new John Travolta, is dancing with Baby in a meta-theatrical sequence, and this enables Baby to be transformed into a rebel leading her own personal teenage revolution.

Dan Rebellato's rather harsh, but realistic, view of the "McTheatre" industry informs us that the new trends require the choreography to be "fixed, and the movements are largely determined by the automated sets and standardized lighting designs, which means that any deviation from the pattern risks injury."[43] The stage work feels like a close companion to the film, an unashamed continuation. Katie Phillips insists that this one is "definitely one for the girls."[44] In agreement with that, I cannot help thinking that perhaps the effect that the film *Dirty Dancing* had on a whole generation of women in the 1990s resembles the effect that *Wicked* and *Legally Blonde* have today. Perhaps these new works are designed exclusively for a younger, heterosexual female audience.

The association/memory/imagined pasts fit in well with the imagined future of the youth ticket. The producers managed to strike a chord primarily with the teenage population, but one that can also be enjoyed by a more universal audience. The artistic team has created a non-inclusive female teenage fantasy, with the male protagonist (in our case the male dancer) being the explicit catalyst for a female teenage revolution. "Dirty dancing" has been exploited as a softcore cover-up for a more explosive erotic representation of teenage female fantasy of desire and sensuality. What is more, *Dirty Dancing: The Classic Story on Stage* has admirably managed to give its (mostly female) audience the power to demand certain kinds of work (nostalgic musicals, film adaptations for the stage, teenage flicks) and thus influence future theatrical developments and trends.[45]

Notes

1. The "teen dance movie" genre originated from films such as *Dirty Dancing*, *Dirty Dancing 2: Havana Nights* (Guy Ferland, 2004), *Grease* (Randal Kleiser, 1978), *Grease 2* (Patricia Birch, 1982), *Flashdance* (Adrian Lyne, 1983), *Footloose* (Herbert Ross, 1984), *Strictly Ballroom* (Baz Luhrmann, 1992), and many others.
2. Amy Nicholson, "Your First Dance," *Footloose: The Dance Musical Official Programme* (2011), 9.
3. Lyn Gardner, "Dirty Dancing," *Guardian*, October 25, 2006, http://www.guardian.co.uk/stage/2006/oct/25/theatre. Accessed on October 3, 2011.
4. The original production premiered at the Theatre Royal in Sydney, Australia on November 18, 2004. It was directed by James Powell, choreographed by Kate Champion, designed by Stephen Brimson Lewis (set), Tim Mitchell (light), Bobby Aitken (sound), Jennifer Irwin (costume), Jon Driscoll (projection), and had additional choreographies by Craig Wilson (Ballroom and Latin) and David Scotchford. This essay will, however, be focusing on the London production, which started previewing on September 29, 2006, opened on October 24, 2006 at the Aldwych Theatre, and closed on July 9, 2011. A subsequent UK tour started on September 1, 2011, and was booked until May 26, 2012. The stage adaptation had a record-breaking £12 million worth of advance (260,000) ticket sales in London. Dominic Cavendish, "A Chick Flick Live on Stage," *Telegraph*, October 26, 2006, http://www.telegraph.co.uk/culture/theatre/drama/3656126/A-chick-flick-live-on-stage.html. Accessed on October 3, 2011.
5. This stage adaptation uses fifty-five songs and has a cast of thirty-five. The main protagonists, curiously, never sing, but mostly dance with some interconnecting dialogue, and the dance and the choreography are put at the forefront of the narrative. An inevitable comparison can be made with the stage work *Footloose*, which has been marketed as a dance musical with all its performers singing/dancing and acting.
6. Gardner, "Dirty Dancing."
7. A form of musical theatre that focuses on dance/choreography in its conception, accompanied by a soundtrack of pre-existing songs. For a more detailed analysis of the term "dansical," see Pamyla Alayne Stiehl, *The Dansical: American Musical Theatre Reconfigured as a Choreographer's Expression and Domain* (unpublished doctoral thesis, University of Colorado, Boulder, 2008).
8. Bergstein was quoted in the website dedicated to *Dirty Dancing: The Classic Show on Stage*, http://www.dirtydancinglondon.com/about/. Accessed on June 30, 2011.
9. George Rodosthenous, "*Billy Elliot The Musical*: Visual Representations of Working-class Masculinity and the All-singing, All-dancing Bo[d]y," *Studies in Musical Theatre* 1.3 (2007): 287.
10. Shelly Ronen, "Grinding on the Dance Floor: Gendered Scripts and Sexualized Dancing at College Parties," *Gender and Society* 24.3 (2010), 356.

11 Christine Mennesson, "Being a Man in Dance: Socialization Modes and Gender Identities," *Sport in Society* 12.2 (2009): 174.
12 Ibid.
13 Rodosthenous, "*Billy Elliot*," 275.
14 Mary Louise Adams, "'Death to the Prancing Prince': Effeminacy, Sport Discourses and the Salvation of Men's Dancing," *Body and Society* 11.4 (2005), 64.
15 Paul Taylor, "First Night: *Dirty Dancing*," *Independent*, October 25, 2006, http://www.independent.co.uk/arts-entertainment/theatre-dance/reviews/first-night-dirty-dancing-aldwych-theatre-london-421531.html. Accessed on June 30, 2011.
16 Wright was quoted in http://www.youtube.com/watch?v=yGrwUBBiBw8. Accessed on July 28, 2012.
17 Jennifer Fisher and Anthony Shay, "Introduction," in *When Men Dance: Choreographing Masculinities across Borders*, ed. Jennifer Fisher and Anthony Shay (New York: Oxford University Press, 2009), 16.
18 Baby is too attached to her father, who is busy striking a balance between a holiday with the family and the presence of his boss in the same resort. Baby's motto is "my father is here, he will take care of everything," and during the summer holidays Baby's ideal summer romance perhaps involves replacing her dad with an older man. Or at least, the audience is nudged toward interpreting her quest for a relationship with an older man in this way.
19 See in particular Adams, "Death to the Prancing Prince"; Ramsay Burt, *The Male Dancer: Bodies, Spectacles, Sexualities* (London: Routledge, 2007); Michael Gard, "When A Boy's Gotta Dance: New Masculinities, Old Pleasures," *Sport, Education and Society* 13.2 (2008); Mennesson, "Being a Man in Dance"; and others.
20 Gard, "When a Boy," 185.
21 Steven Cohan, "'Feminizing' the Song-and-Dance Man: Fred Astaire and the Spectacle of Masculinity in the Hollywood Musical," *Screening the Male: Exploring Masculinities in Hollywood Cinema*, eds. Steven Cohan and Ina Rae Hark (London: Routledge, 1993), 65–66.
22 Michel Foucault, *Discipline and Punish*, trans. Alan Sheridan (New York: Random House, 1979).
23 Susan Russell, "The Performance of Discipline on Broadway," *Studies in Musical Theatre* 1.1 (2007): 101.
24 Burt, *The Male Dancer*, 46.
25 Adams, "Death to the Prancing Prince," 65.
26 Katie Phillips, "Dirty Dancing," *The Stage*, October 26, 2006, http://www.thestage.co.uk/reviews/review.php/14665/dirty-dancing. Accessed on June 30, 2011.
27 Emilyn Claid, *Yes? No! Maybe ... Seductive Ambiguity in Dance* (New York: Routledge, 2006).
28 Taylor, "First Night."
29 Zoe Williams, "*Dirty Dancing*: It's Not Just about Sex," *Guardian*, May 7, 2011, http://www.guardian.co.uk/stage/2011/may/07/dirty-dancing-musical-not-just-about-sex. Accessed on June 30, 2011.

30 Ronen, "Grinding on the Dance Floor," 356.
31 Ibid.
32 Judith Lynne Hanna, "Dance and Sexuality: Many Moves," *Journal of Sex Research* 47.2–3 (2010): 212.
33 Benedict Nightingale, "Dirty Dancing," *Times*, October 25, 2006, http://entertainment.timesonline.co.uk/tol/arts_and_entertainment/article612457.ece. Accessed on June 30, 2011.
34 Faye Woods, "Nostalgia, Music and the Television Past Revisited in American Dreams," *MSMI* 2.1 (2008): 27, 29, 31.
35 Ibid., 31.
36 Gardner, "Dirty Dancing."
37 Ibid.
38 Cavendish, "A Chick Flick Live on Stage."
39 Taylor, "First Night."
40 Chapman was quoted in Williams, "*Dirty Dancing.*"
41 Mark Shenton, "Dirty Dancing," *The Stage*, September 7, 2011, http://www.thestage.co.uk/reviews/review.php/33425/dirty-dancing. Accessed on October 30, 2011.
42 Dennis Kennedy, *The Spectator and the Spectacle* (New York: Cambridge University Press, 2009).
43 Dan Rebellato, *Theatre & Globalization* (London: Palgrave Macmillan, 2009), 44.
44 Phillips, "Dirty Dancing."
45 Many thanks to Professor Jonathan Pitches, Dr Fiona Bannon, and the editors of the book for reading drafts of this chapter and providing me with invaluable feedback.

CONTRIBUTORS

Cynthia Baron is associate professor in the Department of Theatre and Film at Bowling Green State University. She is also an affiliated faculty member in the graduate American Culture Studies Program. She is co-author of *Reframing Screen Performance* and co-editor of *More Than a Method*. She is co-author of *The Politics of Food in Film* (forthcoming) and author of *Denzel Washington* (forthcoming). Recent publications include chapters in *New Constellations: Movie Stars of the 1960s*, *The Wiley-Blackwell History of American Film*, and *Genre and Performance*. She is the editor of *The Projector: A Journal on Film, Media, and Culture*.

Mark Bernard is Visiting Assistant Professor of English and Interdisciplinary Studies at Johnson C. Smith University in Charlotte, North Carolina. His research interests include media industries, horror film, and food in film. His work appears in upcoming anthologies *Cult Film Stardom: Offbeat Attractions and Processes of Cultification* and *Murders and Acquisitions: Representations of the Serial Killer in Popular Culture*. He is co-author (with Cynthia Baron and Diane E. Carson) of the forthcoming book *The Politics of Food and Film*. He is currently at work on a manuscript titled *Selling the Splat Pack: The DVD Revolution and the American Horror Film*.

Richard Dyer teaches film studies at King's College London and the University of St. Andrews. He is working on a book on serial killers in European Cinema and on *La dolce vita*.

Jane Feuer is professor of English and film studies at the University of Pittsburgh. Her main areas of interest are popular culture, television, and musicals. Her publications include the monographs *The Hollywood Musical* (BFI, 1982 and 1993) and *Seeing Through the Eighties: Television and Reaganism* (BFI, 1995). She has also co-authored *MTM: Quality Television* (BFI, 1984) and has published numerous essays in international journals and anthologies. She is currently writing a book on "quality" television drama.

Pamela Church Gibson is reader in cultural and historical studies at the London College of Fashion. She has published widely on film, fashion, gender and consumption. Her edited anthologies include: *The Oxford Guide to Film Studies* (Oxford University Press, 1998), *Dirty Looks: Women, Power, Pornography* (BFI Publishing, 1993), *Fashion Cultures: Theories, Exploration and Analysis* (Routledge, 2001) and *More Dirty Looks: Gender, Power, Pornography* (BFI, 2004). Her most recent book is *Fashion and Celebrity Culture* (Berg, 2011). She is currently co-editing a new anthology, *Fashion Cultures Two* for Routledge and preparing a new monograph. She is Principal Editor of the journal *Film, Fashion and Consumption* and in July 2012 organized the first conference of the European Popular Culture Association (EUPOP) of which she is currently president.

Oliver Gruner teaches film and visual culture at London Metropolitan University and the University of Portsmouth. His research interests include cultural memory of the 1960s, the historical film and film reception. His work has been published in various journals and edited collections.

Amanda Howell is a senior lecturer in screen studies at Griffith University. Her current research focuses on popular music and film, and her book, *Making Spectacles of Themselves: Popular Music in Action Films and the Performance of Masculinity* is forthcoming from Routledge.

Tamar Jeffers McDonald is senior lecturer in film Studies at the University of Kent, UK. She read English at Somerville College, Oxford, before turning to Film Studies and being awarded her Masters by the University of Westminster and her PhD by the University of Warwick. Her current research interests include film costume; genre studies, especially romantic comedy, the gothic and melodrama; and stardom, especially the star figure of Doris Day, the subject of her next monograph, *Doris Day Confidential: Hollywood Sex and Stardom* (2013). Recent publications include two monographs, *Romantic Comedy: Boy Meets Girl Meets Genre* (Wallflower Press, 2007) and *Hollywood Catwalk: Exploring Costume In Mainstream Film* (I. B. Tauris, 2010). An edited collection, *Virgin Territory: Representing Sexual Inexperience In Film*, was published by Wayne State University Press in February 2010.

Siân Lincoln is senior lecturer in media studies at Liverpool John Moores University. Her research interests are around contemporary youth culture, young people and private space, teenage "bedroom culture" and young people and the media. She has recently published her first book *Youth Culture and Private Space* (Palgrave Macmillan, 2012) and is working on her second, titled *Rethinking Youth Cultures: A Critical Introduction* (Palgrave Macmillan). She has published in and guest-edited various journals, including *Leisure Studies, YOUNG, Space and Culture, Continuum: Journal of Media and Cultural Studies, Journal of Sociology* and *Information Technology and People*.

Tim McNelis completed his PhD in film music at the University of Liverpool. His research focused on the role popular songs and musical performance play in regulating agency and constructing identity in US youth films. Tim has co-authored two essays with Elena Boschi. "'Same Old Song': On Audiovisual Style in the Films of Wes Anderson" has been published in *New Review of Film and Television Studies*, and "Seen and Heard: Visible Playback Technology in Film" will be published in a collection entitled *Ubiquitous Musics*.

Claire Molloy holds the chair in film, television, and digital media at Edge Hill University. She is the author of *Memento* (EUP, 2010) and *Popular Media and Animals* (Palgrave Macmillan, 2011) and co-editor of the collections *Beyond Human: From Animality to Transhumanism*

(Continuum, 2012) and *American Independent Cinema: Indie, indiewood and beyond* (Routledge, 2012).

Gary Needham is senior lecturer in film and television studies at Nottingham Trent University. He has published on numerous collections and is the co-editor of *Asian Cinemas: A Reader and Guide* (Edinburgh University Press, 2006) and *Queer TV: Histories, Theories, Politics* (Routledge, 2009). He is also the author of the monograph *Brokeback Mountain* (2010), part of the "American Indies" series, which he co-edits for Edinburgh University Press. He is currently co-editing *Andy Warhol in Ten Takes* for the BFI.

Bill Osgerby is professor in media, culture and communications at London Metropolitan University. His research focuses on twentieth century British and American cultural history, and his books include *Youth in Britain Since 1945* (Blackwell, 1998), *Playboys in Paradise: Youth, Masculinity and Leisure-Style in Modern America* (Berg/New York University Press, 2001), *Youth Media* (Routledge, 2004), and a co-edited anthology, *Action TV: Tough-Guys, Smooth Operators and Foxy Chicks* (Routledge, 2001).

Hilary Radner is professor of film and media studies in the Department of History and Art History, University of Otago. Her research focuses on understanding the representations of gender and identity in contemporary visual culture, particularly in terms of how these evolve over time in relation to second wave feminism. Recent publications include: *Neo-Feminist Cinema: Girly Films, Chick Flicks, and Consumer Culture* (Routledge) as author and *New Zealand Cinema: Interpreting the Past* (Intellect/U. of Chicago) and *Feminism at the Movies: Understanding Gender in Contemporary Cinema* (Routledge) as co-editor. Current projects include co-editing *A Companion to Contemporary French Film* for Blackwell Publishing, a manuscript on regulating the emotions after second wave feminism in the Hollywood romantic melodrama and a further project on the woman's film in New Zealand cinema.

George Rodosthenous is a lecturer in music theater at the School of Performance and Cultural Industries of the University of Leeds. He is the artistic director of the theater company Altitude North and also works as a freelance composer for the theater. His research interests are the body in performance, directing, refining improvisational techniques and compositional practices for performance, devising pieces with live musical soundscapes as interdisciplinary process, the director as coach, updating Greek tragedy, and the British musical. He is currently working on the book *Theatre as Voyeurism: the Pleasure(s) of Watching*.

Millie Taylor is professor in musical theatre at the University of Winchester. Her research interests are popular musical theatre, British pantomime, contemporary music theatre and voice. Recent publications include *British Pantomime Performance* (Intellect 2007) and *Musical Theatre, Realism and Entertainment* (Ashgate Press, 2012) in the series Interdisciplinary Studies in Opera. She recently guest edited a special issue of the journal *Studies in Musical Theatre* (Vol. 6/1, 2012) on 'Voice and Excess' and is currently working on a text book on musical theatre and co-editing a collection entitled *Rethinking Musical Theatre: Song and Dance*.

Yannis Tzioumakis is senior lecturer in media and communication studies at the University of Liverpool. His research specializes in American cinema and the business of media entertainment. He is the author of *American Independent Cinema: An Introduction* (2006) *The Spanish Prisoner* (2009), *Hollywood's Indies: Classics Divisions, Specialty Labels and the American Film Market* (2012), all for Edinburgh University Press, for which he also co-edits the "American Indies" series. Yannis is also co-editor of *Greek Cinema: Texts, Forms, Identities* (Intellect, 2011) and *American Independent Cinema: Indie, Indiewood and beyond* (Routledge, 2012).

Frederick Wasser is a professor and the chair of the Department of Television and Radio at Brooklyn College, CUNY. His scholarly interests are in media industries, contemporary Hollywood and political economy of the culture industries. He wrote an influential book on the video cassette recorder entitled *Veni, Vidi, Video* (University of Texas Press, 2001). His most recent book is *Steven Spielberg's America* (Polity Press, 2011). He comes to scholarly studies after working as a sound editor and other jobs in Hollywood in the 1980s. He helped edit at least one Vestron film in this time period (not *Dirty Dancing*).

INDEX

abortion: abortion subplot, 53, 80, 132, 148, 159, 232; compassionate depiction of, 135; as (narrative) distraction, 163; and feminism, 134, 184; Hollywood portrayal of, 134; and lower classes, 53; mature handling of, 5, 127, 135; progressive representation of, 128, 134; and Reaganite entertainment, 96; and suggestion of recreational sex, 191; and *Roe vs. Wade*, 134, 135, 166n28; and sex education films, 199n12; and teen pics, 46. *See also* Bergstein, Eleanor; *Dirty Dancing*; feminism
Adams, Mary Louise, 304
adolescence, adolescents, 171, 176, 209
Adorno, Theodor, 100, 101
Advancing Paul Newman, 154, 155
Adventures of Ozzie and Harriet, The, 215
affect, 13, 234, 240, 242; and pleasures, 236

African American, African Americans, 22, 77, 80; and Clayton, Merry, 249; and Coles, Charles "Honi," 65, 90; culture, 64; dance, 78; minorities, 5; music, 244; musical culture, 77; musical identity, 82; musicals, 71n12; and Ronettes, the, 157; and "soul" music, 77; and tradition of jazz, 64, 90
AIDS, 135
"Alexander's Ragtime Band," 82
Alice Doesn't Live Here Anymore, 154
"Almost Paradise," 247
alternative cinema, 224
Altman, Rick, 44, 57, 59, 62, 63, 65, 67
American cinema, 7; and girls' dreams, 276; and Hollywood industry policy (*see* industry policy), 88; and independent sector, 5; in the 1980s, 23; and sex, 198; and teen film, 209. *See also* American film; Hollywood; classical Hollywood

American film, 23, 198, 209; industry (see also Hollywood film industry), 4, 12, 21, 25, 26. See also American cinema; Hollywood; classical Hollywood
American Gigolo, 115, 197
American Graffiti, 229, 230, 240, 268, 269; and Californian motif, 217; and early 1960s historical backdrop, 155; and lost innocence, 213; and nostalgia culture, 108, 208, 240, 268; and nostalgia film, 44, 218, 228, 232; and nostalgic teen film, 210-11, 214; and wall-to-wall music, 59, 240, 269
American Retro, 108
anachronism/anachronistic, 239, 240, 245, 246, 247, 248, 249, 250, 252; and historical accuracy, 114; fashion, 136; film scores, 240; hairstyles, 136; music, 205, 242, 245, 247, 248, 249, 250; musicality, 246; popular soundtrack, 136; songs, 13, 87, 220, 239, 241, 242, 245, 246, 247, 248, 249, 250, 251, 252, 254, 255. See also *Dirty Dancing*; "(I've Had) The Time of My Life"; score
ancillary; markets, 3, 21, 28, 34, 224, 266; products, 266; revenue, 275; rights, 28, 29
Animal House, 155, 208, 211
Ardolino, Emile, 2, 35
Arena, 111
arthouse cinema-going, 224
Artisan Entertainment, 3, 40, 272
Astaire, Fred, 61, 302
Athena posters, 107, 122
audiovisual; aesthetic, 242, 249; evocation of nostalgia, 205, 242; humor, 246; representation, 240; storytelling, 269; style, 243
Austin Chronicle, 131

Baby, It's You, 5, 6, 9, 208, 241
"Baby, You Are the One," 301
Back to the Future, 218
Baez, Joan, 158
Bardot, Brigitte, 117
Barthes, Roland, 287
Baum, Frank L., 264
Baumgarten, Marjorie, 131
"Be My Baby," 79, 158, 185, 207, 220, 243, 244
Beach Boys, the, 216
Beauvoir, Simone de, 141, 142, 143, 146
bedroom culture, 170-71
Bee Gees, the, 97, 265, 268
Benjamin, Walter, 61
Benson, Sheila, 162
Bergstein, Eleanor, 3, 122, 135, 137, 138, 152, 155, 252; and abortion subplot, 134, 159; and analysis of the *Dirty Dancing* fans, 274; and *Dirty Dancing's* conclusion, 144; and *Dirty Dancing's* "pastness," 136; and feminism, 133, 154, 163; and the genesis of *Dirty Dancing*, 153; and Jewish culture, 63, 64; and memories of Catskills, 68, 82, 114, 203, 213; and musical choices, 269; and onstage dancing, 298; and the production of *Dirty Dancing* 26, 267; and the relationship between film and stage show, 283; and representation of women, 154,; and teen cultures, 204; and teen songs, 158, 244
Berkeley, Busby, 81
"Besame, Mucho," 305
Big Chill, The, 44, 208, 241, 268
"Big Girls Don't Cry," 207, 220, 229, 244, 270
Big Wednesday, 208, 214, 217, 218
Bill Hayley and the Comets, 295
Billboard, 208, 263, 267

Index

Billy Elliot: The Musical, 299, 300
black culture, 65. *See also* African American culture
Black Fury, 100
Black Swan, 81
Blackboard Jungle, 295
blackface, 85
Blade Runner, 99
Blair Witch Project, The, 40
Blake, William, 95
Blay, Andre, 29, 30
blending theory, 287. *See also* conceptual blending
block booking, 28
blockbuster films, 35, 225, 264, 267
Bloom, Noel, 30, 31
Blow Monkeys, the, 79, 174, 248, 254
Body Heat, 218
Booker, Keith, 217
Bordo, Susan, 148
Born on the Fourth of July, 152
Bourne, Matthew, 300
Boyfriend, The, 43
Brando, Marlon, 110, 197
Breakfast Club, The, 88
Breakin', 34
Breakin' 2: Electric Boogaloo, 34
Breen, Joseph I., 88, 100, 101
Bringing Up Baby, 49
Britton, Andrew, 88, 93, 94, 96, 98, 99, 102, 104
Brockes, Emma, 283
Brown, Josef, 300
Brunsdon, Charlotte, 145
Buena Vista, 36
Burke, Solomon, 55, 79
Burt, Ramsay, 304
Butler, David, 245
Butler, Judith, 148
Buziak, Bob, 269, 273

cable television, 266
Cafferty, John, 242

Calvin Klein, 110, 111
Can't Buy Me Love, 36
Canby, Vincent, 131, 132
Cannold, Mitchell, 26, 33, 40
Cannon, 34, 35, 38
Cannonball, The, 30
Cantor, Max, 132
Cardin, Pierre, 119
Carlson, Marvin, 285
Carmen, Eric, 79, 247, 248, 270
Carolco, 35, 38
Casablanca, 225
Cassidy, Patrick, 37
Castle, Irene, 90
Castle, Vernon, 90
Catskill Mountains, Catskills, 26, 62, 64, 65, 68, 82, 117, 207, 209; and Jewish culture, 64
Cavendish, Dominic, 282, 283, 309
CBS, 29
Chanel, Coco, 118
Channel, Bruce, 79, 268
Chapman, Guy, 309
Chapman, Rowena, 113
chick flicks, 145, 227
Children of the World, 268
Christian Science Monitor, 161
civil rights movement, 99, 107, 153, 154, 156, 196, 215, 283
Claid, Emilyn, 306
Clarke, Cath, 163
class, 12, 14, 189.; conflict, 109, 204; differences, 49, 63, 65, 66, 89, 188, 300; divisions, 251; dynamics, 84; inequality, 80; mobility, 87, 88; politics, 23, 81; struggle, 244, 248. *See also Dirty Dancing;* middle-class; working-class
classical Hollywood, 27, 88, 102, 223, 245; cinema, 93, 95; scoring, 245 *See also* American cinema; American film; and Hollywood
Clayton, Merry, 79, 249, 270

clean teen (music), 158, 244
Clift, Montgomery, 196
Close, Glenn, 153
Coca-Cola Company, the, 32
Cocker, Joe, 250
Cocktail, 8, 9
Cohan, Steven, 110, 302
Cole, Shaun, 115
Coles, Charles "Honi," 65, 75, 78, 80, 90, 252
Columbia Pictures, 29, 30, 32
comedy, 45, 57
coming-of-age, 68, 172, 180, 228, 285; and adult standards, 211; and dancing, 144; and feminism, 132, 160; and genre, 267; and loss of innocence, 204, 213-14; and nostalgic teen films, 208, 209; and *Platoon*, 151; and solitary media practices, 171; and songs, 229, 231, 251. *See also* narrative
complex narratives, 226,
conceptual blending, 285, 286, 293. *See also* blending theory
conglomeration, 23
continuity editing, 5
Contours, the, 79, 220, 230, 270
Cook, Amy, 286
Cooke, Sam, 115
Cosmopolitan Magazine, 146
counterculture, 95, 153, 224, 229, 230
couples-based dancing, 186, 188, 189
Courrèges, André, 119
Cousin Brucie, 207, 244, 248
Crazy, Stupid Love, 10
Cruising, 99
Cry Baby, 197
"Cry to Me," 75, 79
cult musical, 282
cultural biographies, 169, 180. *See also* emerging biographies
cultural capital, 225, 230
Cultural Studies, 113

dance film, 39, 70, 72, 88, 241, 242, 291, 297, 310, 311. *See also Dirty Dancing*; musical
Dance, Girl, Dance, 81
Dance With Me, 72
Dancing with the Stars, 10, 188, 300
dansical, 298, 305
Davis, Geena, 39
Day of the Dead, 99
Dead The, 38
Dean, James, 196, 197
DeLaurentiis, Dino, 34, 35, 38, 39
Denby, David, 162, 163, 267
DeNicola, John, 247, 251
Denisoff, R. Serge, 239
Depp, Johnny, 197
Diaghilev, Serge de, 299
Diamond, Neil, 83
diegesis, 59, 107, 244, 248, 250, 303. *See also* diegetic
diegetic: audience, 81; dancing, 59, 61, 67, 70; music, 59, 62, 70, 230, 255; singing, 59, 60, 61, 62, 67, 70; verisimilitude, 229; world, 247. *See also* diegesis; "(I've Had) The Time of My Life"; musical; narrative
Dika, Vera, 219, 220
Diner, 228, 229, 230
Dirty Dancing: and abortion, 127, 134-35, 159, 184; and African-American culture, 77; and American film industry, 12, 21; and anachronisms, 114, 242, 246, 252, 254; and ancillary markets, 3; as anti-feminist, 146; and backstage musical, 43; and binary oppositions, 65, 66, 67, 69; budget, 34, 37; casting, 35; and cause-effect narrative logic, 5, 6; and character transformation, 7, 174; and choreography, 298, 303, 305, 306, 311; and class differences, 49, 65; and class politics, 81, 109;

Index

and classical Hollywood, 88; and copyright-holding companies, 3; and costuming, 116, 117; and cult film, 224, 225, 235; on DVD, 273; as dance film, 70, 208, 300; and distribution, 36; and diversion from adulthood, 173; and emerging biographies, 171, 172, 173, 175, 179; and *Emmanuelle*, 191; and empowerment, 178-79, 211; and ethnic boundaries, 109; as ethnic musical, 64; as fairy tale musical, 63; and family melodrama, 50, 51; and fans, 203, 239, 263, 275; and the female body, 138; and female identity, 157; and female perspective, 7; and feminism, 13, 128, 132-34, 145, 146, 154, 155, 156, 160, 163, 164; and film location, 64; and franchising, 2-4, 12, 260; and the gaze, 110; and gender politics, 81; and genre, 21, 44, 48, 57; and heroine's intelligence, 112; and helpful media texts, 169, 171, 176, 179; and heterosexuality, 184, 186; and high-concept, 6; and Hollywood formula, 102; and Hollywood industry policy, 88, 100-101; and home video industry, 26; and homoeroticism, 197; and hustling, 184, 192, 194, 195, 197; and ideology, 185; as independent film 5, 36; and intertextuality, 221, 232; as Jewish film, 63, 65, 82; as Jewish folk musical, 62, 63, 64, 66, 68, 70, 71; and Johnny's delinquent look, 197; and Latin American dance influences, 190; and liberalism, 44, 80, 107, 158; as life-affirming, 184; Lionsgate remake, 11, 68; and MGM, 26; and MTV aesthetic, 60; and masculinity, 23, 116; as melodrama, 109, 161; and mise-en-scène, 51, 54, 114, 212, 232, 254, 265, 269; as musical, 45, 60, 62, 64, 70, 76, 88, 89; and narrative, 7-10, 102, 110; and negative reviews, 162; and neo-feminism, 145; and New Men, 109, 112; and the 1980s, 22; and the 1960s, 155; and non-diegetic singing, 60-61, 71n2; and nostalgia, 84, 108; and other Vestron titles, 38; and patriarchy, 96-97; and Patrick Swayze's body, 111; and politicized narrative, 152, 160, 161, 164; and performance (live), 287, 292; and personal recollections, 233, 234; and queer politics, 129, 183; and Reagan-era cinema, 87, 88, 89, 102; and Reaganite entertainment, 87, 93, 96-99, 100, 101, 102; and realism, 81; and relationship between Jewish and African-American culture, 83, 84; and relationship with contemporaneous films, 8, 88, 152, 153, 160, 180; and repeat viewing, 227; and retro style, 114-15; and romance, 212; and romantic comedy, 44, 48, 58; and *Romeo and Juliet*, 191; and second wave feminism, 145, 146; as self-aware text, 48; and sex, 73, 175, 191, 198; as show musical, 63; and songs in, 205, 243; and spin-off television show, 37; and stage adaptation/stage show, 261, 281, 286, 293; and studio filmmaking, 6; and synergies, 268, 269; syntax of, 62; and teenage fantasy, 298; and teenage girls/young women, 129, 161, 169, 171; and teenage lifestyles, 217; and teenage rite-of-passage, 167, 168, 173, 175, 177, 179, 180, 211, 229; tie-ins, 2, 4; and upward class mobility, 97; and use of music, 109, 158, 230, 242, 246, 252, 253, 254; on VCR, 270, 274; and

325

Dirty Dancing (continued)
  Vestron, 5, 21, 25, 33, 38, 39, 40, 136; and voiceover, 105; and whiteness, 83, 84; and working class, 22, 89-92, 93, 97, 101, 157; and wrong partner trope, 49-50
Dirty Dancing: The Classic Story on Stage, 2, 4, 10, 259, 260, 274, 275, 297, 298, 308, 310
Dirty Dancing: The Concert Tour 270, 273
Dirty Dancing: Havana Nights, 2, 4, 14, 15, 66, 67, 68, 69, 272, 273, 311
Dirty Dancing: Live!, 4
Dirty Dancing: Live in Concert, 271
Dirty Dancing: Live the Dream, 271, 272
Dirty Dancing: Official Dance Workout, 274
Dirty Dancing: The Time of Your Life, 4, 14, 199, 273
Disney, 29, 38, 40
"Do You Love Me?," 158, 220, 230, 246
Dolan, Jill, 289
dominant ideology, 94
Donna Reed Show, The, 215
Doobie Brothers, the, 246
Douglas, Susan, 158, 160, 243
Dr. Strangelove, 245
Drake, Phil, 228
Dream a Little Dream, 38
Drifters, the, 79
Dyer, Richard, 110, 116
Dylan, Bob, 158

Earth Girls Are Easy, 38, 39
Ebert, Roger, 48, 152, 163
Eddie and the Cruisers, 242
Edwards, Tim, 116
Eisenhower, Dwight, 218
Elsaesser, Thomas, 226
Elvis, 197
Embassy Pictures, 31

emerging biographies, 168, 169, 171, 173, 175, 179. *See also* cultural biographies; *Dirty Dancing*
Emmanuelle, 191
empathy, 288, 291
empowered consumption, 164
entertainment, 94, 101; industry, 40
Erdreich, Sarah, 134
E.T.: The Extra-Terrestrial, 99
ethnic; conflict, 204; differences, 66; musical, 64
European art films, 27
European dance, 189, 190
Evans, Sarah, 157
event exchange, 289
Everly Brothers, the, 305
Exorcist, The, 28
exploitation films, 27, 35

Facebook, 11, 68, 128
fairy tale musical. *See* musical
Faludi, Susan, 153
Family Home Entertainment, 30, 31
Fast Times at Ridgemont High, 134, 163
Fatal Attraction, 153
Father Knows Best, 196, 215
Fauconnier, Gilles, 285, 286
feedback loop, 289
Feltheimer, John, 274
female: agency, 23, 110, 244; audience, 3, 123, 127, 176, 275, 298, 302, 303, 309, 310; demographic, 259; fans, 170, 180; fantasy, 298, 302, 308, 310; friendship film, 154; identity, 157; perspective, 7, 9, 243; sexuality, 128; subjectivity, 227; viewer, 112, 123. *See also Dirty Dancing*
feminine, 157, 187; culture, 149; movement, 142
Feminine Mystique, The, 45
femininity. *See* feminine.
feminism, 99, 106, 132, 133, 135, 144, 145, 146, 147, 160, 163, 164, 196,

227; and abortion, 134; as corrupting force, 153; and debates, 163; and neo-feminism, 128, 145, 146, 149n49; radical, 155; second wave, 45, 128, 142, 145, 146; and stigma, 137; third wave, 106. *See also* abortion; Eleanor Bergstein; *Dirty Dancing*; feminist

feminist: academics, 138; activism, 153, 155, 164; audience, 134; credentials, 13, 128; critics, 134, 184; debates, 138, 154; film, 128, 132; issues, 154, 155, 160; movement, 45, 153, 157, 160, 164; and neo-conservative texts, 103; plot, 133; text, 127, 146; thought, 137; theorists, 138, 142. *See also* abortion; Eleanor Bergstein; *Dirty Dancing*; feminism

Ferland, Guy, 2, 67

Ferris Bueller's Day Off, 151

Fiddler on the Roof, 64

Fifties, the, 115, 183, 204, 214, 215, 217, 218, 220; iconography, 108; retro, 23, 109; style, 108

film fandom, 224

film musical. *See* musical

Financial Times, 283

First Blood, 34

Fischer-Lichte, Erika, 289

Fisher, Jennifer, 300

Fishof, David, 270

Five Satins, the, 79

Flashdance, 6, 16, 33, 60, 63, 88, 208, 225, 253, 311

Flynn, Errol, 48

folk musical. *See Dirty Dancing*

Fonz, the, 109

Footloose, 33, 63, 186, 208, 241, 247, 261, 311

Forrest Gump, 152, 164

Fort Apache, The Bronx, 30

42nd Street, 43, 81

Foster, Susan Leigh, 143

Foucault, Michel, 302

Fountainhead, The, 118

Fox. *See* Twentieth Century Fox

franchise, 3, 39, 259, 260, 264, 265, 266, 269, 273, 274, 275. *See also Dirty Dancing*

Frankie Valli and the Four Seasons, 79, 229, 244

Fraser, Wendy, 250

Friedan, Betty, 45

Funny Girl, 64

Furst, Austin, 26, 29, 30, 31, 32, 33, 38, 39

G.I. Blues, 115

Gallup, George, 216

Gardner, Lyn, 283, 297, 298, 309

Garland, Judy, 60, 81

Garrison, Miranda, 273

gay liberation, 99

Gaye, Marvin, 114

gender, 14, 186, 187, 189, 196, 227; conflict, 204; differences, 89; identity, 189, 215; politics, 12, 23, 81, 106

generic hybridity, 44

Genette, Gérard, 88

Gentleman's Quarterly, 111

Gere, Richard, 111

Ghost, 111, 261

Gilbert, James, 216

Gill, Rosalind, 145, 146

"Gimme Shelter," 249

Girlfriends, 154

Glee, 10

Globus, Yoram, 34

Go Tell the Spartans, 33

Godfather, The, 28

"Goin' to the Chapel," 158, 166

Golan, Menachem, 34

Goldblum, Jeff, 39

Goldcrest Films, 40

Golden Harvest, 30

Gone With the Wind, 225, 265

Goodman, Benny, 83

Goodwin, Andrew, 253
Gore, Lesley, 248
Got to Dance, 300
goyim, 65
Grainge, Paul, 219
Grease, 33, 108, 109, 114, 169, 172, 208, 225, 241, 311
Grease 2, 208, 311
Grey, Jennifer, 35, 46, 297; and dancing skills, 81; and *Dirty Dancing* poster, 161, 225; and *Ferris Bueller's Day Off*, 151; likeness of, 1; playing a character younger than her, 253; and presence in the stage show version of *Dirty Dancing*, 285–86; and Semitic features, 66, 82; and sequel, 37; and 2009 comeback, 10; and voiceover, 255n19
Grey, Joel, 35
Griffith, D. W., 36
Guardian, 131, 134, 163, 177, 283
Gurley Brown, Helen, 145, 146, 149
Guys and Dolls, 309

Hairspray, 183
Hallelujah!, 81
Hanna, Judith Lynne, 308
Happy Days, 109, 208
Hardin, Melora, 37
Hart, Elizabeth, 286
Harvey Girls, The, 81
Haskell, Molly, 162
Hays, Will, 88, 100, 101
Hegarty, John, 108, 114, 115
Hellman, John, 216
Hemdale, 35, 38
Hentges, Sarah, 211
Hepburn, Audrey, 117
Heritage Foundation, the, 153
heteronormativity, 13, 188
heterosexual romance, 247
heterosexuality, 80, 129, 137, 145, 146, 184, 186, 187, 189, 199; compulsory 183, 198n1

"Hey! Baby," 60, 61, 268
high-concept, 6, 16, 225, 226, 236. See also *Dirty Dancing*
High School Musical, 189
Hill, Evan, 216
Hine, Thomas, 215
Hintnaus, Tom, 111
historical accuracy, 223, 240, 242, 246, 249, 252. See also anachronism; score
historical allusion, 220
historical genre, 45
Hit and Run, 33
Hitchcock, Alfred, 67
Hollinger, Karen, 154
Hollywood, 26, 64, 70, 264; cinema, 7; contemporary, 134; film industry (*see* American film industry), 88, 99, 100, 102; film musical, 189, 275; majors, 6, 21, 27, 28, 29, 30, 34, 39, 226; studio filmmaking, 5. See also American cinema; American film; classical Hollywood
Hollywood industry policy, 88, 100, 101
Hollywood Shuffle, The, 5, 15
Home Box Office, 29
home video, 3, 26, 39, 226, 233, 266; distribution, 30; market, 5, 21, 31, 32, 34, 37, 38, 39; recorder, 29, 30; rental, 26, 30, 226, 266; sales, 266
homosexuality, 194, 196
homosocial gaze, 106
homosociality, 106
Horkheimer, Max, 100, 101
horror films, 27, 31
Hughes, John, 241
"Hungry Eyes," 185, 231, 232, 246, 251, 253, 303
Hunter, I.Q., 235
Hutcheon, Linda, 219

"I Heard It Through the Grapevine," 114

identity, 186, 191, 198; formation, 170; politics, 14
Ienner, Jimmy, 269
Imitation of Life, 51
"In the Still of the Night," 249
Independent (UK), 309
independent film, 5, 7, 40, 176, 267; companies, 28; distribution, 27, 266; distributors, 27, 28, 38; producers, 27, 28, 34; production, 5, 40, 266; video distributor, 40
independent woman's film, 154
indie film. *See* independent film
indiewood, 6. *See* independent film
Inglis, Ian, 227
Internet Movie Database, the, 10, 129, 170, 176, 177, 180, 234, 236
It's My Turn, 153, 154
"It's Raining Men," 188
"(I've Had) The Time of My Life," 212; anachronistic use of, 87, 220, 246, 250-51; as diegetic music, 62; and *Dirty Dancing* television spin off, 271; and evocation of the 1960s, 136; and *Glee*, 10; as leitmotif, 61, 80, 251; music video, 253; and narrative closure, 84; and 1980s music, 81, 225, 230; and self-reflexivity, 183; at the US charts, 208, 239, 268; as white pop music, 78
IVE, 31, 35

Jackson, Michael, 34, 239, 267
Jailhouse Rock, 197
Jameson, Fredric, 107, 108, 209, 218, 219, 220, 232, 233
Jansen, JoAnn, 67, 68, 272
Jaws, 28
Jazz Singer, The, 83, 84, 85
Jessel, George, 83
Jett, Joan, 248
Jewish folk musical, 22, 62, 66, 68. See *Dirty Dancing*; and musical

Jezebel, 134
JFK. *See* Kennedy, John F.
JFK, 152, 164
Joanie Loves Chachi, 208
Johnston, Tom, 79, 246
Jola, Corinne, 291
Jolson, Al, 83
jouissance, 287
Julia, 154
jump cut, 61
Just, Jaeckin, 191
juvenile delinquent movie, 46

Kamen, Nick, 115
Karate Kid, The, 7, 8
Kassabian, Anahid, 73, 76, 230, 244, 253, 255
Kassar, Mario, 34
Katzman, Sam, 265
Kearney, Mary Celeste, 172
Keeler, Ruby, 81
Kellner, Douglas, 90, 103
Kelly, Gene, 61, 302
Kennedy, John F. (JFK), 45, 52, 105, 155, 208, 214, 216, 218, 228, 229
King Creole, 197
Kitt, Sam, 40
Klaus, Nomi, 248
Klinger, Barbara, 223, 227
Kristeva, Julia, 148
Kubrick, Stanley, 245

L'arnacoeur [*The Heartbreaker*], 10
Landis, John, 211
lands-man, 65
Larson, Reed, 171
Lasker, Jay, 266
Last Exit to Brooklyn, 219
Laverne & Shirley, 208
Legally Blonde, 3, 310
Levi's, 108, 109, 114, 115
Levin, Gerald, 29
Lewis, Jerry, 83
liberal politics, 107, 120, 135, 136, 158

liberalism. *See* liberal politics
Lions Gate. *See* Lionsgate
Lionsgate, 3, 4, 10, 11, 40, 260, 272, 274; Television, 272
lip-synching, 60, 61, 62, 70, 87
LIVE Entertainment, 3, 35, 40, 272, 273
live experience (theater), 284, 293
live performance, 285, 287, 288, 289, 292
Living TV, 4
Looking for Mr. Goodbar, 99
Lord of the Rings trilogy, The, 11
Los Angeles Times, 162
Love & Dance, 72
"Love Is Strange," 61, 75, 77, 79, 268
"Love Man," 79, 230
Love Me Tonight, 81
Love N' Dancing, 72
low-budget; independents, 21; producers, 34
lower-class. *See* working-class
Lucas, George, 210, 213, 228, 240, 269
Lyne, Adrian, 6
Lynn, Vera, 245

Macaulay, Alistair, 283
Mad Hot Ballroom, 72
Magnetic Video, 29
Mail Online, 281, 282, 288
mainstream cinema, 184, 211. *See also* American cinema; Hollywood cinema
major studios. *See* Hollywood
Making of Michael Jackson's Thriller, The, 31
Malcolm X, 152
male body, 260, 297, 300, 301;
male dancer, 298, 299, 300, 301, 304, 308, 310
Malnig, Julie, 186, 187
Maltby, Richard, 225, 226
Mamet, David, 17
Mamma Mia!, 309

"Maniac," 253
Marilyn Hotchkiss' Ballroom Dancing & Charm School, 72
Markowitz, Donald, 251
masculinity, 23, 106, 113, 116, 157, 248, 298, 301, 302, 304; cinematic, 110
Matewan, 5
Mathijs, Ernest, 224
Maurice Williams and the Zodiacs, 79, 220, 230, 268
May, Kirse Granat, 217
McCarthy, Eugene, 155
McConachie, Bruce, 286, 288
McDermott, Alice, 162
McEwan, Melissa, 131, 133
McMains, Juliet, 144
McRobbie, Angela, 186
McTheatre, 310
Media Home Entertainment, 31
Medley, Bill, 80, 220, 250, 251, 252, 268, 270, 271
Medovoi, Leerom, 196
Melnick, Jeffrey, 82
melodrama, 21, 49, 51, 109, 127, 161
memory narrative, 68
Mennesson, Christine, 299
merchandise, 259, 264, 265, 274, 282
metrosexual, 123
MGM, 26, 32
Mickey & Sylvia, 79, 268
Mickey Mouse, 108
middle-class, 89, 159, 187, 193, 209, 216, 218, 229, 230. *See also* class; *Dirty Dancing*; working-class
Midnight Cowboy, 197
Miller, Chris, 211
Millet, Kate, 146
mini-majors, 38
Minnelli, Vincente, 61
Miramax, 5, 38, 40, 267
mirror neuron, 288, 289, 293
Mississippi Burning, 152
modern dance, 190

Index

Moi, Toril, 142, 146
Molnar-Szakacs, Istvan, 291
montage, 46, 157, 191, 231
Moon, Michael, 195
Moonstruck, 88
moral majority, 153
More American Graffiti, 208
More Dirty Dancing, 4, 268, 269, 270
Motown Records, 266
MTV, 31, 240, 253; aesthetic, 60, 63, 70
multi-media conglomerates, 265
multiple viewing. *See* repeat viewing
Mulvey, Laura, 116
music, 158.; authentic, 249; contemporary, 223, 225, 230, 234, 242, 250; jazz, 242; Latin American dance 242, 246; period, 223, 225, 229, 230, 239, 241, 242, 248; pop(ular), 240, 242, 245, 246, 250, 253, 269; rock, 246; soul, 242, 247, 248; video, 60, 70. *See also* anachronistic; *Dirty Dancing*; nostalgia; retro; score; soundtrack
musical, 22, 39, 67, 241, 242.; all-black, 64; backstage, 43, 252, 302; and binary oppositions, 65, 66; Broadway, 63, 64; Classic, 60, 70, 76; conventions of, 89, 98; dance, 88, 208; definition, 59–62; and entertainment, 70; ethnic, 64; fairy-tale, 63, 65 ,67; and fantasy scenes, 260; folk, 63, 64, 66, 68, 70, 71n; and gay erotics, 197; Hollywood, 64, 65, 70, 72n20, 189, 275; jukebox, 265; nostalgic, 310; post-classic, 63; and production at Vestron, 33–34; show, 59, 62, 63, 66; stage, 297; structure of, 66, 67; theater, 260, 289, 293, 311; and utopian impulses, 81. *See also* African American; cult; dance film; diegetic; *Dirty Dancing*
My Dream is Yours, 43

narration, 52
narrative, 48, 53, 55, 57; and abortion subplot, 5; and American independent cinema, 5; and anachronistic use of music, 245; and cause-effect logic, 5, 6; and climactic sequences, 8; closure, 9, 63, 69, 211; coming-of-age, 229, 231; and conventions of falling in love, 116; derivative, 223; design, 93; and diegesis, 59; and *Dirty Dancing's* resolution, 102; and the disappearance of Jewishness, 84; and dual focus, 67, 70; and family power structures, 52; and female perspective, 9; and feminist activism, 155; and the formation of heterosexual couple, 5, 8, 9, 50, 89, 275; male-centered, 164; and MTV aesthetic, 60; and *Romeo and Juliet* formula, 7; and links to romantic comedy (rom-com), 44, 48; of male prostitution, 198; of nostalgia, 283; open ended, 211; of overcoming difficulty, 290; and personal change, 45; politicized, 152, 161; and predictability, 98, 99; and relationship with music, 224, 227, 243; and rite-of-passage, 172, 180; and sex, 191; and sexual experience, 175; simplicity, 225; and teen film, 209; trajectory, 229; and utopian vision, 95; and white artists' (music) tracks, 79; and working class, 99; and wrong partner trope, 49. *See also Dirty Dancing*
National Lampoon, 211
Neale, Steve, 44, 49, 57
negative pickup, 27
Negra, Diane, 160, 164
Nelson, Carrie, 133
neo-feminist cinema, 145

neo-liberalism, 128, 145, 146
Never Been Kissed, 9
New Comedy, 63, 67, 71
New Hollywood, 264, 265, 266
New Line, 38, 40
New Man, 23, 107, 109, 112, 113, 116, 122. See also *Dirty Dancing*
new masculinity, 107
new women's film, 154
New World, 267
New York Abortion Access Fund, 134
New York Hustlers, 197
New York magazine, 161, 162
New York Times, 5, 6, 131, 134, 136, 137, 155, 271
News Corporation, 32
Newsweek, 154, 161
Nicholson, Amy, 297
Nightingale, Benedict, 308
Nixon, Sean, 115
No Way Out, 36
nostalgia, 84, 144, 246, 265; and Eleanor Bergstein, 136; commodified, 44, 233, 234, 240; culture, 108; effect, 252; experience of, 215, 227; film, 44, 45, 57, 218, 219, 220, 224, 232, 233, 241, 242, 254, 308, 309; framing, 210; intertextual, 283, 285, 293; marketing, 204; music, 205, 234, 275; and the 1960s, 228, 268; nostalgic recollections, 203; personal, 233, 234, 240; postmodern film, 219; production of, 12, 208, 227, 242; songs, 234, 239; trend, 269. See also *Dirty Dancing*
nostalgic teen film, 210, 211, 216

O'Hara, Maureen, 81
Ochs, Phil, 158
Officer and a Gentleman, An, 250
"Old Man River," 83
one hit wonder, 268
operetta, 65, 70
oppositional reading, 162
Orbach, Jerry, 82, 132
Orion Pictures, 31, 33, 35, 36, 38
Ormrod, Joan, 214
Ortega, Kenny, 11, 37, 272
otherness, 120
Outsiders, The, 35, 155
"Overload," 60, 248
Overy, Kate, 291

Palmer, William, 102
Paramount, 265
Parents, 40
pastiche, 105, 232, 233
patriarchal: authority, 172, 173, 175; ideal, 196; family, 95; viewpoint and Hollywood cinema, 7. See also patriarchy; feminism; Reaganite entertainment
patriarchy, 96, 99. See also patriarchal
Peggy Sue Got Married, 155, 241
Peisinger, Jon, 30, 31, 33, 37, 38
period authenticity, 223
Phillips, Katie, 306, 310
Picasso, Pablo, 118
Pitt, Brad, 108
Plasketes, George, 239
Platoon, 128, 151, 152, 160, 162, 164
Playboy, 110
Pollock, Dale, 213
Polygram, 265
popular culture, 4, 11, 12, 14, 15, 127, 158, 170, 209; contemporary, 168, 215
popular film, 169, 259
Porky's, 208
Portman, Natalie, 81
postfeminist; culture, 160; sensibility, 145
postmodern, 219
Postmodernism, or the Cultural Logic of Late Capitalism, 107
Powell, James, 309
Pretty in Pink, 7, 8, 88, 169, 241, 253
Pretty Woman, 145

Previte, Franke, 247, 251
Price, Lonny, 82
Prince, Stephen, 6, 7
private space, 169, 170, 171
Prizzi's Honor, 32
Production Code Administration, 100
progressive politics, 185
Psycho, 67
Purple Rain, 34
puzzle film, 226, 236

queer: politics, 129; reading, 249
Quigley, William J., 33

R&B, 230, 246, 249, 254, 268
race, 12, 14, 185; politics, 23
racial reproduction, 73
Rambo: First Blood Part Two, 34
Rand, Ayn, 56, 58, 118
Raphaelson, Samson, 83
Raspberries, the, 247
Ray, Nicholas, 109
RCA, 29, 267, 269, 270, 273
Reagan, Ronald, 22, 100, 108, 153, 192
Reagan era, the, 87, 89, 241; cinema, 90, 91, 101, 103
Reaganite entertainment, 22, 87, 93, 163; and abortion, 96; *Dirty Dancing* as, 96–99; and formulaic character, 93; and helplessness, 93; and Hollywood industry policy, 88, 99–101; and negative utopia, 94; and patriarchy, 96; and repetition, 93, 94, 95, 98, 99, 101; and resolution, 98. See also *Dirty Dancing*; patriarchy
realism, 80, 81,; emotional 309; historical, 242
reality television, 188, 189, 199
Reay, Barry, 197
Rebel, 34
Rebel Without a Cause, 51, 109, 197

reception, 13, 152, 160, 161, 163, 299, 300; and identity, 198; of male dancers, 300; and queer politics, 129, 196,; studies, 12; theatrical, 285
Reds, 99
Red Dawn, 35
Redding, Otis, 79, 230
remake, 2, 11, 14 67, 68, 83, 102, 273
repeat viewing, multiple viewing, 224, 225, 226, 227, 233, 234, 235
retro; aesthetic, 168, 204; costuming, 107; film, 228; music, 107; musical, 205; styling, 107, 108
Rhapsody in Blue, 83
Rheindorf, Markus. 252
Rhodes, Cynthia, 75, 132
Rich, Adrienne, 198
Righteous Brothers, the, 220, 250
rite-of-passage, 7, 49, 167, 169, 170, 172, 175, 176, 209, 282, 303; and cultural biographies, 172, 179; break up as, 174,; and empowerment, 211; film, 168, 209; love story as, 173; and narrative, 180; and nostalgia, 220; and reason for liking *Dirty Dancing*, 177; and teenage girls/young women, 129, 168, 172, 175, 176, 180. See also coming-of-age; *Dirty Dancing*; narrative
Ritts, Herb, 110, 111, 119
"River Deep, Mountain High," 220
Road House, 37
Road to Ruin, The, 191
Robin Hood, 47
rock 'n' roll, 64, 158
"Rock around the Clock," 295
Rocky, 46, 90, 98, 100
Rocky Horror Show, The, 282, 289
Roe vs. Wade, 134, 135, 159, 166n28. See also abortion
Rogers, Ginger, 61
Rolling Stones, the, 249

rom-com. *See* romantic comedy
romance, 39, 50, 161, 227
romantic comedy, 21, 44, 48, 49, 57, 58. *See also Dirty Dancing*
romantic drama, 45
romantic narrative, 80
Rombes, Nicholas, 226
Romeo and Juliet, 7, 191, 308
Ronen, Shelly, 307
Ronettes, the, 79, 158, 185, 207, 243
Ross, Steven J., 99
Rubin-Dorsky, Jeffrey, 64
Russell, Susan, 302
Ryan, Michael, 90

Samuel Goldwyn Company, the, 38
Saturday Night Fever, 76, 81; and dance films, 33, 208, 310; and high-concept, 225; and historical realism, 242; and New Hollywood, 266; soundtrack, 239, 265, 268; and synergies, 264, 265, 267; and working-class 90, 97,
Sayles, John, 15
score, 109, 254; *Dirty Dancing*, 208, 239, 242; and anachronistic music, 245, 251; and clean teen (music), 244; commercially-driven, 252; composed, 239, 242, 254; dramatic, 245, 247, 248, 250, 251, 255; and historical accuracy, 246; and nostalgia, 241; and Patrick Swayze, 250; source, 247, 248. *See also* music; soundtrack
Second Sex, The, 142
Sedgwick, Eve Kosofsky, 106
Sense and Sensibility, 246
sensual dancing, 260
Sex and the City: The Movie, 3
Sex and the Single Girl, 145
Sexton, Jamie, 224
sexual narrative, 80
sexual politics, 14
sexual reproduction, 73

sexuality, 184, 185, 187, 198, 248
Shakespeare, William, 67, 71, 308
Shall We Dance, 72
Shary, Timothy, 209
Shay, Anthony, 300
She's All That, 9
"She's Like the Wind," 8, 80, 81, 136, 250, 253
Sheen, Charlie, 151
Shenton, Mark, 309
Shirelles, the, 79, 158
Show Boat, 83
Show musical. *See* musical
Showtime, 31
Shumway, David, 44, 139, 144, 158, 212, 220, 233, 235, 240, 241, 243, 252
Sixteen Candles, 241
Sixties, the, 153, 160, 162, 176, 204, 228, 244
Smith, Jeff, 240
So You Think You Can Dance, 188, 189, 300
social media, 128
Some Kind of Wonderful, 241
"Song of Roland," 67
song. *See* music; score; soundtrack
Sony, 28, 29, 32; and Betamax, 29
soul music, 108, 158
Sound of Music, The, 225, 309
soundtrack, 6, 223, 228, 230, 253; album, 2; *Dirty Dancing: Live!*, 4; formats, 224, 263; *More Dirty Dancing*, 4, 268; and nostalgia, 269, 309; Polygram, 265; RCA, 267; sales, 252; success of, 3; *Ultimate Dirty Dancing*, 273. *See also* music; score
source music, 248, 249, 255. *See also* score
Spector, Phil, 207, 220, 243
Speed, Lesley, 209, 210, 211
Spencer, Charles, 283
spontaneous communitas, 292
Sprengler, Christine, 214, 215, 218

Springfield, Dusty, 248, 305
Springsteen, Bruce, 239, 241, 267
stage; adaptation, 14, 259, 298, 308, 310, 311; musical, 61, 297; production, 274; show, 281, 282, 283, 284, 285, 290, 293
Staiger, Janet, 12, 44, 225
Stand By Me, 210, 228, 229, 230
Stand and Deliver, 15
Star Wars, 11, 28, 100, 232, 233, 264, 265, 266, 271, 273; franchise, 98, 275
"Stay," 220, 230, 268
"Stayin' Alive," 97
Staying Alive, 88, 208
Steel Dawn, 38
Steinem, Gloria, 163
stereographic plurality, 287, 293
Stigwood, Robert, 265, 268
Stilwell, Robynn J., 246
Storey, John, 220
"Stormy Weather," 83
straightness, 184
Street Corner, 191
Streetcar Named Desire, A, 110
Streisand, Barbra, 82
Strictly Ballroom, 60, 63, 66, 69, 311
Strictly Come Dancing, 188, 300
studio era, 26, 264; filmmaking, 6
Summer Stock, 62, 81
Sundance Film Festival, the, 5
Surfaris, the, 231
"Swanee," 83
swashbuckler genre, 47
Swayze, Patrick, 2, 6, 182, 197, 209, 272, 285, 297, 300, 302; body of, 48, 57, 66, 75, 107, 111, 168, 192; death of, 10, 132; and ethnicity, 76, 85; *Guys and Dolls*, 309; and Jennifer Grey, 87, 161, 177, 225, 285; and nostalgia, 303, 304; *Road House*, 37; and stardom, 14, 286; *Steel Dawn*, 37
synergy, 240, 264, 266, 267, 269

Tabashnik, Sue, 234
Take the Lead, 69, 72
Tasker, Yvonne, 111, 160, 164
Tax Reform Act, 101
Taxi Driver, 99
Taylor, Paul. 309
teen/teenage: audiences, 230, 253; culture, 204, 208, 216; fantasy, 308, 310; film, 208, 209, 210, 220, 241, 242, 253, 297, 311; girls, 129, 158, 243; life, 204, 208; pic, 14, 46, 151; years, 168, 169. *See also* young; youth
teenager 167, 170, 171, 173, 180, 233
Telegraph (UK), 283
Terminator 2, 35
Texas Chain Saw Massacre, The, 99
textual analysis, 12
theatrical performance. *See* live performance
Thomas, Danny, 83
Thompson, Anne, 40
Thompson, Kristin, 7
Time, 194
Time-Life, 28, 29, 30, 32
Time Warner, 32, 38, 40. *See also* Warner Bros.
Tin Pan Alley, 64
Top Gun, 89, 103
Top Hat, 63
Travolta, John, 302, 310
Trimark, 40
Tucker, Sophie, 83
Turner, Ike, 220
Turner, Mark, 285
Turner, Ted, 32
Turner, Tina, 220
Twentieth Century Fox, 29, 30, 32. *See also* Fox
Tzioumakis, Yannis, 236

United Artists, 31
Universal, 29
Unmarried Woman, An, 154

"Up Where We Belong," 250
upper-class, 218
upward mobility, 97
USA Today, 163

Vajna, Andrew, 34
Van Sant, Gus, 67
Vassallo, Hannah, 286
verisimilitude, 242
vertical sex, 185
Vestron, 25, 32, 38; Law, 39; Pictures, 5, 21, 25, 26, 30–40, 136, 243, 260, 263, 267, 271, 272; Television, 37, 271;
videocassette. *See* Home video
visual culture, 22, 106, 107
visual style, 6
Vitale, Ruth, 26, 33, 37
Vize, Lesley, 247, 249
Vogue, 162
voiceover, 10, 44, 52, 105, 137, 155, 173, 207, 210, 211, 228, 231, 244, 255

Wall Street Journal, 161, 270
Walt Disney Company, the. *See* Disney.
Walter Reade Organization, the, 3
Wanderers, The, 155, 208, 228, 229, 230
Warhol's Flesh, 197
Warner Bros., 10, 32, 39, 83, 100. *See also* Time Warner
Warnes, Jennifer, 80, 250, 268
"We'll Meet Again," 245
Weather Girls, The, 188
Weber, Bruce, 110, 111
West Side Story, 47, 195
When Harry Met Sally . . . , 145
"Where Are You Tonight?," 246, 254
Wicked, 310
Wild One, The, 197
"Wild Thing," 158
Williams, Zoe, 177, 307
"Will You Love Me Tomorrow?," 79

"Wipe Out," 191, 231, 232
women's liberation movement, 152, 155
Women's Wear Daily, 274
"Wonderful World," 115
Wood, Robin, 95, 96, 97, 99, 104
Woods, Faye, 309
working-class, 186; characters, 89, 90, 93; and class mobility, 88, 97, 218; dancers, 120; fashion and style, 89; and Johnny, 101, 112, 116, 139, 301; versus middle-class, 46; and Reaganite cinema, 99; staff, 157, 212; youth, 91, 230. *See also* class; *Dirty Dancing*; middle-class
Working Girl, 88, 106, 145
Wright, Johnny, 286, 300
wrong partner (trope), 21, 49, 50, 52, 53, 54, 56, 57, 58. *See also Dirty Dancing*; narrative
Wyatt, Justin, 225

Yentl, 64, 68
"Yes," 249, 253, 254
York, Ashley Elaine, 3
"You Don't Own Me," 248, 254
"You've Lost That Lovin' Feeling," 220
young: adults, 173; people, 169, 170, 171, 216; women, 171, 172, 173, 177. *See also* teen; youth
Young Guns, 38
Young, Marion, 138, 139, 140, 141, 142, 143
youth, 253; audiences, 267, 295; cinema, 267; culture, 170, 195, 208, 210, 215; films, 127. *See also* teen/teenage; young
YouTube, 108

Zappacosta, 79, 248
zayde, 65

Lightning Source UK Ltd.
Milton Keynes UK
UKHW020456270221
379370UK00005B/126

9 780814 336243